Men, Masculinities, and Aging

The Gendered Lives of Older Men

Edward H. Thompson, Jr.

College of the Holy Cross
and
Case Western Reserve University

ROWMAN & LITTLEFIELD
Lanham • Boulder • New York • London

Executive Editor: Rolf Janke
Editorial Assistant: Courtney Packard
Marketing Manager: Kim Lyons

Credits and acknowledgments for material borrowed from other sources, and reproduced
with permission, appear on the appropriate page within the text.

Published by Rowman & Littlefield
An imprint of The Rowman & Littlefield Publishing Group, Inc.
4501 Forbes Boulevard, Suite 200, Lanham, Maryland 20706
https://rowman.com

Unit A, Whitacre Mews, 26-34 Stannary Street, London SE11 4AB,
United Kingdom

British Library Cataloguing in Publication Information Available

Library of Congress Cataloging-in-Publication Data Available
ISBN 978-1-4422-7854-7 (cloth : alk. paper)
ISBN 978-1-4422-7855-4 (pbk. : alk. paper)
ISBN 978-1-4422-7856-1 (electronic)

∞ ™ The paper used in this publication meets the minimum requirements of American
National Standard for Information Sciences Permanence of Paper for Printed Library
Materials, ANSI/NISO Z39.48-1992.

Printed in the United States of America

Contents

Contents

Acknowledgments

Clichés come to mind as I begins this: "It takes a village . . .", and "All scholarship stands on the shoulders of others." It does. This book was a welcomed project. It formally began when Toni Calasanti, a sociologist and gerontologist at Virginia Tech, and the Diversity and Aging series editor for Rowman & Littlefield, ask me to consider writing what has become *Men, Masculinities, and Aging*. I have known Toni for some time, admire her astute mind, and was honored by the invitation. She is a principled person, a friend, whose editorial comments and suggestions are pointed, helpful, and always couched by "but it is your book." Such guidance is memorable. Early on Sarah Stanton, sociology editor at Rowman & Littlefield, was encouraging and tolerant of my slow start, and senior production editor Alden Perkins later proved to be a gentle task master and considerate in her timetable of deadlines. My thanks also go to Rolf Janke, the new executive editor at the press, and to Courtney Packard, my assigned editorial assistant.

Dale Dannefer and Eva Kahana, fellow sociologists and gerontologists at Case Western Reserve University, provided me a much-welcomed university home now that I left behind undergraduate teaching and moved to northern Ohio. Case libraries and my access to interlibrary borrowing proved indispensable to doing this book. It was Ann Marie Leshkowich, my colleague at Holy Cross, who convinced me to read Judith Butler's work on gender performativity; David Hummon, another colleague, whose seminal work on sociology of place that kindled my interest in geographies and aging; and my many conversations with Andy Futterman and our friendship, which proved to be an experiential grounding about aging men's lives. Thank you all. I am deeply indebted to a number of my former undergraduates for their interest in, questioning of, and weighing of my earlier thoughts on the gendered lives of aging men. There are too many to individually name all, yet I want to shout out to three—Kaitlyn Barnes Langendoerfer, Julia Bandini, and Ali Leichthammer—who have more recently published with me.

Deeper in background are several colleagues who have been more than colleagues. Particularly, Michael Kimmel at SUNY Stony Brook, Len Kaye at the University of Maine, and I have regularly crossed paths in common work and interests for decades. Their thinking is inspiring and their encouragement much appreciated. So too is Gabriella Spector-Mersel's work and person, and I am indebted to her for her conceptual trigger, "never-aging masculinities." My thanks also go to the anonymous reviewers of this book project's proposal and of the initial draft of the manuscript.

Introduction

Masculinities. Men. The plural nouns brilliantly acknowledge the heterogeneity of men and the variety of gender practices distinctly shaped within cultures, age cohorts and generations, social class, sexualities, religious faiths, and ethnicities. On close examination, even within outwardly uniform groups such as US naval officers (Barrett 1996) or a monastic community (Powers 2009), a search for the modal, or even model, masculinity will disappoint. There are marked variations in men's gender practices within these communities, as in any community, small or large, uniform or not, ancient or postmodern, Western, Nordic, or Asian.

Masculinities always have an age, although too few theorists address this directly. A majority of discussions of aging men continue to propose a view that casts men's aging in terms of diminished masculinity. This "diminished" interpretation erroneously suggests that one masculinity spans all of men's adulthood and later life, and old men's practices no longer represent the principles of masculinity. Ignored are old men's production and performance of "aging masculini*ties*" and how aging masculinities are contextually and temporally cultivated and performed. Making visible old men's lives and some of the many aging masculinities that old men practice is the aim of this book.

The perspective I advance to better understand masculinities and aging is informed by critical theory. It appreciates that gender relations and practices take place within structures of social inequality and within historical, demographic, and sociocultural contexts. Age relations have been and remain a key basis of inequality, and many writers have already called attention to the moral discourses accompanying different stages of life. For example, within most developed societies the praise of youthfulness and the "misery perspective" on aging and late life (Öberg 2003) combine like unequal weights on a teeter-totter to stigmatize aging and marginalize, if not scorn, old people. As well, when the inequalities embedded within masculinities are examined, aging men are routinely melded into the social category of "seniors" and collectively viewed as degendered, even genderless. They drift to and exist on the periphery of other people's daily life, which is centered on education, employment, children, and family responsibilities. The fact of the matter is that aging men are neither degendered nor ungendered. They are men.

A FUNDAMENTAL QUESTION

How do men navigate their corporeal and social aging as they experience later life and very late life? This book aims to answer that question. Turning points, such as grandfathering, the changeover from work to retirement, the onset of health problems or becoming a carer, and for some men widower-hood, can throw into sharp relief the masculinities and identities in later life. My starting point is rooted in sociological theory that posits men's identities as relational, endlessly revised as they navigate time and exit and enter relationships, and evident in their preferences or "tastes" (Bourdieu 1984). The masculinity practices that men and women witness and adopt as their *habitus* (an important construct that I will integrate) reflect their embodied generation, class, ethnicity, and geography. Geographical places are the home of the cultural worlds where people's lives are uniquely constructed, represented, and lived, whether this is in the hallows of the Blue Ridge Mountains, rural communities of Finland, or a village in sub-Sahara Africa (cf. Rowles 1983). Geographies of places stage people's view of "others" and their experience of class, gender relations, and felt age. They frame men's relational selves as brothers, fathers, a guitarist, and so on. Take as an example the way O'Brien, Hunt, and Hart (2009, 371) heard Scottish men linking masculinities to place:

> A number of participants cited examples that exaggerated the "legendary" toughness of Glaswegian masculinities. Some older participants alluded to violent masculine practices relating to male territory in Glasgow as exhibited through the "gang warfare" of the "razor years [1950's] . . . [where] you couldn't go out in certain streets because you . . . were afraid they [other men] would [attack] you" (Bill, 62, unemployed and Retired Men's Group).

O'Brien and her colleagues (2009, 371) continued, "Other participants connected the enactment of this kind of 'tough' masculinity to the heavily industrialised city that Glasgow once was, where 'men used to do tough physical labour' (Sean, 47, Student Group)."

Following on the heels of the second wave of feminism, there emerged international interest in masculini*ties* and men's lives within class, age, and gender relations (e.g., Connell 1995; Hearn et al. 2012; Kimmel, Hearn, and Connell 2005; Whitehead 2002). This has produced the hundreds of references on masculinities cited in the book, thousands more not cited, and a widening public conversation about the enigma "men." Consider Norah Vincent's (2006) intriguing eighteen-month immersion experience disguised as a man living in, working in, and infiltrating several communities of men in the US, including a white working-class bowling league, a Roman Catholic monastery, and a neoliberal men's therapy group. As Ned, she encounters some of the many ways social relations are masculinity coded; and she authenticates discourses about masculinity, or what she calls cultures of "unspoken male codes" that thrive within as much as across her unspectacular alliances with ordinary men. She was struck by the intricacies of solidarity, such as her discovery that a passing-respect handshake, and other times friendly greeting, man-to-man handshake are both practices of inclusion, and that being the worst performer on a sports team will prompt teammates' encouragement and instruction, less often ridicule. Her ethnography of sorts unveils the ways masculinity practices are fluid across contexts, the ways men embody and remake these practices, and how this reproduction naturalizes the gender relations she witnessed. Because gender relations are so deeply rooted in everyday practices, they are typically invisible and have been falsely attributed to being essential. She makes their social construction visible. A reader deciphers, even feels the relations of power between men and women and among men. Vincent never theorizes them. Rather, the contextually bound dynamics of gender relations are witnessed and reexperienced in her narrative. She stories the situated nature of masculinities, how different masculine realities stand alongside each other. In doing so, she speaks as if a critical gender theorist to masculinities as cultural practices and about men as individual agents who practice, perform, and produce gender. Her book is a case in point for how men and aging masculinities could be, and should be, examined.

In most studies of men, it is now commonplace to name men as "men," no longer "males"—recognizing they are more than genderless members of a sex category. It is also commonplace to find researchers distinguishing masculinities as cultural practices, no longer types of manhood or clusters of traits, as was once common; and to find critical studies, some not so much, of the varied masculinities and their nuances of power that coexist in a given time and place. Critical aging studies and critical men's studies are making efforts to dispel the homogenized view of manhood or the notion that one set of (ideal) gender attributes—muscular, strong, hard, in control—is what masculinities are about. Though not yet commonplace in studies of either aging or men, there has been swelling attention to "intersectionality" (Crenshaw 1991), which is the recognition that we live within the hierarchical structures of inequality of class, race/ethnicity, sexuality, and age. Our identities are always a composite of our locations within each basis of inequality.

Coming to be recognized is how context can mask or silence some identities, at least the ways some identities are "present" and performed. For example, if someone identifies as a Japanese American, late middle-aged man whose "home" is Northern California despite presently living in London, this composite identity reveals neither class nor sexuality. His embodied identities as middle class and a married heterosexual father are material yet unspoken. This is consistent with the not fully integrated postmodernist turn in studies of men that underscores how compulsory heterosexuality underlies and shapes gender relations and the discourse about it—(hetero)sexuality is a central axis of identity, which for heterosexual men is taken for granted but for nonheterosexual men is never taken for granted.

Too rarely considered is how corporeal aging and age relations might affect masculinities. The principal portrayals of masculinities in sociology, psychology, and critical gender studies examine gender in relation to class, ethnicity, sexuality, nationality, and historical time (e.g., Kimmel, Hearn, and Connell 2005). Most studies focus on just one or two parts of the intersecting axes, such as masculinities and class or masculinities and sexualities. These ageless endeavors maintain a pluralistic ignorance of 20 percent or more of the population of men in most Global North countries.

In all fairness, within the study of men there is a common understanding that "social clocks" (Neugarten 1974, 1979) and life course stages are age-related and shape masculinity performances. Research probing into the gendered lives of boys, "guys," young and middle-aged fathers, or late middle-aged men with health limitations has flourished, albeit with too little, if any, life course or life span time theorizing (an exception is Kimmel's 2008 *Guyland*). Perhaps this is so because for decades the study of men seems to have been lost in a quagmire that thinks in terms of ageless, or more precisely, "never-aging" masculinities (Spector-Mersel 2006). It is as if one masculinity script universally applies to boys, midlife men, and old men; and, it is as if you asked people about "acting their age," there would be no difference in how a boy and an old man would report how he *should* behave.

Theorizing masculinities in ways that ignore age, in particular late life, prompted Gabriela Spector-Mersel (2006) to persuasively argue that contemporary Western cultures offer old men an incomplete masculinity script. She writes, "In relation to early and middle adulthood [where] we find clear models of dignified masculinity, these [models] become vague, even non-existent, when referring to later life" (73). Her insightful thesis is simple: Western masculinity scripts conclude somewhere before old age. I too have argued, "To all intents and purposes, growing old seems to be outside conceptualization of masculinity. In most discourses one can be masculine and one can be old, but not both" (Thompson 2004, 1).

In a manner parallel to the absence of a life span time perspective in masculinity scholarship and thus men's studies emphasis on never-aging masculinities, the field of social gerontology long employed a lens in which aging adults were portrayed as gradually moving along a life course unaffected by gender relations, practices, and preferences. Early investigations never really challenged the biomedically rooted view of aging as a genderless, wearisome journey into decline, dependence, and surrender. For decades, sociological studies of aging imagined men's lives as the standard for theorizing the life course and would investigate matters such as the consequences of (his) retirement.

When aging and gender were jointly investigated, the social inequalities between old men and old women were investigated at the outset (Calasanti and Zajicek 1993). Prime questions addressed how his cumulative (dis)advantages mediated biological aging to affect mortality or later life morbidity, such as why men on average die years earlier than women. Researchers highlighted the invisible social (dis)advantages old men accrued as a group. Without doubt, the majority of old men in affluent developed societies benefit from many institutionalized forms of patriarchal privilege. Take, for example, how heteronormative patriarch family systems assured the man a spouse and/or other female relatives to provide him body care work and meet his other care needs. Little wonder the cliché exists that "home" is the everyday man's castle.

Whether it was how the theorizing of masculinities in men's studies long ignored old men by the near-exclusive attention to boys or midlife masculinities, or how social gerontology hurled gender into the shadows of aging and sometimes degendered older adults, the knowledge production processes within these two adjacent fields effectively positioned old men to the fringe of manhood as storytelling grandfathers or aging veterans. As outsiders, metaphorically and literally, old men's lived experiences are made invisible. This othering of aging men as elders or as seniors (notice, neither "elder" nor "senior" is a gendered noun) has perpetuated a type of thinking that old men cannot exemplify the lionized forms of masculinities that depict agency, independence, competence, and responsibility. Their biographies once may have. But they no longer do. And even after gerontology researchers acknowledged aging men as a (privileged) group who embody and practice age-distinctive masculinities, the particularity of privilege afforded by the different masculinities among men who are able-bodied or not, white or not, was seldom recognized.

CONCEPTUAL TURN

The argument of this book is uncomplicated: old men are above all else men whose gender practices testify to the growing prevalence of aging masculinities within their communities. In critical gerontology (Minkler and Estes 1991) and feminist gerontology (Calasanti 2004), old men are accurately positioned as men whose lives—privileges, vulnerabilities—are influenced by political economies, policy decisions, the histories of age relations and gender relations. The study of aging men is a nascent field that blends studies of men and studies of aging, and it remains an archaeological expedition of sorts as it investigates the field(s) of aging masculinities. It recognizes that gender and age are omnipresent in all social situations, much like the previous example that sexuality and class can be omnipresent.

Social gerontologists understand aging as a process—a lifelong embodiment of "being-in-the-world." This interpretation is Heidegger's (2010/1953) view of our lives basically involving an ongoing integration of experience, and it is consistent with Merleau-Ponty's (1995) position that the lived body is the starting point for our experiences and actions. Hence, to age means to live with body changes, shifting interests and thoughts, and the transformations in our social connectedness. As men embody the habitus (preferences, tastes, practices) of their generation, class, and ethnicity, which are nested within and staged by their communities, their *differing* habitus distinguish one aging man from another and reflect the aging men's (dis)similarities of experience.

From this vantage point, normal aging ought no longer be viewed as a dreary, tiring journey of bodily decline, social withdrawal, personal loss, and surrender, as it was viewed in earlier times when the tolls of survival caused physiological deterioration years before age 40 and men's life span was much shorter than it is currently. Figure 1 depicts this early image of the life course, which is modeled on "a rising and descending staircase" and with later life divided into a series of stages (or ages) each marked by further decline and deterioration (Cole 1992, 5). If we accept that we are aged by culture more than corporeal changes, the decline metaphor is "as hard to contain as dye. Once it has tinged our expectations of the future . . . with peril, it tends to stain our experiences, our views of others, our explanatory systems" (Gullette 2004, 11). Later life in developed countries need no longer be the descending staircase. Bodies age much slower in regions characterized by greater socioeconomic development and old age welfare systems. The vast majority of 60- and 70-year-old men are healthy enough; many, if not most, have some type of "pensioner income" or other postwork income; and, on average, their life span time is expected to continue go on into their 80s (United Nations 2015).

Later life and late life are now ordinary experiences, and aging masculinities are no longer rarities. They too are normative, empirically and socially. But what is later life and late life, and as experienced by men? Some analysts call attention to an ever lengthening "third age," which Peter Laslett (1991) theorized in his book *A Fresh Map of Life* as a new stage of later life no longer connected with work or rearing children. This third, or postemployment, age is typified by people's gradual aging, continued health, and amassed masculine capital. It is "later life," and it is eventually followed by what he called a "fourth age," formerly "old age," which is still distinguished by the roller coaster drop of health decline and much greater dependency. The bodily decline and dependency that in part characterize men's "late life" might be evident in one man's early 60s and another man's late 80s, given how their lives were differently (dis)advantaged.

My analysis throughout the book avoids use of stage models of the life course; thus I do not characterize aging in contemporary developed countries as involving distinct "ages." I prefer using the vocabulary "later life" and "late life" as loosely descriptive constructs in lieu of adopting Laslett's sequential third and fourth ages. I also prefer to not bring forward any of the Global North culture's "life course imaginaries," which is Gullette's (2004) term for the multiple diffuse narratives about the linear or arc sequencing of

Figure 1: Stages of a Man's Life Source: Life and Age of Man: Stages of Man's Life from the Cradle to the Grave, Currier & Ives (between 1856 and 1907), LC-USZ62-24, Library of Congress Prints and Photographs Division, Washington, DC.

lived time. I sometimes mention an age category like "late middle age," yet referring to an age cohort does not equal offering a narrative about men's life course.

Further, my interest is to avoid any implication that a man's healthy-enough later life is "successful" aging, and by implication when significant bodily decline inevitably happens in our lifetimes, this is equivalent to unsuccessful aging or to "failing." The discourse on aging well and successful aging is addressed in chapter 2, but right now it is important to argue how the construct "successful" aging fundamentally applies to one class in one historical period—the affluent who have the economic capital to resist "natural" aging. It also applies to mostly Anglos.

By taking up an approach that brings together critical gerontology, critical men's studies, and sociological interpretations of gender relations, my intention is to present a fresh perspective that will contribute to an appreciation of men's experiences with growing old in ageist societies and how they navigate the omnipresence of never-aging masculinity ideologies. This is not to say that old men are without some cultural guidelines for being an aging man—ask old men about acting their age, and they will be pretty clear in voicing some expectations for how an old man should behave, what he should and should not wear or do. These men provide a voice about the aging masculinities they are expected to perform in their community, and have usually embodied. My intention is not to reiterate a structuralist presentation about gender inequalities and how privileged old men—such as white, middle-class, heterosexual, healthy old men—reap more patriarchal benefits than other old men and most women. Prior structural analyses have certainly provided invaluable insight into the social inequalities of gender relations and their reproduction. Still missing is the theorizing and investigation of men's lived experiences with bodily aging and getting old in economically developed, typically ageist societies.

It is time for a pointed change of focus within men's studies and within social gerontology to understand aging and its transformation of men's preferences, tastes, and practices, and their subjectivities. This is why I turned to Pierre Bourdieu's (1984, 1990) sociology of practice to address the uniquenesses of old men's later life experiences and cultural capital. In Bourdieu's sociology, there is also recognition of an "implicit paradox" of how the dominated in ageist societies (e.g., old men) may contribute to their own domination as a result of embodying (ageist) social relations, even as the generational habitus of contemporary old men is about resistance. My starting point is that old men remain men throughout life, and the social and cultural constructions of masculinities embedded in cultural practices and social institutions are now faced with the upsurge of aging masculinities.

NOMENCLATURE

Unlike twenty years ago, I now deliberately use the terms "aging men," "aged men," "old," and "very old" throughout *Men, Masculinities, and Aging*, in contrast to "older," for two reasons. First, "older" is a problematical discursive strategy. Even from a life course perspective that envisions sequential stages, "older" homogenizes the vast differences among mature men and blurs the distinctive life experience of middle-aged and old men. It segregates all of these older men as a single group, distinguished from the category "younger." But ask a college student about "older" people, and for many their middle-aged aunts, uncles, and parents are included, which thoroughly masks whatever is distinctive about the social worlds of old men (and women). Colonializing "not young" people together as "older" has impaired recognition of the particularities of the masculinity practices distinctive of old and very old men, as much as it clouds analyses of the existential differences in priorities old men espouse in later and late life.

Second, by intentionally directing focus to "aging," "aged," and "old" men, my aim is to reclaim the category "old" as descriptive and no longer pejorative. I intentionally use language that positions people as both agentic and old. I use the term "old" to defy stigma, to normalize aging, and to acknowledge age stratification. When gerontologists eschew the term "old men" for fear that they are disrespectful and use "older," this practice unwittingly abridges our view of masculinities as never-aging. Orthodox social gerontology has oddly treated "old" as if the adjective is applicable to only the 2 to 3 percent of very old men who are frail, likely bedridden. It would not be uncommon for a gerontology-thinking observer to imagine an "old" man as having moved into old age, that period of life mulishly depicted by the gloomy clout of narratives about "end stage," institutionalization, frailty, and dying. After years of doing this, "old" became an ugly euphemism. It spoke only about some men in very late life.

Another conceptualization of "old" I partly quarrel with is from Gilleard and Higgs's body of work. They proposed that later life, or the third age, "is a [new] generationally defined 'cultural field' which emphasizes the values of choice, autonomy, self expression and pleasure" (2013, 368). By comparison, late life, or the fourth age, "constitutes not so much a set of practices but a 'social imaginary' which operates as a set of often unstated but powerful assumptions concerning the dependencies and indignities of 'real' old age" (ibid., 369). My unease with this distinction is how it can perpetuate an emphasis on the *differences* between two life span times—healthy, active later life taking place within a generationally defined cultural field vs. the frail, care-oriented end of life. Their distinction intensifies a degendered view of very old age where there is no "possibility of agency let alone masculinity" (Higgs and McGowan 2013, 32). And it subtly orients "generationally defined" toward middle-class tastes and practices.

The starting point I advocate is to see the *similarities* across the life span in men's gender practices and identity practices as men, independent of their health. I propose that an old, impotent, blind man in a nursing home *remains* a man who continues to perform masculinity and sees himself as a man, even when a passerby neutralizes the man as the "(male) resident" in the room near the end of the corridor. As detailed in coming chapters, when ageist cultural narratives no longer eclipse the salience of gender, then researchers, journalists, and policymakers become conscious that old men embody and perform masculinities even as their bodies falter, and their place in the world as men shifts to near-complete dependency of being cared for. But gender never recedes when this transformation in life(style) occurs.

Recent investigations of aging "have produced more accurate and positive images that bespeak the vitality, creativity, empowerment and resourcefulness attainable in old age" (Katz 1995, 70). I find this especially the case in nonacademic accounts. Consider the following. When Mitch Albom chronicled his on-again relationship with Morrie Schwartz in his memoir *Tuesdays with Morrie* (1997), what is easily recognized are the continuities of Morrie's atypical, emotion-based masculine subjectivity, history of norm-busting, penchant for critical thinking—all products of a lifetime of experience as a man, mentor, husband, professor, friend. At no time is he genderless. Similarly, Tracy Kidder (1993) displayed in *Old Friends* the appeal of an ethnographic study for teasing out the contextual and specific nature of old men's gendered experiences as "residents" in a 121-bed nursing home in Northampton, Massachusetts. He observed the nuanced ways two men continued to perform masculinity no matter where they were. Kidder underscores a friendship that develops between the roommates who differ in almost every way—the minimally ruffled Lou, who is almost completely blind, 90, widowed, suffers from heart disease, and often repeats his rambling stories about his past; and Joe, a cantankerous 72-year-old who has experienced several strokes, suffers because of his diabetes, and can barely walk. Lou is Jewish, a conciliator, the mensch. Joe is an Italian Catholic, better educated than Lou, but profane. Kidder's narrative quietly details how these two very different men continue to "do masculinity" and exemplify (aging) masculinities, even in "old age," even when their immediate future is death, and despite the indignities of life in a nursing home. Kidder's "story" is about the gendered lives of men (and women), not about the processes of ill health and physical frailty. He exposes the continuities of masculine identities, the quiet intimacies among men, old men's use of masculine capital, their accommodations to illness-ravaged bodies, the transformations of their masculine subjectivities as old men now in a nursing home, and their existential/spiritual musing. Representing Bourdieu's sociology of practice, Kidder's analysis recognizes the possibility of continuous personal chutzpah among frail old men, their gendered practices, and their merriment with the intimacy of friendship. Late life, or the so-called fourth age, is more than failing bodies; it is also about gendered lives.

LOOKING FORWARD

In writing a book about old men and aging masculinities, my problem shifted very quickly from what to include to what to leave out. As I noted at the outset, studies of aging men have, after a rather slow start, begun to intensify. During the twenty-plus years that have passed since the publication of *Older Men's Lives* (Thompson 1994) there has been a richness of new scholarship on aging men, and some of it explores the social worlds of very old men. Within this body of work are the narratives (and memoirs) by old men that critically reposition these men from their status as outsiders to, optimistically, "normals." When we listen to their narratives, we know they are men.

Among academic researchers, men's aging and old men's lives are becoming recognized as worthy of interest. We are beginning to see newer theoretical and conceptual approaches addressing aging men, such as the work, utilizing Bourdieu's sociologies of practice, that no longer regards aging as inevitable or immutable, but instead as a malleable process (e.g., Coles and Vassarotti 2012). These newer works are helpful in interpreting how men's aging bodies are experienced, how learning to be old becomes increasingly central to the aging man's sense of self, and in what ways aging transforms masculinities and men's subjectivities.

Nearly all these new approaches embrace as a starting point the feminist and critical studies' axiom that social relations are power relations. Feminist scholarship also has demonstrated that marginalized groups (old men, more so old men of color) are positioned by experience to make it possible for them to dissent and question orthodoxy vis-à-vis hegemonic never-aging masculinities, to be aware of and resist ageist stereotypes and stigmas, to develop the resilient identities that experiences produce, and to have a voice. This book aims to convey the ways in which old men's lives remain gendered by their inventiveness and construction of age-affirming masculinities.

Most aging men have confronted the humiliation of ageism and social exclusion in some contexts (cf. Ojala, Pietilä, and Nikander 2016). Rarely seeing anyone like them represented in consumer advertisements or, more generally, rarely imaged positively in media representations such as birthday cards, is disconcerting. Witnessing workplace and family conversations focused on the interests and worries of younger generations can be marginalizing, yet ordinary. Aging men also have faced the person in the mirror to confront the existential gap between their bodily aging and their sense of self.

They know their balance is not what it once was, nor their stamina, yet most know they are not "that old," especially vis-à-vis the social imaginary associated with late life. In their everyday lives they regularly encounter other old men much like them who also engage in masculinity practices that affirm self-identity and reflect an unparalleled individualization of aging and aging masculinities. Because of their expected longevity, unprecedented numbers of aging men are paying attention to their health, later life intimacies, and existential quests. They juggle competing experiences—living with ageism, living with their aging bodies, living within the poorly charted later life, yet living with many other aging men whose practices evidence gendered continuities in self more than not. My foundationalist position—that old men are men, in aging bodies and within ageist societies—raises the challenge to investigate their experiences and subjectivities.

Shifting the object of analysis—old men and their gendered relations—from the margins to the center of attention begs for recognizing men's aging masculine subjectivities and practices. Despite my attempt to provide a more comprehensive investigation of aging men and aging masculinities, I am aware of the absences and matters not discussed. Take, for example, the many writings rapidly coming about addressing geographies of place and embodiment, or sexualities and aging, or late modernist misgivings with the legacy of the "old age" imaginary. This book will satisfy and intrigue many, not all. It defends aging men's and very old men's masculine capital and dignity without pushing old women to the margin. Lest it is misunderstood, old men's gendered lives involve real and symbolic relations with other men and with women, and their class, race, ethnoculture, generation, and sexuality contextually shape these experiences.

A PREVIEW

Collectively, not individually, the three sections and twelve chapters of this book consider how aging is embodied by old men or, less often, resisted. *Men, Masculinities, and Aging* incorporates many stories and anecdotes about old men's lives. It is the voices of old men that inform us about their lives. These voices are sometimes drawn from my research interviews conducted at Holy Cross and many times from other researchers' qualitative studies. Sometimes they are anecdotal and retell situations I observed while engaged in everyday activities (playing softball or having lunch, for example). And some of the voices are drawn from the narratives of old men with whom I had several or many conversations. In all instances I alter enough of the contextual information to assure the source's anonymity.

The first section of *Men, Masculinities, and Aging* introduces and examines the concept of aging masculinities: how old men's practice of never-aging masculinities are amended and replaced by their practice of aging masculinities, how men navigate ageist relations and participate in the innovative fields of the third age culture, and how old men's everyday lives reveal their adaptations to their changing bodies. The second section shifts attention to the inequalities among old men's physical and emotional well-being, including the issues of depression and suicide, how later life health challenges become masculinity challenges, and how the most prevalent discourse of old men and their sexual health is medicalized and warrants re-thinking. The final section pulls the lens back to address the social worlds of old men, beginning with a review of their social relationships, what types of intimacy are most salient in later life, what older heterosexual and gay men similarly and differently think about their sexual aging, the rising prevalence of old men becoming primary carers of their partners, and the experiences of the old men who face later life as a widower. The final chapter could well be a section to itself, but I purposely integrate it into the social worlds of old men. It takes on the pervasive view of late life as an "imaginary," or the cliff from which men fall into frailty. Instead, I close the section on old men's social worlds with an argument that the emergent fourth age culture has begun to accommodate late life preferences and old men's resiliency. The epilogue returns to review and discuss aging masculinities as the better alternative way of viewing old men's masculinity practices.

I

Masculinities and Aging

Chapter One

Masculinities

As men age and move through the course of their lives, so too do their identities as men shift to accommodate the changes in their lives. Moreover, what masculinity means at the societal level changes across epochs, and individual conceptualizations of what masculinity means necessarily shift to accommodate these changes as well.

—Coles (2009, 30)

The category of "old man" is composed of two primary social positions, age and gender. As much as aging and age relations shape gender practices and identities, and gender relations shape the aging experience, other social axes affect both. As a result of intersecting social inequalities, old men are always something else, whether it is their body wholeness or not, sexuality, religious affiliation, or ethnicity. Katherine Newman (2003, 204) reminds us,

We are all bearers of a particular history, as it unfolded in specific spaces. The time and place leave their marks on us as we pass through . . . We do wear different shades of gray because the pathways that take us there are not the same. Some are much easier than others, in part because . . . inequalities in resources affect our options at every step of the way.

This chapter begins with an understanding that the diversity of masculinities and men, especially in terms of aging, remains understudied. Reviewed are the paradigms that have defined what masculinity means, why they matter, and the theoretical turn that acknowledged masculini*ties*. The chapter ends with an introduction to Pierre Bourdieu's conceptual architecture and the relevance of his theorizing about fields, bodies, and aging to better appreciate aging masculinities.

DIFFERENCES

The diversity within populations of men has been routinely obscured through the imposition of one or more "binary opposite" comparisons that homogenize all of the variation into a common category, such as when researchers address old men's privileges vis-à-vis women's. Today, no longer unnoticed across many academic fields (sociology, cultural geography, law) are the marked differences among men, even among aging men. This conceptual turn has roots in four developments. First is the theoretical importance of "intersectionality" (Crenshaw 1991), which calls attention to disempowerment when people are subjected to multiple forms of exclusion. Intersectionality refers to overlapping systems of oppression and discrimination, based not just on age and gender but on ethnicity, sexuality, class background, whether one is an immigrant or not, the (hetero)normalcy of marriage, and a number of other axes of inequality. Second, established within feminist inquiry is the field of critical studies of men. This scholarship reminds us that although men as a group are powerful, individual men do not always feel powerful. Critical studies of men is where gendered hierarchies and inequalities among men are explicitly acknowledged (e.g., Connell 1995; Hearn 2004). The premise is that gender relations operate as a, perhaps *the*, primary axis of social inequality. Masculinity hierarchies operate between and within classes, sexualities, ages, or race and ethnic groups; thus some groups of men gain/retain privilege in relation to other men, even when all men benefit from a patriarchal dividend.

The third is critical gerontology, which is also inspired by feminist scholarship on age inequalities and the power dynamics across age statuses. Its premise is that age relations present a decisive basis of inequality such that old men are subordinated in relations with younger men. It probes the connections among age, aging, and gender and is mindful that as individuals and cohorts age, they have embraced gender practices that can be modified by experiences and age relations. Replacing the early nongendered gerontological approaches that studied "old people," critical gerontology adds a framework for exploring old men's social worlds as men and as old men. It recognizes that there is no hegemonic way ageism takes place; rather, its forms (and intensity) differ by class, sexuality, and ethnicity and by local and national contexts.

The fourth is the new scholarship on aging and masculinities. This perspective challenges the premise that inequalities should be the key narrative for discussing later life masculinity practices (cf. Coles 2008, 2009; Meadows and Davidson 2006; Thompson and Langendoerfer 2016). It does not dispute the importance of power dynamics or the institutionalization of patriarchal privileges; rather, it aims to shift attention from inequalities to an examination of old men's *lived realities*, whether or not they are conscious of their privilege or vulnerabilities. Its interest is old men's experiences. It argues for more effort to understand the masculinities old men embody and practice.

Blending these fields of inquiry, it can become taken for granted that every man represents many different categories of men, will engage in different masculinity practices as contexts expect, and embodies many identities. One old man may, for instance, be a working-class, lapsed Catholic, retired Italian-American widower who still lives independently in his home in a northeastern small town in the US and nearby most of his grandchildren. His slightly older cousin retired as an electric engineer, travels often, lives comfortably alone in a large southeastern city, never married, and rarely divulged his homosexuality because his successful employment hinged on masking. Some identity categories extracted from these descriptions (white man, heterosexual man, widower, grandfather) and the performances of masculine subjectivities (not like an old woman, resilient like an aging gay man, caring like a grandfather) are differentially supported by a host of social institutions, including the family provider and breadwinner narratives that affected both men's lives. Strangers might see the cousins only as two "old men," whereas family members see a multiplicity of identities, and each man sees reflected in the mirror even more complexity because his identities are intertwined and "old man" is not likely the central identity he tags to himself.

McGinley and Cooper (2012) make use of this multidimensional turn to teach law students about and to learn to argue against legal policy and social practices that essentialize masculinities, such as the "boys will be boys" narrative embedded in law, or the "old men work too slowly" narrative institutionalized in age discrimination practices. Cleverly depicted on the cover of *Masculinities and the Law: A Multidimensional Approach* is a Rubik's Cube—it is their symbolic representation of masculinities as many-sided, contextual, and comprising intersecting identities. Borrowing from their work (especially McGinley 2013), imagine the white sides of each little cube within the Rubik's Cube to represent both the gender and age of old men. Because each little cube has other sides, we must always bear in mind that the red, yellow, orange, and other colored sides are representative of race, class, sex orientation, and other identities. This visual symbol of multi-dimensional masculinities makes it obvious that old men have multiple identities that are imperceptible if "old man" is the primary identity others see. These other identities—old men of particular races, classes, and generations—are recognizable whenever old men are gathered together in a room or in a sample. One can pay attention to the diversity and subtle differences.

Mere recognition that varieties of culturally distinct masculinities coexist calls attention to how masculinities can vary in terms of men's ethnocultural ancestries and generation. But as Schrock and Schwalbe (2009, 280) caution, to invoke "the existence of Black masculinity, Latino masculinity, gay masculinity, Jewish masculinity, working-class masculinity, and so on is to imply that there is an overriding similarity in the gender arrangements" of the men who are Jewish, working-class, gay, or black. This oversimplification loses sight of the pronounced variations within categories. One paradigmatic example for why we need to avoid categorical reductionism is in Mitchell Duneier's (1992) *Slim's Table*, an ethnographic study of the class- and generation-based African-American masculinities in urban Chicago in the 1980s. Core dimensions of the older black men's masculinity were their "respectable" citizenry ethos and their embodiment of the value of hard work that characterized the working class of their generation. Being principled, honest, and caring defined the older men's masculinity. Another "street smart" masculinity was shared among the young men within the South Side underclass. The competing ideologies and masculinity practices differed sharply at times across the two age cohorts, though their stories communicated some of the intergenerational commonalities of being black men in racialized America. Duneier's study goes beyond dismantling public stereotypes of black men or comparing two generations. He brings his readers into the lives of the aging men who get together for food and friendship at a Chicago diner.

PARADIGMS

Many earlier theories about gender and masculinities have been set aside in the past twenty years. In this section I briefly provide a sociologically informed review of the transition from thinking about the "traditional" masculinity associated with modern, industrial society to theorizing the forms of masculinities associated with the late and postmodern eras. This background is important to more fully discuss the distinction I will make between never-aging and aging masculinities.

    Through most of the twentieth century, the dominant paradigm for thinking about men and masculinities used essentialist arguments, much as had been voiced in earlier centuries. Gender was not yet a construct. Only sex and sex differences existed. It was widely held in most Western and Asian cultures that sex was a dichotomy and biologically determined; it was rooted in bodies. Gender practices were very often imagined as by divine design. Publics and academic scholars accepted universal sexual asymmetry as the starting point: men and boys are males and thus, or should be, masculine; girls and women are females and thus, or should be, feminine. Mirroring the discourse within the literatures and philosophies of antiquity and scripture (cf. Moore and Anderson 1998) and embraced by early work on personality psychology, this paradigm interpreted masculinity and maleness oppositionally—as what is neither femininity nor femaleness. Gender practices were policed to support male/female, masculine/feminine binaries (such as breadwinner/homemaker, herder/gardener). These contextual binaries were under-stood by the mid-twentieth century as "sex roles," and people's attitudinal and behavioral compliance was thought to be necessary for individual and national health. Operating within this regulatory system was heterosexism, which "assumes that men, that is 'real' men, are born male, exhibit masculine behaviors, and are attracted, exclusively, to those of the opposite sex" (Leo-nard, Duncan, and Barrett 2013, 106).

Taking into account the essentializing of gender being biologically deter-mined, it is not too surprising that healthy masculinity was once said to depend on heterosexuality and acquisition of an immutable sex-typed iden-tity, or "sex-role identity." Nor is it surprising that psychodiagnostic tools were developed to ostensibly assess normalcy by charting boys' and men's trait-based self-descriptions, such as how the m-f scale within the Minnesota Multiphasic Personality Inventory tried to assess gender normalcy and psychopathology in the late 1930s and early 1940s. Societies' moral and legal policing of the gender binary was also unmistakable (e.g., men barred from nursing; "weak" or effeminate men bullied, even stoned). In the US and many other nations, until laws changed, men who violated gender norms in occupations, such as any man either teaching preschool or doing the emotion work of a flight attendant, were punitively sanctioned because their skills, dispositions, and demeanors were antithetical to the accepted masculine character, and what manhood was "supposed" to be.

The deconstruction of essentialist ideologies during the transition into late modernity was "slow motion" (Segal 1990). The first wave of feminism across Europe and North America that championed the suffrage rights of white, middle- or upper-class women chipped a bit away from men's exclu-sive control of gender relations. The Great Depression and later the inclusion of women in the labor force alongside men initiated a reform of the male-as-breadwinner paradigm. The identity politics movements of the 1960s (black men, gays and lesbians, second-wave feminism) collectively contested most segregationist practices and traditionalist narratives about gender, sexuality, and race. And, the late twentieth-century processes of individualization moved "life politics" (Giddens 1991) to front and center and transformed conversations to be about the pursuit of personal meaning. Together, these century-long processes freed women and men from the heavy-handedness that characterized traditional societies' gender binaries and restrictions.

Before these changed practices were commonplace, public understanding of "gender-bending" was *National Geographic* exotic, like photographic rep-resentations of the nomadic Wodaabe tribe where young men "do" feminin-ity with delicate posturing, face-painting, and decorative clothing for the annual reunion of tribes at the Gerewol Festival. Gender-bending in devel-oped societies is no longer limited to the tropes of cross-dressing, costumes and fashion, or artistic freedom. Adult men (and women) of all ages regularly "bend" the rigid gender constructions of the past when, for example, men exemplify the emotional agency now expected in contemporary "attention economies" (e.g., Nixon 2009), or women compete alongside men in marathons, white-water kayaking, or other "extreme" sports. Gender-bending reflects the rise of the practice of masculini*ties*, by both men and women.

Nonetheless, some moral and legal policing of rigid, binary "sex roles" persists: US courts continue to permit sex segregation practices in privacy-related jobs such as spa and restroom attendants. There are also the "taken-for-granted ideas and practices [that are] performed 'with consent,' 'without coercion'" (Hearn 2004, 53), such as the voluntary forms of sex segregation among groups engaged in a particular interest (professional team sports, bachelor parties), or men barring women from membership in old boys' clubs (the Porcellian Club at Harvard University, San Francisco's Bohemian Club) and women barring men from women's clubs (the Belizean Grove in New York City).

The demise of essentialist thinking about sex roles was led by the clarification that people's lives are governed by *gender*, not determined by sex. This fresh paradigm distinguished itself with its argument that gender is a socially constructed ideology, and it abandoned the practice of always viewing men as a homogenous category and comparing them to women. It was Mannheim's (1936) writings on the meaning of "ideology," later amplified by Berger and Luckmann's (1967) seminal analysis of the foundations of

Figure 2: Wodaabe Men. Source: Robert Harding picture library.

knowledge in everyday life, that helped me recognize that people's knowledge, beliefs, and practices were products of the contexts in which they were created. As they argued, the ideologies found within places, generations, or classes shape "mind." Although gender ideologies are produced in time and place and in service of particular interests, the dominant ideologies come to be viewed as natural. This is persuasively recapped in Lorber's (1993) "believing is seeing" maxim. Here are two examples: believing that masculinities were biologically determined led early twentieth-century eugenicists to "know" certain national traits are superior/inferior, and led early physicians to "see" physiological differences between men's and women's bodies that do not in fact exist (Martin 1991).

The construct "masculinity ideologies" names the dimensions of culture that script men's lives (Thompson, Pleck, and Ferrera 1992). There is a particular composition that is referred to as the "traditional" masculinity ideology (Brannon 1976), which embodies cultural shoulds and should nots such as avoid femininity ("no sissy stuff"), be willing to take risks ("give 'em hell"), and strive to be respected and admired ("the big wheel"). This ideology emerged with modernity and was thought to be a universal model for boys and men. However, it is specific to the norms of a time (1900s–1960s), place (Global North countries), race (white), class (working/middle), and sexuality (heterosexuality). I place quotes around the word "traditional" to signify that it is a contested term, since one must logically ask, traditional for whom or in what context.

The constructionist paradigm basically emphasized that men and women think and act in the ways that they do because of context-dependent norms and the gender ideologies imbedded within their (local) culture. The paradigm thus challenged the premise that one masculinity ideology was universal. Some theorists using the constructionist paradigm emphasized variations in how masculinity ideologies were practiced or endorsed, even if some practices are common across groups of men and guided by overarching ideologies. Other theorists emphasized how masculinity practices are better understood as "situated accomplishments" directed by the unique ways contextual norms help operationalize the broader ideologies (Goffman 1959). Still others argued that masculinity practices are everyday performances of cultural scripts yet distinctly produced by the interacting parties themselves (West and Zimmerman 1987). All of these theoretical tracks share the thesis that ideologies guide lives.

The initial use of this paradigm soon met criticism, especially from the feminist-inspired sociologies of men (e.g., Carrigan, Connell, and Lee 1985), on two counts: first, for still theorizing an overly static, single masculinity (at times even called the "male role"), and second, for basically ignoring power within gender relations. The sociologies of men emphasized *gender relations*, not gender. Most influential to the revisionary thinking that there is no essential or foundation identity are Erving Goffman's *The Presentation of Self in Everyday Life* (1959), Judith Butler's *Gender Trouble* (1990) and *Bodies that Matter* (1993), and Raewyn Connell's theory of hegemonic masculinity and emphasized femininity (1987, 1995). At the risk of oversimplification, in *Gender and Power* (1987), and later *Masculinities* (1995), Connell expanded people's thinking with her conception of multiple masculinities hierarchically ordered from ideal to marginalized. She saw masculinities as different configurations of gender practice. By the early 2000s Connell argued that one configuration of practice—hegemonic masculinity—is "the *currently* most honored way of being a man; it required all other men to position themselves in relation to it, and it *ideologically* legitimated the global subordination of women to men" (Connell and Messerschmidt 2005, 832, my italics). When institutions such as Wall Street or the military or when individuals strive to represent a hegemonic masculinity ideal, their convincing and unconvincing performances fortify the ideal.

Connell's constructs "gender order" and "hegemonic masculinity" delivered a valuable way of thinking about gender practices, and about men and power. Arising from her conceptual framing has emerged a widely accepted narrative on plural masculinities, each of which is temporally bound and culture contingent, thus whatever is hegemonic having no truly fixed content. Her work became influential to thinking about masculinities as changing across history, as well as across geographies and cultures. She distinctly envisioned one form of masculinity as always the pinnacle. This hegemonic form embodies the local, regional, and/or societal *ideal* standards of manhood (perhaps independence, invincibility, imperviousness to pain) and exerts a constant, back-shoving pressure for men (and women) to conform to it, even across contexts. It serves to morally, then politically govern gender practices. In her writing, Connell recognized that there is no absolute hegemonic masculinity (Connell and Messerschmidt 2005); instead there are ideal masculini*ties* that reside at the top of the hierarchies found in different places and/or times. A result of Western culture's ageism, whatever masculinity preferences and practices old men embody, their masculinities would be subordinate.

Butler's (1990, 2000) interpretation of gender and hegemony helps shift our attention to people's lived experiences and away from cultural and social hierarchies. For Butler (2000, 14), the notion of hegemony "emphasizes the ways in which power operates to form our everyday understanding of social relations, and to orchestrate the ways in which we consent to (and reproduce) those tacit and covert relations of power." I think she conveys a mistrust of master narratives of any sort. Butler's keen insight argues that "one's gender is performatively constituted in the same way that one's choice of clothes is curtailed, perhaps even predetermined, by the society, context, economy, etc. within which one is situated" (Sahil 2007, 57). By directing attention to how masculinities are contextually performed, Butler's perspective appreciates a plurality of authoritative, time- and place-bound masculinities rather than always affirming a hierarchy and one unfathomable ideal. It is the context of everyday social relations, which have their own histories, that actively regulate and empower the performances of (nonhegemonic) masculinities. I lean on this in theorizing old men's practice of aging masculinities.

Never-Aging Masculinities

I find that there are difficulties when it comes to using Connell's masculinities theorizing for studies of old men experiences and sense of self. First, when Spector-Mersel (2006) listened to old men tell their life stories, she recognized that the guidelines for masculinities the men tried to use applied to pre-old age. Restating this, the hegemonic masculinities old men may strive to live by never accommodate corporeal aging, nor old men's later life, postemployment lifestyles. As Meadows and Davidson (2006, 296) comparably noted, being old and being a man "illustrate how old men offer a window to hegemonic forms of masculinity through their *absence* from this space." When viewed through the lens of hegemonic masculinity, men's later life is expected to continue to be the same as it was, never-aging.

Second, hegemonic masculinities are always expressions of established institutions and social practices, and they serve to maintain the privileges and interests of some, not all, men. When Connell published *Masculinities* in 1995, her thinking embodied the modernist prerequisite of hierarchically ordered gender relations, which were evident within the institutions of education, law, class-based employment, and so on. An alternative starting point is what sociologist Zygmunt Bauman (2000) called the "liquid modernity" of the times. In contrast to the "solid modernity" that preceded it and seems to have enveloped Connell's theorizing, he saw the masculinized nature of most organizations, social institutions, and social practices contested rather than affirmed. The deconstruction of rigid gender boundaries and relations had been well underway. Postmodernity's transformation of social life not only began to deinstitutionalize the foundations for gender inequalities, it destabilized the life course such that later *and* late life masculinities freely occur. My argument is that hegemonic masculinities are short-lived in the liquid nature of postmodernity. Since the postmodern turn most men live by the quieter canons of many nonhegemonic masculinities, including aging masculinities. Previously I suggested (Thompson and Whearty 2004, 6) that "hegemonic masculinity may not be the lived form of masculinity at all" for old men, despite the fact that it is a powerful, even dominant, script against which old men may judge themselves and others.

Third, in Western and Arabic cultures hegemonic masculinities were once the configurations of gender practice that supported the dominance and authority of (some) older men—the guild master craftsmen and freemasons, religious elders, property owners, and family patriarchs who retained control of their own households as long as they were able. (Poor and property-less old men could not command respect.) But the transitions associated with modernity gave rise to ageism's new preference for "able-ism" and "youth-fulness." The new ethos of modernity disempowered the gerontocracy of old men and redefined the tenets of masculinity to canonize youth. Old men were displaced, and retirement was introduced as a special place for the growing numbers of old men to go away to. In the solid nature of modernity across Europe and North America in the 1900s, the structure of gender relations made aging men become less and less *present* in vital, mainstream masculi-nized places. Even in the contemporary circumstances of late modernity, or postmodernity, the discourses of hegemonic masculinity's "othering" tell us that men cannot be both men and old. It is principally a discursive practice that positions old men as diminished and that affirms the never-aging model of manhood that I find problematic, because whenever we draw on hegemon-ic masculinity theorizing an old man becomes an oxymoron.

Invaluable as the hegemonic masculinity narrative has been for theorizing and researching gender relations at a structural level—e.g., which men are subordinate and why—I argue that this narrative does not assist in under-standing how old men consciously and unconsciously locate themselves when embodying aging masculinities and struggling with the cultural narra-tives of "never-aging" masculinity. Nor does the hegemonic masculinity nar-rative shed light on the agency of most old men. The lens of hegemonic masculinity ignores, maybe even belittles, old men, casting them as compli-cate and subordinate and more likely as marginalized others. Thus, in tandem with some of Connell's friendly critics (e.g., Coles 2009; Whitehead 2002), I too suggest that a rereading of Pierre Bourdieu's sociological theories of practice and of the body as symbolic and physical capital, and his concepts—habitus, field, capital—enable new insight into the meanings of aging mascu-linities and a better understanding of aging men's social practices.

OLD MEN'S HABITUS AND FIELDS

In Bourdieu's (1984) most cited text, *Distinction: A Social Critique of the Judgment of Taste*, he critically addresses the ways that social inequalities are reproduced. For Bourdieu, the social world is made up of *fields*, which is a metaphor for the social and institutional arenas or domains of social life (e.g., broadly, education; specifically, colleges). It is within fields that people compete for access to economic capital, social capital, and cultural capital. His (1990) theory of practice examines the ways fields are intertwined with distinctive social practices that affirm and modify individuals' habitus as well as reproduce the settings' social inequalities. The concept of habitus lies at the heart of Bourdieu's theoretical framework.

Habitus is the relatively durable patterns of judgment, perceptions, and preferences (collectively called *taste*) generated by a generation, a class, an ethnic group, a college, or a retirement community and embraced by the participants. Consequently, men's tastes are far from individualized. They are the cultural foundations that distinguish one group from another (for Bourdieu, social classes). When we belong to a group and identify with the group (whether class, generation, or village), we make choices that usually reflect the group's tastes. Everything from what kind of clothing worn, to whiskies drunk, to political rhetoric and colloquialisms, to what kind of food and diet, to site of heroin injection (which is discussed below) occur within the social processes that (re)construct inequalities in capital and produce the boundaries between groups. One man's habitus is, basically, his schema of dispositions, preferences, and routines that guide his masculinity and class practices. For Bourdieu, habitus is the subjectivity that constitutes the core of self.

Bourdieu's thesis boils down to this: "Collective expectations . . . tend to inscribe themselves in bodies in the form of permanent dispositions" (2001, 61). "Permanent" does not translate into a deterministic meaning. For Bourdieu, the set of dispositions and schemas rooted in individuals' experiences not only produces different patterns of practice within and across social groups, but people's habitus is fluid enough to be changed and to navigate unfamiliar fields where practices take place. People acquire habitus by internalizing the particular rules operating within fields (whether business, art or antiques, a sport, a marriage, or particular leisure spaces). They embody the underlying *nomos*—the fundamental principles or rules-of-the-game of a field. "You need only think of the impulsive decision made by the tennis player who runs up to the net, to understand that it has nothing to do with the learned construction that the coach, after analysis, draws up," Bourdieu suggests (1990, 11). Bourdieu and Wacquant (1992, 127) explain:

> Social reality exists, so to speak, twice, in things and in minds, in fields and in habitus, outside and inside social agents. And when habitus encounters a social world of which it is the product, it is like a "fish in water": It does not feel the weight of the water and it takes the world about itself for granted.

To illustrate this, an old man talking sports with "mates" in a British pub or, instead, with morning-coffee "buddies" in a breakfast cafe in Boston does not feel out of place. The field of sports and debating with friends in familiar places is his ordinary. The same old man may possess interest in and the reading skills to critically interpret a new novel or biography, but he feels quite out of place in a book club where women heavily populate this field and the styles of talk.

As people maneuver in fields, they express and adjust their actions to the field—from the competitiveness of a ball game to, an hour later, the generativeness of reading to a young grandson. Within a field we accrue knowledge, status, and authority (or, in Bourdieu's terms, cultural *capital*, symbolic *capital*, and social *capital*). Bourdieu mostly focused on the class tastes and inequalities reproduced in different fields, but his theorizing looked beyond class to include generations as fields. The term "generation" can be troubling for sociologists and gerontologists to interpret. Karl Mannheim (1952) defined "generation" as a cohort of men and women born and raised within the same formative historical and social context (the generation of the Depression, or the postwar boom, or the cohorts of gay men self-identifying as gay before and after the 1969 Stonewall riots).[1] It is the formative historical and social contexts that create an influential generational consciousness and predispose members within the generation to engage in social practices, develop certain tastes, and uphold values that are in keeping with the times (and places) in which they were raised. Bourdieu (1993a, 99) recognized that the antagonisms between generations are "clashes between systems of aspirations formed in different periods." Each generation is "an age cohort that comes to have social significance by virtue of constituting itself as cultural identity" (Turner 2002, 16).

Harnessing the idea that generations have their own habitus, many observers argue that the rise of the "youth culture" in the 1960s created desires and values among the young Baby Boomers that differentiated this generation from the generations before and after. Sensed as strongly by members of the working class as by middle class, the Baby Boom age cohort was antitraditional, liberational, rebellious, and in pursuit of the "new." This generation has sustained its habitus of reflexive individualism and its preference for choice and agency. As this generation aged, especially within the US, Boomers took "with them many of the values and tastes of their youth" (Featherstone and Hepworth 1991, 375).

Some scholars contend that only in the late twentieth century did the idea emerge that personal agency can be exercised over how aging will be experienced and expressed—in other words, the newer generation(s) of aging adults are maintaining their independence and agency in old age (e.g., Gilleard and Higgs 2000, 2013). Challenged is the imagery that old age pivots on decline and dependency. Qualitative research and media articles have affirmed how the fields now characterizing later and late life bear the trade-

---

1. There are variations in the way generations are named. The labels and dates commonly used in the academic literature: Traditionalists, also known as the Silent Generation (born between 1925 and 1945); Baby Boomers (born between 1946 and 1964); Generation X (born between 1965 and 1980); and Millennials, or Generation Y (born between 1981 and 1995).

marks of the new generations of old people—their agency, active lives, independence, and resilience that are evident among many practices within sports (e.g., Eman 2011) and later life dating and sexuality (e.g., Beckman et al. 2008). In light of these and many other "cases," we already know that aging (corporeal and social) gradually transforms a man's taste and practices. The habitus of an old man will reflect his fields of experience and his opportunities. As he ages, his habitus will gradually convert to a fish-*in*-water subjectivity from an initial fish-*out*-of-water encounter, such as when aging men embrace postemployment life as "retired." There is much to suggest that Bourdieu's conceptual vocabulary can assist to more imaginatively discuss the existing and rising generations of old men.

Unpacking all this and applying Bourdieu's conceptual framework to old men, we can expect some men's performances, opinions, and tastes to hold more authority than others. As Coles (2009, 36) wrote, "Within the [overarching] field of masculinity, there are sites of domination and subordination, orthodoxy (maintaining the status quo) and heterodoxy (seeking change), submission and usurpation. Individuals, groups, and organizations struggle to lay claim to the legitimacy of specific capital within the field." His and chiefly Bourdieu's argument encourage us to anticipate, for example, that old working-class men who are retired factory workers will talk, eat, swagger, and participate in different conversations compared to old men who attended university, and both groups acquire distinctive cultural capital that is invaluable for their lives, even if a basis of class inequality. Their respective class-related capital can be recognized in their distinctive practices, relations, and subjectivities.

Here is a first-rate illustration of how Bourdieu's constructs of habitus, capital, and field can make sense of aging men's social practices. Bourgois and Schonberg (2007) uncovered certain ethnic dimensions of the habitus of white and African American advanced middle-aged, homeless men in San Francisco who shared fields of daily encampments and indigent poverty and heroin use. The men constructed different income-generating strategies and styles of heroin injection that were rooted in legacies of the underclass and their race.

Most of the African American men remained in active contact with relatives, and by doing so maintained identities as black men, not as down-and-out homeless men. They also endeavored to maintain "a thick dynamic social network of extended family and of friends and acquaintances (some of them sexualized) on the street" (Bourgois and Schonberg 2007, 19). They refused to produce income by either passively begging along highway access ramps for small change or by accepting off-the-books "boy" day-labor jobs such as sweeping sidewalks or unloading trucks, as many white men did. The African Americans interpreted begging as "stooping down"; these men also fervently "criticize[d] the relationships that the whites develop with employers as being akin to slavery" because odd-job work conditions were judged as "demeaning, exploitative and feminizing" (ibid., 15). Envisioning themselves as successful, streetwise outlaws, as men who resist the "apartheid" field of being homeless black men, they championed a habitus that is connected with a discourse of resistance—an "outlaw" masculinity that valued risk, rebelliousness, ingenuity, and sacrifice as well as professionalized and specialized theft. Their body capital and practices included their "commitment to staying well-dressed, to bathing against all odds, to walking energetically with shoulders raised and a steady gaze" (ibid., 19). Despite scarred and virtually inaccessible veins as a consequence of their histories of injection, they repeatedly spent considerable lengths of time to find a functional vein. They did not want to forgo the exhilarating rush of pleasure from injecting intravenously.

By comparison, the white men were outcasts from their families and loners within the homeless population. They had become "down-and-out" failures, looking and acting dejected: "they slump their shoulders, stare at the ground despondently, avoid bathing . . . [T]he constellation of dispositions and techniques of the body that characterize the whites: they dress in rags, are malodorous, limp dejectedly with canes and often drink themselves into a stupor" (Bourgois and Schonberg 2007, 18). The whites also gave up on the quest for the regular heroin rush. Searching for a viable vein was replaced by "skin-popping"; they sank the needle unthinkingly into fatty tissue, very often through their clothing. Heroin use was a necessity, no longer fun, nor a communal occasion. Sustaining the legacy of their upbringing in families who appraised theft as an unacceptable income-producing strategy, the men relied on panhandling to support their heroin habit. Even though they did not enjoy begging, the "hard work" of hours of humbly begging or collecting cans and bottles were practices rooted in class habitus. In addition, the white men's victim discourse and loner practices attest to the symbolic violence of their exclusion from the working-class society from which they originated and from the homeless "community" that black men dominated. Their posture, heroin injection "tastes," production of economic capital, and progressive downward slide within the field of the homeless—these collectively distinguish their masculinity practices and depleted social capital.

Bourdieu's sociology of practice proved valuable for this investigation of the ways in which homeless aging men's habitus and bodies transform into and epitomize their distinctive ethnic trajectories within the field of the homeless and men's heroin use. Though collectively living in abject poverty, the men's masculinities and practices were manifested in differing bodily forms, tastes, and heroin use. Bourdieu stipulated that the "natural" body is materially transformed through, for example, one's activities, food, and social histories into a "distinctive" body, which is manifested in posture, bearing, or even style of walking. Bourgois and Schonberg corroborate. They uncovered the men's distinctive class- and ethnic-based bodily forms, social practices, and habitus. Indeed, the choice of a style of life even when homeless is testament to the usefulness of the constructs habitus and fields.

As will be shown in later chapters, Bourdieu's sociology (of practice and body) proves valuable for understanding most old men's lives, even though I find his view of aging problematic. It was Bourdieu's observation (1984, 110–11) that "Social ageing is nothing other than the slow renunciation or disinvestment (socially assisted and encouraged) which leads agents to adjust their aspirations to their objective changes, to espouse their condition, become what they are and make do with what they have." He also pointed out that the aging process might even entail self-deception as to what we are or what we have. From my vantage point as a gerontologist, Bourdieu's sense of social aging is more consistent with the narrow, if not ageist, cultural views that prevailed in the last half of the twentieth century, when he was writing. His sense of aging precedes the rise of the culture of the third age as a new field (discussed shortly) and how our elongated postemployment life span no longer expects "slow renunciation and disinvestment" of status or capital.

GETTING BEYOND NEVER-AGING MASCULINITIES

I end this chapter with a yet-to-be-substantiated argument that late middle-aged and old men have been and remain vulnerable to the cultural authority of never-aging masculinities. These authoritative voices have deep roots. They go back to the still-persistent male/female binary, and at times to essentialist thinking that nature determines gender relations and inequalities at least as much as nurture. The cultural authority of never-aging masculinities continues to have favorable reception within the discourse on "traditional" masculinity (e.g., Gerdes et al. 2017; Griffith and Cornish 2018) and the medical discourse on "successful aging" (cf. Katz and Marshall 2003).

The cultural ideologies that affirm never-aging and "traditional" masculinities too often ignore that gender is a configuration of practices harbored in time and place. Equally overlooked is the fact that gender always has an age. Young, middle-aged, and old men all practice and produce an array of masculinities, and most are age-specific, such as younger heterosexual men amending their habitus for their first "in a relationship" status, or old men moving into fields of aging masculinities and out of the spaces dominated by never-aging masculinities. The men's amended habitus and new fish-in-water performances can reveal how little or how much their habitus is ageless or age mindful. The performances will also reveal people's embodied class and ethnic and place habitus, something that Bourgois and Schonberg (2007) powerfully demonstrated in their investigation of aging homeless men in an urban sanctuary.

SUMMARY

Connell (1987, 1995) persuasively argued that every community has multiple masculinities, which are distinctive configurations of gender practices hierarchically ordered from ideal to subordinate and marginal. Bourdieu's sociology of practice (1984, 1990) also urges us to recognize that observable configurations of practices (masculinities, for example) are embodied and practiced, thereby reproducing social inequalities. This was illustrated with an ethnographic study of the lives and lifestyles of aging white and African American homeless men. This chapter began with a review of the paradigm shifts to Connell's and Bourdieu's sociologies and ends with the thesis that never-aging masculinities are (ageist) cultural mandates that ignore later life and, in turn, cast old men into stigmatized statuses as diminished, emasculated, or simply "old." Introduced is the idea that old men amend their gendered habitus in fields of aging masculinities and begin to align their masculine subjectivities with their new practices.

Chapter Two

Negotiating Age Relations and Aging

The old Americans I studied do not perceive meaning in aging itself; rather, they perceive meaning in being themselves in old age.

—Kaufman (1986, 6)

Resulting from improving longevity throughout the twentieth century, and then the sheer size of the Baby Boomer generation born during the post–World War II period, the soon-to-be and the existing cohorts of old men within Anglophone countries (the United Kingdom, the United States, Canada, Australia, New Zealand) and "developed" Asian countries (Japan, Singapore, South Korea) are an increasingly larger segment within their nations. They are a diverse group in terms of their gender practices and their aging trajectories. These facts, however, are clouded if not ignored by the ageism within gender relations and the ageist stereotypes within never-aging masculinities. I distinctly remember when I read sociologist Susan McFadden's comment about a needed image of aging—one that does not split frailty from strength, one that does not cast aging into polarities such as successful and unsuccessful. She argues that old age should be portrayed "neither as golden nor as badly tarnished" (McFadden 2012, vii). In this chapter, how old men experience age relations and their aging is appraised and theorized.

AGE RELATIONS

As a starting point for consideration, a brief excursus into "then and now." Over the nineteenth and twentieth centuries, national policies in most Global North nations normalized the cultural narrative of aging as physiological decline and social neediness. A significant transformation in public consciousness took place. The eighteenth- and nineteenth-century ideal of the venerated "elder" with his sagacious mind, white hair and wrinkles, use of a cane, and spirited disposition (Cole 1992; Fischer 1978) was quite rapidly replaced by the modernist veneration of "youth" with his fit body, hardiness, and strength. The calculus that masculinity *and* the wisdom of aging yields social authority was no longer deemed valid in the industrial world. The underlying core values of the emergent modernist discourse extolled youth (not seasoned maturity); virile, competent, healthy bodies (not lessening physical capital); economic productiveness (not just consumption); and an overall antiaging proclivity. It cast aging as decline, loss, and demasculation, and it spawned a medical-geriatrics paradigm of aging as a health problem.

When he chronicled the development of the "cult of youth" in the US from 1770 to 1970, David Fischer (1978) discussed the up-and-coming characterization of old men as oppressors and the modernist rallying cry for all nonaged men to unite against the legacy of gerontocracy. Ideals of masculinity were repositioned to accept new master cultural narratives that valorized youth, fueled stereotypes of old men as frail and dependent, and institutionalized the narratives that framed growing old as a drift toward demasculation. Such values questioned the premise that old men were wise and should be respected and restructured age relations such that old men were "rightly" marginalized. Ageism against elders emerged as a form of accepted oppression.

By the 1960s, "youth" emerged as a status in the life course and "old age" was further stigmatized. The cultural revolutions within the 1960s contested "the old ways," rejected all that was old, and privileged youth as found in young people's "alternative" lifestyles and self-expression. Writing autobiographically as an aging person in *The Coming of Age* (1972), Simone de Beauvoir detailed the pervasive contempt for the aged, particularly among youth, and mused about what growing old and being aged meant in modern societies: "The myths and the clichés put out by bourgeois thought aim at holding up the elderly man as someone who is different, as *another being*" (ibid., 3, italics original). Her next provocative proposition was that the aged man is viewed as "no more than a corpse under suspended sentence" (ibid., 244). Recognizing modern capitalist societies' revulsion and devaluation of old people as unproductive and rightly tossed aside when no longer of value, de Beauvoir daringly diagnosed old age as at once personal and political.

Embodied Ageism

Perhaps more than most other axes of social inequality for men, the distinction between the fit and the frail is one of the greatest social divisions and directs attention to another axis of inequality—dis/ablement. Old age, whenever it begins, involves the uncertainties of becoming old and then very old and living with corporeal disabilities. In cultures where there is the lingering "narrative of decline" that emerged with modernity (Gullette 1997), aging bodies and the old men in them were/are devalued.

This cultural narrative coaches people to study their faces, necks, skin, posture, and movement for signs of getting old, which in the stereotype's worst-case scenario signals impending debility and social exclusion. The early corporeal warning signs for men:

> Their bodies become weaker and more susceptible to illness and injury; their hair eventually turns grey and thins; their skin loses elasticity and becomes more wrinkled and sallow; layers of fat begin to cover once toned muscles and coarse body hair sprouts in places unimaginable to the younger self. (Coles and Vassarotti 2012, 33)

The cultural narrative also describes, or rather it scripts, old men's diminishing cultural authority and falloffs in masculine capital that trail the men's diminishing physicality. This is because the decline narrative exemplifies never-aging masculinities.

Such cultural narratives influence, might even corrode, how people experience age and aging. In her longitudinal studies of the consequences of living with ageist narratives, Becca Levy (2003) demonstrated "mind matters"—our age identities are based on negotiating the negative cultural stereotypes associated with aging. In cultures that discursively characterize age-related changes as decline, old men are imagined as smarting from one after another perilous personal loss—their occupational status vanishes with retirement, their social capital shrinks and community of coworkers fades away, their cultural authority diminishes, all as their masculine capital crumbles. Old men are figuratively positioned on the sideline of manly fields such as the workplace or bedroom. Men who had earlier adopted these negative views of aging were found to experience poorer functional health in later life and were more likely to die earlier than people with positive views of aging (Levy et al. 2002). The opposite is also correct: positive self-perceptions about growing older appear to *improve* men's subjective health and increase longevity. Levy's studies were of US adults, but her argument may not be limited to one country.

Recall Spector-Mersel's thought-provoking thesis on how old men must live with masculinity scripts that are truncated at middle age and fail to acknowledge later life at all. The ageism within never-aging masculinities basically demasculates old men as a population. Spector-Mersel (2006, 75) summed this group as

> a sort of "aging melting-pot." Metaphorically, when people cross the barrier of age sixty-five, they cease to be Jewish or Christian, American or English, and even, women or men. They are now being identified, first and foremost, by

their aged status. By no means, it should be stressed, do gendered images vanish in relation to old age. Nevertheless, they are pushed aside.

Consequently, men might consciously resist this; below are two examples.

Among aging Australian men who remained working in pharmaceutical sales well after the ordinary retirement age, the men had to negotiate their aging and sustain their identities as mature, not old (Foweraker and Cutcher 2015). Without viable scripts in the workplace to recognize workplace aging masculinities such as mentor, the men continued to draw on "traditional" scripts but tweaked them by using the capital available to them—leveraging their visible signs of aging (gray hair and wrinkles) to signal maturity and wisdom. They rejected their earlier testosterone-fueled selling strategies and, instead, placed emphasis on their experience of how to "read" the buyer. These aging men proudly became "material signifiers" of the company's older, well-accepted drugs, and they choose to "wear" their age as a mark of social distinction rather than decline. Foweraker and Cutcher's analysis also revealed that a principal discursive strategy for the men was to talk about themselves in terms of never-aging stories, and to emphasize how much their practices remained in sync with the masculinities of their earlier adulthood. They positioned themselves as superior to nonworking, "nonproductive" older men, thereby mimicking the common othering of "old" people. Remaining employed literally positioned them in the mainstream, even if they had also participated in "senior" or "veteran" social spaces with fields of aging masculinities such as found in motorcycle fraternities similar to the Grey Knights in the US, or "senior" arenas for competitive running, golf, bowling, or cycling.

Saxton and Cole (2012) analogously demonstrate the "incomplete and inchoate scripts" for old men in their critical analysis of the protagonist in *No Country for Old Men*, Sheriff Ed Tom Bell. The sheriff seemingly struggles as if a "broken man" when he faces the static, never-aging image of masculinity and his "impending retirement and death, which [in masculinity terms] are ultimately the same thing" (ibid., 112). However, Saxton and Cole propose, the sheriff's postemployment search for meaning "implies that there *may* be numerous ways of being an old man—not a one-size-fits-all image to which one must conform" (ibid., 113, my italics). Cormac McCarthy's titling of the novel title suggests maybe not.

Knowing that people's experiences with their aging take place within historical contexts raises the question: Are the contemporary generations of largely healthy-enough old men as constrained by the divisive ageism their fathers and grandfathers faced? All evidence strongly suggests that the rising generations of old men are less likely to encounter the full blunt of the institutional ageism or the ageist discourses their fathers and grandfathers lived with, since law prohibits many forms of blatant age discrimination. As well, most old men live active lifestyles that belie negative ageist stereo-types, including those besieging retirement. Most old men's self-defined "healthy enough" status is delineated in opposition to the social imaginary of "old age" and thus softens the meaning of ordinary aches and discomforts. In addition, the opportunities within the expanding field of aging masculinities offer most old men protective places.

Still, the discourses of corporeal decline and later life demasculation re-main threatening, even if they no longer fit the demographics of postmodern societies' healthier generations of old men and women. The irony is, despite the existence of ageism, the majority of old men maintain a positive sense of self and of well-being. Perhaps this is because they do not identify as "old"—that tag is reserved for someone else, not them. Further, as studies of Cana-dian and Finnish men suggest, old men negotiating their aging experience report fewer encounters with ageism than researchers generally expect. Al-though old men know ageism exists, unless the ageism occurs within an institutional context such as age "redlining" in residential options, Canadian men typically report they have not personally experienced ageism (Hurd Clarke and Korotchenko 2016). For Finnish old men, when they experience age-based "teasing" in a hunt club, they pass off the ageist commentary as a jocular masculine activity (Ojala et al. 2016, 52).

THIRD AND FOURTH AGE HABITUS

Gerontologists' mixed use of "third age" and "fourth age" nomenclature can be problematic when it comes to discussing later life and aging masculinities. There is the lingering conceptualization that nourishes a view of later life separated into two life course phases—the newer, initial, elongated and rela-tively healthy postemployment time, followed by the cliff of decrepitude, dependency, dysfunction, and death that is associated with very old age. This dis/able distinction paints a very rosy imaginary of the third age and a horrid imaginary of the fourth. For example, Weiss and Bass (2002, 3) comment at the beginning of their book, *Challenges of the Third Age*,

> The post-retirement years are, *for many*, a time when there is no longer respon-sibility for childcare nor need for paid employment, the two obligations that would have structured much of preceding life. *Many* in these retirement years have available to them pensions and savings adequate to maintain middle income styles of life and, in addition, health and energy not much diminished from their later years of employment. Their freedom and resources permit them to enter into any of a very wide range of activities. (my italics)

The *many* people within this imaginary of later life are assumed to not depend primarily or solely on Social Security for survival, to not face serious health challenges and their strain on mobility and finances, and to not have to help raise grandchildren. They are also less likely to be racial and ethnic minority men. Most retirement-age men in the bottom two-thirds of the income distribution do not have sufficient, if any, retirement savings and *many* will continue to work out of necessity. Such inequalities of retirement time and other capital in later and late life cannot be overlooked when we think in terms of old men's involvement in third age and fourth age cultures.

Whenever a stage of life is the prime focus, too easily ignored are the social inequalities and, in turn, the diversity of masculinities that aging men practice and embody. The conceptualization I use to draw attention to the fields of aging masculinities focuses on two cultural fields, not life stages. As Bourdieu would argue, viewing the third and fourth ages as fields, we can see that they have subcultures and distinctive habitus. The third age field might emphasize venues such as participation in "silver sneakers" workout programs, a weekly gathering of buddies for a card game or an inexpensive round of golf at a public course, senior-only online dating forums to find companionship, or fishing with grandchildren at different camping sites. The fourth age field could include welcoming the assistance of meals-on-wheels visitors and visiting nurses after downsizing to age-segregated communities or congregate housing. In the words of Higgs and Jones (2009, 66), the pervasive view of aging imagined several generations back could be said to be "dying out."

A "cultural field" conceptualization is what I rely on to understand and theorize the diversity of old men's experiences which take place "in-between their ideals and their realities" (Cole 2015, 6). The culture of a third age is recent because it is a generationally defined field that emphasizes the values of choice, autonomy, and self-expression. To some extent it involves an extension and expansion of midlife preferences and practices, yet with distinct new "rules of the game." Core in a third age habitus is resistance to social categorization as "old," chiefly through maintaining personal agency but also through active lifestyles.

In the (sub)cultures of the third age, men's aging trajectories are freed from preestablished masculinity blueprints (cf. Thompson and Langendoerfer 2016) and no longer determined by the pace of corporeal decline that was common among their grandfathers. Sociologist Anthony Giddens (1991, 147) discusses how the modernity processes that lengthen people's life span time also intensify later life with a new emphasis on individualized aging. Aging trajectories are now characterized by people's choices within and across classes, not just by class and people's capital. For instance, guided by their generational habitus, the old men of the Silent Generation who are in their 80s or older may gather most mornings for coffee and conversation with other "old guys" and continue their stoic-mindedness by silently managing their bodily aging. I do not think there is a fast-food chain restaurant that I have gone into any morning anywhere in the US or Canada and not witnessed several tables of old men huddled over inexpensive coffee and in animated conversation, with canes hanging off some men's seats at the table. For the younger cohorts of aging men, their generational habitus embodies postmodernity's overarching orientation to personal agency and the (relative) privileges of people's freedom to design their later life.

Generally speaking, participants in the fields of the third age construct "late lifestyles." These have often been misconstrued as leisure lifestyles, given the neoliberal emphasis on individuals underwriting their own postemployment living. With new generations of aging men's and women's life course radicalized by their longevity and the opportunities of late lifestyles, they may knock off bucket list items such as an annual motorcycle trek, a hot air balloon ride or a parachute jump, volunteering as a fictive granddad at a childcare center, or visiting turning-point places such as Birmingham, Alabama or the beaches of Normandy. These few examples of adventure, mentoring, and travel only apply to the majority of men who are not constrained by the early onset of corporeal decline, and they apply to men who have sufficient economic capital.

The fourth age is a more poorly understood and studied cultural field, but it seems to involve an acceptance of becoming "old" and the varied tastes people have regarding living with disability and frailty in old age while retaining their agency. It embodies the dialectic of decline and personal and spiritual growth, the paradox of preparing to let go while actively maintaining control. A greater dependency on and acceptance of others' care chiefly defines one's involvement in fourth age cultures, whether the care occurs through in-home geriatric services or within the new wave of "retirement" or "senior living" campuses that offer full services as needed. Participants in the field of the fourth age are differently active. Their physical disabilities or incapacities have often shrunk their mobility options to short walks with assistance, creating meaning through stories of past experiences and artistic activities, or seizing opportunities to argue sports and politics—all of which are means for resisting an existential vacuum.

My foregoing claim is that the third and fourth age are cultural fields where old men embody their age, build later lifestyles, and eventually embody their frailty and disabilities. This competes with the ubiquitous "new aging" discourse that tries to set apart "successful" aging from "usual" aging. Invoked by Rowe and Kahn (1998, 2015), this late twentieth-century discourse on so-called successful aging has other descriptions, including "positive aging," "healthy aging," "active aging," "optimal aging," and "aging well." Its trademarks are the encouragement (if not moral expectation) for people to maintain good health and remain socially engaged despite their chronological age. Indeed, some observers have argued that to age successfully means not to age at all.

Successful aging narratives originated in the medical community and have morphed into a neoliberal prescription that benefits the more affluent and healthy among aging men. The successful aging enterprise targets the men who are more likely to have the capital to maintain lives that extend middle age and subtly shames the men who do not. Holstein and Minkler (2003, 294) sum up, "By suggesting that the great majority of those elders in wheelchairs could indeed have been on cross-country skis had they but made the right choices and practiced the right behaviors can burden rather than liberate older people." Reviewing how the successful aging narrative evolved from a biomedical interpretation for privileged men's longevity, Calasanti (2016) notes that the discourses of successful aging reinforce the legacies of both hierarchal masculinities and ageism. Viewing biophysiological aging as a personal responsibility brands the men whose morbidities become limiting or disabling as "failures"—which occurs in much greater numbers among lesser privileged men whose work histories exact more from their bodies and whose resources may be too limited to contest "usual aging." By overlooking the structural and social factors that (dis)advantage men's lives, the successful/unsuccessful dichotomy levies a "message that an ideal aging citizen is someone who chooses to age successfully" (Rozanova 2010, 220).

Critics have suggested that successful aging narratives too closely approximate a Peter Pan, never-growing-old make-believe and are discursively "antiaging." The narratives are supported by aspects of a "new aging" enterprise that informs middle-aged and old men that retention of their masculine identities and patriarchal dividend is on them. In Global North economies the discourses on successful aging have metamorphosed into a new consumerist culture that chastises usual aging by promoting agelessness through products and policies encouraging an active aging consciousness. Old men whose aging trajectories are "usual"—not "successful"—can be prejudicially othered. Too infrequently noticed, the old men whose aging trajectories are "usual" are more likely disadvantaged socioeconomically and worked in demanding wear-and-tear occupations.

In all, old men's lived experiences with aging have long been embedded within ageist masculinity discourses that both other and shame them. They live surrounded by the inescapable narratives of success/failure that advocate unscripted masculinity trajectories, voices of demasculation, and the pervasiveness of "separate spheres" narratives that aim to segregate the aged and nonaged in many communities. Their subjective experiences of corporeal aging and later life could very well leave many of them bound up by the narratives of the inevitable decline of "usual aging." This seems to be the case for the disadvantaged old men who begin later life in poor health, and may ultimately adopt the negative, stereotypical images of demasculated men (e.g., Levy et al. 2002).

AGING MASCULINITIES

The way in which aging men retain and acquire masculine capital in later and late life reflects two processes—amending if not relinquishing their habitus of never-aging masculinities and embodying aging masculinities. It is arguable that old men perform and perhaps embody a variety of aging masculinities that reveal their generational habitus, corporeal experiences, class (or occupational grouping), and crafted lifestyles. Aging men may, for example, convert the never-aging masculinity penchant for risk-taking from strenuous hiking or aggressive financial investing or ignoring routine health concerns to a landscape consonant with aging masculinities, such as old men's preferences for gifting wisdom and capital and listening to their physician's advice before hiking treks (e.g., Gast and Peak 2011). For many old men who do not participate in consumerist-driven late lifestyles such as traveling, they may put into effect their late lifestyles within traditional fields such as active involvement in a faith community and its generative house-building and international ministry projects or as grandparents, perhaps even raising their grandchildren. Further, even when financial circumstances necessitate remaining involved in paid work, which is the case for many old men in the US, the men will also spend a significant portion of their later life in fields less characterized by never-aging masculinities and emphasized femininities. Consider, for instance, the finding that grandfathers who remain employed have more contact with their grandchildren than retired ones, and that at the turn of the millennium one in five grandfathers in the UK helped their eldest child with childcare (Gray 2005). What is observed are men's performances of various aging masculinities.

My argument is that aging never trumps men from being men, and old men will act their age. Repeating an earlier comment, gender always has an age; thus later life and late life masculinities are not the same as men's earlier never-aging masculinity performances. To age is to change, and this relates to how masculinity can be and is performed. Stephen Whitehead (2002, 199–200) notes, "The masculinities that become inscribed on the youthful male body become transformed just as the boy is transformed through aging . . . [and] the dominant discourses around ageing appear to be undergoing some profound shift, ushering in new and possibly less restrictive ways of thinking about age and the body."

It is generally acknowledged by sociologists that as modern and then postmodern societies embraced individualization, the structure of the life course was destandardized (Giddens 1991). This means that chronological age is no longer the primary way of organizing people's lives. It also means that no longer is the school-to-work transition to adulthood or the work-to-retirement transition to old age the sequenced pattern for most people, as old age has been transformed into later and late life. What was once thought to be an ordinary biographic turning point, the work-to-retirement transition, has lessened in importance to understand old men's late lifestyles. Old men may remain in the labor force out of need or choice and never "retire"; they may outlive their spouse and develop new intimate relationships in later life; they may return to school to pursue an unfulfilled interest in history; some may prefer living alone whereas others prefer housing options that are age homogeneous.

Supported in postmodern societies are new masculinity niches strengthening late lifestyles. Others have made similar arguments. Inhorn and Wentzell's (2011) observation of the "emergent masculinities" within the Muslim Middle East as well as Coles and Vassarotti's (2012) theorizing on the "field of aged masculinity" equally recognize that aging masculinities may well soon eclipse the "traditional" never-aging masculinity that once dominated men's lives. In the Middle East and Mexico, aging men are enacting "emergent masculinities—living out new ways of being men in attempts to counter forms of manhood that they see as *harmfully* hegemonic" (Inhorn and Wentzell 2011, 801, my italics). Old men confronted by the fog of mystery that still surrounds crafting postemployment lifestyles invent novel, aging masculinities through their preferences and practices. This reasoning recognizes that earlier cultural narratives on masculinities may linger to partly guide old men's preferences and practices in later and late life (cf. Thompson and Langendoerfer 2016). These decades-old masculinity ideologies were part of old men's generational and personal habitus when they were younger.

Knowing that aging men's earlier habitus is not expunged, rather it is amended, aging men's agency strategies may emphasize what they can "still do" (Meadows and Davidson 2006). One example of this is the masculinity narratives voiced by men aged 85 and older in northern Sweden (Aléx et al. 2008). "Being in the male centre" was a dominant narrative; it laid emphasis on values consistent with younger-aged hegemonic masculinities, including the old men's very active life, own ability, independence, and unremitting sexism. Another narrative, "striving to maintain the male façade," was noticed more among the old men who were anxious about their bodily aging and no longer in "the male centre." This narrative emphasized the men's preferred adherence to past cultural norms, but more so discursively through stories than in practice. Both of these narratives existed alongside men's rejection of the misery perspective that was prevalent and guiding their (initial) thinking about how getting old equals demasculation. The narratives were consonant with the men's subjectivities as men and, to different degrees, being comfortable in their "own skin" as old men. Pirhonen and colleagues (2016) similarly observed that Finnish men aged 90+ would use frail aged peers as their point of downward comparison; the old men talk about their functional limitations, but distinguish their limitations from frailty and center their narratives on their intention to be independently able to "continue the habitual aspects of gendered life" (15).

Other research also indicates that old men at times will be complicit with the directives of hegemonic masculinity yet transgress them in practice. For instance, this can occur when grandfathers disclose their agency in doing regular care work and position themselves in ways challenging cultural stereotypes about minimalist grandfathers (e.g., Bartholomaeus and Tarrant 2016) or when husbands who occupy a feminine space to be their wife's primary caregiver do not ask for assistance, even encouraging their daughters and wife's sisters to stay back. In both cases, the old men engaged in forms of unpaid family work, yet spun their stories to attest to their independence and proficiency.

A common thread running through most aging men's narratives is that they are not bowed by the stereotypes that held merit twenty years ago. The dispiriting message about aging and demasculation in late life, which old men heard and witnessed as young men, has been upended by most aging men maintaining busy lives. Their later life trajectories are more personalized and less defined by the masculinized spaces they occupied earlier in their lives. Old men position themselves in new callings that provide masculine capital inside fields of action that value self-expression and autonomy such as environmental work, spiritual quests, storytelling within intergenerational programs, and encore careers. None, or maybe few, of these fields of action are esteem sites for "doing masculinity" if viewed through the lens of never-aging masculinity, but these fields of action are many old men's preferred spaces. They represent the field of aging masculinities.

When Coles and Vassarotti (2012) shift attention to aging masculinities and investigate the experiences of old men, their work highlights the importance of studying old men's subjectivities, identities, and masculine capital. This is in line with Bourdieu-inspired analyses of aging men, where gender relations or the structural arrangement of masculinities are not the best starting place to understand the social worlds of old men. Rather, it is men's subjectivities and identities, which are repeatedly transformed through time and always constructed through their aging body.

For instance, old men's everyday strategies in realizing their gendered identities are linked with claiming or rejecting symbolic membership in particular groups and improving their positioning within these groups. Drawing on interview data, Coles (2008, 245) details the case of "Charlie," a 62-year-old retired gay man and how he reformulates hegemonic masculinity to deliberately exclude heterosexuality and sporting prowess, which marginalize him as a gay man, yet includes the masculinity emphasis on manual labor, which affirms his continuing physical capital of "getting his hands dirty." Quoting Charlie:

> [My father] lived through the war years. And that's what I, as a kid, grew up to see as masculine. So I have a lot of that about me . . . that comes from my father. And not being interested in sport, not being able to kick a footy around or throw a ball, not being interested in women's tits, I don't think makes me any less of a male.

Scholars (e.g., Phoenix and Sparkes 2009) argue that such storytelling as Charlie's functions to impose order on experiences and make sense of men's experiences with aging. Narratives involve the performance of identity. They blend together "big stories" that reflect broader cultural narratives about working hard to make the most of life *and* the "small stories" that disclose the individual's circumstances and experiences. Phoenix and Sparkes (2009) discuss Fred, an active 70-year-old who came to their attention when a news story reported how he organized and played in a football (soccer) game. He framed his narrative in terms of a "big story" about maximizing masculine capital—"Life is what you make of it" (230). His episodes of illness and his aging experiences were storied as ordinary parts of living (225), not as biographical ruptures undermining his sense of himself as a man. The notion of "getting on with it" was core to this man's aging masculinity (225), as shown in the following quote (226):

> I think it's like everything, what people need to realize is that nothing comes easy and you've got to keep going back and trying, whatever it is. But that means enjoying each day as it comes along . . . from my point of view, I do believe that you are what you can make of yourself and you've got to keep going haven't you for as long as you can.

A masculinity script that stresses being successful and respected infuses Fred's narrative; his core taste represents a man who is striving to be a fit old man with a full, "leisurely" life. His identity and habitus are centered on maintaining a busy everyday life (231). As Fred's story demonstrates, aging masculinities can include involvement in competitive sports and some commitment to never-aging masculinities.

Thus, unlike stereotypes, most aging men do not experience a negative existential crisis as they "grow" older or construct their postemployment lives. The narratives old men commonly present within interviews and personal stories are not aligned with decline or dependency or demasculation. Instead, emerging from these and other studies of old men's negotiation of the fields that they are imbedded in in later life is the subjectivity of being freed from (e.g., Saxton and Cole 2012) the rigidity of "traditional" and never-aging masculinities. Later life can liberate. Old men may never feel fully retired from the bindings of never-aging masculinities; however, more of their everyday lives are within fields where they are capable and that offer promise and possibilities. For example, in the field of later life sexuality, a couple's intimacy practices can supersede the (hetero)sexual coital mandate. As Linn Sandberg (2013b, 277) notes, "Something social [intimacy] shapes, in this case, is older men's sexual subjectivities and bodies." Coles and Vassarotti (2012) support this argument: What takes central stage in later life is aging men's preference "to operate in the *field of aged masculinity* (a subfield within the field of masculinity) in which the capital that they owned was valued (such as experience, maturity, and wisdom as part of cultural capital)" (36, italics original). Men appear to find value in later life in developing a sense of self that is not culturally allied with hegemonic masculinity.

Take, for example, Drummond's (2003) observation that as the level of bodily proficiency diminishes with age, men who were once fit sometimes reclaim masculine capital by taking up different challenges. Old men often maintain a competitive posture even when engaging in solitary activities; in mall walking, their competitiveness leaks out by attempting to walk farther, longer, or faster. Similarly, a 67-year-old man in Wiersma and Chesser's (2011, 254) study of masculinities, aging bodies, and leisure talked about his *relative* capability:

> At this last Tai Chi thing . . . I was working together with a young woman . . . I think maybe she was 45 or 50. Somebody would say that's not young but anyway we worked together doing our thing . . . And she said, "Oscar, you've got good muscle tone in your shoulders, you know, not like most of the old people I work with." And I was hugging this beautiful younger woman and feeling very masculine and not particularly sexual but just feeling that kind of thing and she was comparing me to these old people that she works with.

Eman (2011) found in her study of old athletes aged 68–90 that all but one of the nine men had stopped competing; yet the majority positioned themselves in activities that preserved feelings of competitiveness and success, such as golf or fitness walking. One man talked proudly about how he engaged in physical activities that would hinder his age peers: "I have cousins of the same age as me who can't even touch the floor, whilst I am able to ski 20 miles" (Eman 2011, 52). A retired man's "small story" describes his continuing need to garner respect from his achievements: "It's like I need to keep proving to myself that I can do stuff, so whenever I commit to something I say it has to be on my terms, so it has to be when I'm able to do it but I'll do it. I need to keep having accomplishments" (Oliffe et al. 2013, 1633).

Accumulating evidence also shows most old men recognize the paradoxes of corporeal aging as the new *normative* (cf. Carstensen et al. 2011; Lomranz and Benyamini 2016). This means that for some old men the sense of inconsistency or discontinuity between being as old as you are and not feeling as old as you are, or conversely the gap between age-related functional limitations and feeling neither frail nor dependent, is recognized as this age group's tolerance for and acceptance of incongruity. Old men's subjectivities and narrative identities attest to living with fluid situations, which include the inconsistencies, discontinuities, and paradoxes of corporeal and social aging.

REFRAMING THE DISCOURSE

Whitehead (2002) mused that there may dignity and opportunity in aging for some men and existential chaos with lost selves for others. I would prefer to argue that it is not either/or, rather that *every* old man encounters new opportunities and existential bumps, and will experience dignity and ignominy. Aging is a complex process that research tends to still-frame as a 35mm camera may.

I end this chapter closely paraphrasing Whitehead (2002, 200)—the masculinities once inscribed on old men's bodies and part of their habitus become transformed just as the body is transformed. Through a lens that sees men not as old but as *old men*, the masculinity practices we witness among aging and very old men are just that: gendered practices, reflecting gendered selves in later and late life. Aged bodies are old men's "home," and just as young bodies were their home years earlier, bodies always hover ambiguously between nature and society. Old men continue to be men. Their subjectivities as aging men are bodily informed and socially constructed.

SUMMARY

In the nineteenth century, veneration shifted to youth from the aged, part of the cultural effect as modernity replaced tradition. Another cultural shift is occurring in many developed nations as a result of postmodernity and most people's healthier, longer lives. More and more people now have the opportunity to cultivate personally rewarding postemployment lifestyles within later life. Old men now practice and embody (or amend their never-aging habitus) a variety of culturally and socially sponsored aging masculinities.

Chapter Three

Aging Bodies: Our Corporeality

It is difficult to imagine a disembodied social gerontology. And yet the body is something that is more often implied than discussed.

—Powell and Longino (2001, 199)

Bodies matter, including the aging body. The aging body is increasingly a prevalent body in graying societies, certainly not omnipresent but no longer invisible even if mostly ignored; it is the medium through which we experience growing older; it is always unfinished; it mediates social relations; it is a marketing touchstone, employed by the expanding antiaging enterprise to hawk motorcycles, lifestyles, various forms of insurance, pharmaceutical products, and surgical-medical interventions; it continues to have the capacity to surprise, as when someone's touch quickens respiration; it can be unruly, as when sleep is disturbed by a leg cramp or when mindfulness is interrupted by thoughts of an in-law's bullying; clothed, it can be a sign of generation; it signifies old men's dis/able status; it is phenomenologically both "me" and "not really me."

My use of the word "body" in this chapter refers to the material, fleshy entity in which we find ourselves. We have bodies and we are bodies and we live with the corporeality of aging. This is what is meant by "our corporeality" in the chapter title—our forever-aging corporeal bodies, which age at different paces as a result of who we are. Examined in the chapter is the advent of the corporeal body that was long ignored in sociology and recognition of old men's social body, which was virtually ignored in gerontology. The chapter includes discussion of how men commonly take their body for granted until "it" hurts or, less often, until a situation makes them self-conscious, such as when a man's functional capabilities become concerning. Those situations draw attention to the gap between people's felt (younger) age and their ongoing corporeal aging. Also addressed in the chapter is how much old men's body consciousness hinges on their physical functioning, not their "looks," and how the majority of old men reject consumerist concerns with aesthetics as both unnatural and inauthentic masculinity practices.

ABSENCE, PRESENCE

In *The Body and Social Theory*, Chris Shilling (2003) referred to bodies as an "absent presence" within social theory. What he means is that the body itself was long ignored in sociology, even when medical or sport sociologists might have indirectly studied it. I find his comment applies equally to the theorizing in gerontology and critical men's studies about aging bodies. Old men's bodies have presence in the sense that they were acknowledged on occasional by researchers as consumer bodies or medicalized bodies (Shilling 2003, 35). Yet old men's bodies themselves are quite absent. I found Peter Öberg's (1996) essay on how the (gendered) body had been largely excluded from investigation in aging studies striking, because about the same time I had called attention to the invisibility of old men in both aging and masculinity studies, yet I too, embarrassingly, barely mentioned aging men's bodies (e.g., "Bodies are not virile, rather pleasantly plump," Thompson 1994, 12).

There has been increased attention to bodies in gerontology since Öberg's observation, yet too little empirical work has addressed men's aging bodies outside of a biomedical lens, which more likely than not speaks to the "natural" biophysiological deterioration of cells, muscles, organs, and function. Gerontology's long-term geriatrics-leaning interpretation of bodies combined with the sociology of the body's past thirty-plus-year habit of neglecting bodies was my second wake-up call. Together they compel my attempt to try to discuss men's aging bodies in a chapter not wedded to health matters. I want to underscore "try to," because there is so little prior work to grab onto to affirm my and others' theorizing for a research-grounded discussion.

In sociology, past practice has emphasized how (younger) bodies are regulated by institutions such as religion and medicine (e.g., Foucault 1965) or how bodies are constrained by the inequalities that result from people's social location, particularly socioeconomic inequalities (e.g., Marmot 2005). Scholars taught us how a natural body is regulated and made "docile" through discourses and norms that act on and produce a social body (e.g., Elias 1982). Without doubt, much has been learned about the oppression of bodies, especially racialized bodies, women's bodies, and the bodies of a class of people.

Drew Leder (1990) directs our attention to a different absence, presence that I find compelling. Most of the time, he suggests, the (aging) body is also *absent* in our own everyday experience. From the first-person point of view, our ordinary, daily experiences with our body disappear from awareness or consciousness (Bourdieu 1990; Leder 1990). It is absent. Our body seizes our awareness at times of disturbance, as when pain surfaces as an "alien presence" (Leder 1990, 70–79); or, when we are in new situations interacting with strangers, the body is propelled forward, in front of the person in it. It becomes the object subjected to both our own and others' gaze. A case in point: Aging heterosexual and gay men's bodily experiences are (un)consciously registered as experiences of a straight/gay man. Their bodies do not routinely become objects of their own attention as straight or gay. Bodies remain absent or taken for granted, until something like unwanted attention disrupts and threatens the shielding cocoon (Giddens 1991; Sparkes 1996, 465). For instance, in encounters with younger men, the bodies of aging straight/gay men can become present and spark a reminder that they are at odds with the fitness ideals in contemporary Western cultures.

EMBODIMENT

Amidst all current theorizing around the body, Bourdieu's work on habitus stands out because of the sophistication it provides in understanding the processes of embodiment, and the ways in which our internal and corporeal bodily processes are connected with and fashioned by social life. Bourdieu's (1984) recognition is that we are our body, in both its physical and symbolic capital, and as we age we engage in struggles in pursuit of our own interests. Bourdieu's sociology of the body also fits the postmodern cultural emphasis on personal responsibility and agency.

In *Distinction* (1984) Bourdieu also addressed how the body is a living expression of the hierarchies of social power. Drawing on his theorizing, critical sociological and cultural studies have taught us not to ignore the symbolic violence within racialized experiences (cf. Bourgois and Schonberg 2007). Take an impeccable example involving the intersectionality of ethnicity and generation and the literal embodiment of social relations: Old Japanese American men born in the US prior to World War II embody their stigmatized otherness and childhood horror of being forced into prison internment camps because of their ethnic ancestry; many came to practice docile bodies, unlike the experience of their children and unlike the experience of nearly all now-old white German American men who were not imprisoned or othered (Nakagawa 1993; Rostow 1945). What other bodily consequences arise from people's literal and/or symbolic imprisonment? The ethnic components of habitus express themselves as everyday practices, emotions, and beliefs that can constrain life choices.

Or consider an example of men's sexuality and generational habitus: Compared to middle-aged gay men who have benefitted from the ongoing destigmatization of sexualities, most old gay men now in their 70s or 80s have a very different relationship to their bodies because of the years of living "closeted" and marginalized if they did not perform the body practices of "traditional" (heterosexual) masculinity (Leonard, Duncan, and Barrett 2013, 112). I introduce these examples of the regulation of the (social) body because as the chapter unfolds and draws on the available research and theoretical work, bodies matter and body practices ought not be overlooked.

THE SOCIAL BODY: ME. NOT ME.

To strangers, we are all known by our body and its signs of age, ethnicity, and class. For an aging man, his sophisticated salt-and-pepper hair color, facial wrinkles, and motion will transmit age-related messages, as his clothes also might. Men's perceived interpersonal age as late middle-aged or old, however, often diverges from their felt age and self-image. Bodily aging often masks the old man's sense of himself, feelings of physical vigor, and experience of age. Thompson and Kaye (2013, 133) illustrate this difference:

> The way our body changes with aging is commonly framed in words such as "I'm in pretty good shape for my age," even if the man's appearance suggests otherwise. Meet a weathered-faced man in his late sixties who uses a cane, and he might confidently tell you that he doesn't feel old. You think he looks it. What you do not know is that he has been using a cane for 30 years, ever since his horse stumbled and threw him in a steeple chase, requiring several surgically implanted pins in his leg. Because he still works outdoors with horses—he is a trainer of racehorses—his skin has a distinctive weathered look. His physical appearance is consistent with his livelihood and age, and his body image is consistent with his resilience and functional ability.

Perspective matters. The stranger sees only the body. The old man looks into the mirror and does not routinely see his weathered face or gray hair. He sees the old man he is—the whole man, how "the self of the past is an underpinning for the self of the present" (Thompson and Whearty 2004, 8). Sarah Matthews's (1979) study of old women's everyday life distinguished how being among friends also displaces the stranger-perspective: Familiarity brings forward the person inside the aging body and makes the body virtually invisible, for the moment. Friends see one another, and only occasionally is the other's body front and center. But out in the general public the aging women more acutely sensed being viewed as old. My observation is that old men's social worlds are not too different. Friendships and familiar places provide old men a relevant context for the aged body to be unimportant. However, unfamiliar settings thrust the aged body to the foreground. When encouraged to begin yoga exercises as therapy for hip osteoarthritis, it was not easy for Ted (age 71) to blend into or feel at ease within local yoga classes populated by much younger women. He quit. Living in a smaller town, it is not surprising that Ted could not locate a Yoga for Old Stiff Guys group. We all prefer to congregate with age peers—it breeds a sense of comfort.

MASK OF AGING

The disparity between one's outward appearance and felt age is what Featherstone and Hepworth (1991) propose in their "mask of aging" construct. They argue that many old men view their corporeal aging as a troubling camouflage; it projects an image at variance with the way the man feels and conceals beneath the aged exterior an essential younger self. Bryan Turner (1995, 257) similarly commented, "With ageing, the outer body can be interpreted as a betrayal of the youthfulness of the inner body." This paradox was once called "the ghost in the machine," where a younger-feeling ghost inhabits an old(er) machine, or body (cited in H. Gibson 2000). This masculinist discourse about the body as a machine dates back to the early 1900s' merging of industrialization and modernity (e.g., Benedict and Carpenter 1909).

Following on, Featherstone and Hepworth (1991, 379) exemplify masking:

> When asked at the age of 79 to describe what it felt like to be old, the author J. B. Priestley replied, "It is as though, walking down Shaftesbury Avenue as a fairly young man, I was suddenly kidnapped, rushed into a theatre and made to don the grey hair, the wrinkles, and the other attributes of age, then wheeled on stage. Behind the appearance of age I am the same person, with the same thoughts as when I was younger."

When people aged 59–86 were asked "Do you think of yourself as old?" Thompson, Itzin, and Abendstern (1990) discovered that nearly seven in eight replied categorically "No." This is not surprising. Studying subjective age across the life span, Rubin and Bernsten (2006) found that from midlife on, individuals feel about 20 percent younger than their actual age. This pattern of denial of being old, or as I prefer, old people discursively positioning themselves as not yet old, is part of a more general pattern whereby normative assumptions about being old are rejected. When old people "declare 'I don't feel old, I feel young inside' what they are trying to express is that they do not identify with the false stereotype of what an 'old person' is commonly supposed to be" (H. Gibson 2000, 775).

The rift between our age and our felt age is often presented as an existential quandary. It surely can be a taproot for ontological uncertainty—"Am I *really* 'old?'" Living with the pervasiveness of ageism, it is not uncommon for old men to talk about aging in narratives that distance them from their aged bodies and from old age. Take, for example, a study of older adults who were living with multiple chronic conditions. Hurd Clarke, Griffin, and their colleagues (2008, 1088) note, "One man, aged 76, who had eight chronic conditions, expressed . . . 'I don't feel old even though I'm going on 77. I don't feel old. I still think I'm 50.'" Similarly, one old man interviewed by Coffey (2012) in Sturgis, South Dakota, at the annual motorcycle rally summed up, "You know, age is your body, mostly. In your mind, I'm not sure you age much."

BRIDGING AND MASQUERADING

The gap between what is hidden (felt age) and what is manifest (the aging body) can be regularly bridged, Biggs (2004) theorized, by "masquerades." Masquerading is doing one's (younger) felt age, as in continuing to ski or trekking in snowshoes or remaining in the labor force by choice. According to Biggs (ibid., 48), purposeful social masking becomes more pronounced whenever a group or individual becomes socially excluded from sources of value and esteem—e.g., the marginalization of aging men in many work-places. Biggs proposed that social masking or masquerading, especially in intergenerational contexts, is an intentional rebuff of the stigma of old age. Recall the way aging men in Australian pharmaceutical sales masqueraded. Biggs argues that social masking is not so much the pursuit of a perpetual state of ageless adulthood or an ageless self. Rather, it is the agency people use to resist the negative overtones of age stereotyping and/or the ageist prescriptive norms of social clocks that encourage aging men to disengage from much of social life.

Scandinavian research suggests that masquerading may begin in men's mid-30s; Öberg and Tornstam (1999) also found men's felt age hovers roughly ten years younger than their chronological age throughout the life span. In a study of midwestern US grandparents, Kaufman and Elder (2002) found, on average, that a 60-year-old man felt 54 years old, a 70-year-old man felt 62 years old, and an 80-year-old man felt 70 years old. The pattern shows that as men get older they progressively feel younger than they are. This pair of studies jointly suggests that social masking is very likely a longstanding embodied experience and that many old men who feel younger are probably as active as they feel. Notably, Öberg and Tornstam report that old men generally feel satisfied with their bodies.

Drawing on Biggs's theorizing, I suggest that whenever an aging man dons a social mask to evoke or maintain a particular self-presentation, such as a 67-year-old retired carpenter (Matt) rarely trimming his thick, graying "biker" beard or a 71-year-old administrator (Rob) dying his hair to hide its gray, each man is engaged in "body work" (practices undertaken to modify or maintain the body in some way) to blend in among the esteemed bodies within his social world. It is a matter of identity management and preservation of masculine capital. Postmodern times champion each individual to construct his body to support his identity (Shilling 2003), which is based on his felt age as well as his reading of the bodily expectations of others. These "others" are his social groups far more so than the "generalized other" of a man of a particular age. The old carpenter, Matt, is a member of the internet-based Brotherhood of Grey Beard Bikers, whose stated aim is to preserve and enjoy the biker lifestyle. He is otherwise unaffiliated with an organized riding club but is part of a group of "old guys" who regularly ride together on weekends. His beard is "just me. I've had it for a long time." As an emblematic postmodernist, Matt explains his appearance in saying, "Everybody has their own way." In northern Ohio, Matt is one of many gray-bearded old men continuing a riding lifestyle. Wander around an Ohio village or rural small-town craft fair in the spring or summer, and you will be stunned at the range of aging bodies present and the herds of bikes in the parking areas.

A 66-year-old New England janitor (Stan) I interviewed for a study of men's aging concerns had been unable to ride because he had severely ruptured his bicep, but hoped to ride again in a year. Stan embodied his lifestyle even though he was temporarily not riding: he had several forearm tattoos; maintained his full, thick goatee; and often wore a stars-and-stripes bandana at work. He commented, "I miss riding. The only good news, though, because I'm big, they [his supervisors] expect me to be the mule lifting and carrying furniture. I can't now for at least a year. Ha!" On the cover of the April 2013 *Gerontologist* is the photo of a fit, balding, 70+-year-old appliance technician with his gray goatee: "Zip," his nickname, who rode from his home in Dallas, Texas, to the Sturgis motorcycle rally in South Dakota for twenty-three years before he died in 2014. These old men—Matt, Stan, and Zip—exemplify ongoing lifestyle embodiment despite aging bodies, with some of their current preferences and taste largely consistent with their earlier experience and habits. Their gray beards or goatees signify their age. Their attire symbolizes the social world of men with motorcycles. Because of the continuities of their lives, their embodiment of being older may go unremarked, unless they make passing social comparisons to men less fit (Laz 2003, 517), or they laugh about the fact that they now need more pit stops or breaks when riding a distance. Quite similarly, Minello and Nixon (2017) explored the meanings and experiences of road (bi)cycling among predominantly white, middle-class aging men. Not unlike working-class men's experiences with their bikes, the road cycling men Minello and Nixon interviewed lived a lifestyle such that they strived for the camaraderie of cycling, the joy of the ride, feeling well and being fit, and resisting as long as possible but then adjusting to the limitations imposed by their corporeal aging.

AGE PERFORMANCES

I suppose what Biggs called masquerading may first seem an odd construct, given its dictionary meaning, to "pretend to be someone one is not." However, a masquerade is quite simply the *performance* of felt age and thus one's own identity. I am reminded of Erving Goffman's (1959) discussion of everyday performances. In light of the greater healthiness of most aging men compared to their grandfathers' later life, and given the new moral requisite to take personal responsibility for and control of one's body shape, weight, and appearance, are old men who are socially and physically active really "masquerading" their age? Inversely, are old men who are not able-bodied and are in fair-to-poor health "inauthentic"? I think "no" answers both questions. Repeating Matt's observation, "every*body* has their own way." Judith Butler (1988, 1990) points to how commonplace communication—speech, a biker beard, gestures—is performative and serves to define one's identity. She (1988, 521) elaborates, "One is not simply a body, but, in some very key sense, one does one's body and, indeed, one does one's body differently from one's contemporaries and from one's embodied predecessors."

Biggs and Butler direct us to understand that whatever the ways late middle-aged and old men manage their performative and embodied identities, it involves expressing oneself though one's body. These performances are phenomenologically the reassertion of a contextual "me," which scholars have interpreted as an old man purposively contesting ageism. Each point of view may be true. An aging man dons multiple social masks, such that the "younger" self-presentation of a senior professor who spends much of his time in the company of young colleagues and students is accomplished by his preference of regularly wearing blue jeans and a sport jacket, whereas his mask as adviser and authoritative professor is accomplished through his voice, gestures, body demeanor, smiles and frowns, and aging face (cf., Goffman 1959, 1967). The same 64-year-old professor playing fast-pitch softball is unacknowledged as a professor. Rather, he is known as one who singles and is often a designated runner for less agile teammates—his legs work well, but his upper body strength limits his hitting power to singles. No passing observer of the team would be familiar with his CFO and tow truck driver teammates' off-the-field "masks"; it is their agile bodies, constant banter, and much better legs that draw attention as they threaten to push a double into a triple or coast under and catch a deep fly ball.

In sum, and paraphrasing Butler (1988, 521–22), the body is not merely fleshy material; it also is social, is contextual, and has history. The body is more than the corporeal exterior; it is the "I am" that continues to symbolize performances and possibilities. Butler's discussion of performative acts as both corporeal and gendered (ibid., 523) supports my observation that aging men's body presentations and body projects in and of themselves affirm their felt age and enactment of never-aging as well as aging masculinities. The remainder of this chapter will show that old men may feel constrained by their bodies' *capabilities* but they also normalize most bodily aging as part of aging.

REPRESENTATIONAL MASCULINITIES

In popular culture, there has been a dramatic increase in images of the male body, and two bodily standards—muscularity and fitness—continue to define the desirable male body in most Western societies. This is unmistakable by the men presented on the covers of men's magazines and their representation in women's magazines. The prototypical young man mimics the classical body form of the youthful Greek god Adonis, a symbol of masculine beauty. Over the past thirty-plus years male bodies featured in popular magazines have remained youthful in appearance and even became more lean, muscular, and V-shaped (Law and Labre 2002). The image is frequently an "eroticized aesthetic showing a toned, young body" (Gill 2003, 187). Very few men aged 65 and older have Adonis bodies, and most never had.

The representational masculinity in media can create photographic myth-scapes. On the one hand, there is a prevailing imaginary where flabby old men serve as comic relief. Their corporeal aging is as comical as their grumbling and stumbling. They no longer represent the body ideals of manhood and may be portrayed as "going to pot," "over the hill," "old goats," and "old farts." On the other hand, the irony is, of the limited portrayals of men in later and late life, most media representations—whether in magazines, film, video, or television—are not explicitly ageist in a negative masculinist sense. The inverse occurs. Based on their early study of British television, Rodwell and colleagues (1992, 7; cited in Hearn 1995, 109) concluded, "[T]here was a tendency to present a *selective* view of old age that played down the possible connections between old age, disability, ill health and death" (my italics).

Recently, old men were absent in men's magazine advertising and interest stories. When they were occasionally present, the representations almost exclusively were in a favorable light (Hurd Clarke, Bennett, and Liu 2014). Typically the old men portrayed never-aging masculinities; they were experienced and powerful, healthy and happy. From their analysis of magazine photographic representations of old men, Robinson and Callister (2008) noted that the health status presentations were overwhelmingly favorable, even when inactivity (e.g., sitting) was imaged twice as frequently as being active (e.g., walking, jogging, swimming).

In all, even though old men's rare representations in visual and textual media may well be "not negative," perhaps this is because old men's bodies are nearly always hidden, or at least clothed. In an analysis of the advertising industry's war with the aging body and with age itself, Katz and Marshall (2003, 5) suggest that the industry has constructed portrayals only of a "senior" who is an independent, healthy, sexy, flexi-retired citizen. This "senior" does not represent old men. Men no older than late middle age personify the senior. Such advertising casts an agreeable aesthetic, since this guise proposes that aging men need not look (too) old. The media representations are absent the many ways time marks men's corporeality with wrinkles, lines, spots, sagging skin, and larger bellies. Rarely is a man's experience of his aging body directly addressed, outside of heteronormative comedy representations about able-bodied men such as Jack Nicholson as 63-year-old Harry with a reputation of dating "girls" a third his age in *Something's Gotta Give*. More rare would be a representation of a very old body, and especially a positive representation. There are a few exceptions, such as the performance by the late Peter O'Toole as Maurice in the 2006 film *Venus*, where the character embodies the wisdom of being an old man and the physical frustrations of being old.

INSTRUMENTAL AND AESTHETICS

With the *lived* aging body, and maybe the shame of it typically ignored in cultural representations, does this neglect affect men's bodily experiences? The answer is, of course. Bodies are judged by others and, in turn, by us. When the corporeal signs of aging are masked, such as when film and print representations veil old men's bodies in clothes, the embarrassment, perhaps revulsion, of sighting an aging naked body is assuaged. The aesthetics of never-aging masculinities also are encouraged, but not necessarily endorsed by old men themselves. Take, for example, the work of Ward and Holland (2011), who studied the expected self-image dilemmas associated with graying, thinning hair. They found that "very few [UK] men touched upon the topic of self-presentation and appearance at all when discussing discrimination in later life" (296). In a sample of Finnish and US men, Ojala et al. (2016) similarly noted that the majority of the men rejected consumerist strategies focusing on aesthetics as both unnatural and inauthentic masculinity; the men, particularly those from the working class, favored "natural" aging bodies and maintaining physical functioning to preserve their respectability as men. They snubbed aesthetics, but cared that their bodies look like they can still perform.

Similarly, age-related "change in looks" was not an important factor among aging Swedish men (Öberg 2003). There seem to be two interwoven reasons: First, the proportion of men who "think they look masculine" actually began to very slowly diminish at the time they were in their 20s (Öberg 2003: 120). Second, three-quarters of the men aged 65–74 believed they continued to look masculine, and more than half of the oldest men (aged 75+ in the study) perceived themselves as looking masculine. This study's findings regarding still "looking masculine" are not likely restricted to Swedish men—aging appearances do not outweigh men's embodied sense of self as "looking masculine." Rather, it is when flexibility, strength, and stamina begin to diminish that troubles arise. In all, wrinkles, hair color, and saggy necks are not demasculating. Loss of bodily capacity and becoming dependent can be. In Lodge and Umberson's (2013) study of middle-age men talking about their bodies, a 55-year-old man commented on his existential awakening when he confronted the midlife threshold leading to later life: "Until you are 45 you just think your body is going to be as receptive as it always is, but when that [aging] starts happening, you just go, 'Oh.' You have got to start working harder at just staying even and not go backwards."

The obligation to negotiate body aesthetics may occur more commonly among old gay men, as gay communities place emphasis on appearance (e.g., Jones and Pugh 2005). There is a "lookism" sexual culture (Bergling 2004, 212, 228). The obligation to negotiate body aesthetics also occurs among men who depended on their healthy-enough "look" for work. In Japan, men aged 60–65 are typically pushed out of their employment in large companies to make room for the younger generation, and those old men wanting to reenter the work force in small companies must manage to look "fit": "There is no age limit . . . If you are healthy, you can work" (Warnock 2016, A4). The third age culture's aesthetic obligation may also occur among working-class old men who work in construction and know their older body has changed when compared with their younger body; any perceived erosion of bodily capability can lead to worries about continued employability, and the men mask their aging body by chewing handfuls of ibuprofen and wearing flexible knee sleeves. Any review of the research literature will find this paradox: men's body image becomes of lesser importance with age, yet the bodily changes that affect appearance and function throughout the aging processes—e.g., graying, spreading, sagging, and stooping—still oblige aging men to negotiate the gerontophobic messages imposed by the youthful masculine ideal.

Most aging men know they eventually will come up short in terms of their aging body's appraised physical, masculine, and sexual capital (Lodge and Umberson 2013; Suen 2017). Yet men's body (dis)satisfaction appears to not be linearly related to age or be age dependent. Most middle-aged and old men report positive feelings more often than negative ones regarding their bodies (Öberg and Tornstam 1999), particularly when their bodily function and instrumental capabilities are scrutinized. My interviews with old men in New England about their aging concerns strongly suggest that appearance changes are neither too troubling nor an enduring unease. "It is not what you look like but what you do that defines you, before and after old age" (Skip,

68-year-old retired painter). Other research has shown men report low aging-appearance anxiety. Men in a UK study (Halliwell and Dittmar 2003) typically discussed their body as a singular and complete object, rather than as many distinct parts, and a common theme in their narratives was what the body could do. They focused on functionality and fretted about becoming less active as they aged. A 61-year-old man in the study commented,

> I'm not looking forward to having less stamina, quite definitely. I don't know whether the fact that I, I do find hills steeper than I used to. I don't know whether that's because I've been too sedentary for the last 5 or 6 years . . . or whether, what my doctor said, it's the aging process, and if I thought I was going to err, if my stamina was going to continue to degrade as fast as it has in the last 5 years, I'd be pretty distressed. (ibid., 680)

My sense is that so long as aging men maintain sufficient physical capability and do not become too thin or way too heavy, their enduring body functioning is valued masculine capital and compensates for corporeal aging's effects on appearance. This premise has roots in research that finds that men see the body as a process and men focus on the efficacy of its functioning. Thinking of the body as a process leads to being less critical of one's appearance. Here are several supporting examples. In Liechty et al.'s (2014) study of Canadian men's body image, the men aged 60–70 placed more emphasis on physical abilities than appearance. A 62-year-old in the study commented about the value of "healthiness": "The male body should be fit, no belly fat . . . physically strong, not muscle bound. I see far too many men with large stomachs walking in parks with their grandkids, but can't run or play because of their physical stature, which is too bad because they're missing out on so much" (ibid., 11).

In a nuanced quantitative study, Reboussin and colleagues (2000) provide evidence that old men in the US (aged 65+ in the study) value body function more than body appearance. The researchers theorized that men's personal criteria for body evaluation adjust with age, shifting to function and away from appearance when functional capability could be taken for granted. This change may be more characteristic of able-bodied, aging white men's experiences of aging, since the Reboussin study also found aging African American men were more satisfied with their body function and appearance than were white men.

In her intriguing study of older adults suffering from Parkinson's disease, Solimeo (2008) found that the men focused more on their appearance of physical competence; it was body movement and body capabilities that were voiced as worrisome. The old men agonized about appearing physically impaired and thus less of a man. Similarly, Kaminski and Hayslip (2006, 29) contend that declines in functioning may affect old men in a particularly negative manner, as "more of a man's identity and esteem are likely to be tied to what his body can do." Both of these studies affirm aging men's continued taste for the body practices of never-aging masculinities.

From interviews with Australian white men aged 55 and older, Smith and colleagues (2007, 332) also noted that maintaining physical functioning was "important for supporting aging men's independent state of being" and affected how the men discursively positioned themselves as men. The researchers concluded that aging men worry about body malfunction—the loss of corporeal capacity—and how this might detrimentally affect their physical and masculine capital. From a very different vantage point, the message is the same: old men worry about the end of life in terms of "being a burden (i.e., needing help)" and feeling "the impotency of a drawn out death (i.e., being weak, sequestered)" (Broom and Cavenagh 2010, 874).

Pulling together these varied studies, bodily aging is troubling for most heterosexual men when independence is jeopardized, and for both aging gay and straight men the effects of bodily aging on appearances seem based on class norms and generational narratives.

SUMMARY

Bodies are the ultimate personal resource aging men make use of to gain/ retain capital, to negotiate, accommodate, resist, and contest ageism and manage potential demasculation. Influencing these accomplishments, the corporeality of aging—the material changes that come about over a lifetime—occurs unevenly among men as a result of their positioning within class and racialized societies. Bodies bear meanings about social location— class and race/ethnicity are two of the more consequential. Men from different classes, for example, tend to develop distinctive masculinity practices and orientations to their bodies, which affect the men's corporeal aging as much as their sense of self as they age. As Gullette (2004, 101) recognized, "We are aged more by culture than chromosomes."

Noted at the beginning of the chapter, scholarly work in the fields of sociology and gerontology has rarely scrutinized the meaning of the body among men. We cannot ignore the summoning of bodily changes and how these corporeal shifts impact the subjectivities of the men growing older. But we are handicapped in our understanding of the full impact. The common wisdom is that old men fret little about their appearance, or "looks." Is it true? There remains only a limited amount of research, yet it regularly finds most aging and old men fret little about their changes in appearance but worry about "the ways in which the aging body works, and doesn't work" (Featherstone and Wernick 1995, 2). Most old men's embodied masculinity tastes and practices specify their physical capabilities as primary, not the body's aesthetics. It is the lessening capability to continue to "do masculinity" in ways the old men are accustomed that can become troubling.

This chapter also reviewed how old men's corporeal body is usually absent in public representations of old men, and it is usually absent in terms of old men's own bodily consciousness, until "it" does not work as was customary. This is one matter addressed in the next chapter, namely that old men may feel constrained by their bodies' *capabilities* but they also normalize bodily aging as part of growing old.

Chapter Four

Bodies, Habitus, and Age

We have bodies, but are also, in a specific sense, bodies: our embodiment is a necessary requirement of our social identification.

—Turner (1996, 42)

Giddens (1991) and Turner (1995) draw on Bourdieu to argue that the body and the self emerged in postmodern times as *projects*. This means that the body and self are ongoing, codetermined creations that remain socially and personally crafted through midlife and into later and late life. Prior to modernity, bodies were essentialized and adorned according to local cultural traditions. But by late modernity, with the rising authority of societal and global conventions over the local, men and women are constrained differently. They are expected to *cultivate* bodies that personify the likings of their generation, their class position, their ethnic underpinnings and sexuality, and their age. In this chapter, I shift the focus from aging bodies to old men's experiences with their bodily aging. I begin with a summary of Bourdieu's concept "dispositions," then discuss the common age reminders and types of body work that are ordinary among old men as they manage their aging bodies. With the pervasiveness of the (bio)medicalization of aging and discourses on aging well, most old men amend their health habits to slowly grow older. My observation is that most old men do not fret too much about how later life transformations—bodily or social—affect their *masculine identities*. They subjectively know they are still men, but men who are growing old.

BODIES AS CAPITAL

For Bourdieu, the body is always unfinished, whether as a social or corporeal entity. Though he never said much about the aging body itself or what exactly becomes the body project for aging men, as Shilling (1991, 655) observed,

> Bourdieu argues that as working class taste is formed in contexts in which its members have little time free from necessity, they develop an *instrumental* orientation to the body. The body is a *means to an end* . . . In contrast, the tastes of the dominant classes develop in spaces marked by greater "distance from necessity" . . . [and] they treat the body as *an end in itself* . . . Class division in taste and orientations to the body can, though, be *re-formed* by changes in cultural and economic capital and available spare time. (italics original)

Bourdieu's argument holds that many sources of habitus are incorporated into people's aging trajectories, which unquestionably affects the materiality and experience of aging. For instance, corporeal aging for men who are not white or able-bodied and are without much disposable income typically occurs earlier. This is because of the nested way lesser access to capital (economic, social) operates as a force to affect the orientations people adopt toward their bodies, and how social practices embodied from social positions differentially expose bodies to wear and tear to affect men's health and physical capital. Men in subordinate social positions (class, ethnicity) also will have less time and fewer resources to engage in practices of modification/maintenance that public health policy or consumer culture advocate. Men's social positions regulate what kinds of foods and diet are available and preferred. Despite class or access to resources, some men's body project results in developing a basketball belly through an acquired habitus of "eat well and let yourself go" (Lupton 1994, 40). Put simply, bodies are contextually made and remade across lives as men experience aging. The observable corporeal differences across individuals are the *material* result of the embodiment of experiences.

A caveat: The body is more than an inscribed tablet documenting a biography of embodying social identities and statuses (Bourdieu 1984, 190). It is directly involved in social action. The body is a form of *capital* itself, an asset that helps determine aging men's other capital and their overall status depending on the field of activity. As Tulle (2003, 102) noted, "All bodies have capital." But unlike her argument that the bodies of dominant groups have more capital, my sense is that what types of bodies are esteemed will depend on people's social location and the values different groups ascribe to bodies. Imagine the midwestern working-class aging man whose Harley, large forearms and biceps, and hulking beer belly are displays of his social identity; his bigness and the sleeve of tattoos on his arm are as basic an asset as is his bike to his status *within* his everyday later lifestyle. By comparison, one of the old men Tulle (2007) interviewed was in his later 60s and a "Master" runner whose weekly mileage might range from 35 to 100. His lean, toned body would be dominant in this field of sport and also probably highly valued among affluent aging men engaged in exercise regimens to resist corporeal aging. But his runner's body would be subordinate among the aging working-class men whose field is "still riding" and whose social relations pivot on Harley clubs and biker pubs.

DISPOSITIONS

The way aging men are oriented to and treat their bodies reveals their inculcated masculinities, class, and taste—"the deepest dispositions of the habitus" (Bourdieu 1984, 190). These dispositions refer to people's intractable second-nature habits appropriated from class, generation, and ethnic preferences in dress and consumption, language and speech, body techniques, and orientations toward aging. In the more affluent middle and upper classes in Europe and North America, this valued older body is "healthy enough," aged but not old, aesthetically appealing, and able to trek mile after mile on walks or hikes. It is more often displayed in media representations. In the working class, the valued body is "functional enough," aged but capable. The physical capital quests for aging men have distinct trajectories—including, perhaps, later life membership in a health and fitness club, or occasional weight lifting in a garage mixed with evening stops at beer pubs (cf. Featherstone's 2010 cultivation of appearance).

Dispositions also frame the existential worries originating from old men's bodily experience. For example, a healthy old man in his 70s who regularly takes walks and presents no sign of arthritic discomfort may well interpret knee pain as near disabling. By contrast, another same-aged man with a history of daily use of inflammatory medication to manage arthritic pain while he continues to be a self-employed builder of concrete patios interprets the knee pain as "oh-hum" (cf. the discussion of runners by Tulle 2007). The first man worries about his bodily aging's effect on lifestyle; the second normalizes it as work (and class) related. Each older man's body is his physical capital to take walks and maintain honored status, or to retain economic and masculine capital as a creative landscaper.

Which body reminders of corporeal aging are more unnerving? Barrett and Gumber (2016) found that everyday body problems (e.g., pain, imbalance) exert stronger effects on age consciousness than either body repairs (i.e., surgeries and medication) or body aids (e.g., hearing or mobility aids). Yet, most age reminders that give rise to aging consciousness are social in origin and become obvious in people's 50s (Karp 1988), and thus are not limited to the body reminders of aches and pains, changes in appearance, and mobility issues. Age reminders can originate from others' mortality, generational events such as a grandchild completing high school, and contextual messages such as becoming one of the oldest men on the job. The reminders can be different for aging gay men, who less often have intergenerational reminders—children and grandchildren—to cue their aging and who face looking "old" earlier than heterosexual men (cf. Lee 2004; Slevin and Linneman 2010).

Once the body is recognized as a project constructed and reconstructed within different times and contexts, we can appreciate how recent generations of aging men and women are more conscious of their body as a personal project rather than a "natural" entity, compared to their great-grandparents' generation. This is the gist of postmodernity, and it is at odds with the (historical) importance of bodies in agrarian societies. In modern affluent countries, many men have the resources to maintain, intervene, and/or alter their body's aging trajectory. The range of "body work" practices undertaken may include simple morning stretching exercises, replacing eyeglasses with contact lenses or improving vision with cataract surgery, and regular use of anti-inflammatory drugs.

BODY WORK

A number of social theorists (e.g., Bauman 2000; Featherstone and Hepworth 1991; Turner 1996) propose that bodies in postmodern communities are means of displaying self, sometimes in guises. Proposed is a "reflexive" body rather than a corporeal body. The reflexive body is a *site* of personal self-expression and, at times, reinvention. Body practices are one of the ways individuals "work on" themselves by self-regulating their fleshy bodies and their conduct (Foucault 1988). This "work on" is what I mean by "body work."

Middle-aged and old men's lived bodies, especially in terms of what they do as their everyday "reflexive practices" (Crossley 2005), remain underresearched. Based on interviews with late middle-aged, working- and middle-class obese British men, one study found the men joined weight-loss programs to improve their body aesthetic; they were motivated by "contemporary appearance-related expectations and pressures" (Gough, Seymour-Smith, and Matthews 2016, 89). Before participating in the weight-loss program, they had discursively minimized their "large" bodies, and despite slimming several belt holes in size, the men intended to remain "big" in order to retain masculine capital. Their big bodies symbolized, they believed, masculinity, and by reducing some but not too much weight, they sought to reclaim earlier "manly" feelings of being fit. These men's body techniques sought to modify, maintain, and thematize the body (Crossley 2005, 9), ostensibly to improve the men's symbolic capital.

Along with the embodiment of class or ethnic tastes, men embody their experiences within age relations and with growing older. At times those growing-older experiences come to involve intentional body projects. Exercising (swimming, Tai Chi, mall walking) or relearning to play a musical instrument (guitar, piano) in later life are good examples of aging men purposefully working at the body to modify it. Breathing rhythm and endurance are worked on and altered; finger dexterity and strength are trained; new habitual knowledge is embodied; physical capital is produced. Consider as an example the intentional forms of body work that a 74-year-old retired high school teacher (Ralph) undertakes. He and I sometimes talk while on side-by-side rowing machines. His regular cardio workout is all about having a later life morning routine and then making and maintaining personal connections. As a widowed grandfather, he aims to stay fit. Ralph has tattooed his grandkids' names one after another down his left arm; his right arm sports an eagle atop a globe and anchor, the official emblem of the US Marine Corps, with the words "Semper Fi" across the top and "USMC" underneath. His tattooing is pro-social body art and, frankly, masculine emotional work (Elias 1991). With the body art capturing "turning point" life experiences—the Marines, grandfathering—and his regular exercise aiming for continuity in his social, healthy-enough self, each form of body work is intrinsic to his reflexive project as an aging man.

The postmodernist maxim "Just do it" suggests that aging men can and should control their bodies through consumer and lifestyle choices and thereby liberate themselves from "normal" aging, while simultaneously defending themselves against ageism's demasculating account of getting older. To thwart the deftly marketed terror of sinking into the "black hole" of infirmity (Gilleard and Higgs 2010), consumer advertising targets old men's body functioning rather than aesthetics. It urges old men to resist the stigma and shame of becoming old by actively engaging in all manner of the antiaging body work found in exercise and fitness programs, stress reduction and mindful meditation, hormone enhancement, use of vitamins and herbs, and resexualizing pharmaceuticals; less often are old men represented in advertising for dental care, clothing choices, or dietary control. Rarely noticed in such advertising are the race and class privileges that underlie the recommendations for white men with sufficient capital resources. Equally glossed over is how sexopharmaceuticals are marketed as a way of "ensuring the maintenance of healthy, heterosexual relationships and not as an adjunct to stimulants that enable [aging] men to maintain their erections during periods of prolonged sexual engagement with one or more partners" (Leonard, Duncan, and Barrett 2013, 114).

Marketed body work has a moral expectation. Featherstone and Hepworth (1991, 183) and later Calasanti (2016, 1095) remind us that the postmodernist ethos advances self-responsibility and agency, including taking responsibility for one's own body shape, health, virility, and look. Whether the marketing is a recommendation for a regime of very modest physical activity to promote "healthy aging," or the purposeful "resexing" (Marshall and Katz 2002) of aging bodies with pharmaceuticals promising to reaffirm virility and "firm the floppy penis" (Calasanti and King 2005), my counterinterpretation is that the body work old men do aims to assure late lifestyle options more than enhance market definitions of masculine capital.

ORDINARY BODY WORK

Studies of old men's body work are few in number, partly because researchers have maintained the precept that body work is mostly appearance-oriented and thus not something most men do. There are some exceptions: aging men toning muscular appearance or lifting to build/maintain muscle size (cf. Crossley 2005) or the aesthetic body work of a gay widower to reenter the relationship market (Bergling 2004). But the "no-look" convention creates an environment of profound cultural silence about the ordinary body work among aging men, and it has kept invisible many aspects of old men's experiences with their bodies.

A major exception is Kate Slevin's (2008) influential essay on how healthy-enough old men may discipline their bodies, sometimes through exercise/dieting and sometimes through the embodiment of clothing choices, each practice designed to avoid the stigma of looking old: "William (age 75) was adamant in this regard: 'I don't go around wearing old folks' clothes.' At age 80, Wayne also appears to have such concerns on his mind: 'I don't dress like an old man'" (ibid., 41). Clothing choice is part of older adults' everyday body practices and evidence of embodied masculinity. It can reproduce ageist standards when men judge whose clothed bodies are "old." From their point of view, their embodied clothing choices "just happen." As a 67-year-old retired Canadian stone mason in one study (Liechty et al. 2014, 10) commented, "You want to look smart in the way you dress and the way you are, you're clean and tidy and everything but other than that I don't think [appearance] is a big concern."

Existing conceptual work, or theorizing, on old men's ordinary body work also might reflect an unwitting narrowness within some interpretations of "body work." I think Mike Featherstone (2010) may have narrowly imagined body work when he split body work into two *purposeful* types—techniques and strategies aimed at the "inner body," where the concern is with health and optimum functioning, or the "outer body," where the body's appearance and men's control of their movement are the foci. This inner/ outer distinction about purposeful body work is invaluable to understand why, for example, the bearing of musculoskeletal complaints among older Dutch construction workers lowers the men's ability and willingness to continue working after age 65 (Hengel et at. 2012) or why the coerciveness of the norms of youthfulness for aging gay men threatens to chip away at self-esteem (Bergling 2004).

Largely missing is any sense of the myriad of ways *ordinary* body work is undertaken, whether the work is directed to the inner or outer body. To illustrate: Are the ways many old men discipline their body in everyday relations—e.g., to not lean on a shopping cart as if it is a "walker," to walk the stairs whenever possible rather than use an elevator for one floor—practices of a long-embodied masculine taste or consciously intended age-related body practices to distance themselves from being seen as old? Are these practices ordinary or purposeful? Has the experience of "being defined as 'old' for many more years than would be the case if they were heterosexual" (Slevin and Linneman 2010, 499) led aging gay men to employ masking unlike similarly aged heterosexual men, and, if so, is the masking ordinary or purposeful? Does the bombardment of advertising linking aging bodies to demasculation, maybe even emasculation, affect old men in rural geographies involving physical labor less, or differently, than age peers in urban environments? Old farmers, for example, may rarely modify their gender-affirming body practices as they grow old; they continue to wake early and do what they can do as farmers, husbands, grandfathers, and neighbors with or without knee replacement. Elite heterosexual aging Baby Boomers may groom themselves with hair coloring, anti-wrinkle skin care creams, and A to Z potency multivitamins and medications to uphold the "bodily time" norms within their social worlds. But do they? To date, researchers have systematically studied the body work of aging runners, swimmers, tennis players, and homeless old men to illustrate techniques of body work, but rarely studied is the ordinary body work that distinguishes populations of old men.

In sum, usual conceptions of the body have focused upon its perceptible features—skin elasticity, age spots, and body art—and the body work men may do to mask age and retain masculine capital. This is usually, according to Crossley (2007, 82), an "outside-in perspective." Though sometimes profoundly informative, the observer's perspective and narrative are what we discover and missing is an understanding of aging men's embodied "body action and coordination [that] 'just happen'" (ibid., 83).

THE MEDICALIZED AGING BODY

In one of the early publications to use the term "medicalization," Irving Zola (1972, 487) commented that medicalization "is largely an insidious and un-dramatic phenomenon accomplished by 'medicalizing' much of daily living." It occurs when "conditions" that were not previously subjected to the medical gaze are appropriated by medicine, construed as a medical problem, and judged in need of treatment by some form of medically guided intervention, including "alternative" therapies such as chiropractic care or yoga. In Western societies men are surrounded by the ongoing biomedicalization of aging bodies, from hip replacement to laser eye surgery to invisible hearing aids that aim to mask getting older.

Notable trends now include an escalating medicalization of masculinities (Rosenfeld and Faircloth 2006), whereby age-related bodily changes among men are recast into *masculinity* problems. One example is the recent creation of "andropause" (erroneously thought of as the male equivalent to menopause) as an age-related "condition" that produces corporeal demasculation through impotency or baldness (Marshall 2009, 259; Szymczak and Conrad 2006). So too is the creation of testosterone replacement therapy as an elixir for the masculinity "problems" arising from the decrease in androgen production and serum testosterone levels that are common after middle age, such as fewer spontaneous erections, sleep disturbances, reduced muscle strength, and trouble concentrating. Whether or not most men find these slowly arising bodily changes troubling, aging men are being encouraged by direct-to-consumer advertising to reconsider their options. What makes these options so interesting—and medicalized—is that the conditions for which treatments are touted are social in nature and often a result of the influence of the ageism within never-aging masculinities.

Take the case of the expansive medical intervention associated with prostate enlargement. Perhaps half of men in their 50s and 60s begin to develop benign prostatic hyperplasia (BPH), which is the medicalized labeling of prostate enlargement; and by age 80 as many as 90 percent of men will experience prostate enlargement, where symptoms can vary from a need to strain or push to get urine flowing to frequent urination. New treatments range from laser therapies to transurethral microwave therapy and pharmaceuticals. The Food and Drug Administration has approved many drugs and drug therapies to relieve symptoms, some of which yield adverse side effects such as increased male breast size and challenged sexual function.

Many medical sociologists and men's studies researchers have called attention to the expansion of medicine's social control and the making of "sick" bodies out of ordinary aging, particularly how men's later life impotency, once assumed to be an inevitable consequence of growing old, was rewritten into treatable "erectile dysfunction." The term "medicalization" literally means "to make medical." Medicalization of the aging male body underscores the near-hegemonic narrative that natural bodily aging becomes the problems of senescence. The notion that aging processes require treatment has become ingrained in public consciousness and braced by the cultural verdict that being "old" is undesirable and unnecessary.

People have come to recognize the malleability of the aging body within economically developed countries. Aging men and women would be hard-pressed not to take notice of the neoliberal messages for health-related self-care, nor is the plethora of antiaging medications and technologies routinely advertised likely unnoticed. "Healthy aging" public health campaigns prioritize people's responsibility to prevent early aging by maintenance of good physical and mental health. By comparison, consumer products and services prioritize forestalling and unwinding aging; they aim to counteract aging-related "decline" and empower aging men to revitalize manhood. Together, the three-pronged onslaught—public health self-care campaigns, consumer culture's antiaging commodification, and the rise of antiaging medicine—embeds into the habitus of the new generations of aging men the perceived plasticity of an aging man's body. As Peter Conrad (2005) noted, the engines of medicalization have in fact shifted more exclusively to biotechnology's direct-to-consumer advertising of "lifestyles" and to the consumers' desire and demand for body-enhancing products and services. Pharmaceutical promotion of so-called lifestyle drugs targets conditions understood not as life threatening, but rather as life restricting (Mamo and Fishman 2001, 16). In direct-to-consumer promotion for pharmaceutical treatment for aging men's hair loss, for example, Harvey (2013) identifies several discursive strategies such as representing the balding man as outcast, promoting the attractiveness and self-assurance of a man with hair, and situating hair loss in a scientific but masculinity discourse.

For the past thirty or more years, it has become more and more ordinary for aging men to seek out medical assistance to alter and reformulate the body through technologies like joint replacement, Lasik surgery, dental implants, and heart valve replacement, or through body enhancement techniques like reflexology and micro-acupuncture to assist a man's accumulative bodily troubles with diminishing spinal flexibility and his waning ease of putting on a pair of socks. The body is more present, and aging men's awareness of their body has intensified. Thomas Cole (1992) and a number of others since he wrote have cautioned against the medical gaze and its advocacy of health-related self-care overseen by a scientific or medical interpretation of "successful" aging. Their concern is that when corporeal aging processes are viewed through the medical gaze, medicalized discourses on successful, vital, active, and healthy aging percolate up to become proper. As Flatt et al. (2013) asked, are "anti-aging medicine" and "successful aging" two sides of the same coin? I think so, and this can result in sustaining the

problematic never-aging masculinity directives that undercut old men's subjectivities as men.

A separate concern is whether or not the medical gaze is a slippery slope
toward cyborg-aging. I do not think so. Paraphrasing Kelly Joyce and Meika
Loe (2010, 171), science and technology have become central to the lived
experiences of aging men and all others. From pharmaceuticals to GPS de-
vices, old men interact with many everyday technologies to maintain their
lives and lifestyles. They are ordinary men using technologies; they are not
the "cyborgs" portrayed as Robocop or Frankenstein, or even Dr. No with his
prosthetic mechanical arm.

Some people are hopeful that the medical gaze on aging and rise of new
medical technologies and services might have the beneficial effect of releas-
ing old men from the stigmatized status that modernity built for everything
old. Two unstated preconditions for such benefits: most options are available
only to economically privileged men (who have acquired desire), and the
men must embrace the postmodern dictum that "old" is undesirable.

SLOWLY GROWING OLDER

Tulle-Winton (2000, 64) once wrote, "Old bodies are problematic: they can
cause us pain, devalue our social and cultural status and in the end they
remind us of our finality." This is a perceptive outside-in assessment of late
life, that period of time where the aged body is subjectively present more
than it was at the onset of later life. There have been plenty of other, similar
outside-in interpretations of getting old, such as when the listener may mis-
hear and impose an "ageless self" interpretation to an account of an old
man's narrative about his sense of identity remaining subjectively "him"
throughout his later and late life. There also is an immense geriatrics literature on many aspects of internal, physiological aging; it speaks to the objective age-related changes in movement, posture, balance, and health/well-
being. But this literature's outside-in assessment makes no attempt to link
these bodily changes to how and when aging men subjectively perceive
themselves growing older—when felt age embodies feeling old. Take, for
example, the vast library of geriatrics research on aging and vision loss and
the presumption of disability and dependency. But not until work like Ainlay's (1989) qualitative study of aging-related vision loss in *Day Brought
Back My Night: Aging and New Vision Loss* did sociologists, gerontologists,
and others better understand late-blinded people's experience of spatial and
temporal disruptions, and their resilience. What we still do not know much
about are similar lived experiences of being old and how aging is a lived
body.

In postmodern times, where men's life span trajectories are no longer standardized within a class or country, late life and the bodily experience of old age could commence as early as one's 60s or beyond one's 80s. The internal and corporeal bodily processes that lead to old bodies are distinctly fashioned by people's economic security or insufficiency, embodied preferences, time spent living with someone or alone, the type of work formerly done, and geographies of place (cf. Rowles 1983). We also know that age reminders such as grandparenting and retirement are not standardized. In the US, the average age men become grandfathers is 54, and retirement commonly occurs during one's later 60s, if retirement is an option. Each age reminder could trigger the subjective sense of "old age" approaching, well before the pileup of chronic comorbidities that define the man's body as old.

Whether subjectively moored to "old age" or not, each man's later life journey involves his waning body capabilities. The old man has given up competing in the Boston Marathon, but he may still run. Another old man retired his "bike." A third enjoys long walks, but no longer the more strenuous hiking. They all remain sexually intimate, adjusted to the possibilities of their aging bodies. They may still participate in strengthening and exercise programs to slow muscular aging. Some old men enjoy growing summer vegetables, attending the theater, mulling over pre–World War II foreign coin collections, eating in restaurants with friends, Friday night grandkid sitting, or strolling a beach each year while on the annual vacation. Their preferences and taste (habitus) through which they express their identity as men will continue to be tweaked to accommodate bodily capabilities. They might begin to read larger-print books, and later might need to use a hand-held print enlarger to continue to savor the data within a newspaper's baseball box scores.

EMBODYING AGE AND AMENDING HABITUS

Most old men do not agonize much about how late life's bodily transformations affect their masculine identities. They know they are (still) men, men who are growing old. Join a group of regulars congregating over coffee or the late afternoon group in animated conversation with a shot and beer, and what you usually hear are stories of how they embody their slow corporeal aging and resist others' designation that they are "old." What they do worry about is their diminished performance capabilities, evidenced in a round of storytelling about being frustrated in opening a hermetically sealed, infant-proof bag of chips or, more seriously, the age-related bodily changes such as vision loss that would deny a man the quality of life to act independently (cf. Smith et al. 2007). The men I listen to normalize by storying how they seek out and shift fields of activity to match their aging bodies—e.g., from leisure activities that emphasized physical capital to ones that depend on mental capital, such as when rowing and running are replaced by intensive hobbies or the quietness of gardening and environmental volunteering. Liechty and Genoe (2013, 448) offer a discerning example in their study of old men's (aged 60–70) perceptions of leisure activities: "After discussing his son's interest in kite surfing, Jacob remarked, 'I probably won't try that. (laughs) And [getting older] isn't a barrier really, it's more common sense . . . that would take a lot of time and some strength and stuff you'd have to develop and I'm just not stupid enough.'"

My argument differs from thinking that aging bodies pose an ontological challenge to identity. Late life is best not represented by a *loss* of functional capabilities, nor is it best measured by the infirmities, dependencies, and suffering often linked to fourth age cultural imagery. Such thinking narrowly frames "old age" in biological terms—as a body in decline and a time of dependence and disengagement. It problematizes old bodies as dependency prone. Missed from this point of view is the mindful old man who continues to see himself as a man and engages in masculinity practices. Awareness of his old body and the experience of growing older are inherent components of the self for most old adults.

This is analogous to the suggestion by Diehl and Wahl (2010, 340) that men's awareness of age-related changes—or, their subjective experience of aging—takes into account bodily and interpersonal experiences that collectively "make" the old man, who is keenly aware his life has changed as a consequence of having become older. This perspective is also in sync with Linn Sandberg's (2013a) view of "affirmative old age," where the changes in the aging body provide men new ways of doing masculinity and rethinking what masculinity means (also see Coles 2008). Old men come to embody and enact transformed masculinities, and their late life is not limited to medical idioms of decline.

To conceptualize aging and old age through a lens of decline/failure patently ignores how aging bodies and growing old are affirmative, whether the affirmation is of an embodied consciousness of having suffered and being able to tell stories about it, or of the mindfulness of pleasurable time with family and friends. Most old men slowly come to terms with their corporeal aging, stop using a body ideal that is not achievable, and choose to operate in the narrower field of aged masculinities that value experience and similar things. Yet, they resist self-identifying as "old." The Swedish men aged 63 or older that Bullington (2006, 76) interviewed commonly experienced getting older as "the way things are"; one participant commented, "I have the insight that I am getting old, and I accept that. I know that I will have less and less energy and all that, but I see it as a part of a natural process." Studying old men in Cuernavaca, Mexico, Wentzell (2013a, 14) reported a 77-year-old informant's comment, "Your body is like a car—the older it gets, the more problems you've got." This working-class old man had begun to experience decreased erectile capability and other age-related bodily changes, yet similar to many of the other men in her study, he rejected pharmaceutical medical aids that might enable "youthful" sexuality and preferred instead to embody his aging and a "mature" masculinity focused on affective family relationships (ibid., 15). Wentzell's article title, "Aging Respectably by Rejecting Medicalization," smartly captures the Mexican old men's embodiment of their culture's belief that an old body is acceptable. Similarly, a man Coles and Vassarotti (2012, 36) had interviewed commented, "[You] just become more accepting of what is, you know, rather than try to fight it all the time."

Men's personal adaptations to their aging bodies become expressed in their lifestyle practices and are consistent with the continued possibilities of agency within late life. The findings of a study of very old Swedes (Fischer, Norberg, and Lundman 2008) noted that the body was more than a reminder of change; it was evidence of both being old and feeling old. The researchers conclude that growing old was described as "maintaining one's identity in spite of the changes that come with aging and embracing opposites—being changed, and feeling being the same" (ibid., 266). A similar study of very old Finnish men and women (Nilsson, Sarvimäki, and Ekman 2000) identified when "feeling old" began and replaced "being old." The turning point was when the physical changes of advanced age became bodily burdensome—such as when moving and walking or difficulties in balancing were troubling and restricting.

Using data on life satisfaction among Germans aged 60 and older in 1984 and followed annually for sixteen years, Schilling's (2006) analysis found that individuals maintained their relative level of life satisfaction across the years; there were no tendencies for growing older to improve some people's subjective well-being as others declined. Brännström, Bäckman, and Fischer (2012) studied the experience of living in an aged body and using a walker in daily life among old community-dwelling Swedes aged 79–95; the narratives reflect a sense of "walking on the edge" between independence and dependency; the walker provided a means to remain independent. Aside from these studies, the lived experiences of having old bodies are more untold than recorded.

Slowly growing older, the body can be a catalyst for identity musings and late life quests that might be spiritual in nature and again amend the habitus. Aging as a process involves discovery and pondering, reminiscing, integrating, and meaning making. Here is an example of age-related "spiritual" quests and men's musings. The voice is of a narrator, akin to how a researcher might retell the musings of an old man. In his memoir of sorts, *The Earth Is Enough*, Harry Middleton (1989) came to embody the "simple" (natural) world that three old men thrived in—his widowed, in-his-80s grandfather, Emerson; great-uncle Albert; and their Sioux neighbor, Elias. Middleton storied how and why these old men appreciated their own old age and inevitable mortality. They would neither damn the creek nor cut the trees to convert their land into a profitable farm, and consistent with their austere and unconventional way, they appreciated the "success," as they laughed about it, of being the "failures" as other people perceived them. They embodied aging—theirs, the stream and its trout, the trees. The backstory is Middleton being sent "home" from the island of Okinawa, Japan, by his military father in 1965, after an accident wounded him and killed his friend. But "home" was not somewhere within the progressive cultural America of the mid- to late 1960s; instead it was the Ozark mountains and his discovery of the old men's taste for the simple life of subsistence farming, avid reading, and catch-and-release trout fishing. Middleton's mentors taught him well. His own, later existential questing, especially after losing his job with a prominent magazine, kept turning him back to the "simple" life and spiritually journeying with nature, especially near the wildness of streams.

Men's complex embodiment of aging and resistance to getting "old"/giving up is decisive to an existential experience of late life. What leads one person to actively embody and enjoy his old age and another person to deny it and age so differently? It might be some men's greater resiliency and experience of purpose in life. In their study of how very old (aged 85 and older) Swedish men experience and reflect on purpose in life, Hedberg and colleagues (2013, 102) heard men's talk about past achievements, living an honorable life, being able to adapt to bodily changes, maintaining everyday activities, and continuing to feel contented despite functional decline. Yet despite these "big stories," they offered the example of one of the oldest men saying, "For me, purpose in life is being able to get up in the morning and get dressed. That is worth a great deal. If you can't do that and you just lay in bed, there would be no purpose in life at all." Rephrased, continuing to be bodily capable to enjoy daily life, and to make plans for the future despite very old age, matter.

IMPLICATIONS AND SUMMARY

For an outsider listening to the men talk, their self-deprecating comments about their aging might hint at a fading or lost past masculine self (whether real or imagined). This is exactly what some researchers seem to have heard when listening to men's stories about their bodily aging (e.g., Cecil, McCaughan, and Parahoo 2010). Researchers' narratives about "lost manhood" and aging-determined "demasculation" arise because the listener interpreted the men's stories through a framework of never-aging masculinities. When never-aging masculinities are the only instructions, then all men can be threatened as they age. However, this if/then discourse does not make sense, because old men's habitus transforms along with their bodily aging and social involvement in fields of aging masculinities. Never-aging masculinities might be what people presume old men singularly use to navigate lives, but this assumption ignores their aging-amended habitus and taste for and performances of aging masculinities. Aging men's priorities and preferences change, and their masculine subjectivities change, just as the body is transformed though aging (Whitehead 2002, 200). The "lost manhood" discourse would also make sense if the vast majority of men's bodies had actually personified the idealized, proportioned "mesomorph" qualities when they were young men. But few aging men ever had the idealized male body to refer back to. To recap, when old men are asked about their bodies and aging experiences, filtering the heard stories through a lens of never-aging masculinities twists the content of the stories to affirm the legacy of an idealized masculinity, and the content storied by the men about their lives is left on the cutting floor.

Any further analysis of aging men's bodies and body work needs to begin with and build on Giddens's and Bourdieu's postmodernist ideas of our embodiment of lived experiences and the ongoing modification of habitus. Embodied masculinities and identities are not cast in stone by midlife; they are transformed with corporeal aging and the ordinariness of body work and other forms of individual agency. I am in agreement with the thinking of early cultural studies scholars Featherstone and Hepworth (1991) and Turner (1995), who argue that for any passable analysis of old men we must recognize aging men's bodies and identities as both durable and unfinished constructions. The men move through lived time and their social capital shifts over time. The construct of embodiment invites us to rethink how our bodies, each and every day, accumulate and integrate lived experiences and affect new experiences. For all classes, the actual fields old men inhabit will range from some of the same fields they negotiated earlier in their lives (e.g., recreation, intimacies) to newer arenas and places that represent sites of struggle over a principal interest—honor, masculine capital, cultural authority, interpersonal persuasiveness.

II

Health as Men Age

Chapter Five

Wrestling with Aging

My eyesight. My gallbladder problems. My weight. My energy level. My legs. My arthritis. These are among the things participants in a study refer to when asked to talk about age.

—Laz (2003, 503)

Wrestling with aging involves both troubling ageist encounters and the brute reality that bodies do age. In the US with direct-to-consumer advertising of pharmaceuticals, the nightly news and other targeted television programming bombard their audience of mature and aging adults with cartoon-like depictions of "our product will help you age better." Whether or not you pay attention to the commercial, you are repeatedly instructed by an authoritative voice to age well, as it is your future and your responsibility. In each thirty-second narrative, the proposed treatment of an age-related health "problem" reminds the aging man how he can reclaim his waning agency. Each ad treats aging as involving yet another trouble.

In this chapter I call attention to men's aging and illness stories, which are regularly told to friends and acquaintances more than family. Friends listen and concur; families worry. Within the stories often is an emerging recognition or flat-out acceptance of men's impermanence. Their aging and illness stories range from restitution to chaos to quest narratives; they are narratives on a *process* of becoming old men. I also call attention to men's health practices and how these are among the practices of aging masculinities. As men adopt aging masculinity, their "don't care" health attitudes shift to "should care." I end the chapter with the premise that wrestling with aging involves letting go of the cultural never-aging masculinity blueprint and men amending their practices in sync with the comfort of aging masculinities.

79

RECOUNTING AGING BODIES WITHIN STORIES

One participant in Tannenbaum and Frank's (2011, 246) study of masculinity and health among later life men remarked, "Like my father always said, if you treat a cold it will last 7 days, if you don't treat it it'll last a week. So I never bothered treating myself. My philosophy has always been that my body will heal itself." Is this stance toward health maintenance typical of old men—to turn a blind eye to symptoms of ill-health or the ways corporeal aging might silently chip away at functional capabilities until the alarm of impairment? Ask most old men with comorbidities how they are doing, and they ordinarily report, "as well as can be"; they are more interested in a conversation about politics, faith, or sports than their health. They will light-heartedly talk about their lesser ability to hit a tennis ball or softball, or lessening capability to walk up and down a flight of stairs without using the handrail for balance.

To contribute to theorizing about old men's lives and taste for aging masculinities but without the goal of developing a grand theoretical synthesis, my interpretation of old men wrestling with their health is different. First, within the social worlds of old men, age-related health issues are normative, and the older the man, the more likely he has increased contact with health professionals to help manage his declining health. Most old men live with and come to normalize their age-related health, its trajectory, and whatever functional limitations they have, not cavalierly with a "manly" shrug of the shoulder. They recognize the aging body is present, unequivocally so, and still unfinished (Shilling 2003). They know their health will present them with chronic hitches to be wrestled with as they journey through later and late life, and they accept the responsibility and need for health maintenance. For example, it is statistically likely that two in five men aged 65 and older in the US already have either undergone cardiac catheterization and perhaps had a stent added, lived through a heart attack, or been treated for a cancer (e.g., Ko et al. 2013). Age is not causal risk, but getting older increases the odds of multiple comorbidities and experiencing a serious cardiovascular disease or a cancer. Aging men know this, if by no more than talking with age peers or from exposure to direct-to-consumer pharmaceutical advertising.

Their illness stories can reveal a biographical disruption and their strategies for preserving self and embodiment of aging (Charmaz 1994; Tulle 2015). Stories are nuanced. The onset of osteoarthritic pain, for example, brings the body into a daily awareness previously not part of a person's experience. Research from Britain and Australia finds that, faced with these physical realities, aging men are increasingly aware of their health. Rebecca Coles and her colleagues (2010) studied men in a socially disadvantaged area of Britain and found that the men no longer shunned medical care but wanted routine screenings. In their South Australian study, Smith and his colleagues (2008) similarly found that aging men monitored their health status and made conscious decisions to seek medical advice. These findings are suggestive that aging masculinities embody health maintenance. Yet old men's health practices and preferences remain poorly documented and perhaps altogether misunderstood as a result of researchers interpreting their stories through the astigmatism lens of never-aging masculinities.

Second, at some point old men come to integrate the permanence of impermanence. Imagine that later life represents the postmodern era in our lives as individuals. As Randall (2013b, 12) suggests, journeying into it we come to view later life and aging from a more ironic stance—one that is more flexible, more expansive, and more accepting of uncertainty, more able to appreciate the lighter, less serious sides of situations, past and present. In doing so, old men engage the here and now in terms of their capabilities, even if they look back at times and use a "retrospective yardstick." They are aware that future time is finite and are uncertain about what later life and its possibilities entail. For example, Idler (2003) has noted that men's self-ratings of their health reliably take into account their lifestyle *and* acquired mortality risks. The large body of research on subjective health assessment attests that old men certainly experience their aging body as present and they understand the implications of their changing health. When an old man rates his health as "poor" or "fair," no longer "good (enough)" or "excellent," his self-assessment *reliably* weighs in his comorbidities, functional capabilities, and estimate of future time (cf. Idler et al. 2004).

IMPERMANENCE AND STORIES

The men within Western cultures now facing old age—the Silent Generation and the Boomers—may have been intermittently aware that their lives are impermanent, as when their sense of mortality was drawn up by the death of a buddy, close relative, or coworker, or when they purchased life insurance to protect their families' welfare. Still, these men are not inclined to consider their impermanence. Instead, their early experiences were enveloped within generational cultures where the habitus resisted being "old." They grew up and worked in generational cultures that make their elongated lives statistically and social normative, and morally not the same as "old age." They are aging men in societies where public health and medical care sequester dying and death to the very end of life span time and relocate both to foreign places such as hospice and funeral settings. The contradiction is, what became normative—the liquidity of both postmodernity and later life—has not meant people integrate into their consciousness their impermanence before bumping up against their own late life.

To acknowledge our own impermanence is to acknowledge our death. In Western cultures we can reconcile the rolling impermanence of employment-based and postemployment relationships, our geographical sense of where "home" was/is as we relocate, and other aspects of our postmodern-wrapped social worlds, but our own death remains an existential impasse. A "rule of the game" in postmodern Western cultures is that contemplating impermanence, or our death, is one of the "don't go there" rules, largely a result of the death-anxiety hangover from the rise of medical authority that casts death to the periphery as unnatural, something to be fought, hidden, and *not* discussed.

When it comes to accepting our own mortality, people have to relinquish the antiaging, never-aging narrative that thinks in terms of curing and restoring function (Frank 1995). My thinking draws on one of Arthur Frank's (1995, 96) observations that for most old men lived experiences can be more than a "life of busy pretense." Mature and aging men busy themselves with managing their bodily health and a convoy of legacy work to survive them—children, a vintage car, genealogies, trees and gardens (cf. Ekerdt and Baker 2014). But at some point during late life, the permanence of impermanence is weighed and eventually embodied by most people. As an 89-year-old who had been living with Alzheimer's disease for five years noted, "You can't stop the ageing process, no point worrying about it" (Tolhurst and Weicht 2017, 31).

Whenever impermanence becomes embodied, men let go of narratives about survival and begin accepting old age and its uncharted trajectory. They know there will be bumps. For example, they may experience a "stiff" shoulder that a regime of physical therapy or chiropractic care might resolve, somewhat. Or they faced a new cancer, were successfully treated, and now make use of a survival narrative, though they know they've become honorary members of "the remission society" (Frank 1995) who are well but never cured. Yet this experience also affirms their sense of impermanence. The prospect of death is foreseen rather than continually rebuffed.

As the embodiment of their impermanence begins, aging men and their partners are apt to downsize their possessions. The men are more apt to take advantage of what is important, be it a day without the nagging presence of arthritic pain, a phone conversation with a daughter, regular morning coffee and pastry or evening pub gatherings with a handful of men friends, or sitting quietly nearby one's intimate other as both read and listen to music. This is consistent with the axiom that when time is perceived as limited, emotional goals assume primacy (Carstensen, Isaacowitz, and Charles 1999). It is also consistent with the existential position about the inevitably of impermanence, a position that has long roots in Socratic thought and Buddhist traditions, and that is reiterated in Romantic poetry (cf. Hirschberger and Shaham 2012).

The stories aging men tell and can tell about their everyday lives are an important resource for making sense of men's experiences with their age-related health. Through stories old men structure and interpret experiences; construct, display, and reinforce their sense of self; and relate this sense of self to others (Randall et al. 2015). In such narration, men make choices about what to include, highlighting some events and omitting others. It is precisely this inclusion or exclusion that makes it a story. Storytelling is an ontological activity that imposes order on experiences. Stories are also performative. Intermingled are "small stories" that disclose the individual's experiences and identities and "big stories" that reflect broader cultural discourses about masculinities or making the most of life. The men surviving a severe myocardial infarction in O'Brien, Hart, and Hunt's (2007) study told "big stories" and "small stories"—background stories about manhood in Scottish terms, and immediate stories about being family men now living a postwork life with health limitations. Their stories of wresting with illness revealed their cache of masculine capital and discovery of new capital-bestowing practices (e.g., exercise).

When we listen, we hear old men discursively define later and late life through stories. They will narrate their intimacies (e.g., Sandberg 2013b), how time is navigated (e.g., Ekerdt and Koss 2016), whether or not athletic body projects continue (e.g., Sparkes 1996), and other dimensions of their lives. The men's stories provide voice to what old age is. As Frank (1995, 23) advised, "An anthropologist recommend[ed] while attempting to explain a native oral tradition to a white audience: 'You have to learn to think *with* stories.' Not think about stories, which would be the usual phrase, but think with them" (italics original). The stories old men tell about later and late life are not necessarily the men's lives as lived; rather, the stories are our medium to understand old age. In telling their stories the men affirm the self as responsible, which is a core dimension of mature masculinity.

NEGOTIATING AGING-RELATED HEALTH

Compared to the studies that have examined how men negotiate their experience with health challenges such as a heart attack, few studies have asked what health actually means among old men. In their ethnographic work Calnan and Williams (1991) attempted to identify whether health was salient within the everyday lives of middle-aged British men (aged 40–55) from different social classes. They found that matters of health rarely surfaced spontaneously in discussions. It was in the context of illness that these middle-aged men spontaneously mentioned health matters, or it was in response to a researcher's probe. Otherwise, health was part of the men's everyday "practical consciousness" (Bourdieu 1990) and their health practices were undertaken as a matter of course. When directly asked to define health, a working-class man replied:

> It's very difficult to say what you define as "fit" and "well" . . . I mean it is easy to take it for granted. I mean, if you take a man who, for arguments sake, has suffered with rheumatism, then you appreciate that you are probably better off and fitter. It is very difficult to describe, something that I suppose you *take-for-granted*." (Calnan and Williams 1991, 513, italics original)

As men age, however, more ill-health occurs, and the more the aging body is present. When Scottish men aged 65 and older were asked to describe health, the old men presented stories about their control of their lives and their bodies (McVittie and Willock 2006). When they narrated their thinking about ill-health, the theme of being in control gave way to themes of happen-chance and loss of control. Emergent was the accounting, "You get ill health through no fault of your own" (ibid., 794). One other Scot vividly portrayed his claim of being powerless to illness, saying, "You can't fight windmills."

When men's narratives involve the discursive dualism of their own agen-cy determining health and fate determining ill-health, their stories shore up masculine identity and self-worth (McVittie and Willock 2006). My thinking is that the agency stories ought not be misinterpreted as old men's conscious, deliberate performance of masculinity. Rather, the agency and fate narratives reveal men engaged in health practices without much consideration of their everyday actions (cf. Robertson 2006, 178). As men, their health-related practices are of course masculinity practices, but these practices are not consciously organized as such. They are embodied, routine health practices that observers might see as gendered or evidence of a class habitus. It is noteworthy that the agency and fate narratives also embody the neoliberal moralizing within recent public narratives that emphasize men's responsibil-ity for their own health and divest the state of responsibility for health in-equalities.

Having lived in sync with a common class habitus that includes narratives about external forces such as fate causing men's "failed" bodies, an old man's retold experience of his health-challenged self can be empathetically understood by other aging men. Frank (1995, 23) commented that hearing "a story is to experience it affecting one's own life and to find in that effect a certain truth of one's life." The content of the story—of an old man reeling a bit when ill—would not be misheard by the other men as manhood chal-lenged. Instead, the story told is personal; it is about the man and his body and his interrupted practical consciousness that took for granted health. If what one heard was reduced to masculinity lost (and never-aging masculinity ideals affirmed), my argument is the listener is not listening. Even if the consequences of illness can be connected to cultural discourses about gender, the stories told by the men are about the men's slow embodiment of their changing, age-related health and rising preference for living with the impermanence norms within aging masculinities.

As McVittie and Willock's (2006) study revealed, some old men may well bring into later life quite rigid gender identities, which will be wounded by aging-related illness experiences. Charmaz (1994, 283) similarly observed, "traditional" masculinities "narrow the range of credible male behaviors for those who subscribe to them. Hence, they foster rigidity in stance and set the conditions for slipping into depression." The message is that illness and disability are difficult for anybody to embrace, and health declines may be especially compromising for the men who resist their aging and still prefer the idealized masculinity practices of being in control and resisting dependency. This message is supported by ample research evidence on how co-morbidities disrupt, in particular among the men striving to retain/recapture a past, masculine self. Living with diminishing health and age-related bodily changes forces aging men to face up to the likelihood of becoming dependent on others' care.

A caveat. Experiencing a troubling illness and getting old are not always similar, and studies of old men's illness experiences are not equivalent to studies of old men's aging experiences. Distinctions between aging and illness have become increasingly blurred. In a Venn diagram, we would see the respective circles of the lived experiences of aging and illness overlapping, yet we see more separateness than overlap. Contingent on when and what men experience through their aging, most old men likely have seen the value in deconstructing and reformulating dominant masculinity messages as their guides for action and for self-worth. As Tannenbaum and Frank (2011, 243) caution, as much as *some* old men will perceive ill-health as a masculinity threat, by age 70 most men in their study had incorporated seeking routine medical care and healthier lifestyles "into their daily lives in a way that does not conflict with their perceived resilience to [impending] frailty" or their self-image as men. I interpret the research findings behind their caution to also mean that at some point in later life, most old men's transformed habitus has *largely* discarded the "taste" for the gender practices of their youth and embraced instead the dominant masculinities that organize the fields of later and late life and better fit their reduced body capabilities.

Nonetheless, there are parallels between the experiences of men with a serious but not terminal chronic illness and aging men's lived experiences with learning to be old. This is where the Venn diagram overlaps. In both cases, there is the reality of bodily changes and personal accommodations to the aging/chronicity reality. Not surprisingly, researchers have identified that acceptance of serious illness is facilitated by being old (cf. Levy and Cartwright 2015). But "acceptance" is a relative term. To illustrate: "A 77 year-old man who had arthritis, back problems, diabetes, heart disease, kidney

disease and a thyroid condition expressed his *resignation* in this way: 'That's
life . . . I'm not happy with it but if it has to be that way, it has to be. That's
all there is to it. You just accept it and move on'" (Hurd Clarke and Bennett
2013, 353, my italics). Or as Charmaz (1994, 274, italics original) wrote:

> Eventually most men realize that their bodies have changed. Subsequently,
> they become aware of uncertainty—uncertain episodes, uncertain treatment
> effects, uncertain complications—an uncertain life. Awakening to death and
> *acknowledging* continued uncertainty is sobering. Reappraisals follow. These
> reappraisals can lead to epiphanies marking major turning points for men and
> their families . . . When men acknowledge continued uncertainty, their reap-
> praisals bring reflection and self-appraisal.

Aging-related bodily changes and the consequent lifestyle changes are
likely to rattle the ontological security that men's habitus provided, challenge
self-efficacy and feelings of control, shrink the breadth of their social capital
as a result of retracting from some relationships, and reorient their presumption of future time (cf. Carstensen 2006; Frank 1995). These biographical
changes that come about with aging are similar to, not the same as, what
occurs with the onset of troubling illness such as arthritis and its attending
chronicity (Gibbs 2005). In her study of the identity dilemmas of chronically
ill men, Charmaz (1994) discovered that men were challenged most by the
lifestyle changes (e.g., forced retirement, shaken marriages) rendered by
their illness and its encroachments. Illness ruptured the taken-for-granted
lives, and the men interpreted their lifestyle disruption as their wake-up to the
reality of their impermanence. People eventually come to embody the uncertainty of later life much like most of the chronically ill men in Charmaz's
study, and in doing so they recognize that aging is not an acute, curable
condition. Continuing to think about their aging in masculinist, modernist
narratives as a "problem to solve" would prove disheartening.

To make clear, aging and illness narratives focus on the *process* of becoming. The narratives contextualize lived experiences in terms of a biographical perspective. Sickness alters identity, aging alters identity, and men
will use narrative to reorganize self. Based on his experience with severe
illness and listening to other people's illness narratives, Frank (1995) identified three types of narratives arising from illness experiences—restitution,
chaos, and quest—and he argued that "both institutions and individual listen-
ers steer ill people toward certain narratives" (77). All three narrative types
are told, alternatively and repeatedly, within illness stories. At one instant,
one narrative type may guide the story; as the man's illness progresses, the
other narratives dominate the story (Frank 1995, 75–76).

In societies distinguished by restorative medical care and medicalized
discourses about illness (and aging) as not normal, it is unsurprising that
aging men confront every illness with a desire for restoration. It is part of

their cultural habitus. Restitution narratives dominate most illness stories, which Frank (1995, 77) heard told with a common storyline: "Yesterday I was healthy, today I'm sick, but tomorrow I'll be healthy again." Restitution efforts and their stories "attempt to outdistance mortality by rendering illness transitory" (ibid., 115). But they "no longer work" (ibid., 94) when a man's health limitation remains chronic or when the aging man is further away from "good-enough" health. He knows that his aging body isn't "restorable." When this awakening occurs, he initially may founder with the uncertainties of later life and the trajectory of his aging body. He is likely to mull over whether his late life will be brief rather than tedious and burdensome for others.

Applying Frank's typology to men's narratives about their aging, their accounts of later and late life heavily use quest narratives and occasionally chaos narratives. If you imagine listening to a very old man who lived fifty-plus years with his wife doing all the meal preparation and homemaking but now faces the chaos of life by himself as a newly bereaved widower living alone, the syntactic structure of his story would most likely be "and then and then and then" (Frank 1995, 99). His practical consciousness and understanding of the "rules of the game" of life as married are in disarray. His chaos-type narrative "imagines life never getting better . . . [and is] as anxiety provoking [to hear] as restitution stories are preferred" (ibid., 97). By comparison, a continuously partnered old man can embody his corporeal age reminders of getting older and social age reminders of being a grandfather and great-grandfather. But he will reach the personal turning point of "Whoa, I got old," and when he does he has little to no reflective grasp of future time and feels no one is in control. Only the immediacy of an "unmade world" exists. Frank's analogy is, "A person who has recently started to experience pain speaks of 'it' hurting 'me' and can dissociate from that 'it.' The chaos narrative is lived when 'it' has hammered 'me' out of self-recognition" (ibid., 103). Old men are quite likely to muse in multiple episodes of chaos, given the uncertainties of later and late life. But they are not likely to remain bullied by the chaos.

In quest experiences and their retold stories, the aging man meets later life, health decline, widowerhood, and recognition of his impermanence directly. "Quest stories meet suffering head on; they accept illness and seek to use it. Illness is the occasion of a journey that becomes a quest" (Frank 1995, 115). Edit this pair of sentences to speak to old men's lived experiences, rather than only about illness, and it is possible to understand men negotiating later and late life as quests and their narratives as quest stories. "What is quested for may never be wholly clear, but the quest is defined by the [aging man's] belief that something is to be gained through the experience [of aging]" (ibid., 115). Quest stories may recount old men's (re)structuring of their time and purpose, reorganizing their lives and social worlds, or restructuring identities as they navigate lessening independence and declining health (cf. Carstensen 2006; Davidson and Meadows 2010).

Does the erosion of old men's health and, in turn, functional capability undermine their gendered identities? I think not, for two reasons. First, if in fact most old men embody later and late life as opportunities to quest, as I think they do (cf. Randall 2013a), the continuity of their identities as men could be accomplished in fields of aging masculinities. The adventures taken up might be in building genealogies through document searches and cemetery visits, or becoming cancer survivor advocates and volunteer drivers for other men undergoing chemotherapy, or reading cookbooks with a magnifying glass and preparing two new adventurous entrees a week. Second, serious illness is a couple experience (cf. Kayser, Watson, and Andrade 2007) for the aging men who are married or intimately partnered. Like the chronically ill men in Charmaz's study, old men routinely turn to and lean on intimate others for identity validation as husbands, lovers, brothers, and fathers. These core identities affirm men's gendered identities and protect against the threats to self. Charmaz (1994, 278) proposed, "Preserving self means maintaining essential qualities, attributes, and identities of this past self that fundamentally shape the self-concept. Thus, ill people relinquish some identities but retain others. By preserving self, men reconcile the identity dilemmas that chronic illness thrusts upon them . . . Through preserving self, men maintain continuity throughout the past, present, and future."

When I imaginatively revise Charmaz's comment from how a serious chronic illness affects men's identities and awakens a sense of impermanence into a more inclusive comment about old men's aging experiences and identity negotiations, it is arguable that most old men who are negotiating later and late life have already met head-on their stigmatized identities as old men, experience the continuity of their gendered self within close relationships, and recognize their impermanence.

THAT'S NOT MASCULINE

Much has been written about (white and African American) men's masculinity practices putting their health at risk (e.g., Courtenay 2000, 2009; Griffith 2015). The basic argument has been that the masculinity practices that men employ to demonstrate "manliness" and gain/maintain masculine capital are the same ones that can undermine their health. Here are two examples. First, for reasons not fully understood, African American men, particularly if they live in impoverished communities, have one of the highest premature cardiovascular disease mortality rates in the United States. A line of research has investigated the likelihood that embodiment of masculine competitiveness, intensity, even impetuousness (Griffith 2015) contributes to the charged emotions elevating blood pressure. A parallel line of research finds that racialized masculinity preferences considered "unmanly" increase the risk of morbidity and early death (e.g., refusing colorectal cancer screening, not regularly seeing a physician for routine exams, not walking for exercise; e.g., Hooker et al. 2012). The supposition is that by "doing masculinity" as socially prescribed in African American men's culture, the same masculinity practices are doing ill-health. However, researchers do not always directly measure racialized masculinity preferences and practices, which can leave their interpretation speculative. Hammond et al. (2010, 1306, italics original) demonstrate that "African-American men move *towards* preventive healthcare when they endorse more 'traditional' masculine norms . . . which prioritize pro-action and interdependence"; it is "medical mistrust rooted in expectations of racially biased treatment, *not masculinity*, [that] may delay African-American men's routine check-up initiation."

Second, also not well understood is why middle-aged and old men may discount heart disease symptoms by interpreting them as tiredness or heartburn or just getting older, not because they cannot feel the discomfort but because they earlier learned to "read" their bodies in a stoic way. Minimizing and believing that troubling feelings would probably go away was a mark of masculinity. "Mike," who had had a bypass, commented: "A man is not likely to go to the doctor as readily as a woman is. You might get a pain and say, 'well I'll not bother going to a doctor.' That's what a man is more inclined to do. He'll not say until it's really bad, "look, I've got a pain. There's something wrong here"" (O'Brien, Hunt, and Hart 2005, 510).

In support of this, Springer and Mouzon (2011) used the multiwave Wisconsin Longitudinal Study and restricted the analysis to men aged 65 and older. They noted that men who kept up a tough-guy persona were almost 50 percent less likely to use preventive health care services. As another man interviewed by O'Brien and her colleagues (2005, 513) summarized, "Unfortunately . . . I know it's completely moronic, I mean, it's caveman stuff, but that is to a certain extent how guys still operate." Other researchers have drawn similar links between the cultural constructions of masculinities—e.g., the values of "give-'em-hell" indestructability and "tough-it-out" stoicism— and assorted patterns of men's health behaviors, such as men's reticence to admit vulnerability and seek health care.

A similar research trajectory has investigated how the dictum to maximize masculine capital resonates with younger, middle-aged, and old men's health practices. Avoiding regular medical visits on the supposition their bodies "aren't yet broken," or even if so their bodies will typically mend themselves, is often proposed as a masculine capital-producing practice. In reporting a study of young heterosexual men living in London, de Visser, Smith, and McDonnell (2009) titled their article, "'That's Not Masculine': Masculine Capital and Health-Related Behavior." For the 18- to 21-year-old

lads in the study, the symbolic capital they accrued was derived from masculinity practices that adhered to a "traditional" conceptualization of gender
relations and how power (or capital) is accrued.

MASCULINE CAPITAL:
THE DON'T CARE/SHOULD CARE PARADOX

I contend that what young men might regard as "that's not masculine" may
be seen differently by old men, especially when it comes to matters of health.
The research evidence to support my argument is equivocal. There is the
evidence that younger men who are not seriously threatened by a health
challenge consider their ability to live with nagging health troubles to be
ordinary masculinity practice. Unlike the healthy-enough (younger) man
talking about his masculinized practice to not seek medical assistance because "enduring" is integral to being a man, O'Brien, Hunt, and Hart (2005)
detected that once a man's health became more seriously compromised, he
reformulated the practice of being "strong and silent" to being "strong and
wise." These men were older. The research by Emslie and her colleagues
(2006) also illustrates that mature men with depression do not uniformly
abide by the "strong and silent" practice; rather, they will seek help for
emotional and mental health troubles.

Thus, leaning on hegemonic masculinity theory to make sense of aging
men's health practices may result in a simplistic interpretation that glosses
over lived experiences. What mature men actually *do* in daily life may differ
from how they *say* they are expected to behave according to stereotypes
about men. As Robertson (2006, 178) understood, only "part of what forms
an individual's 'habitus' are the public meta-narratives regarding what constitutes appropriate, gendered behaviour(s) or expressions of belief." Robertson argued that men strive to balance the moral dilemma of the masculinity
code "don't care" and their lived experiences of "should care." He found that
by the age of 27–43, the British men in his study were well aware of the
gendered narrative that men "don't care" much about health, but "don't care"
was not how they necessarily behaved. In interviews with Irish men aged
18–71, Noel Richardson (2010, 424) also found "a heightened awareness
among men, as they got older, that health was not a bottomless reservoir, and
needed to be managed and maintained through appropriate health behaviors."

Daughters, wives, and public health messages advocate "should care" and
often counterbalance the "don't care" masculinity code. Given the likelihood
of men faced with competing discourses, and researchers' penchant to interpret men's actions through the lens of the hegemonic masculinity paradigm,
it is not surprising that research evidence supports both "don't care" and
"should care." On one hand, unlike the men in Robertson's and Richardson's

studies who were juggling competing discourses and adopting a "should care" stance, Chapple and Ziebland (2002) interviewed British men, most often older than 60 and diagnosed with prostate cancer, who identified with the gendered rhetoric that it was not masculine to disclose "private" prostate troubles or, in general, admit to a need for help. These men felt they preserved masculine capital by their compliance with the stereotypical discourses saying men "don't care." Similarly, for the men aged 65 and older from southeast England in Davidson and Meadows's (2010) study, the masculinity practices engaged by the men centered on *self*-control and meant the men chose to not participate in preventative health screening or go to a physician unless they absolutely had to. Two of these men commented, "I don't give in. Even if I feel awful, I wouldn't tell anyone" and "You've just got to get through it."

On the other hand, equally in sync with the same dictum to maximize masculine capital are the "should care" practices among middle-aged and old men who embrace the adult "manhood value" of *responsibility* (e.g., Hammond and Mattis 2005). Being responsible can be enacted by "keeping myself in a fit state" and through preventative health behaviors, including routine medical exams. Aging men, if they once practiced "don't care," which favors *self*-control (Davidson and Meadows 2010), can transition to "should care," which favors actions and decisions of taking responsibility for self and health. Take, for example, Noone and Stephens's (2008) study of late middle-aged New Zealanders, most of whom were farmers and were reluctant to engage health care services until they felt they needed to. Noone and Stephens heard the men use two on-the-surface conflicting discourses for their health care decisions: they spoke as respectable, "masculine" infrequent users of health services, at the same time they positioned themselves as knowledgeable, "virtuous" men who use regular health care checkups, disease screening programs, and immunizations. By attending to their bodies the old men changed capital-producing strategies, now preferring to maintain control and distinguish themselves from what they deem as easier, less masculine avoidance behaviors.

Oster and her colleagues (2015) report that the Australian men aged 50–74 they interviewed embraced the "should care" principle and emphasized the rationality to engage in preventative health care, in particular colorectal cancer screening. Similarly, Tannenbaum and Frank (2011) observed aging men talk about proactively taking charge of their failing health, and feeling empowered by taking control. The men's narratives subjectively positioned themselves above peers who did not take charge: "I've seen my friends go downhill, so now it's more important than ever for me to take care of my health" (ibid., 247). When diagnosed with prostate cancer, men's illness narratives will often address how managing their survival trumps the value of casting oneself as independent (cf. O'Brien et al. 2007, 187–88).

The old men's discourse centers on owning up to the rotten consequences of fate and external factors: a cancer and its treatment.

My thinking is consistent with Robertson's. Experiences derived from bodily aging and age relations launch opportunities for men's critical reflection and habitus modification. Experience empowers mature men to navigate among the cultural masculinities, and to engage in actions that can seem oppositional to the never-aging tenets of "traditional" masculinity ideologies. The actions may well be consistent with aging masculinities. Perhaps equal to the importance of men's transformed habitus, most aging and old men have banked sufficient masculine capital such that with minimal cost they can engage in practices consonant with the nonhegemonic aging masculinities that are emergent within ageist societies.

Consider Gough's (2013, 2) comment that "help-seeking is customarily avoided by men, but could be reframed as a brave or courageous choice and therefore be congruent with valued masculinities (rather than be feminized as weakness)." This is what Farrimond (2012) uncovered in her interviews with British men aged 20–60. In general, her participants' narratives showed they subscribed to masculinity ideologies that characterized men as resilient, stoical, and reluctant to seek help. However, the men disengaged from these narratives in most matters of health. Many of the men characterized the stereotype of "real" men who do not go to a physician as a "hangover from cavemen times" (Farrimond 2012, 216). A sizeable number of the men divulged they went to doctors for a range of complaints and persisted in their help-seeking when an encounter with a physician was unsatisfactory. These young to late middle-aged men identified themselves as responsible men who take action when their health warrants and positioned themselves as unlike the stereotypical "doctor-phobic 'Neanderthal Man'" (ibid., 213).

McVittie and Willock (2006) likewise noted that, for the Scottish old men in their study, identifying as a "real" man was never given up just because a health challenge compelled the men to seek medical opinion and services. For these old men, their masculine identities were framed by using a moral comparison standard that positioned other men who were irresponsible about seeking help when necessary as "weak." This is consistent with early symbolic interactionist theorizing, which proposed that one way people draw conclusions about their gendered selves is by comparing the self to others.

In another study of Scottish men, O'Brien, Hart, and Hunt (2007) heard mature men profess how they man-upped and endured the stresses of paid work as an unavoidable byproduct of "what men have to do." Then, when hammered with a severe myocardial infarction, severe enough to force the men to terminate their work life, the men shifted their narrative to how they embrace the lifestyles consistent with later life masculinities and now include preventative health practices such as exercise as a surrogate for work. They knew their health was deficient, yet they resisted being treated as a cardiac invalid. As a 67-year-old man lamented, "Neighbors will shout across to you. 'Should you be doing that?' . . . The lass across the road from me. She's up in the accident and emergency unit . . . she's constantly yelling at me for doing this" (ibid., 185). This old man came to embody his health limitations, not others' worry, and he continues to endorse masculinity norms regarding autonomy and independent decision-making. He, like many other old men, cites the importance of responsibility, self-reliance, and perseverance—that is, being responsible for one's self (cf. Farrimond 2012; Hammond and Mattis 2005; Hooker et al. 2012).

SUMMARY: AGING LIKE A MAN

This chapter called attention to the importance of listening to old men's stories and narratives—*listening* to their narratives rather than using their stories to test hypotheses. The canons of deductive research rightly maintain that theory frames hypotheses, which are then sustained or disputed by data. The never-aging model of masculinities theorizes that old men's health practices will shun things associated with "girl stuff," such as not seeking routine medical care or worrying about one's weight and diet. And this is what some researchers hear. However, the "data" within mature and old men's narratives also reveal the men letting go of irresponsible cultural directives and instead exercising responsibility to their family and their selves. Are they not "doing" health like an old man? I think they are. The (white, middle-class, heterosexual) normative standards for never-aging masculinities become superseded by standards of aging masculinities that substitute the "should care" principles and health practices for "don't care."

The never-aging masculinity discourse remains to some degree a directive for aging men's performances and worries (Thompson and Langendoerfer 2016). It is equally important to recognize its ageist discourse, which is something aging men feel and grapple with. With the upswing of the legitimacy of aging masculinities, the majority of aging men maintain lives and lifestyles that raise doubts about the presumption that being a man and being old are dissonant ideas.

In general, there is sufficient evidence that the rise of the third age culture supports old men's embodiment of aging masculinities, which amends tastes, actions, and identity (cf. Meadows and Davidson 2006). There also is enough suggestive evidence that many old men rely on reformulated or amended masculinities as they quest and come to terms with their aging and health (cf. Gray et al. 2002; Wentzell 2013a, 2013b). Questions that now need to be investigated include how men of different cultures, sexualities, and classes feel and act when the chronicity of their ill-health compels them to recognize that their life journey may be on the cusp of ending. Too little is known about old men's experiences with late life, the "fourth age" culture, and others' provision of care for their continued survival.

What is intriguing is that most old men present narratives about their changed health that reflect their intention to maintain "manly" identities. This does not necessarily mean that old men's stories reveal an intention to abide by the standards of never-aging masculinities and ignore their health and medical care needs. Rather, they contest ageist discourses that equate manhood with strength and lost manhood with health decline. These discourses narrowly construe wrestling with health in later life as "successfully aging." Old men embody age- and health-appropriate strategies to gain/maintain masculine capital. In doing so they live in sync with aging masculinities, which encourage being responsible for one's self and persevering in spite of health limitations. One example: In a study of late middle-aged and old African American men, Hooker and his colleagues (2012) note that participants frequently voiced how perceptions of manhood can positively affect health. Reflecting this viewpoint were comments such as, "A healthy lifestyle is the outcome of being a good man" (ibid., 85), and the terms "principled" and "responsible" were prevalent in these men's narratives.

Chapter Six

Health Inequalities

Health is a form of life course capital that individuals preserve or deplete at varying rates over time . . . the health of individuals across positions of advantage and disadvantage confronts forces of senescence and mortality over time.
—Willson, Shuey, and Elder (2007, 1886)

Tailored interventions are needed to address the health disparities and unique health needs of LGB older adults.
—Fredriksen-Goldsen et al. (2013, 1802)

Life expectancy at birth has continued to increase in developed nations, first as a result of public health reductions in mortality caused by infections and hunger, and later as a result of preventative health services and medical care reducing overall mortality, particularly in ischemic heart diseases, which remains the leading cause of men's (and women's) death in the US, UK, and most European countries. Unlike their grandfathers' life span, on average old men may now live 25+ years longer. On average, they regularly experience later onset of chronic, at times disabling, illnesses, whether it is the silent creep of atherosclerosis or the eyes-wide-open experience of prostatitis pain. Unless an aneurysm bursts or a lethal myocardial infarction occurs, the majority of men will be healthy enough to enjoy later life long before they eventually face an erosion of bodily autonomy.

This chapter looks beyond the "on average" and into the inequalities in health status that intersect, for example, with men's own class status and their community's socioeconomic well-being. I bring forward examples from nineteenth-century England and twenty-first-century Appalachian coal mining communities. Health inequities also independently intersect with the masculinities within men's ethnic cultural habitus, as exemplified in the "Hispanic paradox" and by the "John Henryism" found within African

American communities as well as the prevalence of depression and suicide among old white men. The chapter also calls attention to the insults of chronic illness conditions on aging men, and to do so I call attention to old men's masculinity practices as they manage three conditions—Parkinson's disease, prostate cancer, and their own breast cancer.

BEYOND INDIVIDUALS: HEALTH GRADIENTS

It has become a cliché: men live shorter lives than women, but healthier ones. This phenomenon has been regularly documented. It is sometimes referred to as the gendered health-survival paradox. This is because men typically live with fewer comorbidities and lower rates of disability than what women experience, in particular women of color. In Japan, which along with Singapore has one of the longest life expectancies in the world, estimates show that there is a difference of nearly seven years between women's and men's life expectancy, 87 vs. 80 years, respectively (Oksuzyan et al. 2010; West et al. 2014). Japan was the first developed nation where men, *on average*, lived to at least age 80. In the UK and US, recent estimates project the life span gender gap to be five years, ages 81 vs. 76 (West et al. 2014). Comparing people already age 65 or older in the UK and US, the gap narrows to a two-and-a-half-year difference between men's and women's life expectance, with 65-year-old men expected to celebrate their 83rd birthday (Office of National Statistics 2015; West et al. 2014). The projections above are "on average" statistics. This means a growing number of 65-year-old men will eventually celebrate the 90th birthday, and some younger men will not survive to be with their daughters when they marry.

A number of scholars have theorized that the gendered health-survival paradox arises from men's health practices and preferences that may sustain the values within hegemonic masculinity ideologies yet put at risk men's health. In the specific context of depression, studies have found that men who align themselves with "traditional" masculinity scripts end up more likely to experience depression and less likely to seek clinical help or support from peers (cf. Addis 2011; Emslie et al. 2006). Still, reliable explanations for the male/female health-survival paradox are wanting.

Hierarchal systems of gender inequality unquestionably disadvantage the health and life chances of some men, while other groups of men are systematically advantaged. "On average" statistics disguise these health inequalities. Not all men within a country have the same risk of mortality or a similar quality of life in their late years, because there are life chance disparities across populations of men within countries with ethnic and/or socioeconomic diversity. To illustrate the matter of diversity, in Japan there remains virtually no ethnic diversity, very little economic inequality compared to US and European countries, and much greater cultural equality and inclusion; there also is little evidence of life expectancy differences or notable health disparities among Japanese men from different classes or geographies, with the exception of the island of Okinawa (Horiuchi 2011). Japan's socioeconomic gradient in health and longevity is much flatter than found in other countries.

By comparison, UK and US data reveal ample evidence of ethnic and class differences in the length of men's life span and their health status before death. One example of ethnic disparities: Citing post-millennium mortality rates within England, Galdas (2010, 217–18) found that the premature death rate from coronary heart disease [CHD] is 46 percent higher among South Asian men compared with the indigenous whites. As a different example, African American men are at greater risk than white men for suffering with prostate cancer, which is their most commonly diagnosed and most deadly form of cancer (Gaines et al. 2014).

In terms of class disparities, one example is provided by the UK's Office of National Statistics (2014, 2015). Life expectancy for newborn baby boys was lowest in northwest coastal Blackpool (74.7 years), one of the poorest communities in England, and in Glasgow, Scotland (72.6 years), which has deprivation profiles similar to northwest England. In comparison, the life expectancy for baby boys in the relatively affluent west London boroughs of Kensington and Chelsea was 83.3 years.[1] Wherever else one looks, the effect of the socioeconomic gradient continues to show that men of higher social status typically have better health, lower mortality rates, and longer life expectancy.

To provide a historical example: In *The Condition of the Working Class in England*, Engels (1845, 106ff.) detailed the injurious effects of the working class's dreadful dwellings, terrible air quality in their Manchester factory-town neighborhoods, regular exposure to raw sewage, inadequate and poor quality of food, scarce medical care, and overall noxious life conditions. Class matters, and continues to. Michael Hendryx and colleagues (Hendryx and Ahern 2008; Hendryx et al. 2012) have documented substantially higher rates of morbidity, particularly cardiopulmonary disease, and early cancer-related death among residents of coal production Appalachian communities. Residents' poor health and early cancer deaths are not determined directly by being in the mines. Rather, other prime etiological risks were living in proximity to the environmental contamination from the mining industry, particularly the air quality at mountaintops, and the residents' socioeconomic disadvantage and poor access to medical care. Men's life expectancy in McDowell

---

1. Longevity estimates change, sometimes by as much as a year longer or shorter life span within a two- to three-year window, principally because of in- and out-migration patterns within communities.

County, West Virginia, is age 64, nine years less than women's in the county and twelve years less than the US national average for men (Wang et al. 2013). As the title of Wang et al.'s (2013) article notes, there are communities "left behind" as their nation moves into a healthier postmodernity.

I have often used the conditional statement "the majority of men" to passively acknowledge that the particularities of class, ethnicity/race, and other social forces decisively affect men's health and longevity within a generation. Social gerontologists know that what overwhelmingly determines class and ethnic/racial differences in longevity and health status are social factors—the conditions into which people are born, grow, work, live, and age—not the personal decisions. Still, the "social fact" that there is a socially determined health gradient lives alongside an escalating neoliberal attribution that the diversity in men's health status and longevity is the result of lifestyle choices. Too often unacknowledged, more men of color in developed countries are employed in hazardous occupations than are white men, and their health is further constrained by poorer living conditions, including the absence of clean water, the chronicity of stress, lesser education, and limited economic resources. In effect, the onset of the later life comorbidities is heavily determined by men's social, cultural, and economic capital *and* their communities' affluence.

GRADIENTS AND MASCULINITIES

The socioeconomic gradient in health is not invariant, partly because there are often marked differences in health and masculinity practices among men within a class or an ethnic group. There is, for example, a "Hispanic paradox." Arias (2016) noted that, despite their economic disadvantage and greater experience of chronic illness and disability, as of 2014 the life expectancy for Hispanic/Latino men in the US was 79.2 years, which is nearly three years *greater* than for white men (76.5 years).[2] Comparing men of color who share similar social disadvantages and poverty rates and likelihood of premature chronic illness, there is an even greater disparity between the life spans of black and Hispanic/Latino men—whether the benchmark is measured at birth or at age 65. Baby Hispanic/Latino boys have a projected seven-year longer life span than African American males at birth, and by the time men reach age 65, Hispanic/Latino men continue to have life spans nearly three and a half years longer than black men (Arias 2016). This pattern suggests that there may be a mortality advantage for Hispanic/Latino men, and para-

---

2. These US estimates use the ethnic categories Hispanic, non-Hispanic black, and non-Hispanic white. "Black" as a category will include African Americans, English-speaking Afro-Caribbean peoples, and recent Sub-Saharan African immigrants.

doxically the advantage is more concentrated at the lower levels of socioeconomic status (Turra and Goldman 2007).

Some research has begun to question whether indeed every Hispanic group enjoys a mortality advantage. The rationale is that the advantage seems concentrated among more recent Mexican Americans immigrants (Markides and Eschbach 2011). Exactly what mechanisms determine old Mexican American immigrants' advantage remain uncertain. They typically share similar disadvantaged economic profiles as old black men in the US, typically live in rural/urban geographies with similar (dis)advantages, yet Mexican Americans survive much longer. Both populations also experience what is known as a "weathering" effect (Geronimus et al. 2015). The weathering effect hypothesizes that there is a cumulative biological impact of being chronically exposed to socially structured stressors, e.g., racism through social marginalization, and its effect is evident in increased health vulnerability and accelerated aging (James et al. 1992). Nonetheless, it seems that the disadvantages of racism and low socioeconomic status may be a bit offset by Mexican Americans' ethnic habitus. Working-class and poor Mexican and Mexican American men typically embed themselves in their ethnic communities, at times sharing living costs, to maintain prized identities as honorable family men. More than stereotyped machismo masculinity values, the men endorse and perform *caballerismo* ("gentlemanliness") masculinities (Arciniega et al. 2008; Wentzell 2013b), which are associated with social responsibility, protection of family, and problem-solving coping.

Perhaps a cultural shield of family-centered, *caballerismo* masculinities does ward off some of the social disadvantages and chronic stress that usually undermine health and well-being. Research findings now show that the longer Mexican-ancestry men live in the US, the protectiveness of their ethnic habitus diminishes, likely because the habitus is transformed as the men (and their families) embody the individualistic tastes of American culture (Markides and Eschbach 2011).

Research oriented to detect what other masculinity practices old men engage in to *better* their physical and psychological health status will prove to be valuable for clinicians and policy makers. A case in point: It is theorized that some form of "John Henryism"—a strong predisposition among some older African American men to strive against overwhelming odds (James 1994)—increases feelings of self-efficacy and reduces feelings of disempowerment, particularly among the men who also have other capital to buffer their social marginality. Similar studies by Subramanyam and colleagues (2013) found among African Americans with sufficient income that John Henryism lowered rates of hypertension, and Haritatos, Mahalingam, and James (2007) reported that John Henryism is related to better health among high-socioeconomic-status Asians. This evidence suggests that stoic masculinities at times can be beneficial to old men's health, and the "at times" qualifier warns we cannot assume men within a (racial) category engage in similar masculinity practices. Still, too little research has investigated the conditions under which the men's ethnic habitus or the John Henryism form of ethnic resistance to social and economic adversity proves *beneficial* for physiological health.

It has been argued that physiological ill-health results from men's compliance with masculinity norms, such as the contention that norms prescribing stoicism and suppressing emotions increase the risk of coronary heart disease (cf. Courtenay 2009). Thus, African American men's higher rates of heart disease vis-à-vis Mexican Americans has to be partly explained by the men's styles of coping (cf. G. Bennett et al. 2004) and use of "cool pose" masculinity as a way of surviving in a restrictive society (Majors and Billson 1992). As one older African American man in Hooker and his colleagues' study (2012, 84) commented, "A lot of times you were denied opportunities . . . so sometimes that takes away your manhood. It becomes a matter of struggle or survival and, you know, as a man, you do what you have to do . . . it's not fair . . . you just discover your manhood in a different manner." It seems probable that the ethnic habitus of perseverance among old African American men significantly contributes to their lesser risk of clinical depression and much less risk of suicide than white, Asian, and Latino men of the same age.

DEPRESSION AND SUICIDE

My argument is that aging men's experience with depression is both gendered and raced. However, the intersection of race-ethnicity and masculinities on depression and suicide ideation is regularly blurred. Unützer (2007) presented the following case to begin his *New England Journal of Medicine* review essay on depression in later life:

> A 71-year-old man, whose wife died 6 months previously, presents with foot pain from diabetic neuropathy, poor sleep, lack of energy, and increasing frustration about his inability to "keep his diabetes under control." On examination, he also notes lack of interest in usual activities, decreased appetite, a weight loss of 4.5 kg (10 lb.) over the past 3 months, and intermittent thoughts that he would be better off dead.

This case omits race by presuming whiteness. From their meta-analysis of twenty-five international studies, Kraaij, Arensman, and Spinhoven (2002) note that men aged 65 and older become more vulnerable to depression after transitioning to their postemployment lives because of their shrinking support networks; as men became more socially isolated they were less able to cope with the distress that piles up from both daily hassles and disruptive life events. This interpretation is implicitly heteronormative and more applicable to white men, not all men. In Hammond's (2012) sample of African American men, for example, most men aged 40 and older were unmarried and had less evidence of depressive symptoms than younger black men; it was their experience of everyday racism that spiked depressive symptoms, but less so among the men who embodied the self-reliance masculinity norms. Simply put, depression is variant across groups of men, and significantly associated with masculine subjectivities and practices (cf. Addis 2011).

Most aging men episodically experience minor depression (or depressed feelings), but this transient experience is more often a bout of loneliness or anomie or stress pile-up, such as when grieving the loss of a sibling or coping with nagging thoughts about financial uncertainty. Depression in late life ranges from subthreshold (mild) to moderate to major (severe), and among men it is often undetected and untreated (Unützer 2007). The symptoms typically associated with men's depressive episodes vary from unruly sleep, including insomnia, to memory complaints, concentration difficulties, lack of energy, and loss of interest. A clinical diagnosis of major depression requires at least five key symptoms from the following set to be present: depressed mood, diminished interest, loss of pleasure in all or almost all activities, feelings of worthlessness or inappropriate guilt, weight loss or gain, insomnia, fatigue, reduced ability to concentrate, psychomotor agitation, recurrent thoughts of death or suicide. Moderate depression requires two symptoms.

In US community samples, major depression is less prevalent among old men than younger men or old women (e.g., Fiske, Wetherell, and Gatz 2009); prevalence of major depression (or a major depressive disorder) for old men is low, estimated to range from 1 to 5 percent in US as well as in Taiwan and most European countries. But estimates remain guesstimates. They may underestimate because of the way aging men are inclined to neither interpret their depressed feeling as "symptoms," even when asked directly, nor consult medical care to divulge "feeling blue" (e.g., Addis 2011; Hammond 2012). Research also strongly suggests that, unlike younger men, old men are less likely to wrestle with ill-health as an identity threat. Instead, they see their declining health more as the inevitable incursion that comes with aging (Hurd Clarke and Bennett 2013), and consistent with their past they may wrestle with health limitations stoically.

Analyzing the accounts for distress and depression among working-class white and Mexican-heritage men aged 65 and older in central California, Apesoa-Varano et al. (2015) observed that apart from a small number of established signs for clinical depression (anhedonia, low mood), the majority of men made use of euphemisms such as "rumination," "boredom," "pain," being "afraid," and "feeling lonely." Elsewhere, Apesoa-Varano, Barker, and Hinton (2015) reported that some aging men who strive to adhere to the never-aging masculinity ideologies were more likely to counterattack the betrayal of their declining health and sense of losing control through anger and fury. The health deterioration associated with the men's aging was the wellspring of their distress, which then precipitated a pile-up of distress related to work restrictions, economic limitations, and a shamed masculine self. Drawing on a series of focus group conversations about being "down in the dumps" with Australian middle-aged teachers (and others), Brownhill and her colleagues (2005) found that whenever these men personally experienced feelings of depression, they would displace it, numb it, bury it, escape it, and get angry. The repertoire of strategies and discourses the men used to manage their depression often suppressed and built up negative emotions, resulting in outbursts. Perhaps because anger is a sometimes-tolerated "manly" strategy to relieve distress, and depression is incongruent with cultural narratives about masculinities, aging men's depression might be witnessed as "grumpy" old men, and their anger becomes an overlooked sign of depression.

On the whole, older men maintain and even increase emotional well-being compared to men at younger ages (Carstensen et al. 2011). At the same time, men aged 70 and older have the highest rates of suicide deaths in most regions in the world (cf. World Health Organization 2014). Later life is both a time of enhanced well-being for men and a time of markedly increased risk for suicide. As of 2014, suicide caused more deaths in the US among white men aged 65 and older than Alzheimer's disease (Heron 2016).

Suicide still occurs in the US most frequently among old white men aged 75 and older and secondarily among middle-aged white men, age 45–64 (Curtin, Warner, and Hedegaard 2016), yet the rate of suicide among the middle-aged has been steadily rising since the new millennium (Case and Deaton 2015). There appear to be not just age effects on suicide risk, but cohort effects as well, with Baby Boomers bringing into later life an elevated suicide risk as they begin a time of heightened risk. Within both middle-aged and later life age groups, the rate of suicide for white men in the US is at least three times greater than for African Americans and two to three times greater than for either Asian or Hispanic men (Curtin and Warner 2016). Measured by individual-level socioeconomic position or by community-level socioeconomic deprivation, there is a gradient in suicide risk. Men in the lowest socioeconomic group have a suicide rate that is about three times the rate of men in the highest socioeconomic group (Platt 2017), and old farmers are disproportionately the group most at risk of suicide (Garnham and Bryant 2014).

However, the vast majority of the old white men within high risk suicide demographics (such as living alone and being disadvantaged socioeconomically), with multiple comorbidities including mental ill-health, and within the rural geographies of Montana or Idaho or northern Finland with hunting firearms nearby, do not take their own life, even when terribly ill, in pain, or depressed or feeling disconnected and isolated after the death of their wife or close friends. This qualification about risk factors prods the need to delve below the well-publicized risk factors, such as many old men's access to firearms, to investigate what embodied masculinities are also at root of who does and who does not end their own life. Recent research suggests that old men's embodied beliefs about "doing masculinity" may be related to the decision to take one's own life (cf. Canetto 2017; Oliffe et al. 2011).

To illustrate this, Canetto (1995) summarized the case of "Richard," a white man who engaged in a suicidal act at age 70, shortly after experiencing retirement and deterioration in his health (a stroke). Richard did not fit the profile of being socially isolated nor living alone; he was married. Nor did he fit the profile of being unusually emotionally and cognitively rigid. He better fit a "fallen hero" profile (Bryant and Garnham 2015), whereby a masculine subjectivity imbued with pride transforms to one of indignity as a result of ending employment and/or deteriorating health. Canetto (2017, 59, my italics) contends that "there is evidence that suicide by European-descent, ill older men is interpreted as a *reasoned choice* exemplifying masculine control, power, and determination." Her conclusion is that white men's suicide may be enabled by the cultural and gendered ethos that older adult suicide is a relatively rational response to disabling physical illness. In postmodernity, a "good" death through individual choice and agency may transcend other views of death.

I am confident that life insurance investigators regularly ponder whether the "accidental death" of an old white man crashing into a roadside oak tree was in fact unintentional or his impulsive final breadwinner strategy to provide his heirs the double indemnity that accidental death yields (cf. Sentell 2008). Thompson and Kaye (2013, 60) posited,

> A man ending his own life by choice could be interpreted as his final insistence on control of personal destiny. Viewed in this way, suicide in the face of an unacceptable quality of life may be [self-defined as] an act of empowerment and maintaining dignity. By comparison, men who choose to face chronic illness and their disability with some form of acceptance are equally powerful, representing "grace under pressure."

One of the continuing "what ifs" that may distinguish the old white men who seriously consider or attempt suicide is whether or not it is their compliance with cultural norms for men to not disclose their feelings of indignity, even when help-seeking (cf. Oliffe et al. 2011). Ironically, almost three-quarters of old men who commit suicide have seen a physician within weeks of killing themselves (Luoma, Martin, and Pearson 2002). They may have left their physician visit with a diagnosis of a medical condition that forewarns of never having the same quality of life.

COMING TO TERMS AND AGING MASCULINITIES

This section examines the bearing of the insults of chronic conditions on aging men. It begins with a discussion of research on masculinity and physical disability, and then applies these insights to the cases of Parkinson's disease (PD) and two gendered cancers: prostate and male breast cancer. For each, I explore living with a disease that challenges capacities usually associated with masculinity. Neither Parkinson's nor cancer is just a disease; they are "life ruiners." The study of masculinities and chronic diseases has begun to move beyond investigations that narrowly analyze the onset of diseases and invasive treatment as "ontological assaults" to men's social worlds and their embodied sense of being a man. There is sufficient evidence that chronic diseases have continuing seismic effects, such as how PD (e.g., Gibson and Kierans 2017; Jackson 2016) and even arthritis (e.g., Gibbs 2005) progressively curtail men's physical movement, functional ability, and self-reliance; and how the surgical and hormonal treatment for prostate cancer can have deeply troubling, lingering effects on men's subjectivities.

Old men's bodily aging and lessening capabilities are not too different from how a physical impairment forces men with physical disabilities to recognize that "they are at odds with the expectations of the dominant culture" (Gerschick and Miller 1995, 183). More-normative-bodied (younger) men can usually demonstrate the valued masculinity practices of toughness through physical strength, or independence through the physical capital of body mobility, or domination through self-presentation and agency. But when health diminishes or corporeal capacity becomes at odds with hegemonic masculinity ideals, researchers have noticed that some men renegotiate their gendered practices in ways that "come to terms" with being men with body limitations. Gerschick and Miller (1995, 202–3) argue that men with physical disabilities deal with their less-normative capabilities by utilizing "alternative visions of masculinity that are obscured, but available." The disabled men in their study utilized three strategies to come to terms with being men with physical limitations—reformulation, reliance, and rejection.

Reformulation occurs when men reinvent cultural ideals on their own terms. For example, if a man was unable to walk reliably, he might recast the means by which he accomplishes the masculinity discourse about men being independent. Smith and his colleagues (2007) reported how "Arnold," a 76-year-old who was barely able to walk from the kitchen table to the back door, recast his independence of movement in daily activities by using an electric scooter. "Arnold" commented, "The other day, last month I think, I bought myself an electric scooter, which I can get around in. It takes me down to the corner shop, chemist, post office, hotel, or whatever. I don't go very far on it. I get down there in about 5 minutes. It's good" (ibid., 332). This old man's independence was subjectively important, and his scooter did not signify his limitations, but instead his continued autonomy. Or, with regard to sexual intimacy, a disabled (or aging) man might recast sexuality to the importance of touch, emotional connectedness, and trust, thus away from a narrow emphasis on coital sex. As Gerschick and Miller (1995, 191) suggest, when disabled or aging men are confident in their own abilities and values, they confront standards of masculinity on their own terms. My thinking is that when aging men adopt reformulation strategies, they affirm and embody their aging bodies rather than live with "embattled identities."

Reliance refers to the double-down strategy some men adopt. Despite the men's physical inability to meet many of the masculinity ideals, these men relied even more heavily on the demands of hegemonic masculinities. They were routinely troubled and conflicted, such as when someone offered unsolicited help; their sense of themselves as men was undercut whenever they were treated as disabled. Irving Zola's (1982) memoir, *Missing Pieces: A Chronicle of Living with a Disability*, exemplifies how a man with a less-normative body can maintain his reliance on idealized masculinities. As a result of his childhood polio, which left him with a leg brace, a metal back support, and a cane, and later a wheelchair, Zola spent much of his adult life "passing" as a full-bodied man. As Zola once recalled about his initial "reliance" and later "rejection" strategies, "No longer was it necessary to prove that I was just like anyone else, if not better, a 'supercrip.' Though I was still quite capable of walking long distances, I no longer felt that it was necessary to do so" (Zola 1991, 4). Reliance among aging men might similarly take the form of hiding their health problems. One 80-year-old man Hurd Clarke and her colleagues (2008, 1089) interviewed described his "concealment":

> I don't want to display the pills that I take, and I don't lay them out . . . I don't think many people know I take medication. I think it is something private . . . I don't want to indicate a weakness . . . I don't want people to know that I have to depend upon certain things to keep me going.

The third strategy, rejection, is a complex framework that involves the renunciation of the idealized masculinity standards and purposeful creation of alternative definitions of manhood. In effect, when this strategy is primary, aging men would not view their bodies and daily practices as problematic; rather, they would come to terms with them and see the societal conceptions of the body ideal and usual masculinity practices as the problem. This was Zola's experience, ultimately. It is also the foundation of embodying aging masculinities. Gerschick and Miller (1995) identified "Leo," a 58-year-old polio survivor who earlier in his biography rejected physical performance in favor of intellectual achievement and later upheld a view of masculinity that came from his lived experiences, habitus, and practice of "letting go" of dominant masculinity discourses. By middle age, his experiences with aging offered other ways of gaining/retaining masculine capital. By comparison, Sparkes's (1996, 489) narrative of his own experience with chronic lower back pain concludes,

> I'd also like to report . . . that via my experiences I have been able to whole-heartedly reject hegemonic masculinity and develop new standards of masculinity in its place or, at the very least, reformulate an idealized masculinity in terms of my own abilities, perceptions, and strengths so as to judge my "manhood" along new lines. I have and I haven't. I like to, I'm trying but I'm unsure.

Like Sparkes, I think that most aging men experience a similar struggle to reject never-aging masculinities, but at some point many embody the (reformulated) aging masculinities that their generation has created. Aging men may have complex and ambivalent orientations toward hegemonic masculinity, supporting some elements and rejecting others.

The construct "mosaic masculinities" is applicable here. Tony Coles (2008, 238) proposed that as aging men negotiate masculinity, they draw upon fragments or pieces of never-aging masculinities, which they have the capacity to perform, and piece them together to reformulate what masculinity means to them. They come up with their own masculinities, which are as likely to involve rejection as reformulation of the never-aging masculinities they embodied earlier in their lives. Coles's observation that aging men create mosaic masculinities also seems to signify aging men's greater reliance on "quest" narratives (Frank 1995), since quest experiences and narratives are unfinished, much as their aging bodies and masculinities are unfinished.

PARKINSON'S DISEASE

Rare are the studies that have listened to aging men tell of their journey of coming to terms with the early chaos experience of a disabling "condition." In *With Shaking Hands*, a study of men and women with Parkinson's disease, Samantha Solimeo (2009, 14) notes that she learned that while PD sufferers recognized the progressive, incurable nature of the disorder, they did not identify themselves as sick. A few people considered PD a disability. For many, PD was embodied as a *condition* with which they lived and aged. Some considered it to be "a layer of their identity—somewhat proudly referring to themselves as 'Parkys' or 'Parkinsonians.'"

PD is the second most common neurodegenerative disorder, and because its onset typically occurs after age 60, many old men suffer the disabling effects of the disease for fifteen years or more. The disease disrupts the habits of old men's lived body and sense of lived time; no longer is clock time relevant because life is structured by symptoms, medication time, and awareness of vulnerability. Solimeo (2009) introduces Leroy, who is almost 70 and has had PD for six years. When she met him, his out-of-pocket cost for his medication was more than seven hundred dollars per month. "Pain and disability seem to shadow his days," she observes. As each dose of medicine wanes, he reports,

> My joints start aching. I get shoulder aches, terribly. And I can't walk at all. I resorted to just getting down and crawling across the floor when I couldn't get someplace. Because you start walking and your legs just won't move. You tend to freeze up. And I swear to myself. [laughs] I would get up and kick something if I could stand up. It is misery. (ibid., 3)

Similarly, Jackson (2016, 95) introduces Peter, a 64-year-old diagnosed with PD six years earlier, whose "erratic, unpredictable, bodily rhythms of living with Parkinson's seemed to invade the masculine illusion of solidity and rational control" of his and other men's ordered lives. Peter recognized his embodied vulnerability, and his anxieties and fears surfaced often:

> When I have [bad] times . . . It's probably associated with mild depression but it's a sense of aimlessness; listlessness; not knowing what to do; not getting anything done; not being able to rest and relax either . . . I'm afraid that the Parkinson's will mean that actually I do degenerate into more of a vegetable than I want to be. (ibid., 98)

Despite bodily deterioration, autonomy struggles, and dwindling friendship networks, Peter and Leroy retain hope that tomorrow will bring enjoyment and the capacity to reflect on life and attribute meaning to it.

The frustrating symptom profile of PD can include a difficulty to initiate movement, to keep movement going, and to stop movement voluntarily, as well as shuffling gait and occasional freezing of movement, slowness of movement (bradykinesia), a distal resting tremor, overall stiffness (rigidity of muscles), stooped posture, and pain. I occasionally played a round of golf with 83-year-old Dave whose swing was flawless despite the power behind the swing being weakened some by age. His PD was never a golf limitation; he slowly exited the golf cart, caught his balance, and began his shuffling leg movement to move from golf cart to address the ball. He would hit it straight, then reverse the "walk" back to the cart. There were noticeable frustrating times for Dave when he was unable to start a round of golf until the third or fourth hole, after his medication had "kicked in," and an occasional morning where he had to end his game early because his medication "wore off."

The treatment protocol for PD becomes increasingly complicated as the disease progresses; treatment focuses on managing the changing symptoms, sometimes includes secondary prevention strategies aimed at slowing disease progression, and involves adjunct pharmaceutical therapies to counterbalance the drug-induced complications of the primary pharmaceutical treatment. Treatment, however, does not return the body to a bodily state characterizing good health (Gibson 2016, 28).

Many aging men living with chronic conditions face similar contradictions: while some may adopt the ideologies of never-aging masculinity that emphasize control and independence, their bodies present them with age- and condition-based limitations in their ability to do so. They struggle. Most men with PD live with confusion regarding the imagined boundary separating ordinary bodily aging from their lived experiences with PD, which accelerates and obscures natural aging. Men will question what is worse, the disease or the medications (Solimeo 2009). Whatever the conclusion, they are troubled by how PD and its treatment are appearance altering (Solimeo 2008). The way PD limits physical capability undermines the aging men's sense of themselves as men. One-third of the old men that Solimeo (2008) interviewed mentioned loss of strength as their primary symptom; no woman with PD did. "Men described their unhappiness with what they perceived to be emasculated and unreliable bodies, particularly with poor posture and loss of strength—symptoms that affected their ability to perform household duties and that led them to avoid public spaces" (ibid., S45). The men agonized about the symbolic impact tremor, rigid muscles, and other somatic symptoms had on their public persona as less-than-whole men. Masculine capital was preserved by not being noticed.

GENDERED CANCERS

Similar to men's slow awareness that their early PD motor symptoms signal impending disease with disabilities and contested masculinity practices, aging men's early experiences of the symptoms of prostate or male breast cancer do not commonly arouse either a decision to consult a physician or worry that their underlying disease can be disabling. Each of these cancers has symptoms that can be initially trivialized, because early on the symptoms are less discernible or troubling. Yet they are both insidious—they grow slowly, nearly asymptomatically, and will have ongoing repercussions for the rest of the men's lives. Both prostate and male breast cancers and their treatment are body altering and challenge masculine subjectivity. One difference is that prostate cancer is "common." It accounts for roughly one-fifth of all new cancer diagnoses among men in the US; and while it is the second leading cause of cancer deaths among men, the five-year survival rate for newly diagnosed prostate cancer is approaching 99 percent. By comparison, male breast cancer is rare, accounting for 1 percent of all breast cancer diagnoses in the US, one-third of 1 percent of new cancer diagnoses among men, and one in one thousand cancer deaths among men (Siegel, Miller, and Jemal 2016). Long term, most men live cancer free after primary treatment for their prostate or breast cancer, or, if not, live for long periods of survivorship with the disease.

In the past two decades the impact of both types of cancer and their treatment effects on men's subjectivities has begun to draw the attention of researchers. Men narrate the experience of each gendered cancer as an uncertain journey, starting with the "you gotta be kidding me" shock and soul-searching of the diagnosis. As Henry, an 82-year-old married man diagnosed with breast cancer, said, "You just don't expect this to happen. As far as I knew, men didn't get this thing" (Thompson and Leichthammer 2010). Breast cancer in men who think they only have chests is incongruous. Men diagnosed with prostate cancer equally had a profound sense of having the "floor disappear beneath them" on hearing the diagnosis (cf. Wenger and Oliffe 2014).

I will begin by addressing prostate cancer. Early-stage prostate cancer may be asymptomatic or experienced as having minor genitourinary troubles (e.g., difficulty starting urine flow or getting an erection). At this stage men could choose among three options: watchful waiting or two forms of treatment—radiation and/or surgery. If prostate cancer remains in situ and small, the advice typically involves watchful waiting. Once tumor size warrants a physician's recommendation to begin medical treatment, presurgical radiation and/or laparoscopic ("keyhole") surgery to remove the prostate and surrounding tissue are ordinary. This is followed by androgen-deprivation therapy, especially when the cancer is advanced, which chemically stops androgens from stimulating the growth of prostate cancer cells, but can result in chemical castration. Adjunct radiotherapy or hormonal treatment can produce breast growth, hot flashes, and loss of libido, as well as interfere with sexual performance. Hagen, Grant-Kalischuk, and Sanders (2007, 211) cited one man's comment about the way his treatment-induced impotence affected his wife's quality of sexual life and marital relationship:

> My wife and I have talked about it and you know when I mentioned to her that I thought I had an erection, she said, "What do you mean thought?! Was it a dream, or did it really happen?! Do you know?" Well, I said, "It didn't go like—like fully." And she said, "Well, next time that happens, let me know!"

In a study of Latino and African American men aged 50–70+ in Los Angeles undergoing prostate cancer treatment, the major challenges discussed were not exclusively body-centered but related to work, control, and independence (Maliski et al. 2008). For the Latino and African American men, incontinence proved to be a prime threat to the men's capability to work. "Work and the ability to work . . . were an integral part of how men in this study viewed themselves as men" (ibid., 1613). Many white prostate cancer survivors were already retired when diagnosed, yet their cancer produced a convoy of troubles: from a man initially feeling "less a man" because of his less-than-whole body, to a couple struggling with the man's impotence, to men renegotiating the aspects of masculinity ideologies that would likely guide their tastes and actions as they continued to age (cf. O'Brien, Hart, and Hunt 2007). There is the case of "Pierre," who was in his late 50s, elected to go for surgery, and then struggled with incontinence. While impotent too, his backward- and forward-looking perspectives framed his account: "Impotence I can deal with because I can love my kids, love my wife, I can socialize, I can flirt . . . impotence is not stopping me" (Gray et al. 2002, 50). Incontinence was more troubling. To endure, Pierre deliberately disrupted the invisibility of a man with prostate cancer by his decision to participate in a men's cancer support group, which helped him not "go it alone" as, he felt, a closeted, less-than-whole man. From his perspective his participation began a quest for new fulfillments in later life.

Regrettably, in public and professional discourses prostate cancer is discussed heteronormatively. Despite how much medicine and researchers have sought to understand the ways age, race/ethnicity, marital status, and socioeconomic status might structure the prostate cancer experience, almost totally invisible is the effect of gender identification and sexualities—e.g., how middle-aged and old gay and bisexual men are likely to be affected differently in all the major areas of impact, from sexuality, to social relationships, to relations with the medical community (cf. Asencio et al. 2009). The occurrence of prostate cancer in trans women has rarely been reported (cf. Dorff et al. 2007). Among heterosexuals, what remains in need of further debunking is the discourse that prostate cancer is inevitably demasculating. Men have many different aging and prostate health trajectories that have been theorized to threaten their performance of previously embodied never-aging masculinities and sense of self as a man, yet I suspect that these "threats" are most often short-lived and that men's habitus is amendable and their lives as men go forward. Wenger and Oliffe (2014) affirm Robertson's (2007) observations that each man living with cancer is challenged to manage an illness-disrupted embodied masculinity and never-aging masculine ideals by drawing on other identities.

The case of male breast cancer has many similarities to men's lives with prostate cancer. There remains a paucity of research that has examined men's experience with their breast cancer, despite the fact that their experiences are compelling stories about breasts and masculinities. Male breast cancer is typically invasive ductal carcinoma, presents as a painless lump, and is clinically managed in ways almost identical to women—mammography, fine-needle biopsy, mastectomy, sometimes chemotherapy, and five years of estrogen-blocking hormonal therapy (tamoxifen). Because of its rarity and the general public's unfamiliarity that men too have breasts, men commonly delay seeking a medical opinion. At the time of the cancer's diagnosis, the tumor can be the size of half of a Ping-Pong ball. There is no "watchful waiting" with this disease; instead, surgery is almost immediate. Men with breast cancer typically live with a "radical mastectomy" because of the tumor size and involvement of surrounding tissue and lymph nodes, leaving some of them functionally unable to lift objects over their head or rotate their shoulder to throw a ball.

As these men undergo treatment for their breast cancer, they encounter an array of distressing side effects. Men may initially feel askew with the mastectomy scar; however, Thompson and Leichthammer (2010) found that men came to embody their disfigured chest. One man, Patrick, used a food metaphor to comment on his postsurgical chest and the loss of muscle behind the breast tissue: "I'm a simple guy. You have a chicken patty and then you go get a chicken nugget, as far as muscle. So now I have a chicken nugget. They took out the chicken patty." Another man named Geoff commented:

> I was kind of self-conscious the first year. But um . . . It is a sizable scar . . . right down to, you know, to the ribs . . . It doesn't really bother me. I go on vacation or go swimming at the beach. I'm not self-conscious. I don't feel like people are staring at me. I really think a lot of people don't even notice.

The gold standard of anti-estrogen therapy following the mastectomy can yield nightmarish hot flashes and weight gain, as well as diminished sexual libido and sexual performance difficulties for one-fourth to nearly half of the men treated. In the Thompson and Leichthammer (2010) study, Kenneth's response to tamoxifen was "forget this" after two months; with his oncologist's encouragement he tried it again for another very brief period, concluding, "nah, nah, nah, ain't doing it!" Another man, Stephen, in his fourth year of therapy and with plans to continue it until its conclusion, described his odyssey as "I have feelings!":

> Being a man you think emotions are like following the Oakland Raiders with a beer in your hand . . . But, uh, to be, uh, ruled by your emotions. I mean, I *have* PMS, I *have* hot flashes, I *have* emotional explosions . . . I have things where I react, where my emotional reaction is the primary reaction. That is not a male experience in life.

Due to the unexpected acquisition of a breast and loss of traditional gender signifiers—a "pec," sexual function, upper-body strength and range of motion, and emotional steadiness—the men have been often described as emasculated (e.g., Bunkley et al. 2000). However, this interpretation may misunderstand the way most men with breast cancer soon reject any further effort to adhere to hegemonic, never-aging masculinity ideologies. To illustrate, one of the men Thompson and Leichthammer (2010) interviewed is a former marine, Golden Gloves boxer, marathoner, and landscape business-man whose habitus rapidly transformed as he embodied his cancer. He de-scribed his newfound comfort doing things that would have threatened his earlier, securely grounded masculinity subjectivity.

> I definitely can consider myself a more complete human that I was before, because I'm able to [feel], you know. It doesn't matter if you're a dude or a girl. You know, it's really unbelievable, as a guy, my age group, you know, a man doesn't cry, a man doesn't show his emotions . . . it's like you're kinda suppose to be like a machine. No more.

This man threw himself into public forums to initiate personal conversations with others about men living with and through breast cancer. His narrative transformed from abject chaos of the diagnosis and mastectomy into forms of questing—to befriend any other man with cancer, to participate in national education programs about breast cancer also affecting men, and to regularly offer "shout-outs" for cancer care nursing.

I have only read about the very rare incidence of a trans woman who develops breast cancer (e.g., Sattari 2015), usually after many years of hor-monal treatment (HT) for her acquisition and maintenance of female secon-dary sexual characteristics. The etiology of trans women's breast cancer is often attributed to the earlier HT; but, like the cisgender men developing breast cancer, what determines risk remains guesswork.

Given the increasing likelihood that aging men will survive breast and prostate cancers, Frank's (1995) conceptualization of the remission society is applicable—this is where people posttreatment become well enough but can never be considered cured. Both gendered cancers fit with the characteriza-tion of cancer survivors occupying a liminal—transitional—space (Blows et al. 2012; Navon and Morag 2004) where they move from "living with" to "living through" to "living beyond" cancer, but do not return to the space they inhabited prior to the diagnosis. I have suggested that aging men living through and beyond their breast or prostate cancer care may often engage in quests that search for amended identities and selfhood. They face and revise their existential questions about life as aging men who also have survived cancer.

SUMMARY: IS CHANGE POSSIBLE?

This chapter provided a review of some of the health inequalities that charac-terize the expanding populations of aging and old men. I have argued that health, like gender and age, is performative and the health practices and inequalities that we observe reflect the men's social location as well as their habitus. From the weathering effects of men's social location to how men negotiate aging-related morbidities, what we see are glimpses of insight into how much old men's health status reflects and affects their masculinities.

There are long-standing (or institutionalized) cultural traditions regarding "right" and "wrong" health practices, and men embody the habitus of these cultural traditions. In the US, Canada, UK, and Europe, there is no longer a uniform "right" way of doing health. The proportion of the population accounted for by non-European ethnic groups has become significant and is increasing. Such diversity underscores the intersectionality of *how* men's statuses—their generation, ethnic/racial group, sexuality, class, partnered status—intertwine to affect their health chances and performances. For example, we know that the disparities among old men with and without atherosclerosis or other determinants of ischemic heart disease are determined partly by the men's cumulative (dis)advantages. But there remains insufficient research on and understanding of old men's health, health practices, and experiences with more morbidity in later and late life.

Chapter Seven

Sexual Health

All older adults, no matter their gender or sexual orientation, should have the opportunity to enjoy a satisfying and fulfilling sex life. In fact, most of them do, even if interest in sex and sexual activity declines to some extent with increasing age.

—HealthinAging.org

In Global North and many Asian countries, with old men and women living healthier lives, many more old people remain sexually active well into later life—through their 70s and into their 80s. In spite of the imperfect information that is available, this chapter addresses the ways that old men experience their sexual lives. The chapter critically reviews the concept of sexual health as it has evolved in relation to old men. I review the state's appropriation of sexuality through the medical gaze, which problematizes and then controls old men's sexual health, initially in terms of their sexually transmitted infections and disease (STIs and STD, respectively), followed by resistance to the more recent reformation of "sexual health" as a we-, not me-matter.

DISCOURSES ON MASCULINITY AND SEXUAL HEALTH

A powerful influence of late is how aging men's sexuality is more openly discussed through the medical gaze, and much less frequently by other moral discourses. Indeed, when aging men's sexuality is currently acknowledged in consumer promotions and discussed in gerontological and masculinity studies, it is addressed in terms of erectile capability, (treatable) erectile dysfunction, and, by implication, coital intercourse. The dreaded word "impotence" was sanitized, removing much of the personal failure and demasculating connotation. The convergence of the sexual medicine discourse about sexual health with the expansion of antiaging medicine—whether allopathic or complementary-alternative—has extended the jurisdiction of medicine beyond managing individual men's sexual problems and toward the management of heteronormative sexuality.

Discussing aging men's sexuality from the vantage of the medical gaze has largely reformed public discourse. Today's discourse is on erectile capability as an ordinary aspect of "natural" (i.e., vascular) aging. This chiefly medical discourse has consequences. Quieted and marginalized by sexual medicine's cultural authority are the hush-hush conversations about aging men's dwindling virility as well as the long-held stereotypes of postsexual or asexual seniors and of the "dirty" old man who has continuing sexual desire. The pervasiveness of discourse, however, has likely constructed anxieties regarding men's personal likelihood of troubles with their erections.

Medical discourse on aging and sexuality transformed the connectedness between masculinity and sexuality. On the one hand, keeping old men's sexuality as penis-centered, and with chemical support "forever functional," has extended the clout of never-aging masculinities. Old men now confront a discourse that they could, if they wanted to, maintain or regain erections forever. To cite Marshall (2011, 394), "the idea of a compulsory 'sexual retirement' has given way to the new promises of biomedicine to make sexual fitness a lifelong project." Failing rigidity of the penis is a man's problem, not merely a matter of aging. On the other hand, the fashioning of erectile capability as a vascular condition that can be managed with "lifestyle" drugs became a *pièce de résistance* defending the cultural discourses of "active aging," "healthy aging," and "successful aging."

Men's sexuality is now "regulated" by the cultural authority of medicine's successful aging (and never-aging) discourse, less so by the nonscientific, religious, or magic arguments that regarded sexual activity among old people as perilous. The comment that sexuality is regulated deserves clarification. Even though Foucault made no direct reference to later life or old age or aging (cf. Powell 2006), he has contributed significantly to sociology, and in particular to understanding discourses affirming age inequalities (Dumas and Turner 2006). Inspired by his perspective on how ordinary aspects of our existence (such as sexuality and aging) can be "problematized" and regulated by the state (i.e., modern medicine), Stephen Katz and Barbara Marshall (2003) discuss how the biomedicalization of men's sexuality has problematized erectile dysfunction "as a potentially epidemic, progressive disease." Katz and Marshall (2003, 9) continue:

> Consequently, both commercial and public health promotion discourses about positive aging have incorporated the fear of sexual dysfunction into more general models of healthy living . . . Paradoxically, the image of the erect penis, long the most vulgar of indecent "exposures," is now elevated to the

status of a vital organ symbolizing the healthfulness of midlife successful aging.

Supporting this, Cole (1984), Minkler and Cole (1991), and others (cf. Hearn 1995; Tiefer 1986) had appraised the accelerating pace of how antiaging narratives are providing a floor for the biomedicalization of sex and securing the discourse on never-aging masculinities. For example, Tiefer (1986) argued that the recasting of aging men's lessening erectile rigidity into a hydraulic issue and genitourinary matter, rather than personal impotency trouble, was part of a broader repositioning of medical boundaries to grow sexual medicine as a subspecialty and redefine aging.

BIOMEDICALIZATION CURES IMPOTENCE

Urologists were the initial practitioners of sexual medicine, and "sexual health" once concentrated on sexually transmitted infections and reproductive matters (Giami 2002). Wholly attentive to the physiological aspects of men's sexual functioning, the International Society for Sexual Medicine got its start in 1978 as the International Society for Impotence Research. It since has expanded to include family practitioners, gynecologists, and others in a multidisciplinary approach to study sexual health, treat both male and female so-called sexual dysfunctions, and enhance sexual desire and satisfaction (Goldstein 2013). Notice how sexual health practitioners basically presumed "health" meant proper physiological functioning, rather than more expansively meaning people's changing levels of desire or changing preferences in terms of sexual practices and partners.

It was the introduction of Viagra in 1998, and earlier discussion of Viagra in 1994 at the American Urological Association (Goldstein 2013), that fueled the advent of the "forever-functional" (Marshall and Katz 2002) and "sex for life" narratives (Potts et al. 2006) that advance the new masculinist imperative for never-aging intercourse. Wentzell (2017) has also called attention to how the biomedicalization of age-related impotence provided a discursive push for healthy aging and "successful aging." Reviewing the rise in public acceptance of the medical discourse that transformed aging-related impotence into a biological pathology, she notes it was "Euro-American cultural ideals of masculinity and sexuality, as well as ageism and ableism," that combined to determine what sexual changes were defined as dysfunction (Wentzell 2017, 486). Gay men were left out of this heteronormative discourse (Leonard, Duncan, and Barrett, 2013); the long-standing cultural meanings given to gay men's "deviant" sexual activity produced a new "alt-fact" space for the development of a malicious discourse about gay men as "risky" and "illegitimate" Viagra users.

It is estimated in the US that nearly one-quarter to one-half of men over age 40 experience some (minimal, moderate, or severe) degree of erectile difficulty. The degree to which erectile difficulties vary systematically with men's social location remains uncertain. There is some evidence that erectile difficulty occurs more often among men with less socioeconomic capital. And it is the intersections of age and socioeconomic status, not race/ethnicity, that contribute to the variance among men (Kupelian et al. 2008): drawing on the longitudinal population-based Massachusetts Male Aging Study, Aytaç et al. (2000) also reported that erectile difficulty occurred significantly more among men in blue-collar occupations, after taking into consideration all the other common risk factors—age, lifestyle (e.g., smoking, exercise, and diet) and medical conditions.

SEXUALITY AND HEALTH IN LATER LIFE

As self-evident as it is, the greater pervasiveness of erectile difficulty within a population is due to men's elongated life span. Erectile difficulties are a consequence of physiological aging (e.g., the lessening of testosterone as men age, decreases in vascularization) as much as aging-related illness such as benign prostate enlargement and endocrine disorders like diabetes. Furthermore, the side effects of a wide range of medications used to manage chronic medical conditions and psychological distress can result in men's loss of libido (sexual desire) and the predictability of an erection. Many aging men may be on a daily dosage of four or more different prescription drugs, which metabolize less effectively as their bodies age; as well, too few health care providers see the necessity of being concerned with the additive or interactive sexual side effects to ask their patient if his medication is affecting his sexuality (Hillman 2008).

Estimating the prevalence of moderate or severe erectile difficulties—as defined by responding "sometimes" or "never" to the question "How would you describe your ability to get and keep an erection adequate for satisfactory intercourse?"—Laumann and his colleagues (2007) affirm the odds of erectile difficulty increased several-fold with age. In the oldest group of men (aged 70+ years), 55 percent of white men, 54 percent of Hispanic men, and 50 percent of black men lived with impotency. Because of health inequalities 40 percent or more of Hispanic and black men had begun to live with impotency during their 60s, due to their higher prevalence of diabetes and hypertension. Noted elsewhere in Lindau et al.'s (2007, table 4) assessment of sexuality and health among US older adults, the primary reasons for lack of sexual activity among men were their chronic physical health problems or limitations: 40 percent of the 57- to 64-year-olds reported health problems and limitations were the reason they had not had any sexual activity in the past three months, as did 61 percent of the 75- to 84-year-olds.

Most evidence of the prevalence of erectile difficulties has been based on findings from cross-sectional studies that show progressively older age cohorts report more evidence of erectile difficulties. One longitudinal study examined individual changes in sexual function over a nine-year period and affirmed declines in sexual function and activity as men aged, whether their age at the beginning of the study was in the 40s, 50s, or 60s (Araujo, Mohr, and McKinlay 2004). Another US study reported that erectile function, ejaculatory function, and sexual drive decreased together over time in a sample of men actively followed for fourteen years, with greater rates of decline for old (aged 70+) men (Gades et al. 2009).

Both of these studies also report very similar results in regard to men's sexual satisfaction. The men were less likely to perceive the declines in their sexual health as a problem or be sexually dissatisfied. As will be addressed shortly, most men come to live with their aging body and changes in their sexual health. Thus, it makes sense that markedly few men with moderate to severe erectile difficulties consult a physician, perhaps no more than 15–25 percent (Frederick et al. 2014; Lindau et al. 2007). Most US men who seek treatment and fill their prescription for erectile medication are younger than 60; their daily lives are complicated by work and family matters or they are involved in recoupling. Hyde and her colleagues' (2012) Australian study of very old men noted that only a minority of the men (8 percent) sought advice for their erectile difficulty from a physician; instead, they normalized their erectile limitations as part of their aging. Among British men who nearly all have access to a physician through the National Health Service, just 19 percent of the men aged 55–74 reported *ever* using medication to assist their sexual performance (Mitchell et al. 2016). No association was found between use of medication and either educational level or socioeconomic classification (ibid., 33). This is counterintuitive given the greater prevalence of erectile difficulty with lower socioeconomic status.

The large majority of aging men with erectile difficulties who do not seek medical help are older and in long-term relationships; they may be "troubled" by the changes but not so troubled to seek a chemically assisted erection in order to resume intercourse. The general pattern is that when aging men encounter barriers to being sexually active—particularly when health problems or widowerhood is experienced—they place less importance on sex (Gott and Hinchliff 2003). As a point of comparison, in the six-nation Cross-National Survey on Male Health Issues, nearly half (47 percent) of the men who experienced erectile difficulty agreed it was something "you must learn to accept," and half (50 percent) also reported that with their partner they were able to work around the erection problem (Perelman et al. 2005, 399).

In addition, because the onset of old men's age-related erectile difficulty is not acute, they typically have encountered a lack of erectile reliability for some time and they slowly adapt to their bodily aging by modifying their sexual practices. When examining the sexual quality of life in a sample of aging men with varying levels of erectile difficulty, Gralla et al. (2008) observed that it was only younger men with an earlier onset of more severe erectile difficulty who reported worries about their sexual performance and relationship functioning. Older men were more likely to experience erectile dysfunction than younger men, yet were less likely to report that it impacted negatively on either their quality of life or their relationship. In this particular study, "worry" was operationalized as "failed" masculinity and measured using items from the Berlin Male Study, including one item that directly asked if the man had felt less of a man because of a weak erection during the past four weeks. Old men did not. These findings strongly suggest that old men are not using models of never-aging masculinities to self-assess; rather, they have amended their gendered habitus in ways consistent with aging masculinities.

THE MARKETING OF LATER LIFE SEXUALITY

Direct-to-consumer advertising of pharmaceutical cures professes to liberate aging men from their erectile troubles. In her analysis of the rise of Viagra (and I enjoy her pun), Meika Loe (2001, 113) argued that Viagra was initially touted as "coming to the rescue" of men's personal troubles with erectile difficulties. It also tacitly suggested it was rescuing generations of aging men who would be emasculated *when, not if,* their virility waned. There is little doubt that the advertising campaigns that marketed erectile medication put forward a discourse that never-aging masculinity is protected whenever men "take control" of their aging bodies and use chemical support to assure reliable erectile quality, or "staying hard." As cited in Potts et al. (2004, 492), "[W]hile the problem is not life threatening [erectile dysfunction] strikes at the very essence of what it means to be a man and can affect your confidence, self esteem, health and happiness" (Pfizer promotional material targeting NZ consumers, 1999).

Bourdieu (2001, 50) shrewdly commented, "The rush to procure Viagra . . . shows that anxiety over the physical manifestations of 'manliness' is far from being an exotic peculiarity." In large part, the marketing of new age pharmaceuticals to assist midlife and old men maintain or reinstall their erectile function has used narratives evoking the precariousness of manhood. Erectile medication is presented as a treatment for diminished, troubled, incomplete, or failing masculinity for heterosexual, usually white, aging men. ED marketing also casts the practice of penile-vaginal penetration as the only natural, normal, and desirable form of men's sexuality (Potts et al. 2004), thus foreshadowing many old men's interest in foreplay and the intimacy of cuddling. The advertising counsels men to not worry, to be whole again and fix "the problem down there," and to avert a manhood crisis.

In addition, second-wave advertisements have drawn on a point of view that "sex" (i.e., coital sex) is a necessary ingredient for a sustaining relationship, and wanted not just by the man but by his partner. Viagra and Cialis are marketed as preserving the intimacy within couple relationships. The underlying implication is that close relationships depend on the sexual intimacy of coital intercourse. Prioritizing pleasure, not just capability, recent Viagra and Cialis advertising will often present midlife couples holding hands, maintaining eye contact, or gently touching and kissing while they engage in a joint activity. These couple-oriented advertisements privilege intimacy, relationships, and relational sex, as well as the man's partner expecting to be satisfied (Vares and Braun 2006, 324). The partner is always a woman and presumably the man's wife. The heteronormative message is that a "relationship without an erection, *without* penile-vaginal penetration . . . [is] problematic and undesirable" (ibid., 324, italics original).

Notably, erectile medication advertising also employs cultural imagery that focuses on middle class heterosexuality, and more often than not only the social worlds of affluent-enough white men who have expensive gentleman motorcycles, antique convertibles, and opportunities to vacation. Åsberg and Johnson (2009), for example, explore the public imagery of masculinity and sexual health created in pharmaceutical appeals. They argue that the ads naturalize a never-aging form of (white, heterosexual) masculinity that is closely related to virility and to erectile capacity for penile penetration of the female body. Contrasting the Swedish Viagra website with websites in the US and New Zealand, they show how the man is always presented as able-bodied and physically active, and how the "Swedish Viagra man" is marked with national signifiers related to a cultural imaginary of freedom, naturalness, wilderness, and an aestheticized form of Swedish summer (not winter) night melancholia.

The narrow understanding of sexuality that is promoted through erectile drug advertising is not widely endorsed by men themselves. In a survey-based study of late midlife and old men in New England, Thompson and Barnes (2013) found most men renounced the precept that erectile ability and intercourse are integral to masculinity, and the older the men the more unsupportive they were. One-third of the men in the sample reported that they experience erectile difficulties, and half of this group disclosed they used medication to assist an erection. However, both men with erectile difficulties and men using medication disavowed the principle that an erection is central to their manhood. On its face this may seem counterintuitive, especially since researchers examining men who experience prostate cancer or have undergone a prostatectomy and faced erectile problems construe sexuality and masculinity as highly interwoven (cf. Oliffe 2005). Unlike studies of clinical populations or young men, the middle-aged and old men in this community-based sample did not (or no longer) perceive masculinity to be anchored to sexual activity.

COUPLES' SEXUAL HEALTH IN LATER LIFE

It is more likely that aging men who are facing erectile problems and use ED medication do so to *reintroduce* sexual intercourse back into their relationship and *reclaim* sexual practices the man and his partner both deem pleasurable, rather than to reclaim sexual intercourse as a sign of reclaiming manhood. Take, for example, the study that examined perceptions of masculinity among men with and without ED from eight countries: US, UK, Germany, France, Italy, Spain, Mexico, and Brazil. The researchers found that men in all age cohorts across all eight nations and regardless of erectile difficulty rated being seen as honorable, self-reliant, and respected as much more important than having an active sex life. Their study suggests that mature men's lives are not as determined by erectile quality as stereotypes suggest, nor does erectile difficulty "strike at the very core of men's masculine self-concept" (Sand et al. 2008, 591).

Let me also call attention to the well-established finding that sexual activity is mostly couple-centered and age-related (cf. Lindau et al. 2007; Sandberg 2011). Yet most men's studies and medical researchers discuss sexual activity in terms of individuals' sexual practices, rather than what couples do to pursue sexual intimacy. The ignored couple need not be long-term spouses or the aging couple who have lived together for many years. The couple could be in a recent, later life living-apart-together (LAT) relationship that gay or heterosexual men establish with a partner, or the occasional dating relationship of a widowed grandfather. The highlighting of individuals' rather than couples' sexual activity is not simply because of the greater ease in survey research of interviewing individuals rather than couples. There is the pervasiveness of medical model's view on sexual health, which rarely makes his or her sexual capability a "we" matter. Without cavalier intent, his erectile capability is a couple matter no differently than her arthritis and discomfort with coital intercourse (cf. Laursen et al. 2006).

Across nearly all national descriptive studies, it was his potency—whether or not weakened by medication side effects, chronic health limitations, or age-related physiological changes—that was the key determinant in old men's and their partner's sexual activity. It is the physical problems associated with aging, rather than age per se, that led many aging men to lower the priority of coital sex. Much has been made of how this is troubling for men's masculine subjectivity; however, the unreliability of an erection created per-formance anxiety among only 25–30 percent of the old men in a nationally representative US study (Lindau et al. 2007). And as Grace and her col-leagues (2006, 303) comment, "When notions of intimacy and relationship are interwoven with coital 'success,' the anxiety is not only about mechanical dysfunction but is also about relationships."

Less frequently noted is that many of the men's partners also find unpre-dictable and declining erectile capability troubling. In a nationally represen-tative study (Lindau et al. 2007), two-thirds of women aged 65 and older who lacked any sexual activity during the prior three months, whether it was coital sex or touching, said their sexual inactiveness was determined by their partner's physical health problem; and between 15 and 20 percent of women attributed their lack of any type of sexual activity to their partner's loss of interest (or loss of libido), not their own. One wife lamented in Conaglen and Conaglen's (2008, 151) study about the impact of erectile difficulty on wives' sexual satisfaction, "Ah, he would enter me, [sigh] and then just when I was about to have an orgasm he would shrink . . . So this was very, very annoying and very unsatisfactory . . . sometimes he would come but most times he couldn't hold the erection." Another commented,

> It has affected me a lot actually . . . you start feeling as though there's outside influences causing it . . . you're getting fat, you're not as sexy anymore . . . you also wish you weren't so wanting of your partner because if you weren't you wouldn't have the problem as much, if you know what I mean. (ibid., 152)

A 72-year-old woman in Lodge and Umberson's (2012, 434) study de-scribed her less active sex life like so: "It is not as intense as it was. There is just not a whole lot of this, 'I can't wait to get you in bed,' like it used to be. And you kind of miss that, you know. You miss that. On the other hand, it is far more relaxed too." When queried about the falloff in sexual frequency, two-thirds of women under age 70 in Wiley and Bortz's (1996) study were "very" or "somewhat" troubled; as well, when asked about their response to their husband's erectile difficulties, a quarter of the women reported that they were "uncomfortable." Wiley and Bortz (1996, M144) remark, "Potency is a couple's issue." The researchers cautioned that it is time to eschew regarding impotency as only a "male issue" and to begin contextualizing potency diffi-culties as part of the cascade of renegotiated intimacy practices associated with aging bodies.

Within the narratives of men and women in New Zealand regarding the impact of erectile difficulties and Viagra use, the researchers were struck by the wide-ranging "erectile dysfunction" stories and Viagra counterstories (Potts et al. 2003, 2004, 2006). This conversational range also disrupts the reductionist medical/never-aging masculinist view of sexuality in three ways.

First, before the man pursues use of erectile medication, the narratives showed that couples may have already altered their sexual repertoires in ways that emphasize noncoital activities. Wives and their husbands may have become more adventurous and experimental in terms of sexual pleasure, because in some cases the wife becomes troubled (and perhaps sore) by the likelihood of several episodes of chemically enhanced coital sex (Potts et al. 2003). Before wives' preferences are faulted for his lessening coital sexual activity, Trompeter, Bettencourt, and Barrett-Connor (2012) pointed out in their study of aging women's sexual activity and satisfaction that nearly three-quarters of the oldest women reported low, very low, or no pain with vaginal penetration.

Second, as Potts and her colleagues (2006, 306) argue, the advertising and cultural push to "restore" erections and penetrative sex to relationships undermines aging men's positive experiences with the "alternative" sexual practices that they have come to recognize as enjoyable and satisfying for them and their partners. One man in Potts et al. (2004, 497) disclosed,

> It's not the end-all to have an erection, you know, whereas I thought I had to, now I know that [it's] not that important, you know . . . What's sort of came through with us is that . . . the idea of a hard erection is to make penetration and all that, but it's not necessary . . . A woman's main sort of turn on is pretty close to the surface and this idea of having a massive penetrating erection [small laugh] is not necessary for good sex.

Finally, some of the men that Potts and her research team interviewed said how they were accepting bodily changes in general as a "natural part of aging," including erectile changes; others revealed that their erectile difficulties were devastating and how restoration with medication was ego-saving and masculinity-restoring; still other men noted that their sense of masculinity was uncompromised by their bodily incapability for penetrative sex (Potts et al. 2004). The many narratives, including counterstories by men developing confidence with their sexual practices without depending on Viagra, disrupt the homogenizing quality of the Viagra-to-the-rescue discourse. The authors conclude, "There is no standard experience of a 'functional' erection, even less so a 'dysfunctional' erection . . . and there is no definitive view of what constitutes 'normal' masculinity or 'being a man' in relation to erectile 'functionality'" (Potts et al. 2004, 497–98).

Though I will return to discuss her work more thoroughly in a later chapter, Linn Sandberg's (2013b; 2016) qualitative study of older Swedish men in relationships reveals that sexual and romantic intimacy remained personally important to the men. Yet demonstrating intimacy through penetrative sex was no longer crucial to seeing themselves as men or to affirming the depth of their relationship to their partner. Wentzell (2013b) similarly found that aging Mexican men adopted a "mature" masculinity appropriate to their age and declining health, and they adopted less frequent, more intimate, slower sex. Wentzell's study also points to how midlife and old men in contexts where aging is not stigmatized can consider their erectile change to be an acceptable aspect of aging. The men interpreted their decreasing erectile capability and increasing interest in interactive family relations and non-coital center sex as their successful aging.

RETHINKING SEXUAL HEALTH

Men's sexual health remains largely equated with sexual function and never-aging masculinities and now with "successful" aging. There is still the public health concern with the risk of STIs and STDs, which have begun to occur nearly as much among adults over age 50 as among people under 40. Aging men (and women) who face an STI will likely be doubly stigmatized as they are branded by both age and their STI/STD status.

The reasons why mature and old men continue to become infected with STIs/STDs have not been extensively researched, but this experience is likely multifactorial. As a group, should they seek new sexual partners, the men who have been recently widowed or divorced may have a poor understanding of the importance of condom use or their risk for a disease. As well, only a minority of mature and old men report having discussed their sexual activity with their care providers (Lindau et al. 2007) or learned about their risk. STIs are sexual health matters that can benefit from a medical lens, should medical providers understand that many old men are sexually active and not always practicing "safe" sex.

SUMMARY

With respect to the graying of men's sexual health, what is interesting is that aging appears to facilitate coping when erectile troubles or other barriers to sex activity are experienced. With advancing age, though men are more likely to experience erectile difficulties, they are less likely to report that it negatively affects their quality of life. This is likely because erectile problems emerge slowly, and are normalized as an expected part of aging and accepted as such. It is also likely that most aging men opt to age "gracefully" and responsibly by rejecting pharmaceutical aids to firm erections (Wentzell 2013a) and instead negotiate with their partner a greater emphasis on satisfying alternatives to penetrative sex (Potts et al. 2003). Sexual health is not independent of men's sexual partner, or other determinants of the men's lives.

III

Social Worlds of Old Men

Chapter Eight

Social Relationships

I've learned that people will forget what you said, people will forget what you did, but people will never forget how you made them feel.

—Attributed to Maya Angelou, 2003

Social relationships—both quantity and quality—have short- and long-term effects on health, for better and for worse, and . . . these effects emerge in childhood and cascade throughout life to foster cumulative advantage or disadvantage.

—Umberson and Montez (2010, S54)

Life course trajectories are similar in the sense that they inevitably encompass alterations in the convoy of social relationships. Changes in the composition of old men's social relationships can arise from normative life events (e.g., retirement, widowerhood) as well as off-time and unexpected events (e.g., later life divorce, men becoming their partner's care provider). Whether normative or off-time, a common sequel is aging men's reorganization of their social lives and their preference to engage themselves within smaller, usually stronger, convivial networks that prioritize emotionally satisfying interaction (Carstensen 2006; Lang 2001). Narrative research on old men's later life reveals many of the old men's taste for stepping back from the rhythms of work-based masculinities and welcoming the experiences that might center on dinners and conversation with friends, and participating in other emotionally enriching loyalties (cf. Coles and Vassarotti 2012).

This chapter calls attention to old men's social relationships in later life. I direct attention to the cumulative (dis)advantages of different partnership statuses. This is *one* way to address the diversity among old men's social lives. I decided to use partnership status as a window into old men's social worlds, largely because their lives pivot on their partnership status, and then are affected by the (dis)advantages of their sexuality, class, and health. Examined in the chapter are the differing social worlds of old men in couple relationships, single old men (whether never-married, divorced, or widowed), and old men who begin a new intimate relationship (whether cohabitation or LAT).

CONVOYS OF SOCIAL RELATIONSHIPS

Until recently, old men's social lives and relational identities tended to be discussed in terms of the retirement transition. This is because the traditional view of gender emphasized men's and women's "roles" and separate geographies. Men's workforce participation has long been theorized as primary to their identities as a man; thus the stresses and privileges of retirement after forty or more years of employment were thought to define later life. Take a common example of when the community of coworkers that previously helped organize everyday relations becomes peripheral with retirement, and the social lives of old men become more concentrated within their smaller, postemployment community of friends and family. How old men from different classes, or men who are or are not in a couple relationship, experience the shrinking of their social network surely varies in significance. To illustrate, for men without the financial security to retire, their later life networks surely continue to include work-based relationships, which continue to bolster the values of never-aging masculinities. For aging men of sufficient economic capital, the opportunity to leave the workforce diminishes the salience of coworker relationships. Friends, intimate partners or wives, siblings, children and grandchildren, and chosen others constitute these men's networks after they retire and breed support for aging masculinity practices.

COUPLES

My appraisal of old men's social lives begins with (married) couples because, as the national profiles show, the vast majority of old men are living with a spouse or intimate partner. Their daily lives pivot on this couple relationship. In order to reduce the complexity of the topic, I oversimplify the discussion to heterosexual couples and to the best of ties, not the worst of ties—to close relationships, not problematic, ambivalent, or abusive relations (cf. Fingerman, Hay, and Birditt 2004). Though many older couples can face high levels of distress following declines in health and the lifestyle transitions fashioned in later life, partners derive a sense of well-being and of purpose by leaning on one another; in addition, older couples show less potential for conflicts and greater potential for pleasure than younger and middle-aged couples (Kulik, Walfisch, and Liberman 2016).

A snapshot profile of the aging population at any one moment will show nearly three-quarters of the men aged 65 and older in the US are living with their *spouse* (US Census Bureau 2015). This estimate is virtually the same in the UK (Office of National Statistics 2015), in Germany (Haustein and Mischke 2011), and in Japan (J. Brown et al. 2002). Likely underestimated is the proportion of old men in a couple relationship, for sometimes cohabitating and LAT partnerships are not considered. As invaluable as they are, each snapshot also only details the moment, not the movement in and out of relationships, the proportion of the heterosexual men who are in a second (or higher order) marriage or the duration of the marriages, or the likelihood that the men who are not classified as coupled are in fact "in a relationship." Middle-aged and old men's movement in and out of relationships has been on the increase in most Global North countries (Bildtgård and Öberg 2017; Brown, Bulanda, and Lee 2012).

Marriage, according to Berger and Kellner (1964, 1) is *"nomos* building"; that is, it is an ongoing process in which the two "Is" entering marriage come to develop a privately felt "we" and a canopy—their marital habitus—which provides a taken-for-granted sense of stability and ontological security. The couple acquires their "protective cocoon" and comes to feel the "bodily and psychic ease in the routine circumstances of everyday life" (Giddens 1991, 127). Piecing together the available research findings, throughout it is the couple's reciprocal "emotion work" (and emotional support) that cements the quality of their felt "we"; as they age together their relationship will typically become more and more equitable and less conflicted (Kulik 2002). Notably, when asked directly about his emotion work, the husband is usually puzzled because he construes his emotion work simply as part of his relationship with his wife/partner (Erickson 2005, 348). He, like his partner, is simply "doing marriage."

Among old men in the US who are of European or Asian ancestry, the estimate is that nearly three-quarters are living with their spouse; two-thirds of Hispanic (of any race) old men live with their spouse; and about half of old non-Hispanic black men live within a couple relationship (Federal Inter-agency Forum on Aging-Related Statistics 2016). As suggested, men's race/ ethnicity unquestionably affects being coupled and the cumulative (dis)advantages of being coupled. The advantages of couples' ties involve five dimensions—caring, intimacy, family feeling, commitment, and reciprocal identity support (Moss and Moss 1985). *Caring* develops through years of mutual concern and affection; *intimacy* is derived from years of being in a dyad where habitual daily interaction and couple "secrets" are created; *family feeling* is the sense of being partnered and with this comes the symbolic and lived intergenerational connections; *commitment* is the intention to maintain the "we"; and *reciprocal identity support* is how each partner becomes and is defined by the "we." There also are the cumulative advantages in quality of life that marital intimacy usually provides. For example, though too few longitudinal studies are available to affirm a "sex for health" causal order as opposed to the finding that people's later life health regulates their sexual activity, most aging couples remain sexually intimate, which promotes a higher quality of life and good physical health (cf. DeLamater 2012).

Perhaps the most identity-defining relationship for old heterosexual men is their marriage (Thoits 1992). Married, the man comes to possess the private and public identities of "husband." For the generations of old men born before World War II, coming to be a husband accomplished normalcy and publicly affirmed masculinity (Townsend 2002). Yet, aging men's self-conception as an intimate partner is under-researched. The evidence that I found comes exclusively from studies of heterosexual husbands. When asked, married men and in particular old men acknowledge their lives as a husband as their principal identity. While studying the retirement transition, Vinick and Ekerdt (1991) unexpectedly discovered that being a husband was a "master status" that bridged the men's pre- and postretirement autobiographical narratives. The man's identity as a skilled tradesman, marine mechanic, dentist, or divisional manager for a multinational corporation may linger in his consciousness well after he exits the workforce. But Vinick and Ekerdt discovered that being a husband and part of a marital dyad remained men's predominant identity while employed and became even more important to the men's social anchorage and quality of life once their participation in the labor force ended. Similarly, Sand et al. (2008) found that married and partnered men (age range 20–75) from eight countries—UK, US, Germany, France, Italy, Spain, Mexico, and Brazil—rated "having a good relationship with a partner/wife" nine times more important to quality of life than a "satisfying work life or career." They concluded that despite the mandates of masculinity that direct men's lives toward self-sufficiency and achievement performances, men's identities are aligned more with the spousal/partner relationship than the workplace.

Lifelong marital relations remain the comparative norm whenever later life living arrangements are scrutinized. Even though the lagging romanticized image of the lifetime, one-and-only marriage no longer reflects the only reality in most developed nations, there is a grain of accuracy in the image. As examples from the UK show, 65 percent of marriages in England and Wales that began in 1968 celebrated their silver (twenty-fifth) anniversary (Wilson and Smallwood 2008), and 45–50 percent will celebrate their golden (fiftieth) anniversary, should both spouses live that long. For the US, the Census Bureau (2012, table 131) notes that 60 percent of the men married in 1960–64 celebrated their fortieth anniversary. For the old men whose marriages ended, becoming a widow still outpaces divorce, though a rising share of marital endings after age 50 are voluntary (Brown et al. 2016).

To avoid any hint of Pollyannaism, it must be acknowledged that some proportion of the old men in these long-term marriages are in ones (i) of low quality, which negatively affects both spouses' well-being and health, hers more than his (cf. Hawkins and Booth 2005); and (ii) where he relies nearly exclusively on her for emotional support, especially as his postretirement circle of social relations shrinks. This will result in further privatizing of his social world and greater dependency on the partner relationship (e.g., Stevens and Westerhof 2006), which may constrict her autonomy and trigger her likelihood to criticize and weigh the option of a divorce (Lin et al. 2016). Consistent with this, aging married men experience considerably more social loneliness than women, and both spouses' emotional loneliness rises with high levels of marital disagreement regarding spousal attentiveness (de Jong Giervrld et al. 2009).

Despite the fact of a greater incidence of "gray divorce" (Brown and Lin 2012) and the stereotype that old married men drive their wife crazy after retiring, most of old men's time is spent within a couple relationship that provides mutual companionship, enjoyment, satisfaction, and intimacy as opposed to quarrelsome or stressful exchanges, although the latter certainly occur (Szinovacz and Schaffer 2000). Closeness and intimacies typically improve with age (Fingerman, Hay, and Birditt 2004), probably because spouses spend more time with one another. In the context of satisfactory marriages or similar relationships, closeness is performed as "support"—a responsiveness to one another's needs that communicates caring.

Speculatively, one could argue that the reason aging men are interested in spending time within intimate and family relations is because the intimacies accrued strengthen men's core identities and health. Although not always voiced directly by men themselves, families provide them a haven, and if there are children and grandchildren, pronounced intergenerational connectedness and a sense of legacy. Numerous studies attest to the regularity of exchanges of support within families and the benefit men derive from being married or partnered throughout middle adulthood and later life, whether this benefit is operationalized in terms of his nourished feelings of "being a man" or overall well-being (cf. Davidson and Fennell 2002).

The long tradition of research on the benefits of being coupled has provided compelling evidence that couple relations advantage men's health (cf. Ploubidis et al. 2015). These benefits are not limited to aging heterosexual men within marriages. Partnered aging gay men have better self-reported health and less evidence of depression, irrespective of relationship duration, when compared to single (unpartnered) aging gay men (Wienke and Hill 2009; Williams and Fredriksen-Goldsen 2014). Similarly, compared to men who were either "daters" or unpartnered, Wright and Brown (2017, 845) report that heterosexual men who were cohabiting also derived substantial health benefits of being partnered—they reported fewer depressive symptoms and less perceived stress than the married men, and unsurprisingly they expressed much less loneliness. A caveat is that health benefits do seem to hinge on the quality of the couple's relationship, not merely being coupled. For example, the association between aging husbands' life satisfaction and marital quality seems especially contingent on wives' marital appraisals; his life satisfaction is lifted when his wife also reports a happy marriage (Carr et al. 2014), and he is more likely to report considerable feelings of positive marital quality and little evidence of loneliness. As well, with few exceptions, longitudinal research shows us that exiting marriage rather than occupying an unsatisfying marriage shores up men's and women's life satisfaction and well-being (cf. Williams 2003).

Reliable empirical information on gay men's couple status is scarcer. The status of the aging gay men living as couples is on the rise; so too is marriage. Fredriksen-Goldsen, Bryan, and their colleagues (2017, table 2) reported that fewer than 13 percent of the aging gay men in the National Health, Aging, and Sexuality/Gender Study (NHAS) had never partnered/ married. Such large proportions of aging gay men in couple relationships— currently or previously—was unimaginable a generation ago, when LGB people much more routinely had to live with the stigmatization, discrimination, and criminalization that thwarted recognition of partnerships.

Among gay men in their early 60s and residing in one of the thirty-two states with legalized same-sex marriage in 2014, Goldsen et al. (2017) recently reported that 19 percent of the aging gay men were currently married and 25 percent were unmarried partnered, leaving just over one-half of the men living in single households. Drawing on the national Caring and Aging with Pride study, Kim and Fredriksen-Goldsen (2014) reported, unsurprisingly, that gay men living with a partner or spouse experienced markedly less loneliness than aging gay men living alone or with someone other than a partner. Partner status, not necessarily living arrangement, contributes to well-being. The cumulative advantages and disadvantages that affect the trajectories of gay men's health and well-being in later life are just beginning to be detailed; however, being partnered/married, especially if long-termed, is health promoting and capital producing (cf. Goldsen et al. 2017).

Altogether these findings suggest that the salience of aging men being someone's intimate partner is, as Berger and Kellner (1964) theorized, central to how most aging men prefer to navigate later life: as partners or spouses. But research on later life couples has to date tended to examine the influence of marital status instead of the dynamics within relationships over time.

SINGLE OLD MEN

The population of single old men is a heterogeneous group. The diversity within the group consists of the many cultural groups that cultivate a variety of life experiences and tastes, men with varying access to social and economic capital and different living conditions, and the diverse ways single old men perform masculinities or express their sexuality. Whether someone's involvement with this population is at some distance as a researcher or involves directly working with single old men, when attention is paid to the diversity what arises is a sensitivity to these men's unique and shared experiences, including the contextual ways that regional, local, ethnic, and class differences affect the men's lives.

Never-Marrieds

Research has largely neglected never-married old men, who make up 4 to 8 percent of the cohorts of old men in the US and most European countries (cf. Manning and Brown 2011; Wang and Parker 2014), with some exceptions such as Ireland, where there are more never-marrieds. Never-married old men are a diverse ethnic/racial population in the US (Lin and Brown 2012), populated more by men of color. Never-marrieds also are bimodally split between those with low and high socioeconomic status, and they differ in terms of why they never married and why they may live alone. Never-married old men comprise several distinct subgroups—(i) those who dated and would have loved to marry, but "things" just never worked out; (ii) those who choose to live alone and are not socially isolated—these men have sufficient social capital derived from relationships with friends and family, and experience above-average life satisfaction, even compared to their ever-married age peers (e.g., Pudrovska, Schieman, and Carr 2006); (iii) those who may contemplate marriage but do not marry because they ended up cohabitating or partnering within a LAT relationship (e.g., Shapiro and Keyes 2008); and (iv) those aging men who are on the social margin, live reclusive lifestyles, are more likely economically disadvantaged, and often are in poor health.

Never-married men who prefer their lifestyles of living singly may very often date, and date regularly. But they do not couple; rather, they desire to maintain their independent lifestyle and to live separately and distance themselves from the "trappings" of being in a relationship. As Amir, age 80, expressed, "When I ask myself how come I stayed single, my answer is that being single is a result of a certain narcissism. Here, I'm used to a life of peace and quiet. I have what I want and when I want. It doesn't work that way when you have children" (Band-Winterstein and Manchik-Rimon 2014, 388). Never-married "singles," whether heterosexual or gay, who live alone and maintain intimate friendships and family relationships, particularly with siblings, are not likely to be either emotionally or socially lonely (Pinquart 2003; Shippy, Cantor, and Brennan 2004). Yet compared to the men who have coupled, never-marrieds are typically more vulnerable in later life to having less social capital and support, since few have children to assist them when care is needed and, for most, no live-in partner to monitor unspoken needs (Rubinstein 1987, 1996).

Among heterosexuals, never-marrieds' greater vulnerability to social isolation is well documented, such as Davidson's (2004) finding that these men are more unlikely to entertain in their homes and hardly ever or never visit friends or relatives when compared to men who are or have been coupled. Yet, as she suggests, it may be that many (heterosexual) never-marrieds prefer "social isolation" and not visiting or hosting friends and do not feel compelled to maintain a complex network of kin. They have established themselves in their place of residence and are accustomed to living alone. As her study suggests, never-marrieds are alone, but most are not lonely. Shippy and his colleagues (2004) found that unpartnered older gay men in New York were no more isolated than older men in general, and in fact reported a greater number of friends than among the general population of New York's older adults.

We know from other research that never-marrieds who cohabitate often have long relationships (Brown, Bulanda, and Lee 2012). But the proportion of never-marrieds who otherwise couple in some form is poorly understood. Even among the men that census data classifies as never-married and living as singles, many may date one person and never define themselves (in Facebook terms) as "in a relationship" because they infrequently get together with their dating partner, who lives far away. As well, they may be actively involved in a living-apart-together relationship that provides intimacy with the autonomy of living alone (de Jong Gierveld 2004; Strohm et al. 2009).

Divorced Men

Amongst the aging men who were previously married, US, UK, and Japan demographics reveal that what ended men's marriage has shifted in recent decades. A larger proportion is divorced and a smaller share is widowed, though for the majority their marital dissolution was caused by death of a spouse. To help explain the rise of "gray divorce," Brown and Lin (2012, 732) proposed, "Lifelong marriages are increasingly difficult to sustain in an era of individualism and lengthening life expectancies; older adults are more reluctant now to remain in empty shell marriages." Reinforcing this, Lin and colleagues (2016) noted that lesser marital quality, not so much the actual onset of an empty nest or partner's retirement, was what elevated the risk of "gray divorce"; marital breakups among graying couples occur more commonly among the "younger" couples, some who had been married at least twenty-five years.

These dissolutions seem to reflect the wives' decision to move on, not the husbands' (cf. Wu and Schimmele 2007). Marriages may endure despite emptiness, but research suggests that wives reach the breaking point sooner than husbands when personal happiness is low enough, when there is interference from in-laws, and when she sees her future time as alone and in control and perhaps repartnering as a better option (cf. Montenegro 2004; Taylor 2011). Wives who leave are most likely not economically dependent. An analogy I have sometimes heard suggests that aging couples' "gray divorces" are not preceded by an "emotional earthquake" that sways the marriage; rather, it is the small cracks in quality of marital life that eventually push the wife (or husband) away. Another analogy uses the metaphor of a balloon slowly leaking air, not bursting. Life on the other side as "single again" for women is expected to be, and seems to be, less burdensome and less distressing (cf. Gregson and Ceynar 2009).

By comparison, many aging men will experience their uncoupling as an unwelcome, surprising turning point; many end up sheltering themselves in work and will narrate feelings of emptiness in living alone and a keen interest in repartnering. That men's repartnering is often desired is supported by the evidence on aging divorced men's movement out of and into relationships. Almost half of middle-aged and old men's divorces ended a marriage that itself was a remarriage. Family studies researchers have noted that divorce has a self-fulfilling character about it—the first makes the second more probable, and many married older adults are in second or higher order marriages (cf. Lin et al. 2016). A Canadian study (Schimmele and Wu 2016) determined that within ten years of their divorce, about 20 percent of the men formed a cohabitation relationship and 30 percent remarried. That means half have repartnered. The older the men at the time of their marital dissolution, the less likely they were to repartner. Drawing on US data, within roughly ten years of their marriage's dissolution nearly half of divorced men (compared to one-quarter of the widowers) had repartnered, and they were as likely to cohabitate as remarry (Brown et al. 2016).

Profiles, especially demographic ones about divorced men's relationship trajectories in later life, inevitably homogenize lived experiences. Aging men construct the meaning of the same event, divorce, in many contrasting ways that go missing within profiles. Bitterness, resentment, regret, hurt, and loneliness are examples of the negative emotions that are known to leak into divorced men's narratives; positive feelings also exist and might range from being "relieved" that the tensions have abated to feeling unconstrained. As a man named Jeff stated, "I'm way more . . . independent. I feel a lot freer" (Canham et al. 2014). The dearth of qualitative studies handicaps our insight into how old men experience being divorced and getting older.

Meaning-making of the divorce itself and the lived experience of being divorced in later life is emotionally complex and will embody masculinity discourses. Given the scanty theorizing and research comparing the aging men's repartnering patterns, available findings provide mainly food for thought. Suppose, for example, a late middle-aged man (a "young-old") and an old man both experienced an unwanted divorce and neither wants to spring back into a relationship—what are the cumulative (dis)advantages the men experience following this decision? Does emotional healing alone following his wife's decision to terminate the marriage prove to be more advantageous than sheltering himself in a new relationship and hoping that repartnering heals his wounded masculinity? For the divorced aging men left by their former wives/partners, are they more cautious about starting a new relationship or are they feeling vulnerable and want companionship? With younger generations of aging men living longer and generally in better health than the older generations, are there generational inequalities in the cumulative (dis)advantages?

The paucity of studies also challenges our understanding of how context differentially affects how men experience being divorced, being single again, and getting older. There is the "deliberation" phase and then "resolution" phase (Canham et al. 2014) that may substantially differ among men from different faiths, ethnic communities, classes, or localities. Divorced men's narratives would expose an array of discourses on masculinities that reveal the habitus of their faiths, classes, ethnic communities, and localities. Divorce narratives can include the "angry, wounded soul" who feels aggrieved by her alleged emotional infidelity arising from her close relations with friends and family; the "lonely, lost old man" who mourns a different dream and feels unnerved and empty by her decision to walk away; and the "resilient single" who feels freed and excited by becoming a bachelor again. However, analyses of later life divorce have been predominantly gender-comparative, leaving the variability among old men's narratives poorly heard.

Based on my irregular conversations with divorced old men, my sense is that their talk about living alone, interest in new intimacies, and restructured relations with their adult children is not solely the personal narratives of the individuals but discourses on embodied masculinities. Two examples: Terry, a controlling head of the family and STEM professor, was in his early 70s when his younger wife decided to end "his" marriage and rupture "his" retirement dreams; stunned, he sheltered in an apartment and in work for a few years, retired, and moved far away to begin living as a bachelor. His narrative was a discourse of a resilient "sturdy oak" masculinity that offers fresh opportunities for reclaiming oneself. Randal, a Catholic and traditionalist, was in his early 60s when his wife, without warning, he thought, ended his identity as a husband, leaving him a note telling him to move out immediately and then promptly selling "their" home. He sheltered in the continuity of his work and identities as a successful IT support specialist and father. His narrative used discourses on the "absent marriage," his awakening to a needed reflexivity, and "How shall I live" musing as still a man but not a husband.

Divorce stories do not often end "all is okay" or with no regrets. One partner is aggrieved enough with the quality of the marriage to initiate the uncoupling, she more than he (cf. Wu and Schimmele 2007), and the other is either "relieved" or feeling "blindsided." Initiators may contemplate the dissolution for a number of years, prepare emotionally and mentally for the divorce, and find positive meaning in terminating the relationship. Identifying who initiated the marital breakup can be rather arbitrary since who initiated is storied after a decision to divorce has been presented and the couple weigh that decision. Divorce stories are an ongoing interpretive process, and among later life couples both the initiator of the divorce conversation and the other partner are likely to face an extended time in the unwinding of the relationship (even after legally divorced), yet likely engage in less overt conflict because of their heightened ability to effectively manage (or ignore) negative emotion and leave well enough alone (Holley, Haase, and Levenson 2013).

Unfortunately, few qualitative or narrative studies of men's experiences with their "gray divorce" exist to tell us much about old men's lived experiences with being divorced. For instance, is there an appreciable difference between the aging men who are living through their first divorce and men in their second or higher order divorce in their masculinity subjectivities, or sense of themselves as men? Even though what follows is anecdotal evidence rather than carefully analyzed interview-based data, among six old men (all older than age 65) that I knew well enough to talk with about their divorce experience, none said he initiated the divorce, none remarried, and all had opted to live alone and find the companionship and intimacies offered by dating or participation in a LAT relationship. They are a small, diverse group who shared a common interest in softball. All six were gun shy of repartnering. Feeling valued by a (dating) partner was more important than living with a partner and the consequent obligation of involvement with her adult children. Sex was viewed as only part of their interest in dating relationships; instead they emphasized the closeness of occasionally sleeping with someone and the intimacy of cuddling and touching. Because of his prostate surgery, one man had become unable to engage in coital sex for some years before his divorce, thought that was one reason his wife left, and said he now preferred to stick to the intimacy of dinners and conversation with friends and occasional dating partners. All had adult children they regularly talked or spent time with, and only two voluntarily talked with the former wife or mailed her a holiday card. Yet, despite my many conversations, they are not generalizable. Unknown are what distinguishes old men's experience as divorced men, or how their habitus and masculinity practices are modified by the transition from being married to living solo, dating again, or repartnering.

Widowers

"Widowerhood" is not a commonly spoken concept. It feels clumsy. It has its origins in medical-related investigations of men's health following their wife's death, particularly how the "broken heart syndrome" may explain widowers' elevated risk of cardiovascular death in the stressful first six months of bereavement (Parkes, Benjamin, and Fitzgerald 1969; Stroebe 1994). A "broken heart" does not necessarily cause elevated risk of death; rather, a widower's social relationships and daily practices are altered when his wife dies, which may trigger changes in his health behavior such as heavier alcohol use, becoming housebound and not engaging in exercise, troubled sleep, irregular eating and a poor diet, and not maintaining his medications (e.g., Vesnaver et al. 2016).

For many years, spousal bereavement and people's lived experience as a widow(er) were discussed as if both experiences were gender neutral, until Helen Lopata (1973, 1979) focused research on widowhood, rather than bereavement alone. She flagged the brute realities that in nearly all nations it was women who commonly survived the death of a husband and were social-ly disadvantaged vis-à-vis widowers. They still are, but likely less so now than when Lopata assessed widows' financial and social well-being (cf. Per-rig-Chiello et al. 2016). Nonetheless, heterosexual widowers now experience later life with better economic and social capital, and the opportunity to establish new intimate relationships with a wider age range of partners, if they so choose.

Men's transition from marriage into widowerhood can be more challeng-ing, and each aspect of this transformative process is affected by the men's other statuses and identities. Generally speaking, widowers' narratives will story their shock, profound sadness, and numbness as they live through their wife's/partner's life-ending illness and death (especially if the death was unexpected). What follows bereavement is a jarring discontinuity in daily routines as they reconstruct their social world and identity as widower. More so than their divorced peers, old widowers experience high levels of "single strain," which Pudrovska, Schieman, and Carr (2006) defined as the chronic stresses aging men (and women) attribute to being unmarried. Perhaps this difference is related to widowers becoming single involuntarily.

The initial phases of becoming a widower are known to be painful as much as awkward. They have few comparisons to others who are widowed. Their marriage may have included the intensity and closeness of men's unan-ticipated care work to ease a wife's/partner's dying and a roller coaster of emotions. There is the existential crisis that comes about by loss of the ontological security that marriage provided (N. Thompson 2001). Throughout the bereavement phase of becoming a widower, there also may be a persistent psychological bond to the deceased partner (Moss and Moss 1996) as much as difficulties finding solace within the old man's diminishing network of friends (e.g., Isherwood, King, and Luszcz 2017).

For aging gay men who lose a partner or spouse, other people's lack of respect for their partner relationships and of their new life as a widower can complicate, if not exacerbate, grieving (Piatczanyn, Bennett, and Soulsby 2016). It would not be uncommon to hear about an aging gay man whose place of employment denied him the same bereavement leave that heterosexually married coworkers normally receive. Nor would it be unusual for the widower to be denied the opportunity for the couple to share a headstone in a religious cemetery.

For aging heterosexual and gay men, the construct "widowerhood" immediately recognizes their experiences as gendered. There are few widower issues—mostly man issues. Superseding the legacy of the research that problematized the phenomena of becoming and being a widower, which systematically emphasized the initial and lingering troubles (mostly related to bereavement), researchers have begun to probe the diversity of widowers' experiences. Questioned is the way the old men's social worlds without a wife transform and extend their biographies as men. This newer generation of research recognizes that class, ethnicity, duration of marriage, geographies and cultures, and thus masculinities intersect with bereavement and widowerhood.

Early studies (e.g., Parkes and Weiss 1983) cued a distinctive aspect of heterosexual widowers' initial responses to the loss of their wives: the men narrated what happened as if they had been "dismembered," rather than abandoned. They experienced the death of their wife as a loss of protection and reassurance, leaving them disoriented. Most of the heterosexual widowers that Parkes and his colleagues followed for four years related how thoroughly they had embodied marriage and felt its importance for their identity as men (cf. Moore and Stratton 2002; van den Hoonaard 2010). Consequently spousal loss was a *whole body experience*—their identities as husbands severed, their everyday lives as a couple ruptured, their appetites smashed. Part of the ontological foundation on which their masculine subjectivity and capital were based was no longer secure (N. Thompson 2001)—they were not husbands. Not uncommonly storied, men say, "She was like a right arm." Aging gay widowers equally narrate the whole body experience of spousal loss, many speaking in terms of having lost a part of themselves after the death of their partner: "Part of my soul had been amputated" (Shernoff 2013). In all, old men who have been married or partnered for several decades experience loss—often half or more of their lifetimes were spent in the relationship. As Moore and Stratton (2002, 5) contend, "Surely something that is so beneficial in its presence—a supportive marriage in older age—is very keenly felt with its loss."

There is increasing recognition that culture (including the culture within one's family), class, religious or spiritual tradition, and, not least, masculinities all have a powerful impact on what might be called emotional grieving. Widowers have a range of patterns of grief work, sometimes guided by hegemonic masculinity ideologies. In her study of widowed men in England, Kate Bennett (2007; Bennett, Hughes, and Smith 2003) examined the ways the old men managed bereavement in terms of the dilemma about men showing emotional vulnerability. The majority of widowers disclosed how they tried to keep their grief hidden and maintain a "front stage" performance of "keeping a stiff upper lip." Even though many could not maintain the guise— "Well there's hardly a day goes by without having a good cry" (Bennett 2007, 351)—the men chose to suffer in private, away from the public eye (ibid., 354). They divulged that they did not cry in front of others because to do so is stereotypically "sissy stuff." Even as grieving widowers, they felt they needed to masquerade their grief and present a stoical image.

Core to Doka and Martin's (2010) interpretation of men's bereavement grieving is their argument that masculinities influence but do not determine grieving. They theorize that most widowers engage in gender-related, not gender-specific, forms of grief practices as they strive to fill the emotional void and reconstruct their solo lives. Widowers' grief practices are described as putting emphasis on thinking through what has happened, such as trying to make sense of her death to their children and grandchildren, rather than viewing grief only as a series of emotional waves.

Similarly, in her study of British widowers, Bennett (2007) noted that many of the men regarded themselves as independent and resilient "sturdy oaks," and their emotional expressions of grief took place in private. These men disclosed in composed, utilitarian individualistic rhetoric how troubled they were by their loss of their life partner and how much they missed their wife socially and emotionally; they

> describe[d] their emotions in terms of control, rationality, successful action, and responsibility towards others. Their delivery is calm and deliberate . . . although the content is emotional, it is presented in a masculine fashion using the language of control, reliability and success . . . It is not that they are denying their experiences; it is rather that they are demonstrating their masculinity and incorporating their feelings into their masculine personae. (Bennett 2007, 354)

For some widowers, the "hole" in their lives felt during bereavement can linger years into widowerhood. As Davidson (2001, 309, 312) commented in her study, "Not one of the ten widowers who had cared for their wife admitted to any sense of relief when she had died and said that they felt lost without the routine they had established while looking after her;" only two of the twenty-six widowers "positively wished to remarry."

Noted in their longitudinal studies, the most emotionally troubled men at onset of widowerhood are more likely to remain troubled (Parkes and Weiss 1983). It seems that the turning point in widowers' acceptance of their wife's death coincides with no longer feeling the need to avoid reminders, and being able to recall their wives without the intensity of emotional pain. This does not mean that widowers (and widows) no longer maintain a tie to their deceased spouse. Moss and Moss (1996, 165) call attention to how a "widowed person's relationship with the deceased spouse includes strong themes of both letting go and holding on. These two themes are intertwined and not polar opposites." As much as their marital relationship had once provided them with a sense of normalcy and stability, most old widowers do come to accept their wife's death and their unexpected status as widowers.

Old men who are functionally independent and accept their wife's death may begin to seek companionship, love, and sexual intimacy (Carr 2004; Koren 2016). Alinde Moore and Dorothy Stratton's (2002) research on a cohort of old widowers adjusting to their new life illustrates this point nicely. Their interviews reveal the expected roller coaster of men adjusting to widowerhood, which involves a renegotiation of much of daily life and re-configuration of men's sense of self and relationships with family, friends, and others. What Moore and Stratton unexpectedly found was widowers' resiliency, even if some were less resilient than others. What distinguished the more resilient widowers was how they consciously changed their lives. The men sought out companionship, which is similar to what Davidson (2001) found. One of the widowers she interviewed made clear his interest in repartnering, including remarrying: "Yes, I'd be delighted to. I mean, the trouble about being on your own is, it doesn't matter how busy you are, at times, you are very lonely. And certainly if the right person came along, I would be only too pleased to get married. Just like that" (313).

Old widowers who have limited social support and want companionship often enter a new relationship, and the intention to repartner might be related more to men's weaker support ties and subsequent vulnerable feelings created by the void the wife's death created. Wives are not replaced. As Moss and Moss (1996, 170) counsel, "There is no replacement or substitution for a deceased spouse." In fact, they propose that the widower recognizes he is tied to his deceased spouse. He had expected to continue the previous marriage, it did not end voluntarily, and his memory holds together past and present (ibid., 165–75). Some old men seek and find companionship through dating, at times living-apart-together relationships. They do not seem to be the majority. In Bennett, Arnott, and Soulsby's (2013) analysis of sixty British widowers, some of the old men reported that they would not consider remarriage because of their deep feelings for their late wife; others were uncertain about repartnering for the same reason, and only a small number were interested in repartnering.

NEW INTIMATE RELATIONSHIPS

You hear stories. About the widowed grandfather who locates his high school sweetheart on the internet, writes to her, and soon begins a living-apart-together relationship. About the retired man—with one ex-wife and a rebound cohabitant partner—who wants to again be "involved" and enrolls in an over-60 dating service for divorced men seeking divorced women. About the gay husband, now widower, who is thoroughly put off by the gay dating scene and relies on coupled friends to canvass their networks for a possible companion for him. About the unpartnered old man who moves to a large age-segregated community in Florida and goes "clubbing" a few times a week within the community complex. About a widower in the same community who discovers he has acquired an STI. About a man divorced fifteen years earlier who begins seeking companionship by attending community center activities and day bus trips designed for seniors. About an aging couple matchmaking unpartnered neighbors by inviting them over for cocktails and dinner. Many unpartnered aging men maintain undeniable interest in dating, romance, and intimacy, perhaps even sexual intimacy, and there is no age limit on falling in love.

A result of the greater cultural acceptance of old men and women creating later life lifestyles, aging men who were once partnered have more options in their living arrangements and intimate relationships. They can live singly within networks of friends and chosen family, live solo and pursue dating, or form a new couple relationship. Drawing on the National Social Life, Health, and Aging Project study, Brown and Shinohara (2013, 1197) reported that among unmarried men, 27 percent of those aged 65–74 and 24 percent of those aged 75–85 were dating. The old men who were dating compared to those who were not had greater economic and social capital, better health, and were more likely to have been divorced rather than widowed. In a qualitative study of single gay British men in their 50s and 60s, Suen (2015) also found the primary factors encouraging the men's dating included their surrounding social climate that privileged couple relationships, how dating provided them companionship and a more active social life, and that dating met an emotional need for intimacy. As one of the men said, "When you hit a psychological or physical setback, not having someone make you a cup of tea and tell you how good you are . . . that's an obvious disadvantage to me" (Suen 2015, 147).

Because of men's longevity and their children's tolerance of or acceptance of recoupling in later life, old men's repartnering has become more and more common. In the UK and US a rising proportion of old men are remarrying. As well, based on the Health and Retirement Study (HRS), adults aged 60 and older in the US are as likely to cohabitate as to remarry, should they form new later life partner relationships. Just shy of half of divorced old men in the 2010 HRS had repartnered either by cohabitating or remarrying (Brown et al. 2016, table 2), and cohabitation now appears to operate as a long-term alternative to remarriage in late life.

There are alternatives to old men recoupling. Research shows that four in ten US widowers who live alone preferred dating relations based on companionship, and many of the widowers already enjoyed high levels of emotional closeness in relationships with friends (Carr 2004). A study of the relationship goals in personal ads written by older adults from the US found the "young-olds" (aged 60–74 and mostly divorced) were the aging men more interested in starting life over with a new romantic partner, whereas the "old-olds" (aged 75+, largely widowed) sought a companion with whom they could share activities (cf. Alterovitz and Mendelsohn 2013).

A caution: One estimate found that among the divorced and widowed old men aged 65+ in the US, slightly more than 80 percent had not repartnered through cohabitation or remarriage during an eight-year period, 1998–2006 (Vespa 2012, table 1). It was the "younger" men, aged 50–64, who had divorced who more often recoupled—23 percent remarried and 16 percent cohabitated. Age and why the marriage ended matter. Brown et al. (2016, table 2) similarly report that among men who divorced after age 50, more than 40 percent remarried or were cohabitating within a decade of the marriage ending. Only one in four of the men becoming widowers after age 50 repartnered, largely because they were older when they became single. Why these "younger" and "older" age cohorts differ so in their repartnering is poorly understood. Is it each age cohort's generational habitus and view of (or taste regarding) repartnering, or does the length of marriage before becoming single again significantly shape formerly married aging men's repartnering trajectories?

These studies may underestimate aging men's recoupling because the estimates were limited to cohabitation and remarriage and did not include the LAT alternative. Information on later life LAT relationships remains meager, yet these relationships are becoming a more common choice among widowers than divorced old men. Lewin (2017) noted that 7 percent of aging men and women in the US reported their involvement in LAT relationships, with men three times more likely than women to be involved. LAT relationships were twice the prevalence of cohabitation. In Canada, it was cohabitation (or "living common law") that was preferred twice as much as LAT relationships. Yet almost 3 percent of the Canadian men aged 60+ were in LAT relationships (Turcotte 2013). In a national Swedish study where one-third of the age group 60+ identified as single, up to a third of these "singles" were in fact in a relationship, whether coresidential or LAT (Bildtgård and Öberg 2013; Öberg and Bildtgård 2014). This latter finding too may underestimate men's later life coupling, since it reports on "older adults," not distinguishing between aging men and women, and the latter are much less likely to form a new couple relationship.

A study of ten aging couples (aged 60 and older) from the midwestern US found that participating in a LAT relationship necessitated reconciling personal beliefs about the meaning of commitment and partner expectations, which had been shaped by prior beliefs about romantic relationships and prior participation in cohabiting (including marital) relationships (Benson and Coleman 2016b). As well, LAT meant coming to terms with the personal unimportance of marriage in later life. As one man viewed it, "I think relationships develop differently when you're aged than they [do] when you're young . . . I'm not entirely sure I seen any substantial point in being married other than, than having kids" (ibid., 803). Couples wanted to retain their separate places, home maintenance standards, and use of personal leisure time, all of which could be in jeopardy if they lived together. Funk and Kobayashi (2016, 1108) similarly underscore how later life LAT participants perceive their arrangement as not tying them down, providing an "unencumbered life that respects individualities." A study of Swedish older adults in LAT relationships also concluded that the relationship is an opportunity for combining intimacy with autonomy (Karlsson et al. 2007). Some partners, often the aging men, see a LAT relationship more in terms of a conventional marriage-like relationship, while others, usually women, see it primarily as a type of relationship that is more open, guaranteeing the possibility of maintaining an independent while partnered life.

The likelihood of later life (re)partnering is about constraint as well. Whether an old man's later years are spent alone or coupled will be influenced principally by his age, income (dis)advantage, social capital, and health burden, as much as his own decision (cf. Brown, Bulanda, and Lee 2012; Davidson 2002, Vespa 2012). In most Global North countries there is a rising slope in the proportion of old men living alone, and it is the aging widowers and men with health disadvantages who heavily weight this statistic. Another prevalent finding is that people later in life, particularly women, tend to be reluctant to reenter coresidential relationships because living together results in less independence, may signal future care work, and may trigger serious tensions with existing families regarding feelings of disloyalty. For example, de Jong Gierveld and Merz (2013) studied older divorced and widowed Dutch parents' decision-making about their living arrangement after repartnering and the attendant difficulties later life couples may face when they reconstruct family boundaries with children and stepchildren. A 62-year-old man storied his experience of first cohabitating, then retreating to living apart together:

We, my new partner and I, tried sharing a household. Her daughter reacted very strongly. "What's that guy doing in our house?" And her son didn't say a word to me at breakfast, not even "Good morning" or anything; . . . that feels awful . . . not good. So I decided to move out and live separately again. (ibid., 1106)

Children adversely affect later life couples' repartnering/living arrangement decisions in two ways. First, adult children usually are a valued source of unspoken emotional support for aging men, and close relationships with their children may reduce or even eliminate old men's desire to recouple (Wu, Schimmele, and Ouellet 2015). Second, as Vespa (2013) proposed, aging men may refrain from repartnering *and* living together because coresidence may threaten the quality of the intergeneration relations—e.g., alienating adult children and raising concerns with matters of inheritance. However, as Bildtgård and Öberg (2017) recognized, a new partner restructures the "relationship chain" so that the aging man's time and energy will be redirected to the new partner. Still, most often adult children "appeared to be generally supportive of their parents' new intimate relationships." The caveat is, as Bildtgård and Öberg (2017, 399) note, "at least as long as they did not plan to marry." The adult children see many personal benefits of a parent's repartnering. As one 78-year-old woman noted:

Peter's children, for example, think of all the work I've unburdened them from. Every time that he [is ill]—we went to the hospital the other day—they would have had to go with him instead. We ought to have a new collective moral code: Encourage your mother or father to find a new partner as soon as the former partner dies. (Bildtgård and Öberg 2017, 396)

SUMMARY

For aging heterosexual and gay men who are coupled, there is an underlying continuity to their *relational selves* as they transition with their partners into later life and very old age. For men who end an intimate relationship in midlife or later, or who repartner in later life, research shows that these men also reorganize their social convoy (cf. Guiaux, Van Tilberg, and Van Groenou 2007). For aging heterosexual and gay men who move out of primary relationships and into new ones, their relational selves undergo alterations. The chapter asked to what extent aging men's relational selves are reconstructed as their social worlds are renegotiated, and if relational selves and aging masculinities are linked.

It was the research by Vinick and Ekerdt (1991) that noted aging men's relational identity as a husband superseded their "breadwinner" identity that inspired me to emphasize relationships, not retirement. There surely are lingering employment-based identities as aging men develop their postemployment lifestyles. Yet Carstensen's (1992, 2006) theorizing and affirming research on socioemotional selectivity strongly inspires a conceptual turn to investigate and rethink old men's relational selves, especially among the generations of old men living in third age cultures. Scholars are now starting to investigate old men's relational identities and experiences in later life, yet too little of the published research has sufficiently acknowledged that sexual identity, race/ethnicity, class, religious identity, and the traditions within geographies of place are intertwined to, in all probability, show marked variations. An intersectionality framework from the onset in future studies is more than needed.

Chapter Nine

Intimacies and Sexuality

How many times have we heard the phrase, "All men want is sex?" When I was 17 years old I was sure it was true. When I was 37 years old, I suspected it might not be true. And now that I'm 73 years old, I know it's not true.

—Diamond (2017)

"Sex is being warm and caring; sex isn't just sex," says Christopher Rhoades, 66, a San Francisco Bay Area college professor who's been married for 18 years. "It feels good to lay next to a naked woman's body."

—Stern (2017)

I started this chapter with these (heteronormative) quotes because they discursively throw into the wind the common story that sexual practices for men always revolve around "me" and penetrative sex and orgasm. Much of the sexist imaginary about men and their sexual practices ignores many partnered men's interests in intimacy. Similarly widespread is the ageist presumption that old men and women become asexual. Consistent with this imaginary, ask both aging and old men about their "sex" life and, if they answer, expect to hear most men adopt a masculinity discourse and narrow their story's message to incorporate masculinity's sexual gold standard—intercourse. But ask any one of these men about "sexual intimacy" and many responses will reveal the man's relational self, no longer only his self-awarded ribbons for his sexual capability. Manhood stereotypes aside, when an old man talks about his sexuality we will likely hear a response similar to the two extracts above, where the emphasis is on *intimacy*.

This chapter examines old men's sexuality—their sexual practices, preferences, and intimacies. Both the constructs "sexuality" and "intimacies" are defined early in the chapter to ground my writing and readers' understanding, and the limitations of the chapter are detailed in a set of caveats that immediately follow this introduction. I again use the distinction between never-aging and aging masculinities to characterize most old men's preference for sexual intimacy and, in turn, their comfort with less hurried intercourse. Based on descriptive national studies, I summarize the information about men's practices and preferences, that is about who's doing what and why they are doing what. The chapter closes with a discussion of "intimate sexuality," followed by a brief summary of what research shows us about gray and gay sexuality.

A set of caveats: First, most information introduced in the chapter is about partnered heterosexual activity. This is because most of the available research studies draw on community-based and representative samples that are almost exclusively represented by heterosexuals, given their prevalence within populations. These samples are more often white and clustered nearer the median of class diversity. With a few exceptions (reviewed later), there is limited published research on the patterns of sexual expression among older self-identified gay and bisexual men, which may reflect their lesser numbers and the fact that aging gay and bisexual men may remain closeted and wary of talking with researchers. As well, there are few reliable studies of Mexican American or African American or other non-white old men's sexual practices and sexuality.

Second, despite the likelihood that old men are in a coupled relationship, there is still too little information on the *meaning* of "sex" in the lives of aging men and what sexual activities are common and preferred as men and their partners age together. This severely limits conversation and analysis. We know from population-based descriptive studies (reviewed later) that a significant proportion of men and women with partners remain sexually active well into later life, and this recurrent finding repudiates the prevailing myth about aging and sexual dysfunction being inevitable or old people as postsexual (cf. Lindau and Gavrilova 2010). We also know that public discourse regarding the positive benefits of men's and women's sexual activity to their quality of later life has been affirmed within large sample survey research (e.g., DeLamater, Hyde, and Fong 2008). But the varied meanings old men derive from their sexuality and its changes remain clouded.

Third, typically the identity work men do as they age sexually is relationship-based. A nationally representative study (Fisher 2010) underscores that whether a person engages in sexual activity at all in the preceding six months is principally determined by partnership status—being (re)married, living apart together, or cohabitating. As I will discuss in more detail shortly, the longer the duration of couples' relationships, the higher probability that men's sexual life is "we" centered and his sexual identity is primarily relationally based, rather than hinged on cultural ideals of manliness. The private "we" and his embodied sense of aging masculinities regulate sexual practices. Starting with an understanding that aging masculinities are most often relational in context, this chapter reviews and theorizes old men's sexuality and want for intimacy.

SEXUALITY

The first task is to define sexuality. For most old men (and women) sexuality encompasses far more than genital organs. It includes all the physical intimacies of sensual proximity, touch, and taste—e.g., snuggling on the couch, lightly stroking the back of the neck, hugging and kissing, massage, slow dancing, playful butt-bumping, solo and mutual masturbation, oral sex—that express admiration, passion, affection, and high regard for one's partner's body and one's own. It includes the performance of identities as a man (or woman) and as a partner. It entails an ability to value the "we" through giving and receiving. This is particularly the case for men in couple relationships, heterosexual and gay; they typically want a connection that feels good, where sexual practices are relational as well as can be recreational and pleasurable with or without orgasm or intercourse. By comparison, the late middle-agers and old men who are not partnered and have sexual relations with different people may prioritize recreational and "me" pleasurable sexuality apart, unlike sexuality functioning as a medium of the "feel-good" connectedness of being with their sexual partner (cf. Seidman 1989). They too have embodied active sexuality as part of their identity as men, but they are much less likely to engage in sexual practices with the same someone to affirm a relational self.

It is important to recognize that aging men's sexuality is not simply an equivalent to having or not having an erection. Sexuality is not a discrete set of practices. Rather, it is a complex affair tied to sociocultural contexts, embodied self-images and lived subjectivities, and couples' biographies. Historically, the sexual lives of aging individuals and old couples have been pathologized and marginalized, with the assumption that sexual deterioration will be the inevitable accompaniment to (bodily) aging and the inevitable result is "sexual retirement" (Gott and Hinchliff 2003). The majority of research studies on the sexual activities and relationships of men and women in later life have tended to center only on the negative dimensions of sexual activity: physical decline and compromised function. New studies that show sexuality is lifelong and a desired aspect in later life disrupt the legacy of the decline discourses.

It is also important to underscore that sexuality is not natural at all. It is learned and performed within generations and classes, constructed through moral discourses, and lived differently by gay and straight men. Studying sexual beliefs, desire, (consensual) activity, and sexual pleasure exposes the connectedness of men's lived sexual scripts, health and sexual health status, partner status, and, importantly, the habitus that couples develop and revise regarding their everyday lives, sexual preferences, and intimacy practices. Yes, Bourdieu would accept that couples build a habitus—coupling is no-mos-building. This couple emphasis upends the misunderstandings of "essential manhood" found within masculinity discourses that intone "natural sex" as his self-centered act of release, which is driven by biological desire and his social need to demonstrate his manliness sexually. I mean to disrupt misunderstandings about men's aging and sexuality that fail to look past the ageist narratives within the never-aging masculinity discourse to see that penetrative sex (in its various forms and with or without pharmaceutical aid) becomes secondary, in enduring midlife and later life relationships, to intimacy. To disrupt means to change the conversation to how intimacy and sexuality are experienced and storied in aging men's lives.

LATER LIFE INTIMACIES

Of the many constructs addressed in the book, later life intimacies is one that is worth trying to clarify in terms of how I understand and use it. Intimacy already has a range of meanings in contemporary usage: sometimes it is a euphemism for sexual intercourse or more broadly sexual activities; it can be interpreted as warm and close familiarity; it is often equated with the emotional and physical experiences inside relationships that become the glue for the take-for-granted sense of "we"; it has been theorized as a social form that embodies the couple's secrets and private habitus; and it has been sometimes made synonymous with privacy. In this chapter intimacy is understood not as an outcome generated through relational closeness, but as the mode of sensual interaction. It is less a "thing" and more the "doing." It involves distinctive touch and other sensual activity as expressions of feelings of love. Doing intimacy—touching the check or forearm, lying naked together, using a vibrator to induce his partner's orgasm, or walking closely together, touching, and enjoying one another's company—produces the feelings of being intimate, which are the pleasures of physical contact and closeness and shared moments. My understanding of intimacy is very similar to Linn Sandberg's (2011, 2016): we both point to intimacy as a modality of sensual activity. Hers emphasizes intimacy as a form of sexuality; mine makes sexuality a dimension of intimacy. Either way, sexual intimacy is understood as sensual and often genital but maybe not.

de Vries and Blando (2004) cleverly noted that sexuality and aging are unfamiliar bedfellows. Perhaps the unfamiliarity of old men's and women's sexual lives is the way in which aging and sexuality remain an oxymoron in public discourses. Perhaps it is little more than old men's sexuality being overshadowed by the disproportionate attention given to younger people's sexuality—their hook-up culture, being less relationally oriented and more sexually open (e.g., Emmers-Sommer, Hertlein, and Kennedy 2013). There also is the idea that intimate sexuality among old people frightens most other people. Whatever the reason for the unfamiliar bedfellows, research affirms that aging couples do think about sex less often and have less compelling desire than they had twenty or forty years earlier. These changes are age effects, perhaps also cohort differences. However, enough research also is at hand to disrupt the ageist suggestion that there is a "falloff" in sexual practices or interest and that sexual intimacy becomes less important for many aging couples over the course of their relationship (cf. DeLamater 2012; Dodge et al. 2016). Research findings about old couples' lesser frequency of coital intercourse mistakenly power the "falloff" discourse. Unfamiliar to many people is that the quality of sex increases as the frequency decreases among late life couples (Lodge and Umberson 2012).

My worry is that geriatrics researchers can discursively cast a shadow that darkens people's thinking about sexuality and aging. Most aging men's sexuality does not embrace the third age culture's emphasis on penetrative "sex for life" (Potts et al. 2006). Ignored is the fact that old people renegotiate the frequency and types of sexual practices they enjoy and prefer in their own right as old couples with old bodies. As a roundabout, the age effect on sexuality is presumed to be continuous biophysiological decline. Whenever a "lessening" finding is presented, it also whispers that reductions in sexual frequency are likely experienced as a threat to masculine subjectivities, for both midlife and old gay and heterosexual men (cf. Lodge and Umberson 2013; Slevin and Linneman 2010). In my view, whenever social gerontologists and masculinity studies researchers survey the patterns of sexual frequency across age groups and find old men and women reporting less frequent sexual activity, they likely emphasize the "shaken masculinities and femininities" (e.g., Lodge and Umberson 2012, 434). However, should the researchers examine sexuality close up in terms of couples' sexual habits and draw on what the couples say, they likely would discover how intimacy *and* relational sex are the "story" (cf. Sandberg 2011, 2013b).

Later life sexual practices reveal how couples adapt to one another's bodily aging and may prioritize sensual intimacy without sexual activity, orgasm, or intercourse, such as occasional showers together and regular touching and cuddling. Their sexual intimacy should disrupt the discourse on old men's failing erections and lost masculinity, which is still depicted in film and magazine's cultural narratives of old men as impotent "old geezers" (cf. Gatling, Mills, and Lindsay 2017). Familiarity with their relational sexual intimacy should help disrupt the corrosive stereotype of the "unduly sexual" "dirty" old man; it can infuse grandfathers' cautious interactions with (grand)children, at times vigilantly establishing boundaries with young granddaughters to avoid misinterpretations of touch (Lesperance 2010).

In this chapter I draw on poststructuralism and queer theory to discuss old age, masculinity, and sexuality, more often heterosexuality. In *Transforming Masculinities*, Seidler (2006, xix) commented, "We need to reflect upon the new orders of gender and sexual relationships that are emerging within different societies in a globalized world. This means challenging theories that have tended to identify men with prevailing masculinities." His urging surely applies to challenging the place of never-aging masculinities in old men's lives. We need to be able to imagine later life (or aging) masculinities embodying new forms of sexuality—less frequently intercourse to orgasm and more commonly intimate touch and, perhaps, orgasm. As generations of aging men quietly became intimate and caring in their relations with their partner, their narratives about their intimacy experiences problematize the reckoning that when old men want to live up to the standards of never-aging masculinities, they feel inadequate when they "fail" in bed. Whitehead (2002) smartly asked, Is there such a thing as "male sexuality"? He continued:

> What do we mean by this term, one that is so loaded politically and ideologically? What form of sexuality is being presumed there—bisexual, homosexual, transsexual, heterosexual? Of what cultural origin is this sexuality—white/Western/Latino/Chicano/black/Oriental [sic] . . . Invariably, the term "male sexuality" assumes heterosexuality as the "norm." But as with gender, what is considered "normal" is not necessarily "natural" . . . Like gender, sexuality is not a given, it is learnt, imposed, acquired, worked at, experimented with, negotiated and, often with difficulty, experienced. To even talk of such a thing as male sexuality is to collaborate in discursive [sexism]. (2002, 163–64)

Amidst Whitehead's musing and warning he cited Lynne Segal, and by doing so he encouraged me to reread her provocative thinking in *Slow Motion*. She commented, "Male sexuality cannot be reduced to the most popular meanings of sex acts, let alone to sex acts themselves. It becomes intelligible only if placed within actual histories of men's intimate relationships with others—or the lack of them" (Segal 1990, 215). This is my starting point—aging men in relationships.

OLD MEN'S SEXUAL PRACTICES AND DESIRE

In later life, sexuality is less a matter of urgency and more an expression of love, affection, the pleasure of touch, and closeness. Hegemonic masculinities differ somewhat across age cohorts, sexualities, classes, and other bases of men's lives (Connell and Messerschmidt 2005), yet they all have discursively fashioned men's sexuality as penis-centered and based on strong, fiery urges—or, quite crudely, the little head controls the head and heart. Cultural

narratives still promote a consciousness that (hetero)sexual intercourse vali-
dates manhood, and that masculinity is symbolized through penetrative sexuality. Virility and masculinity are synonymous. Both are confirmed through a
proper erection, and secondarily through sexual performance. The cultural
maxim is, so long as the man sexually "performs," his manhood is unques-
tioned. But should he fail to get and sustain an erection, his sexual health
isn't in question; his masculinity is. Even in critical men's studies, men's
sexuality has almost always been deemed as integral to masculinity, and this
point of view has been strengthened by medicine's normal-pathological binary (cf. Tiefer 1986; Weeks 1985). The "almost always" exception in the
preceding sentence is possibly the historical period where monastic life and
celibacy characterized ideal masculinity. But as Baglia (2005) argues, the
prevailing sexual script for men strongly emphasizes erections as the sine
qua non of manliness. In the same way, in his study of the cultural history of
impotence, McLaren (2007) concluded that impotence signals "failed" masculinity.

The never-aging masculinity and successful aging discourses jointly attest
to what is "manly" and what is "failure." My observation is that these paired
discourses frame men's sexuality by using binary pairs: masculine/feminine,
natural/artificial, heterosexual/homosexual, able-bodied/impaired, and
young/old. One illustration of the dualisms: masculinity is affirmed by hard
erections; old men not staying erect long enough or not getting erect equals
emasculation (cf. Wassersug 2009). Another illustration: manly men have
some intense inner need to have sex; old men have memories of those by-
gone times and come to think of themselves as sexually retired (cf. Wentzell
2013b). Rife in the initial national surveys of adults' sexuality was the embodied lens of medicine that equated men's successful aging/failure with
erectile (dys)function.

Should an index in the back of an authoritative book link together aging
and sexuality, it would not be uncommon to see the listing read as "Sexuality: activity, age-related changes in, desire, Foucault on, of men, of women,
virility and; *see also*: dysfunction, extramarital, loss of libido, impotence,
medicalization, Viagra." Missing from this exemplar listing (and in reality
most indexes) are references to "and intimacy, and sensual, relational." The
practice of talking about "sex" as if it means only fiery coital intercourse is
not limited to the textbook indexes. Its history shaped the narrative about the
"traditional" heterosexual script's coital imperative, which Gagnon and Simon (1973) theorized as governing the generations of men coming of age in
the 1940s, 1950s, and early 1960s. This heterosexual script posits an active/
passive binary for the social organization of sexuality, namely that men are
the initiators of sexual activity and women are the gatekeepers, responsible
for controlling the boundaries of the couple's sexual intimacy, whether the
couple are dating partners or long-term marrieds. In all, the practice of speak-

ing as if "sex" is synonymous with coital intercourse has become common discourse, and it is epitomized in President Clinton's decades ago masculinist disclaimer about his sexual involvement with a White House intern—"I did not have sexual relations with that woman." Likening sex to coital intercourse also underpins the narratives of age-related *impotence* as the natural emasculation of men in their postsexual phase of life (Gott and Hinchliff 2003).

Representative national survey-based studies of later life sexuality (which are reviewed below) have identified a variety of background social forces that shape aging individuals' sexual expression, such as religion, generation, and marital status. Perhaps the most significant, however, is involvement in a couple relationship. In every study, being coupled (whether through marriage, cohabitation, or LAT) is the critical determinant of engaging in nonsolo sexual activity. As self-evident as it may seem, widowers, old divorced men, and old never-marrieds who are without a partner lack opportunity for anything other than solo sex (i.e., masturbation) and are also twice as likely to lack interest in sex (Lindau et al. 2007, table 4). The next most influential predictor seems to be the physical health in older men, followed by the quality of the relationship. That said, in spite of bothersome health problems, couples' sexual activity does not decrease substantially with increasing age (cf. Lindau et al. 2007). Sexual practices can be maintained until very late in life; it is the availability of a partner, the man's and his partner's health, and how the couple negotiates the age-related changes in sexual functioning that determine the continuance of these practices.

Before continuing and discussing relational sexuality and what sensual intimacy means to many aging adults within a couple arrangement, it is helpful to review the descriptive research on the sexual experiences of older adults—who's doing what, and why.

Who's Doing What

The definition of "sexual activity" by Linda Waite and her colleagues (2009, i56) in the National Social Life, Health, and Aging Study captures its negotiated character: "Sexual activity and functioning are determined by the interaction of each partner's sexual capacity, motivation, conduct, and attitudes and are further shaped by the quality and condition of the dyadic relationship itself." Unfortunately, comparatively less research exists that either makes the aging couple the unit of analysis or recognizes their negotiation of sexual intimacy. Instead, in most studies sexuality is an individual matter.

Until recently, survey information about aging men's and women's sexual activity was limited. This is because old men and women were rarely included in survey samples. The work by Alfred Kinsey and associates in the late 1940s and Masters and Johnson in the late 1960s were principal sources for informing public discourse about US adults' sexuality; however, men aged 60 and older comprised less than 2 percent of Kinsey's participants and just 3 of 824 pages described their sexual lives, and the Masters and Johnson studies included only thirty-one subjects over 60 years of age (cf. J. Levy 1994). As well, the 1990s survey of US adult sexual behavior—the National Health and Social Life Survey—limited its focus to young and middle-aged adults aged 18–59.

After the millennium, a better understanding of aging men's sexual activity became available from national surveys in the United States and Europe. In a German study (Beutel, Stöbel-Richter, and Brähler 2008), sexual activity was assessed by the yes/no question, "Were you intimate with someone in the past twelve months?" The researchers found that 79 percent of the 61- to 70-year-old men and more than half (54 percent) of men aged 70+ with an intimate partner were sexually active. A different picture emerged for those men with no partnership, where only a third (34 percent) of the "younger" men reported being sexually active and hardly any (2 percent) among the men aged 70 and older did so.

Based on the Spanish National Sexual Health Survey, Palacios-Ceña and associates (2012) reported that 90 percent of Spanish men aged 65+ had a partner and two-thirds remained sexually active, even though roughly 40 percent rated their physical and/or sexual health as "very poor/poor/fair." The most common reasons for sexual inactivity among the "younger" men were health limitations, and for the old men it was the absence of a partner.

In a qualitative study of seventeen midlife and later life US couples in long-term marriages, where the spouses were interviewed separately, sex meant vaginal intercourse (Lodge and Umberson 2012) and thirteen of the seventeen couples were sexually active. Narrating past lives, participants reported a decline in the frequency of sex, and most attributed the decline to his bodily aging and health complications, not hers. At the same time, the researchers noted that men's (and women's) narratives "belied the assumption that a decline in frequency . . . necessitates a decline in quality" (ibid., 434). As one man, "Matthew (age 69) said, '[Sex] has gotten better and less frequent.' His wife, Pat (age 68), agreed" (ibid.). Interestingly, of the seventeen men, only three elected to use Viagra. For two of the three men, their wives were feeling neglected by their husbands not initiating sex or revealing sexual desire; they felt the husbands' absence was a sign that they were no longer feminine, attractive women, and they encouraged their husbands to use Viagra. This is not uncommon among couples. In a study of Asian men from China, Japan, Korea, Malaysia, and Taiwan, the man's partner/spouse was the most common influencer of the man to seek treatment in all regions except Malaysia (Tan et al. 2007).

The National Social Life, Health, and Aging Project (NSHAP) sampled US adults aged 57–85 in 2005–06 and assessed the criterion of having had sex with at least one partner in the previous twelve months (Lindau et al. 2007; Waite et al. 2009). Nearly 90 percent of the men aged 57–64 had a current sexual partner, as did almost 80 percent of the men aged 75–85. The researchers noted sexual activity declines with age, beginning with 83 percent of "younger" men (aged 57–64), 67 percent of those aged 65–74, and 38 percent of the old men (aged 75–85) having had some type of recent mutually voluntary sexual contact (Lindau et al. 2007). Among the men who were sexually active, more than half of the old men (aged 75–85) and two-thirds of men younger than 75 reported being sexually active at least two or three times per month. Nine of ten of these sexually active old men reported foreplay "usually or always" occurred, and vaginal intercourse was usually or always part of 80 percent of men's sexual activity (Waite et al. 2009). Oral sex was quite common among the "younger-olds," aged 57–64 (62 percent), but less so among the men older than 75 (28 percent). This age cohort or generational difference makes some sense when viewed through the lens of history: the "younger-olds" are the Boomer generation who came of age during the 1960s and witnessed and experienced many liberalizing conventions about private and public sexual expression. However, it is not known if this is a generational difference in the men's sexual activity or an age effect captured in the older cohort.

A Swedish study (Beckman et al. 2008) assessed the proportion of married/cohabitating men and men in LAT relationships who had engaged in sexual intercourse within the past year in three samples of 70-year-olds living the same community in 1971–72, 1976–77, and 2000. They found 52 percent, 53 percent, and 60 percent, respectively, of the old men in coresidential relationships across the three waves were sexually active, compared to 30 percent, 30 percent, and 54 percent of men in LAT relationships. Beckman and his colleagues concluded, "The proportion of 70 year olds reporting that they were sexually active, that sexuality had been a positive factor in their life, and that had a positive attitude to sexuality in later life increased during the study period, both among married and cohabiting participants and among unmarried participants" (2008, 152).

The 2009 National Survey of Sexual Health and Behavior (NSSHB) in the US reported on a broader range of sexual activity for a nearly exclusive heterosexual sample ranging in age from 14 to 92 (Herbenick et al. 2010). During the previous month vaginal intercourse was reported by nearly 28 percent of old men aged 70+. Among men in the sixth and seventh decades of life, more that 75 percent who were in LAT relationships reported vaginal intercourse in the previous ninety days. The survey did not restrict assessment to intercourse. Patterns of giving oral sex to a female partner were similar to those for receiving oral sex. Yet, oral sex was not common: among middle-aged men (aged 50–59) with a female partner, 48 percent reported receiving and 44 percent reported giving oral sex; for men older than 70 the proportions were 19 percent and 24 percent, respectively. The findings of the NSSHB and the NSHAP reveal the expected lesser sexual activity as men reach their 60s and sharper decline among men aged 70+, which is associated with partner loss and poorer health (cf. Karraker, DeLamater, and Schwartz 2011).

In sum, statistics on men's lesser sexual activity at older ages affirm our need to better determine if the frequencies in types of sexual activity at different ages reveal aging couple's changing preferences for more intimacy practices and less coital sex, as well as what are the continuities and changes in meanings and experiences of sexuality intimacies across individuals' lives. When change is the emphasis, this may continue to unwittingly convey a decline discourse about the waning of sexuality in later life, as when a presentation skews the message to be an "inability to maintain the sexual relationship" or limits sexual activity to coital sex. Too infrequently noted is how survey-based descriptive studies are cohort-based and how cohorts have their own sexual and moral codes; or how a cohort of old men includes its representative number of African American men, who are at greater odds of being unpartnered. Ignoring cohort effects or within-cohort differences in who has a sexual partner can mislead us into thinking that the research findings are equally generalizable to religious and nonreligious men, whites and men of color, long-time widowed and recent widowed, and so on. Also rarely addressed is whether habitation takes a toll on sexual activity and how much the duration of a relationship is a determinant of couples' types of sexual activity, whether married or cohabitating.

Why They Are Doing What

Across many of the national studies the sexual partners cite *his* physical health as a critical reason for *their* lesser sexual activity, and at times lesser satisfaction (cf. Karraker, DeLamater, and Schwartz 2011; Palacios-Ceña et al. 2012). There are studies that also point to her health as being an issue (e.g., Gott and Hinchliff 2003; Kontula and Haavio-Mannila 2009), yet the preponderance of evidence shows us that it is his heath. Studies usually begin with this fact and examine how couples willingly work around his erectile troubles by adopting nonpenetrative practices.

The conceptual turn to assess sexual intimacy as relational may have begun in earnest. Sarah Murray and her research team (2017) questioned the vestige of individual-oriented research that positions men's sexuality and sexual desire in contrast to women and/or in terms of masculinity scripts and "me" interests. Whenever researchers shift the starting point to what couples negotiate, matters of men's sexual intimacy as relational intimacy are no longer buried below the perceptual threshold. In their exploratory study of what elicited or inhibited sexual desire among middle-aged men (average age

43 years) in relationships (average duration thirteen years), Murray and her colleagues note that although men "did not explicitly use the term *relational* or *intimacy*, the way they talked about their experiences implied that what was desired (or missing) was the perception that sexual encounters were mutual and cocreated" (2017, 326, italics original). The men described their sexual desire as crucially related to the relational context. Intimate communication was reported by the majority of the men as important to sexual desire and intimacy. Cody, age 65, commented, "So for me sex is communication. It's not just physical intercourse. It's communicating while you're having the intercourse, and fun, and talking about 'What can I do?' And I think once you start asking the other partner what they want, it embellishes the relationship. And it gives the partner the feeling of acceptance and love and belonging" (ibid., 325). Also noted was the way men deviated from their past and from masculinity scripts about initiating sex; whenever their female partner initiated sexual activity, for some men it was the "ultimate expression, or reassurance" of a "we" feeling. These researchers conclude that without a relational lens, much of men's narratives about how couples intimately interact would be invisible or misinterpreted as individuals' masculinity- or femininity-scripted practices.

Sexual intimacy for old men in partnered relationships comes to emphasize relaxing, gentle sex, and mutual enjoyment. From an Australian study of midlife and later life adults, Rowntree (2014, 154) notes that "sexual expression not only has a comfortable place in their lives, it is experienced as more comfortable as they age." With age, the expression of sexuality became more relationship centered and about sensuality and intimacy. A common characterization of sexuality was people being "comfortable in my own skin," which reflects how they actively do a wide range of sexual practices and negotiated pleasure. Examining a large sample of couples who were married or cohabitating and had been living together 39 years on average (range 1–71 years), Waite and her colleagues (2017) used dyadic data—that is, both partners' interviews—then aggregated the partner's individual responses. The research team was able to make the couple's sexual activity a unit of analysis as well as compare partners' perspectives on their sexual practices. A majority (53 percent) of the couples engaged in sexual activity at least two or three times a month; 37 percent had no partner sex within the past year, chiefly because of his age and health. Couples' frequency of sexual relations was associated with men's and women's reports of relationship satisfaction, opinion that sex was "very/extremely" important to them personally, and tendency to think about sex at least a few times a month.

One interesting finding from the Waite et al. study (2017) needs greater attention: When women reported conflicts with their husbands, the dyad experienced more sexual activity. But when men reported conflict, the couple had less frequent sexual activity. As Linn Sandberg (2016) recognized, old men's sexual desire is regulated by intimacy and should men feel, rightly or not, that their relational interaction is conflicted, they may convey sexual disinterest. There is also some evidence that conflicts may influence partners to try to match their level of sexual desire to that of their partner, thus his pulling back when her interest is low and/or her doing the emotion work to raise her desire when his interest is greater than hers (cf. Tetley et al. 2016). This recognizes that old men's sexual practices are situational as much as contextual. However, conflict within relationships has not been commonly investigated in terms of how it affects the couple's sexual life. One source of conflict still poorly understood spins on men's sexual fidelity. Extramarital sex (EMS) is regularly defined as a partner's violation of norms of exclusivity in committed relationships, including sexual exclusivity. Researchers estimated that a quarter of married heterosexual men have engaged in extramarital coital sex in their lifetime, and as many as 4 percent in the immediate past (Labrecque and Whisman 2017). This estimate does not reveal to what extent men's age is associated with EMS.

Using a nationally representative sample contracted for the AARP Survey of Midlife and Older Adults, Fisher (2010) examined the extent to which sex and intimacy were regarded as an important part of life. Eight-four percent of men aged 60–69 and 80 percent of those aged 70+ indicated that a satisfying sexual relationship was an "integral part of their quality of life"; however, a majority of men aged 70+ did not endorse the principle that sexual activity was of critical importance. Instead, they had come to believe that sexual activity is a pleasurable but not a necessary part of a good-quality relationship with their partner. One takeaway from this study is that sexual intimacy is a desirable aspect of old men's and women's (romantic) lives and relationships, and this is a key reason the majority of old couples strive to remain sexually intimate.

A few years earlier, Gott and Hinchliff (2003) reported on a study of British men's and women's views on the importance of their sex life. The old married men (aged 70+) rated sex as moderately to very important to them, whereas younger (aged 50–69) married men reported sex as very important. Widowed or divorced old men rated having a sex life as of little importance or no longer important, at times because they felt at their age their "luck had run out" and they were not likely to again develop an intimate partnership. The importance of a sex life as expressing commitment and unspoken reassurance was a prevailing reason for why the old couples engaged in sexual relations. Hinchliff and Gott (2004) elaborate: all participants but two felt that sexual intimacy was important to their own quality of life and to the meaningfulness of a long-term relationship. Even when there was a cessation of coital sex, the participants adapted to include more physical contact such as touching, fondling, and hugging.

Ménard and her research team (2015) examined aging men's and women's "very pleasant and welcome surprise" that their sexual experiences had steadily improved in quality over their lifetimes. The participants (aged 60–82) had been in a relationship at least twenty-five years and credited their sexual experiences as something that they worked at. What "working at" involved was letting go of the negative beliefs about aging and sexuality they acquired much earlier in their lives; continuously cultivating new practices by being sensitive, attentive, and responsive to their partner; and resisting the easy route of settling into a personal comfort zone. One man described his experiences with his wife as "a life of sexual exploration and adventure and excitement" (ibid., 84). It was through narratives of intimacy that men expressed their continued interest in sexuality, and it was the rising caliber of their sexual intimacy and satisfaction that reinforced why the study participants quested for sexual intimacy.

It is crucial to not lose sight of the diversity among aging men's sexual practices. In fact, there may well be a greater range of sexual practices among old men than younger age cohorts. The latter are actively involved in work and family matters and may have less recreational time for extended foreplay, cuddling, and other noncoital sex, or the lived experience of needing to renegotiate satisfying sexual practices with their partner following the slow onset of erectile difficulty. Most aging men remain sexually active partly because sexual desire continues throughout their later years, whether gay or heterosexual (Kontula and Haavio-Mannila 2009; Wierzalis et al. 2006). Libido, or desire, needs to be thought of as a desire for sexual intimacy, and the sexual activities that affirm intimacy are not restricted to coital sex. Among aging men who remain sexually active, and most are, the activity for some men can shift to largely kissing, hugging, sexual touching, and other noncoital intimacies. Among old men who maintain sexual interest, and most do, many experience reliable-enough erections to include coital sex. As noted in the Sexual Health chapter, roughly half of very old men (aged 75+) will face erections unreliable enough for coital sex, and most of these men will not take up use of erectile medication. There is the case of Sven, a 75-year-old Swede who survived prostate cancer and worried about becoming impotent, yet despite some initial problems after his cancer treatment he regained potency and continued to have coital sex "thanks to herbal medicine and a 'loving wife'" who helps him acquire his erection (Sandberg 2011, 115). Sandberg (2011, 116) concludes, "Men's ways of making sense of sex and sexuality in later life are much more diverse and complex than the simplistic 'use it or lose it' rhetoric."

The evolution of the meaning of sexuality as men age, and the shift in sexual activity from always including intercourse to other forms of sexual intimacy, more than likely reflect aging men's and their partners' preferred sexual practices. Preferred practices remain not often investigated.

INTIMATE SEXUALITY

When a relational lens frames queries about men's sexual desire, pleasure, and activity, it is no longer advantageous to structure discussions of men's sexuality in terms of never-aging ideologies or medical explanations for failing erectile function. In this section I want to discuss the intimate sexuality among many old couples. The voice of a 66-year-old sums this well, as he depicted sex in his younger years as "urgent" and presently as slower, more prolonged and relaxed: "I suppose it's like a good wine, it improves with age . . . I can't really say it's because of your age, ah, it's because of closeness, perhaps, you know, taking time, not rushing things" (Potts et al. 2006, 320). A 73-year-old widow, Louise, who began her new relationship with a man in his 80s, reported the same recognition that people's sexual lives can improve with age. Louise explained,

> He wants so badly to have an erection, but it's hard for him . . . It might be the heart medication he's taking that causes the problem, because he's a very virile man. So we just have sex in a different way—I don't mind at all—and we're also very affectionate. He says it's so nice to wake up next to me . . . I expect to make love as long as I can. (Stern 2017)

Small stories of increasing intimacy in sexual relationships are, as the foregoing examples point to, part of bigger narrative about old people becoming more considerate and less self-centered in bed in later life (Sandberg 2013b).

In a review chapter, Schwartz, Diefendorf, and McGlynn-Wright (2014) called my attention to an interesting pair of findings from Wiley and Bortz's (1996) study of a small number of older adults in Palo Alto, California. The old men (mean age 68) desired a higher frequency of sexual activity than what they currently experienced; the frequency of their sexual relations had declined compared to ten years earlier, yet their sexual desire had not diminished over the decade. What stands out is how the old men's sexual preferences changed significantly. Ten years earlier intercourse and orgasm were the preferred forms of sexual activity. Their importance declined appreciably. What rose to the top of old men's current preference was "satisfying (their) partner"; "loving and caring" was ranked as almost equivalent to intercourse (see also Grace et al. 2006).

Wiley and Bortz explained this reprioritizing of the types of preferred sexual activity with a biophysiological lens: changes in men's potency compelled the men to compensate and pursue other sexual behaviors. Perhaps so, yet I believe the men in Wiley and Bortz's study who prioritize their partner are not simply compensating for changes in their erectile capability. Rather, I am intrigued by how later life couple relationships may intensify men's relational selves and concentrate on "we" interests, a possibility that is also consistent with Carstensen et al.'s (2011) thesis that aging is associated with seeking more positive emotional connections and experiences. Among long-term couples, future time is too short to be all about "me." An older couple's everyday life and intimacy practices are we-centered. Thus, rather than highlighting how one-fifth to one-fourth of the men in Wiley and Bortz's (1996, M143) study were "very troubled" by the falloff in sexual frequency (recall, this meant *any* type of sexual activity), I find it more interesting that the vast majority of the men (and women) aged 70+ reported enjoyable sexual relations. One-third of the old men, in fact, reported more sexual enjoyment now compared to ten years earlier.

"Hold me" and the tenderness of touching sex are among the types of intimate sexuality that Linn Sandberg (2013b) calls reciprocal "less selfish sex." Hinchliff and Gott (2004, 604) similarly characterize later life couples' sexuality as more unselfish, particularly as they navigated health-related barriers to sexual activity. Consideration of a partner's painful arthritis and the need to adapt to less preferred sexual positions, or postponing sexual activity when a wife's cardiac-related barriers indicated any sexuality was a bad day, reveal men's later life taste for intimacy. The argument I find easy to make is that for old men sexuality is not "all about" the penis and penetrative sex; rather it is about pleasurable sex, intimacy, and affirming feelings of connectedness. Take, for example, Elliott and Umberson's (2008) detection of some aging couples' *joint* emotion work—for example, some married men made a concerted effort to match their wife's lesser level of sexual desire by tapering down their own desire; instead of focusing on frequency, they concentrated on the quality of their sex. Their joint effort of managing personal desires and emotions aimed to "enhance intimacy and help the spouse feel better about himself or herself" (ibid., 403).

Linn Sandberg's innovative perspective on old men's sexuality encourages social gerontologists and gender studies scholars to shift their focus to later life intimacy and away from life span changes in sexual activity:

> Intimacy may, for one thing, be understood as enabling anti-ageist narratives on later life sexuality, where what it means to be sexual emerges from and is adjusted to the possibilities of the ageing body. Intimacy may also be analyzed as a non-binary concept, where male bodies can re-emerge as sexual in new ways and decentre a coital imperative for men. (2013b, 277)

Sandberg's pioneering interpretation is based on her interviews with old Swedish men born between 1922 and 1942 (aged 67–87 at the time of the research); all were heterosexual, no longer involved in paid labor, and coupled. The majority of the men were married and several others were in LAT relationships; more than half of the men were in a second long-term relationship. Like so many other studies of aging men's sexuality, Sandberg notes that her study draws on men situated in "an *intersecting knot of privilege* springing from heterosexuality, able-bodiedness, whiteness, and for most a middle-class position" (2011, 82, italics original). Rephrased, and in sync with most other studies, hers does not represent the population of old men who live with precarious health and without the social capital of a harmonious-enough long-term relationship.

What Sandberg (2013b) uncovers is how aging bodies and later life's renovated masculinities merge to generate for some old men the lived experience where intimacy comes to eclipse the desire for penetrative sex. The old men's narratives prioritized how they came to embody intimacy and distance themselves from the coital imperatives of "manliness" or lure of Viagrastories. "When men in my study speak about sexuality in later life it is not all about 'staying hard' but rather about *getting intimate*" (Sandberg 2013b, 278, italics original). Later life sexuality is an orientation no longer determined by the intercourse-focused sexuality of men's earlier years or mourning the loss of erectile reliability; it widens to include the sensuality in caresses, touch, fondling, a dance, talking and walking together. Noncoital expressions of intimacy can be pleasurable sexually and affirm men's and women's desirability—the feel of a partner's gentle brush of a kiss, her foot stroking his leg under the table while they have breakfast, a massage, "just feeling a naked body next to you." These all nourish men's sexual, age, and masculine (inter)subjectivities.

For Sandberg (2011, 2013b, 2016), later life intimate sexuality is two things: it is a fluid middle ground between the sexual and the nonsexual that is in accordance with "traditional" masculinity discourses, and it is something "more," for it reshapes male sexuality into something less phallic and remakes the old man into a more sexually free, better lover. Intimate sexuality can be discovered early by some aging men when their bodily aging makes their erections not always reliable, and by other aging men when their everyday lives are no longer regulated by the rhythms and stresses of work and family matters and their partners express their changing sexual desire and preferences. To clarify, Sandberg (2011) argues that narratives on intimacy are what many old men will talk about when they talk about sex and sexuality, and she notes that men's narratives on intimacy were not something she expected. The intimacy narratives were a way the old men made sense of sexual desire and activities. She concludes, "Signifying and making sense of sexuality in terms of intimacy is a positive and unthreatening way of presenting the sexual subjectivity of old men" (Sandberg 2016, 205).

GRAY AND GAY SEXUALITY

Presenting a separate section on aging gay men's sexuality feels awkward, as if doing so casts one group of aging men again into a segregated space, as if "forgotten" (Pugh 2002). To this point in the chapter the emphasis has been on heterosexual relationships with occasional snippets of thinking about gray and gay sexuality. One reason for adding this section is because the majority of national studies did not ask about sexual orientation, and if they did ask their probability samples had very small numbers of old gay men (cf. Fisher 2010) to effectively address if and how sexual orientation may affect men's sexual tastes and sexual activities. Recent studies of adults' sexuality still likely underestimate the population of gay men, because, for example, the men in the older cohorts who lived years with severe discrimination and maintain a LAT relationship may remain guarded and not disclose their sexual orientation to the researchers. Studies also regularly miscalculate gay men's relational statuses because heteronormative martial statuses are assessed, which effectively blends many gay men, living together as partners or not, into the "single" category with the heterosexual men who are divorced, widowed, or never-married. As de Vries and Blando (2004) report, one of the striking differences between heterosexuals and gay men is the greater frequency of singlehood among the latter. Only about half of gay men were estimated to be in committed relationships.

Consistent with de Vries and Blando's estimate, Fredriksen-Goldsen, Bryan et al. (2017) note that 46 percent of the aging gay men in the Aging with Pride: National Health, Aging, and Sexuality/Gender Study (NHAS) were currently partnered or married. But contrary to stereotypes built by snapshot demographics, less than 13 percent had never been partnered or married. One-third of aging gay men in the sample had experienced the death of a partner, a turning-point experience much more common among the oldest men. One-quarter of the aging gay men had once been in an opposite-sex marriage and were fathers. And again consistent with de Vries and Blando, nearly 41 percent of the men were currently "alone." Bisexual men were similar in terms of current relationship terms, but twice as likely to have been in an opposite-sex marriage and half as likely to be in a same-sex marriage.

Best estimates suggest that self-identified LGB adults now comprise about 3.5 percent of the US adult population; at least 2.7 million US adults aged 50 and older self-identify as LGB; and, while the size of the self-identified LGB population decreases with age, the size of the older LGB population will increase dramatically given the aging of the US population (Fredriksen-Goldsen and Kim, 2015, 2017). Moving beyond such demographic profiles, although there is an emergent body of research on aging gay men to begin to consider their sexuality, the available information is still heavily weighted toward the white, well-educated, higher socioeconomic, younger age cohorts of gay men who are out and active in their communities. For example, within a recent nationally representative study of US adults aged 50 and older, the men who self-identified as a sexual minority—gay or bisexual—were more likely to be white, single, live alone or live with a partner (cohabitate), and less likely to be married when compared to the aging heterosexual men, though about one in five of the gay and the bisexual men in this sample was married (Fredriksen-Goldsen, Kim, Shui, and Bryan 2017). As Wierzalis et al. (2006, 94) snappishly note, "Contrary to stereotypes, aging gay men in American society are not all middle-class white men in jeans." Class, race/ethnicity, and masculine capital surely can impinge on men finding common ground other than their sexual identity and age (cf. Bergling 2004; Schwartz and Graf 2009).

Discourses on sexual infidelity and "affairs" are markers of heterosexual partnerships much more than gay men's same-sex partnerships. Aging gay men, and perhaps old gay men in particular, embody the older gay cohort's general acceptance of nonmonogamous sexual relations (Heaphy, Donovan, and Weeks 2004). This is a second reason to separately address gray and gay sexuality. Cultural norms do not stipulate that two gay men must live in a one-to-one relationship, and it is likely that from the onset the men negotiate and construct their relationship without many of the same guidelines and sanctions that regulate heterosexual relationships (cf. Adam 2006). As men, they have embodied masculine discourses of autonomy and adventurism, and as gay men lay claim to sexual self-determination within a subculture that accepts consensual nonmonogamies.

This is not to say that many aging and old gay men do not develop committed, sexually monogamous partnerships or marriages that are minimally different from aging heterosexuals. They do. But a key difference is that among gay men, these are negotiated "closed" relationships, not taken for granted as part of the heteronormative vows of commitment. Only in the case of negotiated closed relationships does "infidelity" apply should a partner breach the monogamous commitment. Other gay and particularly bisexual men develop consensual "nonmonogamies" or "open" partnerships, whether they are aging gay and cohabitating or in LAT relationships or heterosexually married bisexuals. This explicitly agreed-upon "open" partnership seems to occur more among the older men (Adam 2006) whose occasional freestanding sexual relationships are discreet and somewhat resembling the nonrelational, mostly recreational "hook-ups" of contemporary young men and women. Due to the historical context in which these late midlife and old gay men lived and worked, every member of the cluster born before 1950 very probably experienced periods of harsh social exclusion and severe marginalization during the era when coming out in early adulthood, and again during the first decades of the HIV epidemic (Fredriksen-Goldsen, Bryan et al. 2017). And still other aging and old gay men maintain sexual

lives that principally involve one-encounter relations, which are assumed to
lack a long-term time horizon or any relation-specific investment. The exact
proportion of the aging gay population within these three patterns is not well
documented, but the patterns are. On these factors alone, the sexual lives and
worlds of some aging gay and bisexual men remain unambiguously different
than most heterosexuals'.

My presentation, that aging men who have sex with men have different
sexual histories and lives than their heterosexual counterparts who exclusively have sex with women, does not warrant too heavy an emphasis on "differences." Aging gay men face issues similar to many of the sexual matters their
"straight" peers face, such as a decline in the frequency of sexual activity the
longer the duration of the relationship (e.g., Lodge 2015), or a sense of
challenged masculine self-esteem and lessened sense of sexual intimacy
when battling prostate cancer (e.g., Allensworth-Davies et al. 2016), or reporting that the dearth of sex is not an indicator of how emotionally connected and committed the partners are to one another (e.g., Umberson, Thomeer, and Lodge 2015, 551), or having a desire in late midlife and later life
for both emotional and sexual intimacy (e.g., Pope et al. 2007), or how with
age the focus of sex shifts to the partner and is more relaxed and satisfying
and how sexual intimacy, love, and personal identity may merge somewhat
differently from the experiences of heterosexual men, yet nonetheless merge
(e.g., Wierzalis et al. 2006).

What is different are the histories of late midlife and later life gay men
adapting to restrictive, discriminatory heterosexist communities and coming
to depend on LAT relationships to convey a less stigmatized status of "unmarried," or similarly opting to live alone yet seeking discrete sexual encounters and short-term relations to satisfy affiliation interests and sexual
desire. These strong-armed adaptions that slowly became part of aging gay
men's habitus may be changing. The expanding official recognition of same-
sex partnerships and marriages may provide a never-before context for more
aging homosexual men to consider long-term and, perhaps, monogamous
relationships; as well, the explosive rise of internet resources seems to have
increased the likelihood of aging gay men finding and living with a romantic
partner outside of their local microcommunities (cf. Rosenfeld and Thomas
2012). Unfortunately, the partnering intentions and beliefs about monogamy
among the different generations of aging men having sex with men have
been thinly researched.

Any discussion of the sexual and intimacy interests of late midlife and
later life gay men needs to acknowledge the distinct trajectories among the
men's sexual histories. Aging gay men typically embody one of three different relationship histories: those who have been and remain in long-term
relationships with other men, those who were formerly in a heterosexual
marriage and came out in midlife, or those who for the most part have

remained unpartnered (Fredriksen-Goldsen, Bryan et al. 2017). The men in the latter two categories more regularly seek out sexual relations with other gay men than the men in the first category. The men in all three groups also seek out social camaraderie or companionship and the social capital that involvement in their gay communities offers.

The cumulative disadvantages of being a sexual minority, managing the stresses of stigmatized sexual lives, and remaining actively engaged in the "sexual marketplace" make for a number of inequalities for aging gay men compared to aging heterosexuals in affluent countries: as a group (i) being disproportionally at risk for HIV infections via the transmission route of having sex with men (Emlet et al. 2017); (ii) embodying a cultural habitus which guides "thoughts, tastes, and practices" that pivot more on recreational and instrumental sex, not relational sex (Suen 2015; Umberson et al. 2015); and (iii) trying to armor up against the ageism within gay communities that can diminish the self-esteem of old men as aesthetically unappealing (Suen 2017) and position these men as "trolls" (Bergling 2004; Ramello 2013). Studying what encouraged single British gay men over age 50 to date, Suen (2015, 146–47) noted that some of the men felt a lack of emotional fulfillment and "thought they were missing out on the aspects of relationships, which involve openness, the sharing of thoughts and the expression of feelings. Cuddling, sharing and watching television together could all sound very trivial—but these activities were exactly what many of the participants said that they missed." The men thought that sexual desires were relatively easier to satisfy, but intimacy needs were more difficult. One unpartnered participant who dated, Henry, quested:

> having the warmth of a fellow human being beside you, and waking up in the middle of the night, and just cuddling in. I mean, you can masturbate if you want a climax. You can masturbate; it's not a big deal. It's the intimacy and the warmth that's what I really miss. I mustn't sound like a grumpy old man. (Suen 2015, 147)

SUMMARY

Most old couples engage in sexual relations for relational and recreational interests, and it is the relational aspect of their sexuality—their regular, at times discreet, butt touching, evening snuggling while watching a Netflix film—that disrupts ageist stereotypes of a falloff in sexual desire or activity. Indeed, as much as it is through the body that we all experience sexual pleasure and activity, when the interpretative lens focuses narrowly on aging and frequency of intercourse, this tunnel vision inhibits our ability to see the intimacy practices of old couples.

Many gerontology-related research articles on aging men's sexual lives have commonly "asserted" (Scherrer 2009) that sexuality is important to the old men. Many intend to contest ageist stereotypes about later life sexuality. This chapter too "asserted" that old men are sexual beings, and I tried to outshout the hegemony of ageist stereotypes that protect never-aging masculinities. Perhaps in another twenty years, the lingering negative narratives about sexuality and aging will have withered and research presentations and media stories will attend to the nuances, not the ahhh-struck fact that sexuality and intimacy are integral to later life and long lives.

Commonly argued by critical gerontology and men's studies researchers, and here too, is how any mention of aging men's lesser sexual activity compared to their earlier years keeps afloat the narrative about the "natural" waning of sexuality with age. My point concerns the joined-at-the-hip problem of stereotyping and generalizing. As detailed in the chapter, large national surveys of age variations in sexuality describe patterns—for instance, *on average*, men in couple relationships who are age 75 and older self-report less frequent sexual activity than earlier in their biographies or compared to younger groups of aging adults. Such life span and cohort differences in estimates of sexual activity, factual as they are, inevitably tend to homogenize two ways. First, portraits of very old men's sexuality can merge the men within couple relationships with widowers and other men without a partner, which can tally 20 percent or more of the men aged 65 and older and sharply deflate "on average" estimates of sexual activity. Second, equally hidden is the diversity among old men in their able-bodiedness or generational openness to noncoital sexual expression. Once homogenized, the actual range of sexual lifestyles among old couples is made incomprehensible. Sorely needed are more qualitative studies that retain the narratives of the men and their partners and address much more of the spectrum of preferred sexual practices old couples engage in.

Across many national studies both male and female respondents cite men's physical health as a reason for *their* lesser sexual activity and, at times, poorer marital satisfaction (cf. Karraker et al. 2011; Palacios-Ceña et al. 2012). Restated, the progressive downward slope of involvement in some types of sexual activity as couples move through later life is underscored and presented as men's "natural aging" and the liabilities to old couples' quality of life as a result of old men's physical health conditions and/or medication use. By myopically emphasizing his declining sexual function, for whatever reason, little heed is paid to how old couples (re)negotiate their sexed lives, much as they (re)negotiated their sexuality at earlier phases of their common lives. Focusing on his body is in sync with the medical or male gaze, yet by doing so the intersectionality of what determines old men's lived experiences with their sexual partners is unseen. For example, unanswered is whether old couples' preference for intimacy and intimacy practices (cf. Sandberg 2013b,

2016) trumped some old men's, and sometimes their wives', mourning narratives of his flaccid erections.

Chapter Ten

Caring

Whatever the reason . . . [some] parents have to wait longer for their first grandchild—perhaps to age 70 instead of age 60. They have to worry about whether they will be healthy enough to help out and enjoy the time they have with their grandchildren. Or if they'll be alive at all.

—Tergesen (2014)

Spouses . . . had to learn what the other person needed, in relation to gender; what women "need" for instance, to be *women*. To the extent that spouses did this—and there was variation—they had to also learn to think in terms of a different gender identity.

—Calasanti and Bowen (2006, 261)

Not regularly mentioned is the dynamic transformation of most aging men's *identity* toward more exclusively relational selves as they push back on canons of never-aging masculinities and progressively embody the masculinities associated with two forms of caring—grandfathering as well as within marriage while providing greater care for their partner's spoken and unspoken needs. The gradual changeover in men's identities initially occurs while still striving to maintain the never-aging masculine subjectivities enforced in the workplace. Then a faster makeover of identities takes place in later life within families. For the majority of men in later life, their social world becomes more and more family-centric—centered on the principal couple relationship and extending out to the intergenerational connections of grandfathering.

This chapter on old men's "caring" emphasizes both caring about and caring for. I limit the chapter to typically heterosexual men's experiences as grandfathers and their experiences caring for their partner's needs. Mostly, men's grandfather careers begin in late midlife while the men's lives remain employment-centric, and their social worlds as grandfathers remain poorly sketched by the research community (cf. Buchanan and Rotkirch 2016; Bullock 2005; Leeson 2016). No longer unnoticed are the aging men who gradually become primary carers of wives (or partners) suffering with the unpredictable illness trajectories of a chronic disease. This caring is no more than ratcheting up the ordinary care work men do, even if their lives had previously exemplified the separate-spheres view of "his" limited responsibilities within the home. I direct attention to how aging men care within an intimate dyad and thus his care is a negotiated extension of the "we"; for example, a husband and wife *jointly* labor to meet her limitations and take on her suffering. As will be reported near the end of the chapter, fewer gay men become their partner's carer because there are fewer partnered relationships among old gay men, yet we also know that there are *minimal* differences in aging gay men's care work when the comparison is old heterosexual men.

THE LONG (LONG) WAIT TO BECOME A GRANDFATHER[1]

As noted above, most men's transition through midlife into later life occurs concurrently with the transformations within their families' lives—the "empty nest," grandparenthood, both partners' retirement, and perhaps later life recoupling. Whatever the reason, these life transitions seem to be occurring later in men's lives. Launched children return home in some cases, deferring the actual onset of the empty nest. Grandfatherhood depends on adult children beginning their families, and demographic profiles show, on average, women having their first child later in their lives than prior generations. Thus the age of becoming a grandfather has risen some, to men's early 60s.

The vast majority of men are likely to experience being a grandfather, and many can expect to be grandfathers for decades before and after their retirement years. Yet we know too little about old men's experiences as grandfathers. Just as old men were once invisible in the academic literature, Buchanan and Rotkirch (2016) contend grandfathers remain so. Grandfathers' experiences routinely have been eclipsed by the research attention to grandmothers (cf. Mann 2007), whose opportunities to be more engaged with their grandchildren is expected. When grandparenting begins the identities of most men remain connected to the workplace. As well, there is the legacy of cultural norms defining grandmothers as the prime kin-keepers. Research evidence shows grandmothers were once more "present" in grandchildren's lives, and grandfathers were normally perceived as the "accompanying" grandparent (Leeson 2016) or a supportive associate to grandmothers. Even so, it is problematic for researchers to continue to ignore the experiences of

---

1. This is a riff on the title of a *Wall Street Journal* article by Anne Tergesen, March 30, 2014.

aging grandfathers or summarily exclude grandfathers in research (Reitzes and Mutran 2004a).

IT ISN'T THAT INDIVIDUAL

There is wide diversity in grandfathering across individuals, communities, and ethnic groups, as well as across historical time. Rephrasing this, old men's opportunities and experiences as grandfathers differ in terms of their ethnic and class habitus, embodied masculinities, and marital histories. Acknowledgment of these contextual differences is a crucial starting point to understanding that in Global North societies old men's intergenerational relationships are complex, negotiated, and often only vaguely understood. Take the example of long-term married old men compared to the old men who experience marital dissolution and repartnering. Uhlenberg and Hammill (1998) found that, for both grandmothers and grandfathers, the influence of marital status on contacts with grandchildren went as follows: married grandparents had most frequent contact with grandchildren, followed by widowed grandparents. Remarried ranked third with even less contact, and divorced grandparents who had not recoupled had the least contact.

Most married men have positive histories with their adult children and likely encounter fewer gatekeeping barriers to becoming involved with their grandchildren. By comparison, divorced and repartnered old men are quite likely to have more reserved relations with their adult children (cf. Davidson, Daly, and Arber 2003). Studies indeed show that divorced older men have less contact with their adult children than do married men, and adult children's trust in their fathers may diminish as a result of parental divorce. Repartnered men also become a member in their partner's families and can become stepfathers and step-grandfathers in addition to being biological fathers and grandfathers. In these blended families, the men may be replacement grandfathers for some step-grandchildren or marginalized by some step-grandchildren. In general, divorced and repartnered old men have to continuously renegotiate family boundaries, and their children and grandchildren as well as their partner's children and grandchildren often control this renegotiation.

We must recognize that face-to-face interaction between the grandchild seen most often and a grandfather is at best about once a month, unless the grandfathers are doing regular care work or live with the grandchildren. The frequency of contact diminishes for a number of reasons: the farther away the grandfather lives, when he is no longer married, when he recouples, and in cases where the age gap between the generations is wide (Uhlenberg and Hammill 1998). Ken, one man in Roberto, Allen, and Blieszner's (2001, 417) study, sums up this situation well:

> My relationship with the grandchildren gradually took up less and less of my
> time even though I was retired by then. [Soon, they] began having their own
> friends and doing their own thing . . . We spent more time with them, going
> places together and that sort of thing. But as they got older, particularly since
> [wife] died, for some reason, maybe because I am going with somebody . . .

Ken's diminishing experiences with being a grandfather is more typical than
not, particularly when men are widowed and then repartnering.

There are exceptions: Roberto and her colleagues (2001, 419) report how
Quent, a long-haul truck driver, spent little time with his family and ended up
divorced and marginalized from his children; however, when he gave up the
trucker lifestyle and remarried, he had an opportunity to become a step-
grandfather and took pride in being called "Grandpa." In Tarrant's (2010,
193) study of grandfathers one of the men, Peter (age 65), commented:

> [A]s they're getting bigger it is quite difficult but, when I go and see them
> they'll run across the room, the road, the drive or whatever, leap up in the air,
> arms round my neck and sort of swing on me erm, which at the ages of . . . oh I
> don't know, 4 and 1 or something was quite fun, but erm, now I feel as though
> my neck's about to be broken.

These two exceptions are illustrative of Reitzes and Mutran's (2004a, 2004b)
finding: men with positive identities as grandfathers and who attribute greater centrality to being as grandparent are motivated to succeed. Such men
cultivate masculinities that include grandfathering and strive to maintain
high-quality relations with their grandchildren. However, by spotlighting two
cases of men who embody being a grandfather, I cast into the shadows the
men who have quite distant or negative grandchild-grandfather relations,
which might originate from the men's histories of strained relations with
their children or a wide generation gap between the men and grandchildren.

GRANDFATHERS AND "SOFT" MASCULINITIES

Recent studies suggests grandfathers are "coming out of the shadows," defining and developing relationships with their grandchildren independently of
grandmothers (Mann 2007; Mann and Leeson 2010). Based on a study of
grandfathers in the Netherlands, Leeson (2016, 76) summarizes, "the large
majority of the interviewed grandfathers—where conditions allow it—have
an independent relationship with their grandchildren, *as well as* a relationship together with the grandmothers" (my italics). Grandfathers often initially underestimated how attached they would be to their grandchildren. Many
of their narratives have backward-looking musing where they had not spent
enough quality time with their own children because of their work/career

commitments, and now as older men they aim make up for this with (step)grandchildren (Leeson 2016, 74).

Grandfathering can strengthen aging men's well-being by privileging emotional relationships (Carstensen 1992, 2006). It can be a humbling awakening to old and new masculinities, as Alex notes:

> I was brought up in the years, like a lot of older men, where you didn't show affection, you didn't show hurt, you didn't show pain, you didn't show anything: you were the stalwart of the family and such. And I think the grandchildren seem to undermine all that and bring you down to your knees, and then realize that you're just a human person after all, and you're no different to the next bloke, and all the things you were shown were necessarily that time in my . . . upbringing, was wrong. (StGeorge and Fletcher 2014, 366)

But an aging man's quest to find a later life purpose as a grandfather is not dependent on his motivation alone. As mentioned before, the interaction an old man has with grandchildren is principally governed by the "relational bridge" between the men and their (step)children (Luescher and Pillemer 1998; Mueller and Elder 2003). Ambiguous or conflicted relations with adult (step)children will thwart old men's chances to even offer economic transfers, especially when adult children are among the economically advantaged. Low-resource families who need support and care appear more welcoming of a grandfather's involvement and assistance, and old men are rising to the invitation (e.g., Roberto, Allen, and Blieszner 2001).

Should an old man follow in the footsteps of his own grandfathers and postpone active involvement with his (step)grandchildren until his retirement, as many aging men once did, his deferred relations will likely continue the practices of gift-giving and occasional "doing things together" excursions.

> I also have my own special thing with each of them. When they turn 8, just the two of us take a couple of days to go on a cycling trip to a nearby city, eat a good dinner, stay at a hotel and cycle home the next day. They have all looked forward to that cycling trip with granddad. I have only got the youngest one left now. (Hans, age 66, in Leeson 2016, 79)

How grandfathers interpret such excursion experiences is uncharted. For instance, do old men perceive exchanges and excursions with their (step)grandchildren as close (enough)? This type of exchange-excursion relationship may well dry up. By the time grandchildren enter adolescence, most grandfathers are in their late 60s or 70s or even older. Grandchildren begin investing themselves in peer networks, and past evidence suggests that when this happens aging men typically transition toward less personal relationships with older grandchildren. Strom and Strom (2015) note that the methods of communication preferred by preteens and adolescents, such as texting, tweet-ing, and sending pictures, might result in more age-segregated interaction than intergenerational. When older grandchildren "talk" with grandparents, mundane information is often exchanged (Harwood 2000). A grandfather may wish to "be there," but he knows the maxim is "do not interfere"; even when he has the opportunity to be regularly involved he knows, using Bour-dieu's metaphor, that the rules of the game are to go with grandchildren's ways of living and do not interfere by imposing his generational habitus.

Despite the age-gap barrier, recent evidence suggests that grandfather-grandchild excursions and opportunities to talk about history and biogra-phies, to leave a moral legacy (Lesperance 2010; Leeson 2016), can be formative for enduring, reciprocated relations. Waldrop and her colleagues (1999) comment that grandfathers often educate by disclosing life experi-ences. Studying grandchildren's perception of their relations with grand-fathers (and grandmothers) Mann, Khan, and Leeson (2013, 392) discovered that the normative tilt of children favoring grandmothers was evident among young grandchildren, but became less and less so, as older (aged 16+) grand-children, in particular grandsons, had greater contact with grandfathers than grandmothers: "Grandsons ages 12 years and over are, in fact, more likely to perceive maternal grandfathers as the grandparent they get on with best." Put differently, with grandfathers having more available time in their postem-ployment life and longer lifetimes to nourish relationships with older grand-children, prior studies may have unwittingly cut short our understanding of grandfathers' nurturing experiences, unforeseen delight, and generative ethic (StGeorge and Fletcher 2014; Tarrant 2012).

Robin Mann (2007; Mann and Leeson 2010; Mann, Tarrant, and Leeson 2016) contends the importance of grandfatherhood for men has been substan-tially underestimated. Without explicitly saying so, he draws on a recent cohort effect and takes note of old men's elongated lives and the salience of aging masculinities "softening" the practice of masculinity in later life, com-pared to men's earlier practice of "nonrelational" masculinities. He first the-orized that "grandfatherhood represents an 'alternative masculinity' based on emotion-feeling and nurturing" (Mann 2007, 289). But more recently Mann and colleagues (2016, 605; Tarrant 2012) argue for an understanding of grandfathers "premised not upon an alternative masculinity . . . but rather on a softening of the discourse and practice of masculinity and which is carried out in a more negotiated and reflexive way." This "softening" is what Bates (2009) called "generative grandfathering."

CUSTODIAL GRANDFATHERING

There is also the phenomenon of a sizeable number of aging men in the US and throughout Europe who provide care to their grandchildren. Using the Health and Retirement Study data from the US, Hughes and her colleagues (2007) reported that nearly 30 percent of grandmothers and 22 percent of grandfathers provide some regular care to their grandchildren. Hank and Buber (2009) drew on the Survey of Health, Ageing, and Retirement in Europe (SHARE), which surveyed grandparents in Austria, Belgium, Denmark, France, Greece, Germany, Italy, the Netherlands, Sweden, Switzerland, and Spain, to discover 51 percent of grandfathers provided some kind of care for a grandchild aged 15 or younger during the prior twelve months, and their involvement was greater when no longer working and not living alone. The prevalence of grandfathers "caring for" reflects old men's extended lifespan, their availability when retired, and a perceived need to support adult children; there also are the more extreme cases when grandfathers "rescue" at-risk grandchildren. Grandfathers' closeness to, support of, and care of (step)grandchildren vary as a result of race and kinship: maternal grandfathers, for example, typically are more involved than paternal grandfathers and white grandfathers are typically older than men of color (Keene, Prokos, and Held 2012; Uhlenberg and Hammill 1998).

There is a long tradition of some grandchildren being raised by their grandfathers and grandmothers, especially in rural communities and among economically disadvantaged, nonwhite old men. Keene, Prokos, and Held (2012) drew on the American Community Survey to distinguish four types of grandfather-headed households involving dependent grandchildren: married grandfathers co-residing with the middle generation (mean age 56); married grandfathers living in homes in which the skip generation was absent (mean age 60); and two smaller groups of unmarried grandfathers either co-residing with middle generation (mean age 57.2) or living in homes in which the skip generation was absent (mean age 58.9).

Many grandfathers might feel ambivalent about becoming custodial care providers but obligated. Bullock (2005) noted that their sample of old African American, Latino, and white rural grandfathers felt responsible for a grandchild, yet they were concerned about their long-term ability to care for that child. They have reason to be: all reported they felt vulnerable as a result of their grandchild's persistent belittling, complete disregard, and put-downs. Though distressed, these custodial grandfathers did not appear to recognize their grandchild's behaviors as exploitive or harmful. Relationships matter. So does age. When solo grandfathers (more than half older than age 65) were compared to single fathers (fewer than 7 percent 65 and older), Whitley and Fuller-Thomson (2017) report that both groups of men had poorer health profiles than population norms. However, after controlling for the differences in the men's age, race, income, and education level, solo custodial grand-fathers had substantially higher odds of functional limitations and more often rated their health as fair or poor. It appears that when grandfathering be-comes full-time parenting, adverse effects on old men's health likely follow.

Di Gessa, Glaser, and Tinker (2016) similarly controlled for the cumula-tive (dis)advantages of grandfathers' social and economic capital and health with data from three waves of the Survey of Health, Ageing, and Retirement in Europe. They examined whether intensively looking after grandchildren had any long-term physical health effect on the grandfathers; it did not di-minish or undercut grandfathers' health. Given these contrasting results, understanding the consequences of looking after grandchildren for health of grandfathers is a critical issue and ought to no longer be discounted.

THE SENSE OF TOGETHERNESS

Feminist theorists and researchers once made a distinction between "caring for" and "caring about" when it comes to the care work that exceeds the bounds of what is normative or usual in couple and family relationships (cf. Graham 1983; Ungerson 1983). This discursive distinguished "for" from "about" by separating the practical, instrumental labor of care work from the affective, emotional aspect *underpinning* most care work provided by inti-mates and families. It rests on an asymmetrical carer/cared for dichotomy, and it very often exercised a discourse about "his" and "her" separate spheres and competencies, which overgeneralizes (at times essentializes) women's capability for "caring about" and men's deficit capability of either "caring for" or "caring about." This discourse on gendered styles of care casts men carers as if they were visiting (male) nurses whose caring orientation leaned toward an *unfeeling* "managerial approach" and who never crossed over the usual separate-spheres' gender boundaries to give care.

In fact, a baseline for old men doing care work is their couple relationship and their relational self. Caring for is an extension of caring about. Spousal/partner caring is an extension of shared time and a shared life course that is integrated into his habitus. It includes mutual support. However, the legacy of thinking in terms of a separate-spheres ideology is that researchers too often argue that men would be deficit in caring capabilities. Perhaps so, at the onset of doing care work (cf. Calasanti and Bowen 2006). Men talking about their caring may not have conveyed an emotion work narrative. What re-searchers often heard were men positioning themselves as performing mas-culinity and maintaining the integrity of their "manly" self. Not heard were the aging men's experience of greater closeness and intimacy with their wife/partner, even when caring for was problematic, time-consuming, and emotionally difficult. This relational work triggered an unexpected expansion of the men's emotional framework.

A recent conceptual turn shifted investigations of care work from unidirectional—as what one person does for the other and how/how much the care work is accomplished—to a starting premise that spousal/partner care occurs within the dyad. It becomes much easier to grasp that aging men routinely do care work for their partners *and* are cared for by their partners as an ordinary aspect of being a couple. In calling for a rethink of care as a relationship-based activity and not as individual (gendered) performance, a dyadic perspective takes for granted the fact that husbands and wives (or long-term gay partners, LAT partners, cohabiting partners) have developed a shared couple habitus, and will consider the onset of a chronic ill-health condition a "we-disease" rather than "his" or "hers" (cf. Kayser, Watson, and Andrade 2007). As Richard Russell (2008, 64) noted, "When chronic illness presents itself, it often becomes the center of existence—for both caregiver and care recipient." A researcher adopting a "we-problem" view will predictably observe that when one member of a couple is ailing, the couple engages in a collaborative effort to manage that condition and its invasiveness into their lives (e.g., Seymour-Smith and Wetherell 2006). The literature also attests that jointly managing an illness has a noticeable positive impact on the couple's sense of togetherness. Jointly managing an illness most often elevates both partners' sense of well-being, despite the trying times.

In sum, the early literature on spousal/partner care work tended to look past two matters: First, aging couples often have aged together and have experienced mutual caring for years; whether the length of the couple's relationship is long-term or relatively recent, assisting one another with routine care (instrumental activities of daily living [IADLs]) and, at times, personal care (activities of daily living [ADLs]) can become ordinary, not extraordinary. Second, caring is a dynamic process beginning with the invisible, everyday types of caring by "being there" and "keeping tabs" on a partner's well-being (Torgé 2014).

THE GO-TO CARERS

Spouses/partners are the first to provide care at the onset of need within couple relationships. Considering that aging men gradually take up what becomes care work, the starting point is that the biography of caring for (even in low-quality relationships) is routinized and perceptually absent until a serious health limitation makes the new, extraordinary care work present. The couple's taken-for-granted habitus will be amended. They renegotiate habits and preferences as one spouse silently shifts the teeter-totter to provide more care and the other spouse begins to live with the troubling personal effects of a cancer or movement disorder or cognitive decline. Managing "their-illness" is a collaborative process and will remain so, perhaps well after the time a cognitively ill partner becomes no longer able to communicate—"She is not able to tell me if she has pain or discomfort, if she is hungry or thirsty" (J. Murray et al. 1999, 664). The tandem transitions of aging men becoming carers as their partners confront the intrusiveness of their declining health can thoroughly challenge the relational dynamics the couple has taken for granted—he is now regularly cooking and much of his cooking may be awful at first, and their conversations must at times include her and his worries, her likes and dislikes about his care work. At the onset he might lack certain caring for skills due to their generationally supported division of labor, but their joint management of her health needs redefines "normality."

Aging men's caring for is slowly becoming recognized as it is—an evolving arrangement that couples negotiate through his trial-and-error learning curve. The trial and error can be readily noticed as old husbands retell their early experiences with caring for. Take, for example, the very old, Catholic Portuguese husbands that Ribeiro (2009) interviewed between 2003 and 2006. The great majority of the husbands reached adulthood in the 1930s and early 1940s, where gendered marital scripts made household labor virtually alien to men; the old husbands had lived the "should" of the separate-spheres marital ideals. Their wives' failing health thrust them into basic responsibilities they lacked experience with, especially food preparation. The "musts" of their late life situation necessitated doing the practical, everyday labor involved in caring for, and they learned how. Moreover, these "men did not simply engage in caring responsibilities in relation to a spouse; they engaged in the whole caring relationship as a way of benefitting the marriage itself" (Ribeiro 2009, 112). Similarly, in a study of married and cohabitating aging couples managing one partner's colorectal cancer, Emslie and her colleagues (2009, 1171) comment on how difficult it was to separate "caring for" from "caring about," and they cite a wife's comment:

> I realised then . . . what love is all about. He just accepted everything[,] looked after me, did everything, did the cooking; he bolstered me up. He put up with the accidents I was having (with the colostomy), he helped me clean up, took my nighty off and did all those sort of things that really I would never have expected him to do. And . . . seeing that coming out in him helped me more . . . than any support from anybody else.

Transitioning into a carer for his ailing partner has become a more common experience for late middle-aged and old men in many Global North countries, and spousal/partner caring in later life is projected to be more prevalent and significant in the coming decades. Researchers have been documenting the rising slope of aging men taking responsibility for caring for their partners, largely a result of men's longevity and women's greater morbidities in later life. One recent estimate for the US by the National Alliance for Caregiving (2015) noted the expected: half of spousal carers were the husbands (and nearly half of gay partners were the ones providing care within same-sex relationships). Even when formal care and welfare systems are readily available and able to provide different kinds of help, the old Swedish couples Torgé (2014) interviewed valued their mutual care as "freedom from" dependency on others. In the UK, more men are becoming carers than cared for (Office of National Statistics 2016).

An aggregate profile of aging men doing care work strongly suggests that within their couple relationships the men report little distress with their responsibility for care work, derive reward if not a sense of honor/privilege from their caring, are motivated by the implied marital bargain to care and their deep feelings of love and responsibility, and hardly ever define themselves as "carers." Take, for example, the study (Cahill 2000) of Australian aging husband carers of wives with Alzheimer's disease (AD). The men's stated reasons for caring centered on their love, what marriage meant, and a sense of duty. One man caring for his wife commented, "She's my wife and partner, we've done everything together for 41 years, you take your vows. We've been a team. You just don't stop it now for better or for worse" (ibid., 61).

Ribeiro, Paúl, and Nogueira's (2007) study, mentioned above, on the very old Portuguese men that Ribeiro interviewed notes how few of the men identified with the label "carer." All but two (of fifty-three) identified themselves only as husbands, not carers. Providing care for their wives was viewed as a fundamental facet of their marital relationship, as a moral imperative of being a couple, and as an honor to finally be her carer. When these aging men reflected, what was mentioned most prominently was their sense of commitment to their enduring and affectionate marital relationship (Ribeiro and Paúl 2008, 178). One participant (Álvaro) who had been married for fifty-one years commented, "It doesn't matter if you're a man or a woman, what really matters is that there's a soul that helps the other . . . She's my wife" (Ribeiro, Paúl, and Nogueira 2007, 306). The principal motivators for these husbands were relational and the personal satisfaction of caring for (Ribeiro and Paúl 2008).

Also consistent with what many researchers have heard, the very old Portuguese men's discourse on their care work accented masculine ideals such as how "it takes guts" to care for, or how they discursively positioned themselves as "in control" of a demanding, unfamiliar situation. Old Swedish husbands analogously talked about how they prioritized the "protection" of their partners (Eriksson, Sandberg, and Pringle 2008). The old men aimed to "defoliate" their social commitments and social relations outside the marriage, but this inevitably left the men facing loneliness, an obligation to "do it all," at times regretting the defoliating decision, and the hindsight wisdom to reconnect with others, in particular other old men also caring for their wives.

In their assessment of how aging married men reflect upon themselves during the process of providing for an ill wife, elsewhere Eriksson and Sandberg (2008) commented that most of the men undergo marked identity reconstruction. The nature and context of marital interaction evolved from being an everyday husband, to being a caring husband, to finally being a visiting partner and spectator with her move into a nursing home. In each context, men attempted to regain control of *their* lives—their self-identity and marriage-identity (cf. Russell 2007), and throughout the process the men recognized they had embodied their unconventional practices and had let go of the guidance of "traditional" masculinities. What became hegemonic was their caring.

VARIATIONS IN CARE WORK

Most often the aging man's transition into care work is as gradual as his wife's trajectory of declining health, assuming her ill-health status was not the brute onset of something like a disabling stroke. His care work perhaps begins with unremarkably emptying the dishwasher, vacuuming, cooking/barbequing more regularly, and showering last in order to clean up the bath. Care work can be as narrow as Gil's, a husband who had limited income and no cooking experience, so he fed his wife refrigerated biscuits for breakfast and fast food for dinner (Calasanti and Bowen 2006); nevertheless, he cared for her.

Perhaps a husband's care work expands to include buttoning her blouse or pants since her arthritic hands make these tasks difficult. Perhaps it extends to washing and coloring her hair or painting her toenails. The more intimate tasks of body care work oblige the couple to be closely together. Throughout, the man and his partner likely talk with one another, and more often than not their conversations will be less about his improving skill at doing her toenails and more about the week's agenda or a newspaper story. The body care work he does also becomes ordinary.

Caring for is an extension of caring about. Daughters and skilled nurses and men all accomplish the tasks of caring for differently. Men typically perceive the "instrumental" care work to be an ordinary part of couple life, simply as what a partner is called to do again and again. Adding the responsibilities of body care work is qualitatively different than what their fathers might have faced a generation ago, when only sisters, daughters, or skilled nurses performed wives' body work.

The experience of Glenn Kirkland is a profound example. Glenn became the carer for his wife, Grace, who faced the perplexing, troubling, restricting ways that Alzheimer's disease ravaged her mind and their relationship. Glenn, a physicist from the Second World War generation, spent nearly forty years at the Johns Hopkins University Applied Physics Laboratory before he made a purposeful decision to retire "early" in order to take up the responsibilities of being Grace's carer. At the time (late 1970s), he was alone—there was limited information on AD in the public domain and no support groups for AD carers, especially men carers. Mimicking his generational gender practices embodied while a scientist and nighttime ham-radio enthusiast, he very methodically developed memory puzzles to assist Grace, urged her to sing the songs embedded in her long-term memory, narrated for her the landscape during their evening walks, and normalized her potholed contribution to the ordinary tasks of preparing a daily meal. Controlling, perhaps. But more likely Glenn enacted the gender practices he best knew, and he took up the needed care work both as a devoted husband and in the absence of an alternative. Later, he invited a film company to document his wife's Alzheimer's experience over a period of seven years for others to better understand the disease.

The film *Grace* is actually as much about Glenn, the quiet, inspirational very typical/atypical masculine pillar supporting his wife. The film is a candid rendering of Glenn's caring and Grace's downward spiraling. It opens with Grace's dissociative yelling when frustrated, waving a large kitchen knife, and Glenn's soothing, instructional voice from nearby in the kitchen to encourage Grace to continue with her task of cutting vegetables for the evening dinner. "I can do this," she screams. When it is time for dessert Grace asks, "Did we have dinner?" The couple journeyed through the downhill trajectory of Grace's AD *as a couple*. For Glenn, Grace's AD was a "we-disease," which likely makes him atypical of aging men carers of his generation. Every time I showed *Grace* in an undergraduate course, more and more students had a prior understanding of AD, but few anticipated a husband carer—his musing, initially practical then spiritual questing, and his unrelenting commitment as a husband, caregiver or not. Glenn was a regular participant in a church congregation and faithful. He embodied the Silent Generation ethos where men did not divulge their feelings. But this man leaked those feelings, whether it was through his intimate moments with Grace, or during his respite time with his ham radio, or his seeking solace from his belief system. Stereotypes of old men of his generation cast a "John Wayne" muted stoicism; the documentary film cast a caring husband, one who never embarked on the musing of "why me."

The film reminds me of my step-dad's care work for my mother as she vacillated with her declining cognitive capabilities and memory. Similar to Glenn, Hank kept their couple relationship primary (caring about), yet unlike Glenn he sought out others for much of the work of caring for. He was from the Second World War generation—resilient, a conversational minimalist especially when on the telephone, a retired civil engineer, an avid morning golfer who would then go into the bar for lunch and drinks with the other old men, where my mother would join him for lunch and then play bridge with "the girls." As my mother's capabilities faded, she had trouble with the ordinary tasks of distinguishing a quarter *tea*spoon from a heaping *table*-spoon of cayenne pepper; turning on the oven, not broiler, to reheat a donated casserole; and dealing cards clockwise, not counterclockwise. Hank almost nightly escorted my mother out to a restaurant. He rolled with and masked her cognitive deterioration—always mentioning the names of their friends in order for my mother to recall who she was talking with; preparing a daily breakfast and occasionally grilling; paying for the laundering; driving her to a hairdresser and employing a housekeeper occasionally; sometimes shower-ing with her in order to wash her hair; and helping her dress, even when they sometimes had difficulty with him doing this. His caring was analogous to Glenn's; and his musing was starkly revealed in his rare stories about pro-tecting her feelings and safety, hardly ever disclosing his own frets and distress. Unlike Glenn, his "spiritual" resource was golf and the support group of old men being together. As another caring husband notes, "Respite from caregiving responsibilities is essential" (Russell 2008, 66).

The examples of Glenn and Hank are not intended to portray men care-givers in general. They do not represent, for example, many working-class men whose class and immigrant background cultivated very different views on men's marital responsibilities. Still, they are very similar to the old Portu-guese men mentioned earlier—they progressively care for, though different-ly. Nor does my recounting of Glenn's and Hank's caring sufficiently pro-vide a sense of the mutual caring that partners differently embody. But they do illustrate the benefits the men derived from the couples' togetherness. Glenn mentions with tearing eyes how wonderful he feels when he and Grace share time together; Hank proudly went to dinner with his wife at his golf club, where *their* friends helped normalize my mother's neurological frailty and affirm her "independence." Christina Torgé (2014, 213) illustrated how this "freedom to be yourself" was continually made achievable by couples' mutual support throughout the caring for a partner with long-term disabil-ities:

> Husband: I know that there's a person there, who I'm very fond of, that I can be with in sunny and stormy weather, and we can live with each other—it's very important. I think, if I didn't have her, I would have just sat indoors reading my books or using my computer. That would have been my life, apart from my meetings in the disability organization where I can meet people.
>
> Interviewer: So are you outdoors more often, because you're together?
>
> Wife: We go to the theater, to meetings, whatever. Go out, have some afternoon tea out on the green. It's a good feeling to have someone. Yeah, if I didn't have him, I would probably still be a bitch and would think that I have

to fight through things by myself all the time. I wouldn't have this person who gives me a feeling of peace.

DOES TYPE OF RELATIONSHIP MATTER?

Remarried aging couples like Hank and my mother appear to not differ much in terms of their expectations and practices of care from couples in long-term first marriages (Glenn and Grace). In a qualitative study of aging heterosexuals in long-term relationships in the Netherlands, de Jong Gierveld (2015) examined individuals' *intent* to be a caring partner. When asked about providing care when need arose, one remarried man unconditionally replied, "It is obvious that you would do that" (ibid., 360). Remarried men in the study who were beginning to wrestle with their own health limitations were aware of the limits of their ability to care: a 72-year-old man commented, "but when it comes to intensive care, then it is another story. I don't know if I can manage to carry it off . . . I think I would have problems" (ibid.). Beyond intent, however, nearly half of the remarrieds had already experienced giving and/or receiving care, and they all mentioned mutual care as an indicator of their dedication to their partner.

Little research has examined aging men's mutual care work in couple relationships other than within marriage. Later life cohabitation is becoming common among old men who were formerly married, particularly widowers. The aging men who are cohabitating are, on the whole, less advantaged than their married counterparts, whether defined in economic terms, health, or social support (Moustgaard and Martikainen 2009; Vespa 2012). They report fewer nearby friends than either remarried or unpartnered old men. Their cohabitating partner is their principal source of support and care. In a Finnish study, Moustgaard and Martikainen (2009) reported the care provided by cohabitating partners does not seem to equal that provided by married spouses, resulting in much increased odds of separation when care work is necessary and even a bit greater probability of an old cohabitant's institutionalization. Noël-Miller (2011) similarly found that cohabitors with ADL impairment were less likely to receive partner care compared to married individuals. She advised (2011, 350) that this differential "is in agreement with cohabitors' lesser commitment to caregiving obligations inherent to the institution of marriage, with their lower interpersonal commitment and with prior scattered anecdotic evidence that cohabitation may be preferred by individuals seeking intimacy with limited caregiving responsibilities."

In de Jong Gierveld's (2015) study, she noted that just half the LAT partners expressed an *intention to care* parallel to the remarried; the other half of LAT participants were ambivalent about both providing care and receiving care from their partner. Aging women are more wary of new caring commitments. As Davidson (2002, 51) noticed in her study, more widows want "someone to go out with" rather than "someone to come home to." Given this observation, it is not surprising that for the aging Swedish men and women in LAT relationships that Karlsson and Borell (2002) surveyed, men more than women indicated they were prepared to take care of their partner part-time every day and could imagine taking care of their partners full-time if necessary. While this 2002 report was about men's future projections of providing care, Karlsson and her colleagues (2007) later reported that LAT partners in fact rated their partner as providing more support than any other network member, including relatives. Among those who had an LAT partner needing care, de Jong Gierveld (2015) reported that all had unconditionally provided the care. The bonds of the close relationship normalize caring for. The duration of LAT partnerships may facilitate couples deepening their commitment to care. The sparse evidence suggests that care-providing among LAT partners is not too different from spousal care *when* the partner's need is not taxing, and most partners do not perceive "caring for" as an obligation (Benson and Coleman 2016a).

Among old gay men, one estimate shows about one-fourth are partnered and living as cohabitants or marrieds (Fredriksen-Goldsen et al. 2011). Another estimate suggests the proportion of gay men aged 65 and older who are partnered and living as cohabitants or marrieds now approaches 50 percent (cf. Fredriksen-Goldsen, Bryan, et al. 2017). Whatever the exact figure, at least half of old gay men are not partnered and depend on care work from intimates and friends who do not share the household. Aging gay men's involvement in care work is based on best guesstimates, clouded by the fact that the vast majority of very old gay men live alone, and thus the mutual care that takes place within gay "families of choice" remains hidden.

The reality is (aging) gay men's partner relations and chosen families would crumble without mutual care. Shippy, Cantor, and Brennan (2004) surveyed LGBs aged 50 and over in New York; nearly one in four aging gay men had already provided care to a member of their "family of choice" and one in six aging gay men cared for someone in their "family of origin." Fredriksen-Goldsen and her colleagues (2011) reported a nearly identical estimate. They noted that two-thirds of the care the men provided was to their partner or friend rather than someone in their biological families.

SUMMARY

This chapter on caring, evident in old men's experiences with grandfathering and less prevalently with being spousal carers, was intended to draw attention to old men's later life's emphasis on relational selves and their everyday life as family-centric, no longer workplace-centric. More and more commonly discovered in the children's section of public libraries are books about grandfathers. This discovery would have been uncommon a generation ago, when many grandfathers remained in the workplace and less involved in the lives of their grandchildren. When grandfathers' narratives are listened to, researchers (cf. Reitzes and Mutran 2004b) have discovered a "softening" of their masculine subjectivities and the personal joys and lessons learned through their intergenerational experiences. The aging and old men who have the opportunity to remain involved in the lives of their adolescent and young adult grandchildren have likely further amended their habitus to more fully embody the "softness" of aging masculinities. They mentor through stories and pass along wisdom such as "Everyone has a story; take a moment to listen."

Yet we know so little about old men's experience as "granddads." We similarly know too little about old men's lives as spousal carers. What we do now know is that discourses about men "crossing a gender boundary" to "step up" to be carers largely individualizes care work, and this discourse undercuts a couple's taken-for-granted coupleness and ignores the ordinary couple work that husbands extend into significant caring for. The prior presumption was that care work is burdensome, rather than rewarding and intimate. We also know that whatever caring work he does, it arises from caring about and is surely negotiated with his partner's wants, even should their negotiation at times center on his wife's suicide desire to alleviate her horrible suffering. We do not know how humbled carer husbands and gay partners are by the intimacy and loneliness of their evolved relationships. It is time to redirect research questions from how burdened men might feel with their unfamiliar responsibilities, to how his caring for adds a path for their intimacy and his eventual loneliness, and perhaps grieving.

Chapter Eleven

Facing Later Life as an Old Widower

My wife June has been gone eight years now, and, uh, I'm at times caught off guard when I sense her nearby. The smell of cornbread muffins in the oven will do it. A long time ago I was able to make sense of her death . . . I, we, had enough time, ah, a little over three years, to prepare after she was diagnosed with her ovarian cancer. She wanted to be cremated, and we talked about everything our last year together. I think that really prepared me for her death, if you can really prepare for such a thing. Because we spent so much good time together the last years of her life, sharing everything, I was not at all prepared to be a widower. I was alone! Even though you grieve a bit before . . . waking up without her next to me was tough. And cooking for one, eating alone, finding ways to spend my time . . . it all took me some time, almost two years. I have a couple of friends who are also widowers. One seems to have plugged right along after his wife died, getting right back to his card games. I find that calling and texting my grandchildren, there are three of them, several times a week is much more enjoyable than I ever anticipated. They have made me enjoy using emojis. I have friends and neighbors who also live alone and we regularly get together for afternoon GT [gin and tonic] and rail on and on about the idiots in Washington.

—Will, age 79

It is important to recognize at the onset two things: first, the number of widowed old men within most Global North nations is increasing, but the proportion of unmarried old men who are widowed is decreasing because of the rising share of divorced men the same age; second, the duration of widowerhood in later life is decreasing because marriages are lasting longer (cf. Stepler 2016). That said, this chapter aims to provide a realistically thorough account of aging men's experiences as widowers, even though much of the available research examined the lives of earlier generations of widowers who began their lives as widowers at an earlier age than is now common. I draw a distinction between widowers' initial experiences with bereavement and their settling in to later life as widowers, which is deeply shaped by their embodied masculinities and masculinity practices. Unlike the stereotype about widowers rebounding into a new marriage, the common pattern is widowers' reluctance to repartner, especially to remarry. In national estimates, about one-quarter of widowers repartner, and these men are more often "younger." I end the chapter with a proposal that advocates our need to rethink old men's lives as widowers.

BECOMING WIDOWERS

Exploring the prevalence of widowers and widows in England and Wales, researchers noted that among men aged 70+ only 20 percent of the men had *ever* been widowed, compared to 50 percent of the women (Glaser et al. 2008). Estimates in the US similarly revealed that 23 percent of the men aged 70 and older had *ever* been widowed compared to 51 percent of women (Kreider and Ellis 2011, 13). In the US in 2014, 38 percent of the men 85 and older were *currently* widowed, whereas 10 percent of men aged 65–84 were *currently* widowed (Stepler 2016, 27).

Late life changes are always a challenge, perhaps especially for widowers. Of all life events, the death of a loved one has long been recognized as the most stressful (Holmes and Rahe 1967) and it can trigger a cascade of additional stress, including social isolation (Pearlin 1989). When the loved one who dies is the old man's life partner, his entire world is shaken and he feels emotionally fractured. He is literally and existentially alone after years, perhaps forty or fifty years, of being part of a "we." Many widowers will face a pervasive sense of anomie loneliness with the loss of daily rituals (e.g., nightly meals) and distress with the vexing reminders (e.g., birthdays, particular holidays, the missing person at the table). They repeatedly question, "Who am I now?" Per Howell (2013, 5): "When relationships are shattered, as in the death of a spouse, we lose a significant mirror in which our self was reflected and affirmed. I was a husband, but after Diane's death I was a husband no more. But what then was I now? Who was I now? A widower? What is that?"

The research on widowers' experiences has basically proposed that men see no rewards of being widowed compared to being married or compared to women's independence when widowed (e.g., Davidson 2001). Spending years with marital closeness predicts men's intensified grief and the emptiness of his life (Pruchno, Cartwright, and Wilson-Genderson 2009). As one man, Samuel, commented after the loss of his wife, "The evenings were very sad. And, you know, it was just like a bombshell, remembering Hannah, with the empty house" (van den Hoonaard 2009, 743).

There are, of course, some old men who do not intensely grieve when becoming a widower. Some may feel relief with the cessation of exhausting tasks of care work and will continue their later life as a healthier widower compared to men whose transition from marital life into widowerhood was not predated by the strain of care work (Schaan 2013). Accumulating evidence suggests that among the old men who were carers, their relief and resilience in the face of bereavement may be the norm. There are also some old men who lived many years in emotionally empty marriages, and for them becoming a widower can bring a sense of both relief and having new opportunities. "Keith" found widowerhood freeing: "It's a lonely life at times, but I'm enjoying my independence, too. You know, I can come and go as I please" (van den Hoonaard 2009, 745).

Widowers confront the need to care for themselves—attend to their diet, sleep regularly, and keep up with medications. Aging men who had been coupled for many years came to depend on their partner and the habitus of their "we" for meeting these essential needs. Following her death, or for gay men his death, widowers face the necessity of restructuring their lives, and many do, and without delay. There is a considerable body of scholarly work addressing widowers' intrapsychic processes during the early phases of bereavement. But this prior research emphasis on the psychological and emotional features of bereavement has resulted in a lack of sufficient attention to the old men's "restoration" (i.e., expanding self-efficacy, developing new competencies). For example, heterosexual men who had marriages similar to Will, where their wives were their primary source of emotional, social, and health-promoting support, are more likely to have bouts of depression and have initial difficulties administering their everyday lives as widowers, from grocery shopping, cooking, and eating healthily to sending out birthday cards. But the majority of old men soon recover and rebuild their lives; a minority don't (cf. Bonanno, Wortman, and Nesse 2004; McCrae and Costa 1988).

Before continuing, it is important to distinguish bereavement from widowerhood. People are likely to use the two constructs as if they are synonyms. However, spousal bereavement is the relatively shorter-term circumstance encompassing the posttraumatic distress and grieving that follows the death of one's spouse, perhaps lasting up to twenty-four months. Bereavement involves working through the difficult and painful feelings of losing both her and "we." It involves the absence of companionship and the reciprocity of doing the little things together; it obligates the old man to begin living his everyday life and doing all of the everyday activities of living by himself. By comparison, widowhood refers to the continuing experience of having lived through the death of a spouse and remaining unpartnered, perhaps for the remainder of one's life. Widowerhood is the "status" of having lost a wife, and it does not necessarily mean living alone. Given researchers' interests, we know more about men's bereavement because it has been studied much more than men's experiences as widowers, leaving widowerhood a not well-understood subject.

BEREAVEMENT

The research concentrating on old men's bereavement has leaned heavily on a psychological frame of reference, primarily investigating individual men's coping and grief experience. Little of this work sets out to assess whether heterosexual and gay old widowers grieve similarly, or if there are class and cultural variations in old men's grieving. What has been emphasized is widowers' relative degrees of mental and emotional anguish compared to widows, or to married men. Consequently, the terms "grief" and "bereavement" evoke images of sadness, despair, and loneliness. It is unquestionably true that bereavement can be a very difficult time in old men's life. Yet most widowers are able over time, as much as a year or two, to make sense of their loss, manage their oscillating feelings, "bounce back" and master new tasks, develop new friendships, even foster new companionship relations and positively redefine their sense of who they are following the death of their spouse (cf. K. Bennett 2010; Moore and Stratton 2002).

The early research often questioned whether men grieve differently than do women. The pattern of findings initially suggested widowers had less difficulty with spousal loss and bereavement than widows, and widowers were (much) less disadvantaged than widows in terms of the long-term consequences of being widowed (e.g., Lopata 1973). Studies frequently revealed that widowers had lower rates of depression than widows, even though this finding may speak to broader gender differences in mood in general as well as gendered patterns of disclosure.

By asking who is more (dis)advantaged, research frequently produced contradictory findings. A number of researchers have argued that bereavement is more stressful and encumbering for men than women, providing as evidence that men greatly suffered emotionally and physically (Stroebe, Stroebe, and Schut 2001), bottled up their grief in ways standard measurement scales fail to document (K. Bennett, Hughes, and Smith 2003), and had limited preparatory resources because living as a widower was an unexpected life event (Martin-Matthews 1991). These patterns may not be generalizable and limited to a cohort effect, documenting a particular generation's social lives and patriarchal marriages rather than what old men experience as widowers per se. These patterns also may be a methodological artifact: in any given sample of widowers it is likely that they are older and fewer in number than widows, and *more recently* bereaved. Their distress is ripe. Research evidence has consistently exposed widowers to be at greater risk of death

during the early months of bereavement, compared to their married counterparts or to widows; neither preexisting or continuing good health nor socioeconomic affluence seems to protect UK widowers from the risk of early
death (cf. Shah et al. 2012).

The basic conclusion is that bereavement may not the same for men vis-à-
vis women, but there is a great degree of similarity on most matters. One of
the many similarities between widowers and widows is that death forewarning is not a reliable predictor of grief responses (e.g., shock, depression,
anger, intrusive thoughts) in an older population, perhaps because death is
more normative among old men and women (Carr et al. 2001, S245). An
exception, however, is that for men, the forewarning of her approaching
death may increase his closeness to his spouse and his isolation from others
(ibid., S246). It is also very likely that old widowers who were carers minimized their time with friends and family as they increased their care work for
their dying spouse. While the reasons have not been accessed, Balaswamy,
Richardson, and Price (2004) did find that the social capital of widowers
noticeably deteriorated in the early phase of becoming widowers.

I am reminded of Eleanor Maccoby's (1974) influential argument regarding the early empirical studies repetitively showing statistically significant
sex differences on virtually everything, and her diagramming of two (normal) distribution curves of the empirical variable, one for the variance among
men and the other for women, to reveal that the two curves almost overlap
one another. Any observed difference is found only within the crescent
edges, where the two curves do not overlap. The large center area where the
curves are overlapping reveals there is much more similarly, even if there are
"reliable" differences between the statistical means in whatever was measured. By pointing out Maccoby's critique of researchers' emphasis on sex
differences, I am not proposing that we ignore gender or the inequalities
among widowers and widows. Indeed, we do need to question how gender
inequalities shape bereavement and widowerhood, and how differing masculinities shape bereavement and widowerhood. There are at times marked
differences between men's and women's lives before and after recovering
from bereavement and living as widowed, as well as among men from different faiths, classes, and other sources of habitus. These cross-gender differences are likely no longer as stark as they were a generation or two ago,
when nearly all aging couples maintained distinctive "his" and "her" marriages where he benefitted most, and after his death she faced hard times,
particularly financial or finding cross-sex companionship if she wanted it
(Lopata 1973, 1979). Less understood are the inequalities among old men
and how these affect the men's bereavement and life as widowers; consider,
for instance, the likely differences between aging men whose habitus and
masculinity practices in later life involved developing strong ties with their
(step)children and (step)grandchildren compared to the old widowers who

held tightly to the scripts of never-aging masculinities that emphasized kin work wasn't men's work.

Knowing that widowers and widows sometimes similarly and differently grieve through a range of emotional responses, differentially exhibiting intense feelings of numbness, crying, restlessness, impatience, frustration, sleep deprivation, and wanting to give up, as well as increases in drinking and decreases in appetite, I suspect that there is as much, if not more, variability among widowers in terms of their age and health, relationship with children, lifestyle habitus, and social and economic capital. Some features of widowerhood are contextually unique and warrant attention to understand (different) men's experience. One example is the many similarities among widowers in the import of "traditional" masculinity ideologies on their grief practices (e.g., K. Bennett 2007); however, when we consider the diversity among old men's continued embodiment of never-aging masculinities, we can expect different masculine subjectivities to structure becoming and being a widower.

GAY WIDOWERS

Investigating widowed gay men, Piatczanyn, Bennett, and Soulsby (2016) noted that most of the research on gay widowers has been restricted to HIV/AIDS death. This research team studied twenty British widowers whose partner died from a broader range of causes of death. They found that gay widowers face two competing identity challenges. The widowers felt they were expected to grieve in a socially acceptable manner, while at the same time conform to principles of hegemonic masculinities. Restating this, as widowers they felt they were expected to grieve, but as men they were expected to mask the extent of their grief to be consonant with normative stoical masculinity performances. One of the widowers commented,

> Men don't find it very easy to deal with grief, to burst into tears. On one occasion I remember someone who is a neighbour of mine up the road. I was out just put my car away, and he said "Donald, how are you?" and I said "well you may not know but Raphael died a week ago!" Well . . . erhm . . . I burst into tears and he grabbed my arm and he said, "be careful men don't cry in public!" (Piatczanyn, Bennett, and Soulsby 2016, 181)

This illustrates a quandary that widowers, gay or straight, confront regarding public display of their grief versus other people's inability to deal with male grief, especially gay men's grief. Most of these gay widowers lived with unresolved humiliation and anger as a result of their disenfranchisement from decision-making when the partner's biological family and medical service providers ignored their partnership. Prior to the partner's death, they tried to organize his care and death, but then confronted the social exclusion and the challenges of gay identity, which added emotion work, or grief work.

Similarly, Fenge (2014) noted in her exploratory study of same-sex partner later life bereavement and end-of-life experiences in the UK that the hidden or undisclosed nature of their relationship made it difficult for individuals to grieve for their partners as partners, rather than as merely a friend. Edwin, whose partner died after their sixteen-year relationship, commented, "I had very little support and because I wasn't out, I think that's so important to be out now in hindsight" (ibid., 295). Fenge's participants spoke of their haunting "disenfranchised grief." They had difficulties when their partner's biological family took over funeral arrangements without a thought of the bereaved partner, or when trying to arrange the funeral and burial in a churchyard, which at times meant the faith community's prohibition of an adjoining plot and common headstone.

In a systematic review of thirteen recent research studies on the bereavement experiences of people within the LGBT community, Bristowe, Marshall, and Harding (2016) develop a two-axis model based on LGBT-specific experiences—whether the relationship was disclosed to others or not, and whether others acknowledged/accepted the relationship or not. Their principal thesis is that the bereavement experience of widowed gay men who are "out" within their community and have their partnership acknowledged will be similar to heterosexual widowers. Yet, there are three other groups in this four-cell model whose experiences are uniquely determined by being gay, and for men within each of the groups their bereavement will be more difficult.

MASCULINITIES AND BEREAVEMENT

What we know about heterosexual widowers' experiences may be tainted by how researchers investigated bereavement and widowerhood. That sounds harsh, but it isn't meant to be. In their analysis of heterosexual widowers' reflection on their earlier bereavement, K. Bennett, Smith, and Hughes (2005, 351) perceptively discovered that the old men were more likely to communicate their distress during an extended interview, but not on existing paper-and-pencil instruments that assess sadness, anxiety, and depression. Among the widowers who were not fully able to redevelop their life alone and were less able to discuss aspects of their bereavement in positive terms, their scores on standardized measures of grief responses failed to reveal the depth of their enduring grief (sadness, depression) well into widowerhood. Elsewhere, Kate Bennett (2005, 147) pointed out, for example, "one of the most striking aspects [of my interviews with widowers who were reflecting back on their bereavement] was the openness and frankness with which the men discussed whether or not their life was worth living, what its value was, and what was the purpose of life without their spouse." One 75-year-old widower talked about "the futility of life" eleven years after he lost his wife. An 81-year-old widower whose wife died seven years earlier commented, "Sometimes I felt like ending it all, to be honest with you. I mean I don't think I would have done that, never do that. But I felt that" (ibid., 148). This widower's suicide ideation was not only related to his aghast of being alone but, as Bennett often heard, the void that continued for years (cf. Carr et al. 2001). By contrast, other widowers revealed a more positive outlook and discussed the firm decision they took to continue living.

The early-1970s view of grief and bereavement as a set of sequential stages that men would work though in a linear way toward "recovery" has been set aside. Bereavement theorists and researchers now propose that grieving is not a uniform series of stages; instead, grieving has sharply differ-ent trajectories, and bereavement is experienced in a variety of ways largely dependent upon one's cultural schema and habitus. A growing number of gerontologists also now argue that grieving is not primarily an intrapsychic process, but rather is a complexly social process. Facing life as a widower is recognized as taking place within old men's broader community and cultural spheres.

Consistent with this, Stroebe and Schut (2010) discuss a model of be-reavement (not widowhood) that emphasizes the matters of mundane daily life that follow from bereavement, such as household management. Based on the model, Richardson and Balaswamy (2001) examined the lives of hetero-sexual widowers aged 60 and older in their second year of bereavement. They found that early in the bereavement process, loss-oriented feelings and behaviors were more pervasive as the men managed the intrusion of grief and lived through the "time-outs" characterized by avoidance or denial of the needed restoration changes. Later bereavement was more restoration-orient-ed: the widowers were doing new things, attending to the changes in their lives, and rebuilding identities and relationships. Richardson (2010) noted that white widowers more often than African American widowers reported feeling unhappy, depressed, and/or lonely in their second year. What in-creased widowers' positive affect was the length of time since the wife's death, the number of (new and old) friends, and having a confidant.

Bonanno and Kaltman (2001) introduced a very different perspective that also calls attention to contextual influences on bereavement, such as the perceived availability of social support, the "sense-making" widowers en-gage in, and the spiritual capital widowers bring as a personal resource. In the aftermath of spousal loss, widowers and widows routinely strive to adjust and reconstruct their assumptive worlds. The process involves searching to make sense of the death, and then making new meaning as a widowed person (Coleman and Neimeyer 2010). What Bonanno and Kaltman (2001) discovered was that the expected "normal grief" or "common grief" trajectory occurs infrequently. Rather than an upside-down V-shaped pattern of response in which normal life functioning is interrupted with the spouse's death, there is an elevation of depressive symptoms and distress for several months, and then everyday life is gradually recovered; in later life resilience is most prevalent. This is where the trajectory of emotional pains, yearning, and intrusive cognitions are transient rather than enduring for nearly half the widowed in the study (Bonanno 2004, 24). It seems age matters, and in the face of a "normative" loss in men's later life, resilient widowed persons are basically not rocked, taking in their spouse's death with mild, periodic, short-lived distress. There was no indication of avoidance of thinking about their former spouse. Just the opposite seems to be the case: "resilient" widows and widowers reported great comfort from positive memories of their partners, and they felt relatively little need to search for meaning in their spouse's death.

In my conversations with Kate Bennett, she identified one of those ah-ha moments we have as researchers when we read an article or listen to others present their original work at conferences. After listening to Moore and Stratton discuss one case of a resilient widower, Bennett (2010) reanalyzed her sixty interviews with widowers to assess what proportion of the men were resilient or not around two years after their wives' death, and to consider what processes might be involved in achieving resilience. The "resilient" men viewed their current life positively, were active, and regarded life as having meaning and satisfaction. Within this group, most achieved resilience gradually, often as a result of a "turning point" (e.g., joining a club, receiving advice from a counselor or friend, relocating from the couple's home to new housing). Bennett (ibid., 379) concluded, "Some men could achieve resilience by drawing on internal resources but that others were only able to achieve resilience through external intervention, either intentional or accidental."

MASCULINITIES AND WIDOWERHOOD

There is probably some ageism in the tendency to ignore old people's lived experiences of being widowed. Socially and culturally, surviving a spouse's death is often regarded as too close to end-of-life matters and is almost as hushed as conversations about death. Late life widowerhood is a status increasingly caused by the spouse's chronic illness and often painful dying process, less often an accident or acute event that happens suddenly and unexpectedly (Heron 2016). For women, even though becoming a widow has been a normative part of the aging process because of their much greater likelihood of outliving husbands, women's experiences as widows still remain neglected by policymakers and researchers (Feldman, Byles, and Beaumont 2000). Not surprisingly, the limited research on the experiences of widowers has not scrutinized old men's experiences in much detail at all. For example, I could not find a single study examining how ethnocultural diversity affects old widowers' experiences, much less the intersection of wealth, health, and class. This is principally because cross-sectional and longitudinal research studies were and still are constrained by the very small numbers of old men who are widowed. The majority of the quantitative studies focus on individual outcomes such as changes in psychological health or the composition of the men's social support networks.

Notwithstanding this critique, there is a rising number of qualitative studies that have examined the types of resources the old widowers had available, their masculinity practices, repartnering likelihood, and independence (e.g., Bennett 2007, 2010). This body of research features the stories the men tell about their widower experiences, and how these stories are both individual and cultural. The studies provide enough insight to address widowers' masculinity practices as they rebuild lives.

The widowers' narratives and storytelling detail the men's emotional work and routine practices as widowers. Bennett (2010), for example, heard how some old men becoming and then living as widowers moved from the vulnerability of bereavement to resilience by reconstructing their lives as old, solo-living men. She heard across men's narratives how most of them would initially frame their unexpected experiences as widowers within a "traditional" masculinity framework (Bennett 2007). For example, consistent with their generation's stereotypes of manhood, the widowers would report their deficiency in the skills needed for daily living, including shopping, cooking, and household maintenance. Many of the old widowers Bennett interviewed reiterated this stereotype, revealing through conversation that they believed women were more able to deal with living alone as widowed. Their interpretation was tied to having lived in the separate spheres of "his" and "her" marriage and never acquiring what they *felt* were sufficient domestic skills to live alone. The gender inequalities of "his" and "her" separate spheres initially disadvantaged the widowers. Paradoxically, by divulging their incompetency in "her" spaces, the men avowed their masculine capital. They soon acquired the necessary "survival" skills and again affirmed their masculine self-reliance and toughness. As Bennett observed, most of these widowers had become (or were) "keen cooks and houseproud" (Bennett, Hughes, and Smith 2003, 408).

Many of Bennett's widowers also spoke of how they continued to mask their feelings of loneliness to be in sync with the guidelines of never-aging masculinity ideologies that expect men to not reveal to others their feelings of loss or the depth of their pain (Bennett 2007). The men felt they needed to be stoic in almost all contexts, but they recognized the interview context as a safe place for them to talk with a "stranger" and disclose their anguish, worries, and modest triumphs. Moore and Stratton (2002, 103) similarly commented that sadness was frequently expressed within the interviews in nonverbal ways or verbally expressed as loneliness, along with "a full range of emotional expressiveness in various combinations with differing degrees of loquacity and openness." They painstakingly disputed the premise that "traditional" masculinity ideologies lead to men's inexpressiveness and noted the great variability in expressiveness among their widowers. And, to show how individual cases can lead a false positive interpretation about old widowers' stoic masculinity performances, they singled out from among their fifty-one widowers two men whose grief responses and post-loss lives bordered on super-inexpressive (ibid., 104–7)—a career military man, and a man with alexithymia.

Van den Hoonaard (2009, 2010) also examined how cultural masculinities frame old men's experience of widowerhood and old age. Her study focused on widowers who were either "locals" living in predominately rural New Brunswick, Canada, or northern US "immigrants" living in retirement communities in Florida. She noted that even though the two groups of widowers were quite different, the old men commonly lived their generation's highly valued masculinity practices, which included independence, stoicism, and personal control (2010, 14).

Throughout her analysis she emphasized the ways the men relied on the masculine habitus of their youth, and how their "collective story" was about reclaiming their identities as men when faced with old age and the absence of the signifier of being married. She was sensitive to the proposal that the generations of widowers she interviewed borrowed from the social scripts and masculinity ideologies of their youth to go on with their lives (cf. Spector-Mersel 2006) because they felt there were no viable, culturally accepted models of aging masculinity. In the closing of her monograph, van den Hoonaard (2010, 167) notes, "When I first started working on this book, I chose a tentative title, *By Himself* . . . The title turned out to fit very well because the widowers . . . did, indeed, focus on their competence as independent actors in most areas of their lives. They went to great lengths to explain their self-reliance in rebuilding their lives."

In summary, widowers are men practicing varying types of masculinities. These studies attest that widowers act and behave like most other old men. Some widowers' everyday practices and preferences may be in sync with their generation's hegemonic never-aging masculinities, and striving to protect their masculine capital now that they are without a marriage to affirm their masculine subjectivities. They are also without many widower peers to observe or consult to support masculinity practices consonant with the field of widowerhood, and most people in their pre-loss networks have limited experience with widowers to assist them, or to remain comfortable around them. The passage of time helps, and for many so does religious faith. Moore and Stratton (2002) noted that some widowers spend more time alone, others quickly turn to new relationships, while others are cautious about making new friends. Still others get involved in community projects or have coffee in the cafe in the morning, sitting around with other old men, widowed or not, and chat for a couple of hours as men.

RETHINKING WIDOWERHOOD

Should researchers begin viewing widowers as men, the research questioning and interviews will more likely begin to identify lifetime continuities among the widowers, and the diversities that arise from their different classes, faiths, generations, and even whether they have a military background. Questions would be less homogenizing and about old men's psychological loss of their embodied social and personal world of a "we." Questions could shift to assessing in what ways old widowers' ethnoculture, living setting (neighbor-hood, community), sense of future time, or social capital affect living as healthy-enough old men now living solo as a new phase of more and more men's later life. There is a need for greater exploration of the differences among widowers and how social inequalities limit or enable the men's widowerhood experiences. And there is need for investigations documenting how these old men's masculinity practices "bend" the rules of the (gender) game to make their lived experiences fish-in-water experiences. We cannot lose sight of the likelihood that many widowers may prefer not repartnering while still longing for the emotional habitat of support and care. They differ-ently confront the loneliness that arises from living solo after decades of living as a "we," particularly should they remain in the family home. So recognized, it is the subset of old widowers who are most lonely who are at greater risk of abuse from estranged family members and solicitous others.

Just before the millennium, Stevens (1995) observed that widowers in the Netherlands were as likely as widows to live with a partner (about 5 percent), but they were four times *more* likely to develop a "partner-like" relationship to share their daily lives, without being romantically or sexually involved or living together. The men emphasized the importance of regular companion-ship. The majority of the widows had regular contact with one or more women friends and reported that these friends served as their companions outside the home as much as at home. Restating this, women sought out women friends, and men sought out women friends too. Perhaps neither widowers nor widows aim to repartner. Wu, Schimmele, and Ouellet (2015) find a very high likelihood that the majority of older Canadian widowers (roughly 70 percent) and widows (roughly 90 percent) do not repartner, whether in terms of cohabitating or remarrying, and that at older ages there is very little gap between widowers' and widows' likelihood of repartnering. Still, the gender gap in proportions of men and women repartnering is often emphasized, even using the gap to cast old widowers as less resilient in living alone than widows (cf. Koren 2016).

Most old men who become widowers are said to confront shrunken sources of support and ill-ease seeking and accepting outside assistance. The thinking behind this characterization draws on images of masculinities and femininities that are based on the lives of most white, middle-class hetero-sexuals who have his and her spaces and expected personas. For example, in their separate-spheres relationships, widowers' wives had previously coordi-nated his and their social lives. Several of the fifty-one widowers in Moore and Stratton's (2002) study referred to their wives as a "social director," and the men missed this structure. Often the widowers van den Hoonaard (2010) interviewed made clear that their wives had been their intermediaries with family and friend relations. Some old men also conveyed their logic that an inevitable part of the transition to widowerhood was recognition that their prior social world had revolved around couples, and being single again there was a slow evaporation of some friendships because being a "third wheel" or "fifth wheel" was uncomfortable for the men or their former couple friends. Sometimes widowers "felt let down by the failure of friends to keep up with them" (ibid., 163).

Ironically, van den Hoonaard surmises that most of the widowers "either would not or could not" involve themselves in relationships that build close friendships. To support her interpretation, she noted the widowers neither invited people to their home nor often reached out. Instead, they preferred to "bump into" acquaintances and neighbors in local coffee cafes or while shop-ping. Van den Hoonaard's "would not or could not" is attributed to widow-ers' generational reliance on the never-aging masculinity ideologies of the youth, which she saw as advocating independence and freedom rather than being "tied into" the reciprocity of commitments that are involved in main-taining old and building new close relationships. Perhaps so. However, viewed less in terms "traditional" masculinity performances, the men's scal-ing back on "friends" and "friendly relations" could be a purposeful decision to limit their network to a very few emotionally rewarding relationships, ones that no longer serve to emphasize "widower" rather than "man." This is consistent with the performance of aging masculinities and research on old men's socioemotional selectivity.

Contrary to the message of a defoliated social network, or the idea that old men "would not or could not" involve themselves in sustaining a net-work, in Riggs's (1997) study of widowers aged 73–86, she found that *over time* the men not only maintained friendships but also instigated new ones. Their success of replacing peripheral and sustaining emotionally rich old friendships and making new friends was more common than not. For the widowers whose friendship networks contracted, it was these men's decision to step away from some friends because they perceived a lack of reciprocity in efforts to visit one another. As Jack commented,

> Like it's a funny thing, when you go from the stage of living as a couple and then live on your own, your friends seem to be embarrassed about coming to visit you on your own. I'm not quite sure why this is. Whether it was my fault or whether that it was just a thing that people have, but other widowers have told me the same thing: They'll come and see you if you invite them whereas at one time they would just drop in and come have an evening with you. (Riggs 1997, 184)

Comparing widowers in earlier and later phases of their widowerhood experience (before and after five hundred days), Balaswamy, Richardson, and Price (2004, 79) found that, with time, widowers re-integrate socially, and they suggest that the findings of less support may be a function of doing research early in the bereavement process. In studies that do not control for time since spousal loss, finding widowers with smaller support resources and greater loneliness could be partly a consequence of the higher odds that more widowers are recent widowers.

Based on the Australian Longitudinal Study of Aging and then through interviews with ten very old Australian widowers aged 89–96 and ten widows aged 85–90, Isherwood, King, and Luszcz (2012, 2017) find that the oldest of the widowers were at most risk of social isolation and loneliness because of outliving friends and relatives and declining mobility. In general, the longitudinal data reveal that levels of social engagement remained high over the sixteen-year period, but tapered off more noticeably among the very old widowers and those in lower socioeconomic groups. A key finding from their qualitative study was that the oldest group interpreted others' unsolicited offers of support as an imposition and encroachment on their sense of independence, perhaps revealing a masculinity performance of "I can handle it myself." Or, the widowers' shunning of unwanted support could be (equally) determined by the fact that half of these men experienced the recent loss of their wife, which could prompt a greater frequency of family and friends offering unsolicited support. To remain consonant with their sense of themselves as men rebuilding their lives, most of these old widowers found emotional connections through involvement in voluntary work, including running groups at senior centers and retirement villages, and being active in veteran groups or conservation work.

SUMMARY

This chapter disentangles—as a study of masculinities and aging can do—many of the misinterpretations of widowerhood. Old men lose their spouse/partner and experience the loss as body dismemberment. Their public "we" ends but not their histories of being partnered. They have stories and memories to tell about their married lives. They are not shattered forever, and the vast majority live as solo men. Most widowers reorganize their social world to go it alone, perhaps because they are conscious of their limited future time and regard repartnering as unlikely and dicey. Only about one-third of old widowers do end up repartnering, more often in a cohabitation or LAT relationship in order to keep the peace with their and their partner's adult children and grandchildren. These intergenerational relations are crucial to most men's identities as fathers and grandfathers, and there may be mutually agreed upon promises of social support that the men do not want to disregard. From the available evidence there is on widowers' gendered practices, we can see much substantiation of many of the men's changed habitus, such as some men's preference for the company of other men in fields of aging masculinities—evening dinners in pubs, long coffee chats with age peers. Widowers' reconstructed social worlds also differ in respect to content, context, and resources; it is an issue that is too poorly understood.

Chapter Twelve

Late Life and Its Fourth Age Culture

Resilience provides a useful corrective to the tendency to focus on the negative aspects of ageing.

—Wild, Wiles, and Allen (2013, 142)

Old men navigate late life's (un)welcomed disruptions and transitions, and most men have acquired the capacity and social capital to meet these challenges. Their well-being can be assaulted whenever there is "bad news" such as a cancer diagnosis, theirs or their partner's, or their unwanted but needed dependency on others, perhaps as a result of their driving cessation. In late and very late life, most old men face a series of new challenges ranging from outliving friends and siblings, weighing the decision to relocate to some type of shelter housing, and fretting about their dwindling financial resources to having to amend their masculine subjectivities as their bodily capabilities wane and dependencies on others increase. How the old men manage can range from rethinking priorities; to "slowing down"; to acute episodes of quiet suffering and troubled sleep; to spiritual quests; to challenging themselves with learning something new, perhaps rebuilding an old sports car; to spending as many mornings and evenings as weather permits on a porch or deck quietly acknowledging another good day.

As will be discussed in the chapter, ample evidence underscores how most old men's social relations and adaptive histories promote toughing it out and resiliency in late life. I examine how most old men live with and through late life's challenges, and their experiences reveal an array of ways they do aging masculinities. I propose that late life is being (re)defined from its prior imaginary as a black hole that pulls us toward the unthinkable, death, by the rise of a fourth age culture that supports being "old" and "very old." The chapter closely reviews the meaning of resiliency in terms of old men's late life. Developing resilience occurs regardless of social and cultural backgrounds or physical and cognitive impairments, unlike successful aging (cf. Harris 2008). The evidence shows us that old men interact selectively with the people who "provide value" (and, when needed, instrumental support). Value is all relative. The friends, neighbors, family, and on occasion paid care providers are the men's microcommunities that can give late life added meaning. As Freeman (2014, 4–5) notes, "the experiences and things that generally provide the greatest yield of meaning . . . have little to do with ourselves. They derive instead from what is *other* than self."

WHAT IS LATE LIFE?

Late life, whether it begins for some old men in their late 60s or for other men in their mid-80s, ascends on the cusp of ending one's participation in later life's third age cultural lifestyles. This simple definition presumes the transition into late life is not abrupt, as when a disabling stroke relocates an aging man from the golf course to a bed in a care facility. The transition into late life is more often gradual, as when the motorcycle becomes way too heavy to manage and when the man with progressing cataracts senses he no longer sees well enough to safely go for evening rides. This near-70-year-old man knows it is time to permanently cease riding and, though resistant, he senses he is on the cusp of late life. Another old man became a widower in his mid-80s after caring for his wife with her Alzheimer's, and now in his early 90s congratulates himself every morning with an "attaboy" for his decision to move into a small apartment in a continuing care retirement village and for the cadre of new friends and not eating dinners alone. His late life exemplifies a man's participation in the fourth age culture.

These examples also reveal how old men's resistance to "being old" are predictable, given the hegemony of never-aging masculinities and the third age cultural messages to age well. But like these two examples, most old men are realistic about the amount of time left in their lives and come to acknowledge their impermanence. At some point, they are keenly aware that they are on the edge of transitioning from later into late life. As Simon, a 91-year-old who lives in a retirement village, obliquely commented, "Ninety years of age slows you down a trifle" (Browne-Yung, Walker, and Luszcz 2017, 286).

Andrew Moore and his colleagues (2014) reported on a British man over the age of 90 in no pain, yet who was no longer strident about remaining active; nor was he keenly interested in "keeping fit." The man commented about the closing of his community bath/pool: "It'll be a relief in one way, because I don't like getting up in the morning. And about keeping fit, well, I must be getting to the end of the line now." The man welcomed "slowing down" some (ibid., 768). A 71-year-old African American similarly commented,

To put it simply I'm recognizing that I'm at a stage in my life where I've got to adapt to a whole new lifestyle, and as long as I can make it enjoyable, that's all I need. I'm not anxious about the future. As I move through the twilight years, I do so with neither dread nor apprehension. You need to accept the reality of what is and develop ways of coping with it. (Harris 2008, 50)

These "cases" reveal that old men are not likely to become "old" at a particular age, and the cases imply how environmental factors can decrease some old men's risks of becoming "old," such as their class, financial resources, and social capital. Lest we forget, periods of economic recession and growth have produced greater social inequality (and diversity) in men's aging experiences. Still, the vast majority of old men are likely to experience most of late life and old age with a life partner and an awareness of their greater frailty, yet with a subjective sense of "things are good enough" given their age. In this chapter, late life from the perspective of old men is examined.

THE FOURTH AGE AS A CULTURAL FIELD

Very late life (or advanced old age) has continued to be treated as a period of deteriorating health, mobility problems, cognitive decline, and finality. Partitioning people's lengthening later life into an elongated third age and the residual fourth age, the imaginaries cast the fourth age as "a terminal place from which there is no escape": it is the objectification of frailty and finality; it encompasses an irredeemable abjection; and it intensifies the othering of very old people with labeling as "untouchables," "vegetables," or "gomers." As Blaikie remarked, "Increased longevity means more incontinence, more dementia, more bodily betrayals and breakdowns in communication" (1999, 109, cited in Higgs and Jones 2009, 75).

Unlike the past, the sheer number of people in very old age in need of significant care has grown every decade. Living in societies with growing numbers of very old people, the dominant discourse is about how very old people's lives are associated with dependency because of bodily or cognitive decline. This discourse affirms a social imaginary of a fearful fourth age with its "community of otherness, set apart from the everyday experiences and practices of later life" (Gilleard and Higgs 2013, 368).

To Gilleard and Higgs's credit, the third and fourth ages are not conceptualized or discussed as two stages of life. Similar to Bourdieu's discussion of fields, they propose that the third age identifies a cultural field that emphasizes people's embodiment of lifestyles that represent "aging is not being old" (cf. Katz and Marshall 2003). As a field with its own (largely generational) habitus, the third age culture is described as encouraging old men and women to develop their late lifestyles in keeping with their capabilities and preferences, and to maintain bodily fitness and vitality to enjoy their late lifestyles (which is also the antiaging consumerist-driven mantra). But Gilleard and Higgs do not equate the fourth age to a cultural field; instead, in their terms it is only an "imaginary."

The fourth age continues to function "as a social imaginary because it represents not so much a particular cohort or stage of life but as a kind of terminal destination—a location stripped of the social and cultural capital that is most valued and which allows for the articulation of choice, autonomy, self-expression, and pleasure in later life" (Gilleard and Higgs 2010, 123). Rereading their interpretation, what they call the fourth age has always existed in modern cultures. It was not created by the emergence of the third age; almost the opposite is true. It is, they argue, the pernicious symbolic imaginary about "aging without agency" and resisting the fourth age that helped give birth to the culture of a third age. Their interpretation positions the fourth age as an imagined *life stage* that has always existed within cultures, not as a distinct field or culture.

Precisely what the fourth age is, however, remains ambiguous. For example, Higgs and Jones (2009) argue it is the loss of agency over the body that characterizes the boundary between the third age culture and the imaginary cliff of the fourth age. When Gilleard and Higgs (2010, 125) write, the fourth age is a metaphorical "black hole" that cannot be really understood, but creates within cultures a great fear among those old men and women (just) outside its draft.

> In astronomy, a black hole creates a massive gravitational pull that sucks in everything that comes within range including light itself. This generates the phenomenon of the "event horizon" which is a point where light disappears completely. Any light emitted from beyond this horizon can never reach the observer. To many people in or approaching "later" life, the position of those in the fourth age can be likened to that of an object that has strayed too close to the event horizon and has now gone over it, beyond any chance of return.

By contrast, Grenier and Phillipson (2013, 57), who also draw as much on life course stages as social imaginary, propose that the fourth age demarcates "experiences that occur at the intersection of advanced age and impairment." Their position is that "fourth agers" retain the possibility of expression, communication, and agency. In her discussion of the fourth age, Liz Lloyd (2015, 261) opines, and I wholly agree, "The fourth age is a troublesome concept, an inevitable outcome of the third age as a period of personal growth and active engagement." Elsewhere she commented, "and there is a lack of understanding of the perceptions of those who might be considered to be living in it" (Lloyd et al. 2014, 1).

Ever since the rise of modernity, the dread of being "old" became part of the apprehension of aging past youthfulness. In the cultural imaginary, the uneasiness is a loss of agency over our bodies (and thus all physical capital) as well as a loss of capability to make choices. It is this slippery slope toward frailty and dependency that continues to earmark the negative meaning of "old," even among very old people. Crossing the boundary into dependency and frailty can occur for some men in their 60s, when they may have just exited the labor force and now face the existential dread of rapidly deteriorating health. For others the crossover may be well after they celebrate their 85th birthday. For neither of these groups of men has the "event horizon" of dying struck.

From the perspective of an old man who has embodied the third age cultural maxim to "age well," the creep of old age incapacity, disability, and dependency is surely negating. When routine activities, including walking, bathing, eating, dressing, and toileting, require someone's help, these vagaries of becoming "old" are unimaginable at first in any positive way. The independent man dreads that when he is unable to exercise bodily control and do self-care, he will be repositioned to the degendered, dependent status of a nursing care "resident," which is outside the social world he has known for his adult lifetime. This is the fourth age imaginary. It is being aged by culture into accepting age anxiety, bewilderment, and decline as inevitable (cf. Gullette 2004). The imaginary is rooted in discursive othering—casting the old person into a position defined equally by its marginalization and exclusion as his frailty and vulnerability (Higgs and Gilleard 2014, 10).

AGENCY IN LATE LIFE

I propose that these othered fourth agers ought to be thought of as having much more agency than characterized in the horrid imaginary. The perspective falsely suggested is that men and women who are fourth agers are so nearly cognitively and physically depleted that their personal dependency surrenders their agency. However, my own observations, interviews, and conversations with very old men who are unquestionably "very old" and living in different forms of sheltered care facilities suggest that the men retain considerable personal agency and more than enough to sway family decisions and make havoc if they want to guilt others.

To illustrate this position, a man in mid-80s in an assisted living arrangement used a private nurse, was lucid, and thrived on talking about politics, yet was frail and would nod off several times during a twenty-minute conversation. In my thinking, Rob had become "old" and was a spirited participant in the fourth age culture. He had moved into assisted living. He could afford a visiting nurse to assist him with bathing. He defined himself as "very old" because of his deteriorating functional health. He would smirk at his (visiting) daughter's encouragement to "take your meds and take it easy," then negotiate with her his preference for the afternoon's DVD movie, which he always nodded off on. His decisions and interactive style affirmed his agency, despite his very dependent status and congestive heart failure narcolepsy. He was a "resident" to any passerby seeing him hobble along with use of his walker when he took very short daily walks against the advice of his nurse. Unlike this "be terrified of" resident life, his daughters, his nurse, and his friends watched an old man making the best of his life—he continued to be Rob.

Another man in his late 70s suffered two back-to-back debilitating strokes, and with the second stroke lost nearly all mobility and almost all ability to speak, other than two distinct, slurred phrases—"fuck you" and "fuck off." Henry could recognize family and most visitors and would greet them with a gentle-toned "fuck you," unlike his rough response to any one of the "interrupting" nurses. He could process some (not a lot of) details in a conversation, seemed to pay more attention to his daughter when she talked about his San Francisco Giants, and would gently say "fuck off" when wanted visitors, especially his daughter, stood to end the visit. He survived for more than a year listening and "talking" in this debilitated state. Then he slipped into an unresponsive state for almost another half year, during which he continued to eat when the spoon would touch his lip and to sip water and protein shakes. I knew little about the metaphor "event horizon" that Gilleard and Higgs introduce to vividly characterize entrance into the "black hole," but looking back, Henry's horizon was when he became unresponsive (probably after yet another uncharted stroke). To outsiders—including his former work colleagues and golf buddies—his draft into very old age's black hole was when they first heard he had been institutionalized. Visiting family and nurses heeded his "agency with aging" long after his institutionalization.

At issue is how to make sense of the gap between my observations of these two and other very old, sometimes bedridden men's obvious agency in their very late life and the prevalent thesis that what distinguishes fourth agers is people's loss of agency. Lloyd (2015) flagged my attention to the theorizing of Marshall and Clarke (2010), who proposed that personal agency is people's capacity to make choices and act intentionally; they recognized that agency varies widely as a result of the personal and social capital someone has available. They emphasized that all people have the ability to act intentionally and reflexively, until cognitive dysfunction overrules. This means, for most very old fourth agers, personal (and social) agency is not absent. Further, speculatively, it could be argued, the matter of agency does not distinguish the boundary between third and fourth age fields. I think very old men's continued agency (or resilience) punches a hole through the rhetoric that a fourth age is *experienced* as dreadful gravitational pull into darkness. My observation is that this phase of life is experienced as both resistance to and acceptance of dying.

Grenier and Phillipson (2013) similarly question the assumption that agency is either present or absent; that health, activity, and independence are necessary for agency; and that loss of agency is a viable signifier of the cuff of the fourth age. Pondering how agency might be considered among those who are frail, they suggest that agency may *look different* in very late life than men's agency earlier in later life. "This viewpoint—that the forms or expressions of agency from within the 'fourth age' may differ from those which we currently know and expect of agency—is a serious challenge to the state of knowledge in gerontology" (ibid., 72). Grenier and Phillipson continue, "The agency of someone who is in the 'fourth age,' possibly bed-ridden and ill, is likely very different from an able-bodied young person. Acts may be non-verbal or take place through forms of communication that are often difficult to understand (for example, cries, moans or screams) . . . They may also take the form of outright resistance or disruptive acts" (ibid.). I agree. My thinking is that the fourth age is not the pull of a black hole, nor is it defined at the onset by a cliff of frailty. It is a cultural field, not a person's life stage, and this field supports the practice of aging masculinities. A dismal view of whatever follows participation in marvelous third age lifestyles (e.g., holding babies in a neonatal setting, hiking and finding mind-blowing waterfalls, building or refinishing a rocking chair) may be the omnipresent social imaginary, but if gerontologists help maintain this imaginary we ignore very old men's agency and mask their resilient fourth age lifestyles.

LIFESTYLES IN THE FOURTH AGE

Some of these lifestyles will be amended extensions of the men's third age lifestyles, and many will be unlike what the men previously fashioned. On occasion the mass media will report a story about sex in nursing homes. Typically sensationalized but nonetheless to the point: a variety of forms of sexual activity occur within places ignored by the social imaginary of the fourth age. The desire to be touched, for intimate contact—hugging, kissing, cuddling, fondling, intercourse—does not universally diminish in very old age or necessarily end at the doors of care facilities, and old residents have a rather positive attitude about sexuality (e.g., Mahieu and Gastmans 2015). Men who were sexually active before institutionalization may well remain interested in sexual intimacy throughout their very late life. Old men continuing to be intimate with their wives or partners while living in institutional care facilities or coupling with new lovers challenge ageist notions of growing old and the absence of agency in very late life. Remaining intimate is a lifestyle. Rediscovering sexual intimacy with new partners within a community of age peers isn't much different than the context of a college campus.

Intimate coupling in care facilities has raised logistical (and legal) concerns for the institutions that the old people come to regard as their home. The troubles are especially real for the old gay men who encounter staff members' negative attitudes about same-sex intimacy, as well as about heterosexual couples with mixed cognitive capabilities. But the tide of public opinion and policy revision is to preserve the sexual autonomy of old nursing home residents. The changing attitudes across care facilities to recognize old men's sexual autonomy is testament that the lived fourth age is not the same as the imagined.

The fourth age, I believe, is an emergent cultural field situated in the informal, social, and health care–providing institutions of intergenerational family care work, home health care services, brick-and-mortar "service integrated housing," long-term skilled nursing facilities, and residential care facilities for Alzheimer's and other dementias. The field embodies the principle of palliative care. Unlike the past, palliative care is no longer segregated as an end-of-life observance provided by relatives or professionals, or a synonym for hospice care. It has reclaimed the long-standing philosophy of care emphasizing personhood and quality of life and others' help in the management of the outward signs of aging (or illness), including incontinence, immobility, instability leading to falls, and anxiety.

Also unlike the past, the rather narrowly defined types of care and services that were uniformly provided to all residents in an institutional care setting have been displaced by the expectations of third agers for options and choices and their own agency. As Callaghan and Towers (2014, 1427) contend, the promotion of choice and control is a policy priority for social care services in England and "is at the heart of recent drives to personalise services." The policy supports preferences. Quoting residents in care homes in the UK, Cook, Thompson, and Reed (2015) report that the old people did, in fact, want their residential status to involve "living with care" rather than "existing in care"—they wanted the ontological security of "home" yet "cared for." Comparing old people's experiences in extra care housing, care homes, and receiving care at home, Callaghan and Towers ironically found that people aging in place in their own homes and receiving home care consistently reported feeling less control over their daily lives, especially in terms of personalized, responsive services, than the residents in care homes and extra care housing. Unlike their parents and grandparents, some old people living in the emerging fourth age culture seem to prefer not depending on family care and opt for the opportunities fourth age facilities can offer.

My observation is that, similar to the rise of consumerist-driven third age lifestyle opportunities, there has been an upsurge in the commercialization of products to assist very old people with their bodily decline and to sell fourth age care services. The philosophy of palliative care has evolved to have at least two significances—providing old people without immediate care needs an extension of third age amenities along with fourth age care, and providing very old residents the personal (emotional and body) care needed. Howe, Jones, and Tilse (2013) reviewed the new ways "service-integrated housing" has been emerging in the UK, the US, Canada, Australia, and New Zealand and note, "Increasing flexibility has blurred the boundaries between previously distinct forms of housing with set service menus, and widened the range of services available to residents in any one housing setting but not necessarily used by all" (ibid., 27). One noteworthy pair of findings is that the majority of old men and their partners in the UK who move into the newer, extra care retirement communities are without care needs when they move in (Bäumker et al. 2012), whereas residents in long-term care facilities are generally much more incapacitated when they become residents (Johnson, Rolph, and Smith 2010).

The discourse about very late life is shifting from fourth agers' abject dependency to their personal care needs. Howe, Jones, and Tilse (2013, 573) comment,

> Providers have in some cases used positive names to rebrand a variety of forms of existing housing offering different ranges of support and care services, and of varying quality. The spread of "assisted living" in the USA is a positive case in point, and in Australia, the growing adoption of "assisted living" signals the "unpacking" or "repackaging" of care and accommodation components both within and across different housing provision, in name and form, and realisation of consumer preferences and policy goals that have been espoused for many years.

This raises the prospect of leaving behind prior generations' profound dependency in old age on whatever limited care was available and moving toward consumer-based choices in types of acceptable dependency in very old age. The field of the fourth age is expanding. Much as there has been an individualization of retirement as well as an individualization of men's late lifestyles in third age cultures (Higgs and McGowan 2013), are we on the cusp of witnessing an increasingly "improvisational" nature of late life (Polivka 2000) with an individualization of the fourth age? It is not likely that the rising fourth age's cultural emphasis on palliative care will fully disrupt people's worries about very old age, yet will the imagery of the fourth age remain characterized by abject dependency and the underbelly of aging?

RESILIENCY

Aging and late lifestyles are highly related to resiliency, which the research community has begun to recognize as a central component of late life. "Resiliency" conveys a salutogenetic perspective on the gains and possibilities in very old age, instead of the insidious decline ideology. Despite its import, there is no common interpretation of what makes up resiliency or resilience, especially as it applies to late life (Aburn, Gott, and Hoare 2016; Allen et al. 2011). Among life course theorists, coping and positive adaptation when faced with challenging life circumstances and prevailing over the adversity of racism, homophobia, bodily aging, or socioeconomic disadvantage are the usual definitions within empirical research on resilience (cf. Fredriksen-Goldsen, Kim, et al. 2017; Masten and Wright 2010).

The early thesis was that resilience is an acquired capability among a few to weather personal distress; supposedly unlike others, resilient individuals were said to have acquired "hardiness." However, adjustment in the face of adversity appears to be a *common* experience rather than an exception—take, for example, how few people develop PTSD after trauma. Most adapt and integrate the trauma into their experiences; they remember and "move on." Masten (2001) calls it "ordinary magic," because resilience is something common, rooted in *most* people's prior experiences when they work through challenging times or events. It is the adaptive process of living with and through challenging life events and circumstances, and resiliency is contextual. It inevitably entails the flexible use of personal, social, cultural, and environmental resources in the process of responding to stress and adapting.

There is now recognition that resilience at individual-level functioning needs to be contextual, for it can be more evident in one setting or area of life and less in another, and it can differ among men with similar social and economic capital, or similar faiths. Similarities and differences in individuals' resilience parallel the variance in "family resilience" and "community resilience," which describe how social groups differently prevail through periods of struggle.

For example, among widowers, who face one of the most troubling "life events," resiliency involves, according to Robert Rubinstein (1986) and Alinde Moore and Dorothy Stratton (2002), men's reorganization of their lives having "passed through the storm." Of course some men do not effectively adapt or reorganize their lives, but most do. Reflecting on his own experience, Howell (2013, 4) noted,

> An epiphany I had, a year or so after the death of my wife, was the realization that I was in the process of becoming a man that she had never known. My conversations with other widowed men led me to believe that this realization was almost universal. It was certainly one of the most jolting, even frightening experiences I've ever had.

Piecing together the research on widowers' resilience and old men's sense of a resilient self, it is arguable that the resilient widower detaches himself from *continued* psychological participation in his former marriage; lives in the

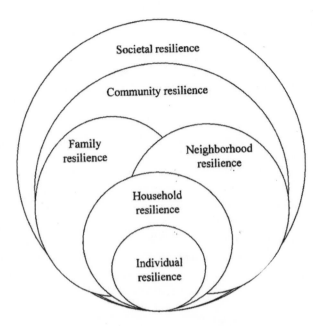

Figure 3: Contextual Spheres of Resiliency Source: Wild, Wiles, and Allen (2013, 153).

present and is future-oriented, even though he keeps connections with his past social identities; appraises and alters his relationships and involvements with friends and family to maximize social capital and shed the unhelpful; and achieves a new lifestyle, whether it involves an intimate companion/ partner or not. As Rubinstein (1986) noted, "present time" is viewed as part of "future time" among the men who reorganize their lives, whereas among the men who do not adapt, "present time" rests heavily on "past time."

The study of resilience among aging men and women has its roots in psychological models of stress resistance and adaption to traumatic events and stress pile-up, as well as in studies of immigrant and military families. After several decades of research, the emergent perspective was that "resilience" indicates positive adaptation in the context of risk or adversity. Rutter (2012), a developmental psychologist, emphasized the outcome of someone "bouncing back" from an unsettling challenge or traumatic event. His model emphasized process, not the person. Shortly following a traumatic event, such as the diagnosis of a life-threatening illness or the death of a spouse, a majority of people report symptoms consistent with maladjustment. But these initial symptoms tend to follow a fairly predictable course, and after three to six months they fade as individuals adapt. From a long-term perspective, social aging itself can lead to the development of adaptive capabilities, allowing one to meet the demands of later life with strength and humor. It is sociologically intriguing to think in terms of the "resiliency" of old men facing uncommon and unanticipated stressful times as encompassing a process of re-restoration as much as the man's emotional sense of bouncing back. This conceptualization interprets the challenges of late and very late life as little different than the challenges and amendment of identities the men confronted throughout their lives. Paraphrasing Gullette (2004, 10), men's latest self might have changed its opinion of an earlier self.

By comparison, Bonanno's analysis of grief names one of the five bereavement trajectories "resilience," because of the observed ability of the widowed person to maintain relatively stable, healthy levels of psychological and physical functioning throughout bereavement. Defined this way, resilience is one distinctive pattern of adaptation, which basically reveals no chaos or marked "bumps" in symptomology of distress caused by the stressful event. The great value of Bonanno's longitudinal studies for theory-building among gerontologists has been in demonstrating that bereavement is more complexly experienced than is proposed by a linear stage model. One "resilient" trajectory of adaptation following the death of a spouse, however, is not the same as the resiliency among most old men who live as widowers or husbands or never-marrieds.

My difficulty with the past emphasis on resilience in bereavement studies, and the developmental psychology tradition of singling out a post-trauma trajectory of healthy or "successful recovery" (Bonanno 2004, 25), is the resulting horse blinders to investigating resiliency among most old men. Take the case of widowers whose everyday life following decades of living within a marriage provides clear evidence of their capabilities of living solo (or, at times, repartnering). Recall, Brown et al. (2016) estimated that about one-quarter of US widowers repartnered, either by cohabiting or remarrying, within ten years of their wife's death; and for Canada widowers Wu, Schimmele, and Oulette (2015) estimate that 29 percent had formed a new union within ten years. This means that in the US and Canada the vast majority of widowers live solo. These old men retain their autonomy and many enjoy the oasis of their home. They live alone, whether their late life leaves unchanged many rituals and aspects of homelife or reveals a markedly new lifestyle compared to their former married life and a "life worthy of passionate reinvestment" (Neimeyer 2009, 228). Widowers' restoration of meaning in late life is an exemplar of the resilience affirmed in several recent studies.

In late life, there always will be a "bump"—the death of the man's wife, acquiring a "funny knee" that inhibits mobility, acknowledging that quality of his eyesight warrants driving cessation. These turning points necessitate dealing with lifestyle change. Resilience involves functioning more adaptively than would be expected given the severity of the "bump"—"thriving versus merely surviving" (Wild, Wiles, and Allen 2013, 139). The man who curtails driving himself about can expand his confidence and social capital in asking for assistance without jeopardizing masculine capital. The man whose diminished mobility now limits skiing or hiking can maintain masculine capital by his involvement within social groups that play competitive pinochle or chess or by wearing a knee brace for less challenging day hikes. As the research on men's bereavement adaptation advises, unless the men's grieving remains chronic, there is restoration and, we can assume, amended lifestyles for the vast majority of old men who become widowers. Most old men's lived experience of widowerhood is rooted in the "ordinary magic" of their resilience. They draw on their acquired experience in other contexts and the external supports old men can derive from their community capital and social environment, such as working-class old men finding companionship within the registered clubs in Australia that Simpson-Young and Russell (2009) describe, or the morning coffee gatherings among Canadian widowers in a Tim Horton's, or the morning pool area card games among widowers in retirement villages in Florida (van den Hoonaard 2010).

We know too little about the import that spirituality or religiosity has on old men's resilience, especially whether spirituality may differently impact the trajectories of "restitution" entailing little change in lifestyle or when widowers build new late life lifestyles and recreate themselves. Not surprisingly, this is partly because most research on the influence of religion or spirituality on bereavement has sampled widows. Dillon and Wink (2007) propose that religious faith or spirituality is a central component of resilience among the very old and intensifies throughout later and late life. It is not the frequency of religious activity, but people's basic belief structure or schema (Berger 1969; Lincoln and Mamiya 1990), their faith or spirituality, that serves as a buffer and pilots their sense of purpose in late life. In an interesting study, Maneerat, Isaramalai, and Boonyasopum (2011) investigated the structure of resilience among Thai elderly and distinguished three components of resilience within the elders' narratives, which the researchers called "I am," "I have," and "I can." The inner strength (or "I am") included positive thinking and a sense of humor. This was attributed to having a strong faith and spiritual support ("I have"), which was voiced by every participant as the foundation of his or her resilience and rebuilding resilience ("I can").

From interviews and a series of participant-led focus groups in New Zealand with older people (aged 56–92) discussing the meaning of resilience, one theme Wiles and her colleagues (2012, 419) identified was called "counting blessings." The participants were commenting on a specific kind of positive attitude, one related to spirituality and specifically their Christian beliefs. For example, within a focus group, one man, Vic, succinctly noted, "I thank the good Lord every morning and say, 'Thank you Lord, another day' and I'm away . . . It's your outlook, I think." What Vic is reporting is how his own sense of social and functional resilience is largely a positive state of mind, which for him includes faith and private religious practices.

Wiles et al. (2012) also heard their study participants discuss resilience in terms of living with illness and disability but still being positive—having purpose and keeping busy rather waiting for the inevitable to "go downhill"; and, finding resilience by incorporating the ability to ask for and accept help from neighbors, friends, and, if nearby, family. Their collective narrative included talk related to individual character and responsibilities, yet, importantly, "resilience was understood as being embedded in social and physical contexts. For example, our participants illustrate that having a positive attitude or purpose in life is not merely an internal state, but is inextricably connected to relationships with others, to the resources available in a giving community" (Wiles et al. 2012, 422). Moore and Stratton (2003) also found almost all of the old men held a secure uncomplicated faith and referred to their religious faith as central to their well-being. The researchers found a few widowers who professed no religious faith, some other men who attended religious services ritualistically and without much consideration of beliefs, and others who searched for spiritual understanding. It "appeared that those men with religious faith—whether derived from strong and unexamined beliefs or from a philosophical quest—were the most at peace in their late life . . . The men with philosophical leanings seemed to have suffered more along the way, but may have come to more satisfying understanding" (Moore and Stratton 2002, 164). In addition, the social interaction associated with public religious activity was noted as a resiliency resource; "the church or synagogue had been a place for social relationships while they were married, and it remained so for them in widowhood" (ibid., 193).

In his discussion of the connection between irony and personal resiliency in late life, Randall (2013a, 166) proposed that old age itself "be thought of as the postmodern phase of our lives as individuals, in which case irony is the genre, the 'narrative tone.'" He continued, "aging itself pushes us (and our *stories* of us) to be more ironic" (ibid., 168, italics original). Randall is comfortable framing his own theorizing about irony in late life using developmental theories of Loevinger on ego development, Fowler on faith development, and Erikson's view of development wisdom and late life irony. He notes that bodily aging progressively makes doing some things more an effort and thus a source of either despair or humor, whereby resilient old men can laugh at themselves and even chuckle, on occasion, with an ageist "joke." Humor, an expression of the irony, reaffirms looking forward and amending our embodiment of the state of the body. Randall hypothesizes that old people who have lived as impoverished are more practiced at experiencing life ironically, because they can assess their status vis-à-vis the "haves." And he hypothesizes that people's sense of irony is intensified through narrative reflection.

I find this latter observation very often voiced in old men's narratives of doing care work for their disabled and dying wives, where they say, "She's not what she used to be . . . yet she is the same, my bride!"; or in self-stories and reminiscence about being the oldest officer in the unit in Vietnam to discover he arrived last at the bomb shelter 20 meters from the tent and said, laughing, "and I thought I was still fast." These old men, talking among themselves with me listening, related life stories of "growing old," not "getting old." The men convey a sense of irony about their embodied masculinities and practices, hinting at their transition to more preferable aging masculinities. Randall calls such people resilient, based on the view that resilience is the "ability to transform adversity into a growth experience and move forward" (2013b, 9). Randall and his colleagues noted that resilient aging men provide rich and complex stories about themselves and their lives in distinctive ways, and often voice the irony of growing old because they "have a certain distance on things, to view them critically or from the 'edge'" (2013b, 10). They actively resist "narrative foreclosure," which de-stories and treats the old man as an "other," no longer present.

SUMMARY

Living within the realities created by the culture and fields of the third age means having to face up to its shadow: the fourth age. The fields within fourth age culture continue to serve as a powerful social imaginary containing the notions of corporeal and cognitive frailty and dependence, which can undermine old men's subjectivities. The fourth age as it has been imagined, and as sometimes lived, casts worries about selfhood and for any public understanding of old men and aging masculinities.

My own interviews and conversations with old men, and my reading of other scholars' interviews and interpretations of men's narratives of late life, have convinced me that paying attention to the social imaginary is awfully inhibiting. Old men's narratives about their late life experiences emphasize how they accommodate aging-related physical challenges, social network changes, and a redemptive capacity to "take on" life challenges. It misses recognition of the fourth age as a cultural field. Very old men, even if their stroke-determined vocabulary is limited to profane, two-word greetings and responses, remain in their eyes *men*, not "cases" or the patient in the room down the corridor. Their embodied masculinities reflect their aging and narrated biographies. Most remain resilient; many retain meaningful lives, but too many remain "othered" by the narcissism of the culture of the third age and its "successful aging" underpinning. Other than when I exit from a brief conversation with a very old person who is no longer "here" cognitively, I have never been pained by my encounter; rather, I have been inspired to know more about their personal lives and about very old men in general. People are incredibly resilient. They have multiple identities that are masked by our misunderstandings, and they retain an underlying continuity in self-presentation even when amended through aging. Old men who are so-called fourth agers can inform gerontological and critical men's studies scholarship, but haven't been granted the opportunity. The National Institutes of Health is not alone in its reluctance to support new research investigating very old men's lives and welfare. So are publishers of textbooks on aging or men's lives.

Epilogue

Throughout *Men, Masculinities, and Aging* the construct "aging masculinities" is used to identify a subset within the field of masculinities. Aging masculinities are eventually performed and in every respect embodied by the majority of old men. It is time to clarify my contribution to the theorizing of the field of aging masculinities.

Spector-Mersel's (2006) elaboration of never-aging masculinity is a productive point of departure. By her account "never-aging masculinities" is not simply another name for the ideal or hegemonic masculinities discussed by sociologist Raewyn Connell (1995) or detailed in social psychologist Robert Brannon's (1976) "blueprint of masculinity." Both Connell's and Brannon's conceptualizations indeed truncate the gender script somewhere in midlife. Spector-Mersel's thesis is that through public discourse and academic theorizing, what people envision, embody, and discuss as the dominant masculinity "script" is abridged in life span time and ignores the import of later life and bodily aging. It is the ignoring that is critical. She writes, while this "preserves an acceptable (i.e., young) masculine self, it runs the risk of denying the aging process" (Spector-Mersel 2006, 78). Never-aging masculinities, and the hegemonic masculinities from the modernist era onward, are ageist and unquestionably ignore men's experiences from late midlife through very late life. Thus, as life span time became decades longer for most men during the modern era, there was an "absence of clear cultural guidelines as to 'how to be an aging man'" (ibid., 79).

Within postmodernity, the absence of clarity as to how to be an aging man is magnified, because there is a near-hegemonic third age cultural field advocating unscripted late lifestyles that extend many of the masculinity practices of early adulthood into later life. There is a needed "well, almost" here. The advocacy within third age cultures applies for the men who decide to practice their generation's new iteration of resistance to "old age" and have sufficient resources to resist in some way. Inasmuch as old men have access to and live with different personal social and cultural capital as well as the variegated community capital within their geographies of place, I have argued that their "resistance" to old age varies. Consequently there is not "an aging masculinity" but many aging masculinities. Slevin and Linneman (2010, 492) smartly caution to not overemphasize "differences"; they capture the core commonality of aging masculinities when quoting an 85-year-old man voicing his identity as a man: "Getting older has made me more real . . . I am freer to say 'Hey, I am not a gay, just a gay. That does not fit me. I'm a man before I'm a gay man.'"

My thinking is that most aging men struggle to reject the never-aging masculinities that steered their lives at least through midlife (Thompson and Langendoerfer 2016), but at some point in later life most men's tastes change, practices are modified by taste and body capabilities, and the men's habitus is modified to reveal the tastes and practices of aging masculinities. If the cliché that it takes a village to raise a child is true, it equally takes a village to free an aging man from the restraints of never-aging masculinities and to welcomingly embody the tastes of an aging masculinity. In doing so, this one man comes to occupy another "subordinate" status from the lens of hegemonic masculinities (T. Coles 2008, 2009). But his masculine subjectivity as an aging man is most consonant with his more frequent experiences in fields of aging masculinities.

While speculative, aging men acquire complex and ambivalent orientations toward never-aging masculinity, supporting some elements and rejecting others as they amend their habitus and practices to be fish-in-water old men. Borrowing Bourdieu's tennis metaphor, they intuitively no longer run to the net when their opponent delivers a drop shot; instead, they complement the opponent with "nice shot." The rules of the game shift to "have fun, don't hurt yourself." They play competitive tennis, but differently. Embodying the masculinities of later life is more than an aging matter; it is a shift in perspective. Later life presents new fields for men to engage themselves in and modify priorities and practices. For example, Sorensen and Cooper (2010) proposed that grandfathering offers the potential of counteracting the expectations of never-aging masculinities because of the opportunity to form new and close relationships *with children*. Mann (2007) noticed men's embodiment of aging masculinities when he studied grandfathers and their "softening" through relational practices, compared to the men's previously practiced forceful, nonrelational masculinities. StGeorge and Fletcher (2014, 369–70) also drew on grandfathers' experiences and emphasized how

> the depth of feeling and the reciprocity in the relationship with the grandchildren were both unforeseen and delightful. However, when this connection

transcended traditional expectations . . . the feelings were catalysts for rethinking lives and priorities. Rather than an identity transformation, the difference
appeared to be a *widening* of what they counted as existing, a *widening* of their
understanding of life purpose and meaning. This is . . . ontological change . . .
to see themselves differently, to change their core beliefs about themselves or
the world. (my italics)

"Softening." "Widening." Interesting assessments on what aging masculinities could be about.

The practice of aging masculinities comes about slowly. Men do not
replace their embodied masculinities any more than a widower who occasionally dates or recouples "replaces" his former wife. She is always with
him—in memory, as a comparison standard of what he is (un)comfortable
with, as an absent coparent with his adult children and grandchildren. Aging
masculinities amend the never-aging masculinities that are part of habitus,
and through time the modifications can be substantial. As reported in chapter
6, Tony Coles's (2008, 238) imagined "mosaic masculinities" are distinctive
in how aging masculinities are constructed, whereby a man draws upon the
"fragments or pieces of hegemonic masculinity" he has the inclination and
capacity to practice, and pieces this together with new practices arising from
later life fields to reformulate what masculinity means to him. Each reformulated masculinity is a mosaic; seemingly incompatible fragments of "doing
masculinity" are crafted together and merged to form a new, evolving ontological whole. Bridges and Pascoe (2014) similarly direct attention to recent
transformations in the performances of masculinities that result in "hybrid
masculinities." They propose, and I concur, that hybrid masculinities position the dominant masculinities as less meaningful than the emergent (aging)
masculinities produced by, for example, old grandfathers and husbands who
may or may not still ride a motorcycle, choose to eat a hearty breakfast and a
healthy light dinner, and remain agentic in deciding their daily experiences
when "institutionalized" in a care facility.

Drawing on nearly one hundred studies, Thompson and Langendoerfer
(2016) examined what aging men voiced as the content of their lived masculinities. We noted that aging and old men appear to have acquired a habitus
that continues to resemble the "blueprint of manhood" that Brannon (1976)
outlined in the mid-1970s. The evidence we mined suggests that older men's
narratives and "small stories" about their masculinity practices retain some of
the "no sissy stuff," "big wheel," "sturdy oak," and "give 'em hell" masculinity injunctions Brannon identified as the "blueprint of manhood," but the
men's narratives are not altogether consistent with "traditional" masculinities. They reveal amendments to and modifications in their embodied masculinities. The available evidence is too "limited to white men whose work
histories represent the middle class and/or the 'settled-living' working class"

(Thompson and Langendoerfer 2016, 136) to generalize. There is little inter-view and narrative data voicing the lived experiences of other than partnered white United States, Canadian, and European men. Considering the cultural vagueness about how old men should and actually "do masculinity," we found the men typically present narratives that recognize their incongruous experiences with the never-aging scripts that seemed to more closely fit their earlier experiences.

My thinking is that three social things distinguish the late life experiences of old men: there is an ongoing experience of oneself as a man, and as an aging man; there is the invariant reality and a subjective recognition of the accumulative effects of morphological and physiological bodily changes in ageist societies; and there is a downsizing of sources of social capital to those relations that assure the affective potential of interaction. The practice of aging masculinities does not equate to untethered, ungendered men just be-cause they are "old" or have presumably experienced the triple Ds—decline, disengagement, and demasculation—associated with the "social imaginary" of old age. First, men understand the importance of bodies in discourses of never-aging masculinities (Bartholomaeus and Tarrant 2016; Coles and Vas-sarotti 2012). They recognize that no matter their prior "fitness," their aging bodies complicate matters and influence decisions and practices to be more aligned with later life capabilities and the affirmation felt when fields of aging masculinities become their touchstone—e.g., a conscious decision to take a daily walk to retain muscle strength and flexibility can be set aside in order to not exercise and just relax. Coles and Vassarotti (2012, 36) also suggest that instead of trying to fit the male body ideal that becomes less achievable the older men become, most men developed other masculine capi-tal-producing strategies to counterbalance their aging bodies. They actually preferred the fields of aging masculinity because in these fields the capital they own is valued. Observe, for example, how athletic participation changes to body-compatible activities—e.g., swimming, pétanque and bocce ball, racquetball and squash, darts, cardio exercise rather than strength exercis-ing—where "muscular intellectualness" is substituted for brawn.

Second, the downsizing of social contacts is predictable according to Laura Carstensen's (1992) socioemotional selectivity theory, which holds that as men grow older their preferences for affectively rich interactions increase and the desire to affiliate with less familiar people decreases. Car-stensen's (2006) theorizing regarding aging constraints on time horizons, and thus old men's appreciation that time eventually runs out, predicts shifts in men's motivational priorities. They adjust their social capital, basing it on a higher proportion of significant others and fewer of the peripheral, instru-mental relations they maintained while younger men. Men may not replace the outer circle of acquaintances as they move into later and late life. They let those relations go. In her research Rosemary Wright (2015, 71) listened to a

67-year-old man talk about his aging-related preferences for intimacies with friends: "I think we're a lot more inclined to go to a friend's house for dinner or have them over to our house for dinner rather than going out somewhere. Also . . . I value closer, less hectic encounters."

As downsizing is guided by the age-related desire to maximize time spent in *emotionally* rewarding interaction, it is not surprising that Thompson and Whearty (2004) found an age-related way that "mind matters" to men (cf. B. Levy 2003). Among the men (average age 72) who did not endorse the tenets of "traditional" masculinity ideology, such as to avoid feelings and other things stereotyped as "feminine," engaging in positive social relations was more common. Men's late life movement into affectively rich interactions has benefits—it diminishes feeling of duress and increases the likelihood of survival (e.g., Giles et al. 2005). And it may well be that the old men who abandon trying to live by the tenets of never-aging masculinities and become comfortable within fields of aging masculinities are the men who benefit most.

The link between body capabilities and constructing one's own mosaic of aging masculinity practices can be directly examined through men's story-telling and reflective analysis within life narratives. Narrative gerontology teaches us that storytelling is a way of communicating meaning in life, what was and what is meaningful. Storytelling is a forum for men to describe their late life experiences from the vantage point of the man himself, and by *listening* to their stories we can better understand their embodiment of aging masculinities. But too frequently the listener customarily only *hears* old men striving to live up the scripts of never-aging masculinities, something Thompson and Langendoerfer (2016) noticed was the case in many qualitative studies that interpreted old men's masculinity performances only through a "traditional," never-aging masculinities lens. This lack of attentiveness to old men's other-masculinity performances that affirm their interests in fields of aging masculinities will continue to cast old men as fallen men and restate the hegemony of never aging. My own thinking is that we researchers have not listened well enough. We can be deafened by the discourses of the cultural field of the third age that shout, "Avoid getting old." When old men have rebuilt their lifestyles and modified their habitus and then "talk" using idioms incongruous with never aging, we may learn more about aging masculinities, and how these masculinities may well continue to reproduce some gender inequalities (between men and women, and among men). Should we listen, we can pay attention to old men affirming the various aging masculinities they embody and practice within later and late life cultural fields.

References

Aburn, Gemma, Merryn Gott, and Karen Hoare. "What Is Resilience? An Integrative Review of the Empirical Literature." *Journal of Advanced Nursing* 72, no. 5 (2016): 980–1000.

Adam, Barry D. "Relationship Innovation in Male Couples." *Sexualities* 9, no. 1 (2006), 5–26.

Addis, Michael. *Invisible Men: Men's Inner Lives and the Consequences of Silence.* New York: Macmillan, 2011.

Ainlay, Stephen C. *Day Brought Back My Night: Aging and New Vision Loss.* New York: Routledge, 1989.

Albom, Mitch. *Tuesdays with Morrie: An Old Man, a Young Man, and Life's Greatest Lesson.* New York: Doubleday, 1997.

Aléx, Lena, Anne Hammarström, Astrid Norberg, and Berit Lundman. "Construction of Masculinities among Men Aged 85 and Older in the North of Sweden." *Journal of Clinical Nursing* 17, no. 4 (2008): 451–59.

Allen, Rebecca S., Philip P. Haley, Grant M. Harris, Stevie N. Fowler, and Roopwinder Pruthi. "Resilience: Definitions, Ambiguities, and Applications." In *Resilience in Aging: Concepts, Research, and Outcomes*, edited by Barbara Resnick, Lisa Gwyther, and Rebecca Allen, 1–13. New York: Springer, 2011.

Allensworth-Davies, Donald, James A. Talcott, Timothy Heeren, Brian de Vries, Thomas Blank, and Jack A. Clark. "The Health Effects of Masculine Self-Esteem Following Treatment for Localized Prostate Cancer among Gay Men." *LGBT Health* 3, no. 1 (2016): 49–56.

Alterovitz, Sheyna S. R., and Gerald A. Mendelsohn. "Relationship Goals of Middle-Aged, Young-Old, and Old-Old Internet Daters: An Analysis of Online Personal Ads." *Journal of Aging Studies* 27, no. 2 (2013): 159–65.

Apesoa-Varano, Ester Carolina, Judith C. Barker, and Ladson Hinton. "Shards of Sorrow: Older Men's Accounts of Their Depression Experience." *Social Science & Medicine* 124 (2015): 1–8.

Apesoa-Varano, Ester Carolina, Judith C. Barker, Jurgen Unutzer, Sergio Aguilar-Gaxiola, Megan Dwight Johnson, Cindy Tran, Peter Guarnaccia, and Ladson Hinton. "Idioms of Distress among Depressed White-Non-Mexican and Mexican-Origin Older Men." *Journal of Cross-Cultural Gerontology* 30, no. 3 (2015): 305–18.

Araujo, Andre B., Beth A. Mohr, and John B. McKinlay. "Changes in Sexual Function in Middle-Aged and Older Men: Longitudinal Data from the Massachusetts Male Aging Study." *Journal of the American Geriatrics Society* 52, no. 9 (2004): 1502–9.

Arciniega, G. Miguel, Thomas C. Anderson, Zoila G. Tovar-Blank, and Terence J. G. Tracey. "Toward a Fuller Conception of Machismo: Development of a Traditional Machismo and Caballerismo Scale." *Journal of Counseling Psychology* 55, no. 1 (2008): 19–33.

Arias, Elizabeth. *Changes in Life Expectancy by Race and Hispanic Origin in the United States, 2013 – 2014*. National Center for Health Statistics Data Brief 244. Washington, DC: US Department of Health and Human Services, Centers for Disease Control and Prevention, April 2016.

Åsberg, Cecilia, and Ericka Johnson. "Viagra Selfhood: Pharmaceutical Advertising and the Visual Formation of Swedish Masculinity." *Health Care Analysis* 17, no. 2 (2009): 144–57.

Asencio, Marysol, Thomas Blank, Lara Descartes, and Ashley Crawford. "The Prospect of Prostate Cancer: A Challenge for Gay Men's Sexualities as They Age." *Sexuality Research and Social Policy* 6, no. 4 (2009): 38–51.

Aytaç, Işik A., Andre B. Araujo, Catherine B. Johannes, Ken P. Kleinman, and John B. McKinlay. "Socioeconomic Factors and Incidence of Erectile Dysfunction: Findings of the Longitudinal Massachusetts Male Aging Study." *Social Science & Medicine* 51, no. 5 (2000): 771–78.

Baglia, Jay. *The Viagra Ad Venture: Masculinity, Marketing, and the Performance of Sexual Health*. New York: Peter Lang, 2005.

Balaswamy, Shantha, Virginia Richardson, and Christine A. Price. "Investigating Patterns of Social Support Use by Widowers During Bereavement." *Journal of Men's Studies* 13, no. 1 (2004): 67–84.

Band-Winterstein, Tova, and Carmit Manchik-Rimon. "The Experience of Being an Old Never-Married Single: A Life Course Perspective." *International Journal of Aging and Human Development* 78, no. 4 (2014): 379–401.

Barrett, Anne, and Clayton Gumber. "How Do Aging Body Reminders Affect Age Identity?" Paper presented at the annual meeting of the Gerontological Society of America, New Orleans, LA, 2016. Abstracted in *The Gerontologist* 56, no. s3, 587.

Barrett, Frank J. "The Organizational Construction of Hegemonic Masculinity: The Case of the US Navy." *Gender, Work & Organization* 3, no. 3 (1996): 129–42.

Bartholomaeus, Clare, and Anna Tarrant. "Masculinities at the Margins of 'Middle Adulthood': What a Consideration of Young Age and Old Age Offers Masculinities Theorizing." *Men and Masculinities* 19, no. 4 (2016): 351–69.

Bates, James S. "Generative Grandfathering: A Conceptual Framework for Nurturing Grandchildren." *Marriage & Family Review* 45, no. 4 (2009): 331–52.

Bauman, Zygmunt. *Liquid Modernity*. Cambridge: Polity Press, 2000.

Bäumker, Theresia, Lisa Callaghan, Robin Darton, Jacquetta Holder, Ann Netten, and Ann-Marie Towers. "Deciding to Move into Extra Care Housing: Residents' Views." *Ageing and Society* 32, no. 7 (2012): 1215–45.

Beckman, Nils, Margda Waern, Deborah Gustafson, and Ingmar Skoog. "Secular Trends in Self Reported Sexual Activity and Satisfaction in Swedish 70 Year Olds: Cross Sectional Survey of Four Populations, 1971–2001." *BMJ* 337 (2008): a279.

Benedict, Francis Gano, and Thorne Martin Carpenter. *Influence of Muscular and Mental Work on Metabolism and the Efficiency of the Human Body as a Machine*. Bulletin no. 208, Office of Experiment Stations, US Department of Agriculture. Washington, DC: Government Printing Office, 1909.

Bennett, Gary G., Marcellus M. Merritt, John J. Sollers III, Christopher L. Edwards, Keith E. Whitfield, Dwayne T. Brandon, and Reginald D. Tucker. "Stress, Coping, and Health Outcomes among African-Americans: A Review of the John Henryism Hypothesis." *Psychology & Health* 19, no. 3 (2004): 369–83.

Bennett, Kate M. "How to Achieve Resilience as an Older Widower: Turning Points or Gradual Change?" *Ageing and Society* 30, no. 3 (2010): 369–82.

———. "'No Sissy Stuff': Towards a Theory of Masculinity and Emotional Expression in Older Widowed Men." *Journal of Aging Studies* 21, no. 4 (2007): 347–56.

———. "'Was Life Worth Living?' Older Widowers and Their Explicit Discourses of the Decision to Live." *Mortality* 10, no. 2 (2005): 144–54.

Bennett, Kate M., Lauren Arnott, and Laura K. Soulsby. "'You're Not Getting Married for the Moon and the Stars': The Uncertainties of Older British Widowers about the Idea of New Romantic Relationships." *Journal of Aging Studies* 27, no. 4 (2013): 499–506.

Bennett, Kate M., Georgina M. Hughes, and Philip T. Smith. "'I Think a Woman Can Take It': Widowed Men's Views and Experiences of Gender Differences in Bereavement." *Ageing International* 28, no. 4 (2003): 408–24.

Bennett, Kate M., Philip T. Smith, and Georgina M. Hughes. "Coping, Depressive Feelings and Gender Differences in Late Life Widowhood." *Aging & Mental Health* 9, no. 4 (2005): 348–53.

Benson, Jacquelyn J., and Marilyn Coleman. "Older Adult Descriptions of Living Apart Together." *Family Relations* 65, no. 3 (2016a): 439–49.

———. "Older Adults Developing a Preference for Living Apart Together." *Journal of Marriage and Family* 78, no. 3 (2016b): 797–812.

Berger, Peter L. *The Sacred Canopy* . Garden City, NY: Doubleday, 1969.

Berger, Peter, and Hansfried Kellner. "Marriage and the Construction of Reality: An Exercise in the Microsociology of Knowledge." *Diogenes* 12, no. 46 (1964): 1–24.

Berger, Peter L., and Thomas Luckmann. *The Social Construction of Reality: A Treatise in the Sociology of Knowledge*. New York: Penguin Books, 1967.

Bergling, Tim. *Reeling in the Years: Gay Men's Perspectives on Age and Ageism*. New York: Harrington Park Press, 2004.

Beutel, Manfred E., Yve Stöbel-Richter, and Elmar Brähler. "Sexual Desire and Sexual Activity of Men and Women Across Their Lifespans: Results from a Representative German Community Survey." *BJU International* 101, no. 1 (2008): 76–82.

Biggs, Simon. "Age, Gender, Narratives, and Masquerades." *Journal of Aging Studies* 18, no. 1 (2004): 45–58.

Bildtgård, Torbjörn, and Peter Öberg. "Attitudes, Experiences and Expectations on New Intimate Relationships in Later Life: Results from a Swedish National Survey." Paper presented at the 20th IAGG World Congress of Gerontology and Geriatrics, Seoul, Korea, June 23–27, 2013.

———. "New Intimate Relationships in Later Life: Consequences for the Social and Filial Network?" *Journal of Family Issues* 38, no. 3 (2017): 381–405.

Blows, Emma, Lynda Bird, Jane Seymour, and Karen Cox. "Liminality as a Framework for Understanding the Experience of Cancer Survivorship: A Literature Review." *Journal of Advanced Nursing* 68, no. 10 (2012): 2155–64.

Bonanno, George A. "Loss, Trauma, and Human Resilience: Have We Underestimated the Human Capacity to Thrive After Extremely Aversive Events?" *American Psychologist* 59, no. 1 (2004): 20–28.

Bonanno, George A., and Stacey Kaltman. "The Varieties of Grief Experience." *Clinical Psychology Review* 20, no. 5 (2001): 705–34.

Bonanno, George A., Camille B. Wortman, and Randolph M. Nesse. "Prospective Patterns of Resilience and Maladjustment During Widowhood." *Psychology and Aging* 19, no. 2 (2004): 260–71.

Bourdieu, Pierre. *Distinction: A Social Critique of the Judgment of Taste*. Cambridge: Harvard University Press, 1984.

———. *The Field of Cultural Production: Essays on Art and Literature*. New York: Columbia University Press, 1993b.

———. *The Logic of Practice*. Stanford: Stanford University Press, 1990.

———. *Masculine Domination*. Stanford: Stanford University Press, 2001.

———. *Sociology in Question*. Thousand Oaks, CA: Sage, 1993a.

Bourdieu, Pierre, and Loïc J. D. Wacquant. *An Invitation to Reflexive Sociology*. Chicago: University of Chicago Press, 1992.

Bourgois, Philippe, and Jeff Schonberg. "Intimate Apartheid: Ethnic Dimensions of Habitus among Homeless Heroin Injectors." *Ethnography* 8, no. 1 (2007): 7–31.

Brannon, Robert. "The Male Sex Role: Our Culture's Blueprint of Manhood, and What It's Done for Us Lately." In *The Forty-Nine Percent Majority: The Male Sex Role*, edited by Deborah S. David and Robert Brannon, 1–48. Reading, MA: Addison-Wesley, 1976.

Brännström, Helene, Margit Bäckman, and Regina Santamäki Fischer. "Walking on the Edge: Meanings of Living in an Ageing Body and Using a Walker in Everyday Life—A Phenomenological Hermeneutic Study." *International Journal of Older People Nursing* 8, no. 2 (2013): 116–22.

Bridges, Tristan, and Cheri J. Pascoe. "Hybrid Masculinities: New Directions in the Sociology of Men and Masculinities." *Sociology Compass* 8, no. 3 (2014): 246–58.

Bristowe, Katherine, Steve Marshall, and Richard Harding. "The Bereavement Experiences of Lesbian, Gay, Bisexual and/or Trans* People Who Have Lost a Partner: A Systematic Review, Thematic Synthesis and Modelling of the Literature." *Palliative Medicine* 30, no. 8 (2016): 730–44.

Broom, Alex, and John Cavenagh. "Masculinity, Moralities and Being Cared For: An Exploration of Experiences of Living and Dying in a Hospice." *Social Science & Medicine* 71, no. 5 (2010): 869–76.

Brown, Joseph Winchester, Jersey Liang, Neal Krause, Hiroko Akiyama, Hidehiro Sugisawa, and Taro Fukaya. "Transitions in Living Arrangements among Elders in Japan: Does Health Make a Difference?" *Journals of Gerontology Series B: Psychological Sciences and Social Sciences* 57, no. 4 (2002): S209–20.

Brown, Susan L., Jennifer Roebuck Bulanda, and Gary R. Lee. "Transitions Into and Out of Cohabitation in Later Life." *Journal of Marriage and Family* 74, no. 4 (2012): 774–93.

Brown, Susan L., and I-Fen Lin. "The Gray Divorce Revolution: Rising Divorce among Middle-Aged and Older Adults, 1990–2010." *Journals of Gerontology Series B: Psychological Sciences and Social Sciences* 67, no. 6 (2012): 731–41.

Brown, Susan L., I-Fen Lin, Anna M. Hammersmith, and Matthew R. Wright. "Later Life Marital Dissolution and Repartnership Status: A National Portrait." *Journals of Gerontology Series B: Psychological Sciences and Social Sciences*, April 30, 2016. https://doi.org/10.1093/geronb/gbw051.

Brown, Susan L., and Sayaka K. Shinohara. "Dating Relationships in Older Adulthood: A National Portrait." *Journal of Marriage and Family* 75, no. 5 (2013): 1194–1202.

Browne-Yung, Kathryn, Ruth B. Walker, and Mary A. Luszcz. "An Examination of Resilience and Coping in the Oldest Old Using Life Narrative Method." *The Gerontologist* 57, no. 2 (2017): 282–91.

Brownhill, Suzanne, Kay Wilhelm, Lesley Barclay, and Virginia Schmied. "'Big Build': Hidden Depression in Men." *Australian and New Zealand Journal of Psychiatry* 39, no. 10 (2005): 921–31.

Bryant, Lia, and Bridget Garnham. "The Fallen Hero: Masculinity, Shame and Farmer Suicide in Australia." *Gender, Place & Culture* 22, no. 1 (2015): 67–82.

Buchanan, Ann, and Anna Rotkirch. *Grandfathers: Global Perspectives*. New York: Palgrave Macmillan, 2016.

Bullington, Jennifer. "Body and Self: A Phenomenological Study on the Ageing Body and Identity." In *The Self in Health and Illness: Patients, Professionals and Narrative Identity*, edited by Frances Rapport and Paul Wainwright, 69–84. Oxford: Radcliffe Publishing, 2006.

Bullock, Karen. "Grandfathers and the Impact of Raising Grandchildren." *Journal of Sociology & Social Welfare* 32, no. 1 (2005): 43–59.

Bunkley, Darrell, John D. Robins, Nelson E. Bennett, and Sherilyn Gordon. "Breast Cancer in Men: Emasculation by Association?" *Journal of Clinical Psychology in Medical Settings* 7, no. 2 (2000): 91–97.

Butler, Judith. *Bodies That Matter: On the Discursive Limits of Sex*. New York: Routledge, 1993.

———. *Gender Trouble: Feminism and the Subversion of Identity*. New York: Routledge, 1990.

———. "Performative Acts and Gender Constitution: An Essay in Phenomenology and Feminist Theory." *Theatre Journal* 40, no. 4 (1988): 519–31.

———. "Restaging the Universal: Hegemony and the Limits of Formalism." In *Contingency, Hegemony, and Universality: Contemporary Dialogues on the Left*, edited by Judith Butler, Ernesto Laclau, and Slavoj Žižek, 11–43. New York: Verso, 2000.

Cahill, Suzanne. "Elderly Husbands Caring at Home for Wives Diagnosed with Alzheimer's Disease: Are Male Caregivers Really Different?" *Australian Journal of Social Issues* 35, no. 1 (2000): 53–72.

Calasanti, Toni. "Combating Ageism: How Successful Is Successful Aging?" *The Gerontologist* 56, no. 6 (2016): 1093–1101.

———. "Feminist Gerontology and Old Men." *Journals of Gerontology Series B: Psychological Sciences and Social Sciences* 59, no. 6 (2004): S305–14.

Calasanti, Toni, and Mary Elizabeth Bowen. "Spousal Caregiving and Crossing Gender Boundaries: Maintaining Gendered Identities." *Journal of Aging Studies* 20, no. 3 (2006): 253–63.

Calasanti, Toni, and Neal King. "Firming the Floppy Penis: Age, Class, and Gender Relations in the Lives of Old Men." *Men and Masculinities* 8, no. 1 (2005): 3–23.

Calasanti, Toni M., and Anna M. Zajicek. "A Socialist-Feminist Approach to Aging: Embracing Diversity." *Journal of Aging Studies* 7, no. 2 (1993): 117–31.

Callaghan, Lisa, and Ann-Marie Towers. "Feeling in Control: Comparing Older People's Experiences in Different Care Settings." *Ageing and Society* 34, no. 8 (2014): 1427–51.

Calnan, Michael, and Simon Williams. "Style of Life and the Salience of Health: An Exploratory Study of Health Related Practices in Households from Differing Socio-Economic Circumstances." *Sociology of Health & Illness* 13, no. 4 (1991): 506–29.

Canetto, Silvia Sara. "Men Who Survive a Suicide Act." In *Men's Health and Illness: Gender, Power and the Body*, edited by Donald Sabo and David Gordon, 292–304. Thousand Oaks, CA: Sage Publications, 1995.

———. "Suicide: Why are Older Men So Vulnerable?" *Men and Masculinities* 20, no. 1 (2017): 49–70.

Canham, Sarah L., Atiya Mahmood, Sarah Stott, Judith Sixsmith, and Norm O'Rourke. "'Til Divorce Do Us Part: Marriage Dissolution in Later Life." *Journal of Divorce & Remarriage* 55, no. 8 (2014): 591–612.

Carr, Deborah. "The Desire to Date and Remarry among Older Widows and Widowers." *Journal of Marriage and Family* 66, no. 4 (2004): 1051–68.

Carr, Deborah, Vicki A. Freedman, Jennifer C. Cornman, and Norbert Schwarz. "Happy Marriage, Happy Life? Marital Quality and Subjective Well-Being in Later Life." *Journal of Marriage and Family* 76, no. 5 (2014): 930–48.

Carr, Deborah S., James S. House, Camille B. Wortman, Randolph M. Nesse, and Ronald C. Kessler. "Psychological Adjustment to Sudden and Anticipated Spousal Loss among Older Widowed Persons." *Journals of Gerontology Series B: Psychological Sciences and Social Sciences* 56, no. 4 (2001): S237–48.

Carrigan, Tim, Bob Connell, and John Lee. "Toward a New Sociology of Masculinity." *Theory and Society* 14, no. 5 (1985): 551–604.

Carstensen, Laura L. "The Influence of a Sense of Time on Human Development." *Science* 312, no. 5782 (2006): 1913–15.

———. "Social and Emotional Patterns in Adulthood: Support for Socioemotional Selectivity Theory." *Psychology and Aging* 7, no. 3 (1992): 331–38.

Carstensen, Laura L., Derek M. Isaacowitz, and Susan T. Charles. "Taking Time Seriously: A Theory of Socioemotional Selectivity." *American Psychologist* 54, no. 3 (1999): 165–81.

Carstensen, Laura L., Bulent Turan, Susanne Scheibe, Nilam Ram, Hal Ersner-Hershfield, Gregory R. Samanez-Larkin, Kathryn P. Brooks, and John R. Nesselroade. "Emotional Experience Improves with Age: Evidence Based on Over 10 Years of Experience Sampling." *Psychology and Aging* 26, no. 1 (2011): 21–33.

Case, Anne, and Angus Deaton. "Rising Morbidity and Mortality in Midlife among White Non-Hispanic Americans in the 21st Century." *Proceedings of the National Academy of Sciences* 112, no. 49 (2015): 15078–83.

Cecil, Rosanne, Eilis McCaughan, and Kadar Parahoo. "'It's Hard to Take Because I Am a Man's Man': An Ethnographic Exploration of Cancer and Masculinity." *European Journal of Cancer Care* 19, no. 4 (2010): 501–9.

Chapple, Alison, and Sue Ziebland. "Prostate Cancer: Embodied Experience and Perceptions of Masculinity." *Sociology of Health & Illness* 24, no. 6 (2002): 820–41.

Charmaz, Kathy. "Identity Dilemmas of Chronically Ill Men." *Sociological Quarterly* 35, no. 2 (1994): 269–88.

Coffey, Laura T. "Slowing Down Is for Sissies: The Septuagenarians of Sturgis." Today.com, August 15, 2012. Accessed December 9, 2016. https://www.today.com/news/slowing-down-sissies-septuagenarians-sturgis-1B5399015.

Cole, Thomas R. "Aging, Meaning, and Well-Being: Musings of a Cultural Historian." *International Journal of Aging and Human Development* 19, no. 4 (1984): 329–36.

———. *The Journey of Life: A Cultural History of Aging in America.* Cambridge: Cambridge University Press, 1992.

———. "Re-reading Simone de Beauvoir's *The Coming of Age*: From a Distance of Some Forty Years." Paper presented at the First North American Network of Aging Studies conference at Miami University, Oxford, OH, May 2015. http://www.thomasrcole.com/s/deBeauvoir_PAPER_3.pdf.

Coleman, Rachel A., and Robert A. Neimeyer. "Measuring Meaning: Searching for and Making Sense of Spousal Loss in Late-Life." *Death Studies* 34, no. 9 (2010): 804–34.

Coles, Rebecca, Francine Watkins, Viren Swami, Susan Jones, Susan Woolf, and Debbi Stanistreet. "What Men Really Want: A Qualitative Investigation of Men's Health Needs from the Halton and St Helens Primary Care Trust Men's Health Promotion Project." *British Journal of Health Psychology* 15, no. 4 (2010): 921–39.

Coles, Tony. "Finding Space in the Field of Masculinity: Lived Experiences of Men's Masculinities." *Journal of Sociology* 44, no. 3 (2008): 233–48.

———. "Negotiating the Field of Masculinity: The Production and Reproduction of Multiple Dominant Masculinities." *Men and Masculinities* 12, no. 1 (2009): 30–44.

Coles, Tony, and Therese Vassarotti. "Ageing and Identity Dilemmas for Men." *Journal of Religion, Spirituality & Aging* 24, no. 1-2 (2012): 30–41.

Conaglen, Helen M., and John V. Conaglen. "The Impact of Erectile Dysfunction on Female Partners: A Qualitative Investigation." *Sexual and Relationship Therapy* 23, no. 2 (2008): 147–56.

Connell, R. W. *Gender and Power.* Stanford: Stanford University Press, 1987.

———. *Masculinities.* Berkeley: University of California Press, 1995.

Connell, R. W., and James W. Messerschmidt. "Hegemonic Masculinity: Rethinking the Concept." *Gender & Society* 19, no. 6 (2005): 829–59.

Conrad, Peter. "The Shifting Engines of Medicalization." *Journal of Health and Social Behavior* 46, no. 1 (2005): 3–14.

Cook, Glenda, Juliana Thompson, and Jan Reed. "Re-Conceptualising the Status of Residents in a Care Home: Older People Wanting to 'Live with Care.'" *Ageing and Society* 35, no. 8 (2015): 1587–1613.

Courtenay, Will H. "Constructions of Masculinity and Their Influence on Men's Well-Being: A Theory of Gender and Health." *Social Science & Medicine* 50, no. 10 (2000): 1385–1401.

———. "Theorising Masculinity and Men's Health." In *Men's Health: Body, Identity and Social Context,* edited by Alex Broom and Philip Tovey, 9–32. New York: John Wiley & Sons, 2009.

Crenshaw, Kimberle. "Mapping the Margins: Intersectionality, Identity Politics, and Violence Against Women of Color." *Stanford Law Review* 43, no. 6 (1991): 1241–99.

Crossley, Nick. "Mapping Reflexive Body Techniques: On Body Modification and Maintenance." *Body & Society* 11, no. 1 (2005): 1–35.

———. "Researching Embodiment by Way of 'Body Techniques.'" *Sociological Review* 55, special issue 1 (2007): 80–94.

Curtin, Sally C., and Margaret Warner. *Suicide Rates for Females and Males by Race and Ethnicity: United States, 1999 and 2014.* National Center for Health Statistics, Centers for Disease Control and Prevention, 2016. Accessed December 29, 2017. https://www.cdc.gov/nchs/data/hestat/suicide/rates_1999_2014.pdf.

Curtin, Sally C., Margaret Warner, and Holly Hedegaard. *Increase in Suicide in the United States, 1999–2014.* Data brief no 241. Hyattsville, MD: National Center for Health Statistics, 2016.

Davidson, Kate. "Gender Differences in New Partnership Choices and Constraints for Older Widows and Widowers." *Ageing International* 27, no. 4 (2002): 43–60.

———. "Late Life Widowhood, Selfishness and New Partnership Choices: A Gendered Perspective." *Ageing & Society* 21, no. 3 (2001): 297–317.

———. "'Why Can't a Man Be More Like a Woman?': Marital Status and Social Networking of Older Men." *Journal of Men's Studies* 13, no. 1 (2004): 25–43.

Davidson, Kate, Tom Daly, and Sara Arber. "Exploring the Social Worlds of Older Men." In *Gender and Ageing: Changing Roles and Relationships*, edited by Sara Arber, Kate Davidson, and Jay Ginn, 168–85. Buckingham: Open University Press, 2003.

Davidson, Kate, and Graham Fennell. "New Intimate Relationships in Later Life." *Ageing International* 27, no. 4 (2002): 3–10.

Davidson, Kate, and Robert Meadows. "Older Men's Health: The Role of Marital Status and Masculinities." In *Men, Masculinities, and Health: Critical Perspectives*, edited by Brendan Gough and Steve Robertson, 109–24. New York: Palgrave Macmillan, 2010.

de Beauvoir, Simone. *The Coming of Age*. New York: G. P. Putman's Sons, 1972.

de Jong Gierveld, Jenny. "Intra-Couple Caregiving of Older Adults Living Apart Together: Commitment and Independence." *Canadian Journal on Aging* 34, no. 3 (2015): 356–65.

———. "Remarriage, Unmarried Cohabitation, Living Apart Together: Partner Relationships Following Bereavement or Divorce." *Journal of Marriage and Family* 66, no. 1 (2004): 236–43.

de Jong Gierveld, Jenny, and Eva-Maria Merz. "Parents' Partnership Decision Making After Divorce or Widowhood: The Role of (Step) Children." *Journal of Marriage and Family* 75, no. 5 (2013): 1098–1113.

de Jong Gierveld, Jenny, Marjolein Broese van Groenou, Adriaan W. Hoogendoorn, and Johannes H. Smit. "Quality of Marriages in Later Life and Emotional and Social Loneliness." *Journals of Gerontology Series B: Psychological Sciences and Social Sciences* 64, no. 4 (2009): 497–506.

de Visser, Richard O., Jonathan A. Smith, and Elizabeth J. McDonnell. "'That's Not Masculine': Masculine Capital and Health-Related Behaviour." *Journal of Health Psychology* 14, no. 7 (2009): 1047–58.

de Vries, Brian, and John A. Blando. "The Study of Gay and Lesbian Aging: Lessons for Social Gerontology." In *Gay and Lesbian Aging: Research And Future Directions*, edited by Gilbert Herdt, 3–28. New York: Springer, 2004.

DeLamater, John D. "Sexual Expression in Later Life: A Review and Synthesis." *Journal of Sex Research* 49, no. 2-3 (2012): 125–41.

DeLamater, John, Janet S. Hyde, and Mei-Chia Fong. "Sexual Satisfaction in the Seventh Decade of Life." *Journal of Sex & Marital Therapy* 34, no. 5 (2008): 439–54.

Di Gessa, Giorgio, Karen Glaser, and Anthea Tinker. "The Impact of Caring for Grandchildren on the Health of Grandparents in Europe: A Lifecourse Approach." *Social Science & Medicine* 152 (2016): 166–75.

Diamond, Jed. "The One Thing Men Want More Than Sex." *Good Man Project*, February 17, 2017. Accessed March 6, 2017. http://goodmenproject.com/sex-relationships/the-one-thing-men-want-more-than-sex-wcz.

Diehl, Manfred K., and Hans-Werner Wahl. "Awareness of Age-Related Change: Examination of a (Mostly) Unexplored Concept." *Journals of Gerontology Series B: Psychological Sciences and Social Sciences* 65, no. 3 (2010): 340–50.

Dillon, Michele, and Paul Wink. *In the Course of a Lifetime: Tracing Religious Belief, Practice, and Change*. Berkeley: University of California Press, 2007.

Dodge, Brian, Debby Herbenick, Tsung-Chieh Jane Fu, Vanessa Schick, Michael Reece, Stephanie Sanders, and J. Dennis Fortenberry. "Sexual Behaviors of US Men by Self-Identified Sexual Orientation: Results from the 2012 National Survey of Sexual Health and Behavior." *Journal of Sexual Medicine* 13, no. 4 (2016): 637–49.

Doka, Kenneth J., and Terry Martin. *Grieving Beyond Gender: Understanding the Ways Men and Women Mourn*. New York: Routledge, 2010.

Dorff, Tanya B., Ronald L. Shazer, Edward M. Nepomuceno, and Steven J. Tucker. "Successful Treatment of Metastatic Androgen-Independent Prostate Carcinoma in a Transsexual Patient." *Clinical Genitourinary Cancer* 5, no. 5 (2007): 344–46.

Drummond, Murray. "Retired Men, Retired Bodies." *International Journal of Men's Health* 2, no. 3 (2003): 183–99.

Dumas, Alex, and Bryan S. Turner. "Age and Aging: The Social World of Foucault and Bourdieu." In *Foucault and Aging*, edited by Jason L. Powell and Azrini Wahidin, 145– 55. Hauppauge, NY: Nova Science Publishers, 2006.

Duneier, Mitchell. *Slim's Table: Race, Respectability, and Masculinity.* Chicago: University of Chicago Press, 1992.

Ekerdt, David J., and Lindsey A. Baker. "The Material Convoy After Age 50." *Journals of Gerontology Series B: Psychological Sciences and Social Sciences* 69, no. 3 (2014): 442–50.

Ekerdt, David J., and Catheryn Koss. "The Task of Time in Retirement." *Ageing & Society* 36, no. 6 (2016): 1295–1311.

Elias, Norbert. *The Civilizing Process.* Vol. 2. Oxford: Blackwell, 1982.

———. "On Human Beings and Their Emotions: A Process-Sociological Essay." In *The Body: Social Process and Cultural Theory*, edited by Michael Feathersone, Michael Hepworth, and Bryan Turner, 103–25. New York: Sage Publications, 1991.

Elliott, Sinikka, and Debra Umberson. "The Performance of Desire: Gender and Sexual Negotiation in Long-Term Marriages." *Journal of Marriage and Family* 70, no. 2 (2008): 391–406.

Eman, Josefin. "Constructing Successful Old-Age Masculinities amongst Athletes." *NORMA – Nordic Journal for Masculinity Studies* 6, no. 1 (2011): 45–60.

Emlet, Charles A., Chengshi Shiu, Hyun-Jun Kim, and Karen Fredriksen-Goldsen. "Bouncing Back: Resilience and Mastery among HIV-Positive Older Gay and Bisexual Men." *The Gerontologist* 57, no. S1 (2017): S40–49.

Emmers-Sommer, Tara, Katherine Hertlein, and Alexis Kennedy. "Pornography Use and Attitudes: An Examination of Relational and Sexual Openness Variables Between and Within Gender." *Marriage & Family Review* 49, no. 4 (2013): 349–65.

Emslie, Carol, Susan Browne, Una MacLeod, Linda Rozmovits, Elizabeth Mitchell, and Sue Ziebland. "'Getting Through' not 'Going Under': A Qualitative Study of Gender and Spousal Support After Diagnosis with Colorectal Cancer." *Social Science & Medicine* 68, no. 6 (2009): 1169–75.

Emslie, Carol, Damien Ridge, Sue Ziebland, and Kate Hunt. "Men's Accounts of Depression: Reconstructing or Resisting Hegemonic Masculinity?" *Social Science & Medicine* 62, no. 9 (2006): 2246–57.

Engels, Friedrich. *The Condition of the Working Class in England.* New York: Oxford University Press, 1993/1845.

Erickson, Rebecca J. "Why Emotion Work Matters: Sex, Gender, and the Division of Household Labor." *Journal of Marriage and Family* 67, no. 2 (2005): 337–51.

Eriksson, Henrik, and Jonas Sandberg. "Transitions in Men's Caring Identities: Experiences from Home-Based Care to Nursing Home Placement." *International Journal of Older People Nursing* 3, no. 2 (2008): 131–37.

Eriksson, Henrik, Jonas Sandberg, and Keith Pringle. "'It Feels Like a Defoliation . . .': Older Men's Notions of Informal Support as Primary Caregivers." *Nordic Journal for Masculinity Studies* 3, no. 1 (2008): 48–61.

Farrimond, Hannah. "Beyond the Caveman: Rethinking Masculinity in Relation to Men's Help-Seeking." *Health:* 16, no. 2 (2012): 208–25.

Featherstone, Mike. "Body, Image and Affect in Consumer Culture." *Body & Society* 16, no. 1 (2010): 193–221.

Featherstone, Mike, and Mike Hepworth. "The Mask of Ageing and the Postmodern Life Course." In *The Body: Social Processes and Cultural Theory*, edited by Mike Featherstone, Mike Hepworth, and Bryan Turner, 371–89. New York: Routledge, 1991.

Featherstone, Mike, and Andrew Wernick. "Introduction." In *Images of Aging: Cultural Representations of Later Life*, edited by Mike Featherstone and Andrew Wernick, 1–15. New York: Routledge, 1995.

Federal Interagency Forum on Aging-Related Statistics. *Older Americans 2016: Key Indicators of Well-Being*. Washington, DC: Government Printing Office, August 2016.

Feldman, Susan, Julie E. Byles, and Rosie Beaumont. "'Is Anybody Listening?' The Experiences of Widowhood for Older Australian Women." *Journal of Women & Aging* 12, no. 3-4 (2000): 155–76.

Fenge, Lee-Ann. "Developing Understanding of Same-Sex Partner Bereavement for Older Lesbian and Gay People: Implications for Social Work Practice." *Journal of Gerontological Social Work* 57, no. 2-4 (2014): 288–304.

Fingerman, Karen L., Elizabeth L. Hay, and Kira S. Birditt. "The Best of Ties, the Worst of Ties: Close, Problematic, and Ambivalent Social Relationships." *Journal of Marriage and Family* 66, no. 3 (2004): 792–808.

Fischer, David Hackett. *Growing Old in America*. New York: Oxford University Press, 1978.

Fischer, Regina Santamäki, Astrid Norberg, and Berit Lundman. "Embracing Opposites: Meanings of Growing Old as Narrated by People Aged 85." *The International Journal of Aging and Human Development* 67, no. 3 (2008): 259–71.

Fisher, Linda. *Sex, Romance, and Relationships: AARP Survey of Midlife and Older Adults*. AARP Publication. No. D19234. Washington, DC: AARP, 2010.

Fiske, Amy, Julie Loebach Wetherell, and Margaret Gatz. "Depression in Older Adults." *Annual Review of Clinical Psychology* 5 (2009): 363–89.

Flatt, Michael A., Richard A. Settersten Jr., Roselle Ponsaran, and Jennifer R. Fishman. "Are 'Anti-Aging Medicine' and 'Successful Aging' Two Sides of the Same Coin? Views of Anti-Aging Practitioners." *Journals of Gerontology Series B: Psychological Sciences and Social Sciences* 68, no. 6 (2013): 944–55.

Foucault, Michel. *Madness and Civilization: A History of Insanity in the Age of Reason*. New York: Random House, 1965.

———. *Technologies of the Self: A Seminar with Michel Foucault*. Amherst, MA: University of Massachusetts Press, 1988.

Foweraker, Barbara, and Leanne Cutcher. "Work, Age and Other Drugs: Exploring the Intersection of Age and Masculinity in a Pharmaceutical Organization." *Gender, Work & Organization* 22, no. 5 (2015): 459–73.

Frank, Arthur W. *The Wounded Storyteller: Body, Illness, and Ethics*. Chicago: University of Chicago Press, 1995.

Frederick, Luke R., Omer Onur Cakir, Hans Arora, Brian T. Helfand, and Kevin T. McVary. "Undertreatment of Erectile Dysfunction: Claims Analysis of 6.2 Million Patients." *Journal of Sexual Medicine* 11, no. 10 (2014): 2546–553.

Fredriksen-Goldsen, Karen I., Amanda E. B. Bryan, Sarah Jen, Jayn Goldsen, Hyun-Jun Kim, and Anna Muraco. "The Unfolding of LGBT Lives: Key Events Associated with Health and Well-Being in Later Life." *The Gerontologist* 57, no. S1 (2017): S15–29.

Fredriksen-Goldsen, Karen I., and Hyun-Jun Kim. "Count Me In: Response to Sexual Orientation Measures among Older Adults." *Research on Aging* 37, no. 5 (2015): 464–80.

———. "The Science of Conducting Research with LGBT Older Adults—An Introduction to Aging with Pride: National Health, Aging, and Sexuality/Gender Study (NHAS)." *The Gerontologist* 57, no. S1 (2017): S1–S14.

Fredriksen-Goldsen, Karen I., Hyun-Jun Kim, Susan E. Barkan, Anna Muraco, and Charles P. Hoy-Ellis. "Health Disparities among Lesbian, Gay, and Bisexual Older Adults: Results from a Population-Based Study." *American Journal of Public Health* 103, no. 10 (2013): 1802–9.

Fredriksen-Goldsen, Karen I., Hyun-Jun Kim, Amanda E. B. Bryan, Chengshi Shiu, and Charles A. Emlet. "The Cascading Effects of Marginalization and Pathways of Resilience in Attaining Good Health among LGBT Older Adults." *The Gerontologist* 57, no. S1 (2017): S72–83.

Fredriksen-Goldsen, Karen I., Hyun-Jun Kim, Charlies A. Emlet, Anna Muraco, Elana A. Erosheva, Charles P. Hoy-Ellis, Jayn Goldsen, and Heidi Petry. *The Aging and Health Report: Disparities and Resilience among Lesbian, Gay, Bisexual, and Transgender Older Adults*. Seattle: Institute for Multigenerational Health, 2011.

Fredriksen-Goldsen, Karen I., Hyun-Jun Kim, Chengshi Shui, and Amanda E. B. Bryan. "Chronic Health Conditions and Key Health Indicators among Lesbian, Gay, and Bisexual Older US Adults, 2013–2014." *American Journal of Public Health* 107, no. 8 (2017): 1332–38.

Freeman, Mark. *Priority of the Other: Thinking and Living Beyond the Self.* New York: Oxford University Press, 2014.

Funk, Laura M., and Karen M. Kobayashi. "From Motivations to Accounts: An Interpretive Analysis of 'Living Apart Together' Relationships in Mid-to Later-Life Couples." *Journal of Family Issues* 37, no. 8 (2016): 1101–22.

Gades, Naomi M., Debra J. Jacobson, Michaela E. McGree, Jennifer L. St Sauver, Michael M. Lieber, Ajay Nehra, Cynthia J. Girman, and Steven J. Jacobsen. "Longitudinal Evaluation of Sexual Function in a Male Cohort: The Olmsted County Study of Urinary Symptoms and Health Status among Men." *Journal of Sexual Medicine* 6, no. 9 (2009): 2455–66.

Gagnon, John H., and William Simon. *Sexual Conduct: The Social Sources of Human Sexuality.* Chicago: Aldine, 1973.

Gaines, Alexis R., Elizabeth L. Turner, Patricia G. Moorman, Stephen J. Freedland, Christopher J. Keto, Megan E. McPhail, Delores J. Grant, Adriana C. Vidal, and Cathrine Hoyo. "The Association Between Race and Prostate Cancer Risk on Initial Biopsy in an Equal Access, Multiethnic Cohort." *Cancer Causes & Control* 25, no. 8 (2014): 1029–35.

Galdas, Paul. "The Role of Masculinities in White and South Asian Men's Help-Seeking Behavior for Cardiac Chest Pain." In *Men, Masculinities, and Health: Critical Perspectives*, edited by Brendan Gough and Steve Robertson, 216–38. New York: Palgrave Macmillan, 2010.

Garnham, Bridget, and Lia Bryant. "Problematising the Suicides of Older Male Farmers: Subjective, Social and Cultural Considerations." *Sociologia Ruralis* 54, no. 2 (2014): 227–40.

Gast, Julie, and Terry Peak. "'It Used to Be That If It Weren't Broken and Bleeding Profusely, I Would Never Go to the Doctor': Men, Masculinity, and Health." *American Journal of Men's Health* 5, no. 4 (2011): 318–31.

Gatling, Margaret, Jane Mills, and David Lindsay. "Sex After 60? You've Got to be Joking! Senior Sexuality in Comedy Film." *Journal of Aging Studies* 40 (2017): 23–28.

Gerdes, Zachary T., Kathleen M. Alto, Stefan Jadaszewski, Francisco D'Auria, and Ronald F. Levant. "A Content Analysis of Research on Masculinity Ideologies Using All Forms of the Male Role Norms Inventory (MRNI)." *Psychology of Men & Masculinity*, October 2, 2017 (advance online publication).

Geronimus, Arline T., Jay A. Pearson, Erin Linnenbringer, Amy J. Schulz, Angela G. Reyes, Elissa S. Epel, Jue Lin, and Elizabeth H. Blackburn. "Race-Ethnicity, Poverty, Urban Stressors, and Telomere Length in a Detroit Community-Based Sample." *Journal of Health and Social Behavior* 56, no. 2 (2015): 199–224.

Gerschick, Thomas J., and Adam S. Miller. "Coming to Terms: Masculinity and Physical Disability." In *Men's Health and Illness: Gender, Power, and the Body*, edited by Donald Sabo and Fredrick Gordon, 183–204. Thousand Oaks, CA: Sage Publications, 1995.

Giami, Alain. "Sexual Health: The Emergence, Development, and Diversity of a Concept." *Annual Review of Sex Research* 13, no. 1 (2002): 1–35.

Gibbs, Lisa. "Applications of Masculinity Theories in a Chronic Illness Context." *International Journal of Men's Health* 4, no. 3 (2005): 287–300.

Gibson, Grant. "'Signposts on the Journey': Medication Adherence and the Lived Body in Men with Parkinson's Disease." *Social Science & Medicine* 152 (2016): 27–34.

Gibson, Grant, and Ciara Kierans. "Ageing, Masculinity and Parkinson's Disease: Embodied Perspectives." *Sociology of Health & Illness* 39, no. 4 (2017): 532–46.

Gibson, Hamilton Bertie. "It Keeps Us Young." *Ageing & Society* 20, no. 6 (2000): 773–79.

Giddens, Anthony. *Modernity and Self-Identity: Self and Society in the Late Modern Age.* Stanford: Stanford University Press, 1991.

Giles, Lynne C., Gary F. V. Glonek, Mary A. Luszcz, and Gary R. Andrews. "Effect of Social Networks on 10 Year Survival in Very Old Australians: The Australian Longitudinal Study of Aging." *Journal of Epidemiology and Community Health* 59, no. 7 (2005): 574–79.

Gill, Rosalind. "A Genealogical Approach to Idealized Male Body Imagery." *Paragraph* 26, no. 1-2 (2003): 187–97.

Gilleard, Chris, and Paul Higgs. "Aging without Agency: Theorizing the Fourth Age." *Aging & Mental Health* 14, no. 2 (2010): 121–28.

———. *Cultures of Ageing: Self, Citizen, and the Body*. New York: Pearson Education, 2000.

———. "The Fourth Age and the Concept of a 'Social Imaginary': A Theoretical Excursus." *Journal of Aging Studies* 27, no. 4 (2013): 368–76.

Glaser, Karen, Rachel Stuchbury, Cecilia Tomassini, and Janet Askham. "The Long-Term Consequences of Partnership Dissolution for Support in Later Life in the United Kingdom." *Ageing & Society* 28, no. 3 (2008): 329–51.

Goffman, Erving. *Interaction Ritual*. New York: Pantheon, 1967.

———. *The Presentation of Self in Everyday Life*. New York: Doubleday, 1959.

Goldsen, Jayn, Amanda E. B. Bryan, Hyun-Jun Kim, Anna Muraco, Sarah Jen, and Karen I. Fredriksen-Goldsen. "Who Says I Do: The Changing Context of Marriage and Health and Quality of Life for LGBT Older Adults." *The Gerontologist* 57, no. S1 (2017): S50–62.

Goldstein, Irwin. "Growth of the Field of Sexual Medicine." *Journal of Sexual Medicine* 10, no. 8 (2013): 1899–1902.

Gott, Merryn, and Sharron Hinchliff. "How Important Is Sex in Later Life? The Views of Older People." *Social Science & Medicine* 56, no. 8 (2003): 1617–28.

Gough, Brendan. "Introduction. The Psychology of Men's Health: Maximizing Masculine Capital." *Health Psychology* 32, no. 1 (2013): 1–4.

Gough, Brendan, Sarah Seymour-Smith, and Christopher R. Matthews. "Body Dissatisfaction, Appearance Investment, and Wellbeing: How Older Obese Men Orient to 'Aesthetic Health.'" *Psychology of Men & Masculinity* 17, no. 1 (2016): 84–91.

Grace, Victoria, Annie Potts, Nicola Gavey, and Tiina Vares. "The Discursive Condition of Viagra." *Sexualities* 9, no. 3 (2006): 295–314.

Graham, Hilary. "Caring: A Labour of Love." In *Women, Work and Caring*, edited by Janet Finch and Dulcie Grove, 13–30. London: Routledge and Kegan Paul, 1983.

Gralla, Oliver, Nina Knoll, Stephan Fenske, Inna Spivak, Marga Hoffmann, Claudia Rönnebeck, Severin Lenk, Bernd Hoschke, and Matthias May. "Worry, Desire, and Sexual Satisfaction and Their Association with Severity of ED and Age." *Journal of Sexual Medicine* 5, no. 11 (2008): 2646–55.

Gray, Anne. "The Changing Availability of Grandparents as Carers and Its Implications for Childcare Policy in the UK." *Journal of Social Policy* 34, no. 4 (2005): 557–77.

Gray, Ross E., Margaret I. Fitch, Karen D. Fergus, Eric Mykhalovskiy, and Kathryn Church. "Hegemonic Masculinity and the Experience of Prostate Cancer: A Narrative Approach." *Journal of Aging and Identity* 7, no. 1 (2002): 43–62.

Gregson, Joanna, and Michelle L. Ceynar. "Finding 'Me' Again: Women's Postdivorce Identity Shifts." *Journal of Divorce & Remarriage* 50, no. 8 (2009): 564–82.

Grenier, Amanda, and Chris Phillipson. "Rethinking Agency in Late Life: Structural and Interpretive Approaches." In *Ageing, Meaning and Social Structure: Connecting Critical and Humanistic Gerontology*, edited by Jan Baars, Joseph Dohmen, Amanda Grenier, and Chris Phillipson, 55–80. Bristol, UK: Policy Press, 2013.

Griffith, Derek M. "'I AM a Man': Manhood, Minority Men's Health and Health Equity." *Ethnicity & Disease* 25, no. 3 (2015): 287–93.

Griffith, Derek M., and Emily K. Cornish. "'What Defines a Man?': Perspectives of African American Men on the Components and Consequences of Manhood." *Psychology of Men and Masculinity* 19, no. 1 (2018): 77–88.

Guiaux, Maurice, Theo Van Tilburg, and Marjolein Broese Van Groenou. "Changes in Contact and Support Exchange in Personal Networks After Widowhood." *Personal Relationships* 14, no. 3 (2007): 457–73.

Gullette, Margaret Morganroth. *Aged by Culture*. Chicago: University of Chicago Press, 2004.

———. *Declining to Decline: Cultural Combat and the Politics of the Midlife*. Charlottesville: University of Virginia Press, 1997.

Hagen, Brad, Ruth Grant-Kalischuk, and James Sanders. "Disappearing Floors and Second Chances: Men's Journeys of Prostate Cancer." *International Journal of Men's Health* 6, no. 3 (2007): 201–23.

Halliwell, Emma, and Helga Dittmar. "A Qualitative Investigation of Women's and Men's Body Image Concerns and Their Attitudes Toward Aging." *Sex Roles* 49, no. 11-12 (2003): 675–84.

Hammond, Wizdom Powell. "Taking It Like a Man: Masculine Role Norms as Moderators of the Racial Discrimination–Depressive Symptoms Association among African American Men." *American Journal of Public Health* 102, no. S2 (2012): S232–41.

Hammond, Wizdom Powell, Derrick Matthews, Dinushika Mohottige, Amma Agyemang, and Giselle Corbie-Smith. "Masculinity, Medical Mistrust, and Preventive Health Services Delays among Community-Dwelling African-American Men." *Journal of General Internal Medicine* 25, no. 12 (2010): 1300–1308.

Hammond, Wizdom Powell, and Jacqueline S. Mattis. "Being a Man about It: Manhood Meaning among African American Men." *Psychology of Men & Masculinity* 6, no. 2 (2005): 114–26.

Hank, Karsten, and Isabella Buber. "Grandparents Caring for Their Grandchildren: Findings from the 2004 Survey of Health, Ageing, and Retirement in Europe." *Journal of Family Issues* 30, no. 1 (2009): 53–73.

Haritatos, Jana, Ramaswami Mahalingam, and Sherman A. James. "John Henryism, Self-Reported Physical Health Indicators, and the Mediating Role of Perceived Stress among High Socio-Economic Status Asian Immigrants." *Social Science & Medicine* 64, no. 6 (2007): 1192–1203.

Harris, Phyllis Braudy. "Another Wrinkle in the Debate about Successful Aging: The Undervalued Concept of Resilience and the Lived Experience of Dementia." *International Journal of Aging and Human Development* 67, no. 1 (2008): 43–61.

Harvey, Kevin. "Medicalisation, Pharmaceutical Promotion and the Internet: A Critical Multimodal Discourse Analysis of Hair Loss Websites." *Social Semiotics* 23, no. 5 (2013): 691–714.

Harwood, Jake. "Communication Media Use in the Grandparent-Grandchild Relationship." *Journal of Communication* 50, no. 4 (2000): 56–78.

Haustein, Thomas, and Johanna Mischke. *In the Spotlight: Older People in Germany and the EU, 2011*. Wiesbaden, Germany: Federal Statistical Office, December 2011. Accessed February 16, 2016. https://www.destatis.de/EN/Publications/Specialized/Population/OlderPeopleEU.pdf?__blob=publicationFile.

Hawkins, Daniel N., and Alan Booth. "Unhappily Ever After: Effects of Long-Term, Low-Quality Marriages on Well-Being." *Social Forces* 84, no. 1 (2005): 451–71.

Heaphy, Brian, Catherine Donovan, and Jeffrey Weeks. "A Different Affair? Openness and Nonmonogamy in Same Sex Relationships." In *The State of Affairs: Explorations in Infidelity and Commitment*, edited by Jean Duncombe, Kaeren Harrison, Graham Allan, and Dennis Marsden, 167–86. New York: Routledge, 2004.

Hearn, Jeff. "From Hegemonic Masculinity to the Hegemony of Men." *Feminist Theory* 5, no. 1 (2004): 49–72.

———. "Imaging the Aging of Men." In *Images of Aging: Cultural Representations of Later Life*, edited by Mike Featherstone and Andrew Wernick, 97–117. New York: Routledge, 1995.

Hearn, Jeff, Marie Nordberg, Kjerstin Andersson, Dag Balkmar, Lucas Gottzén, Roger Klinth, Keith Pringle, and Linn Sandberg. "Hegemonic Masculinity and Beyond: 40 Years of Research in Sweden." *Men and Masculinities* 15, no. 1 (2012): 31–55.

Hedberg, Pia, Yngve Gustafson, Christine Brulin, and Lena Aléx. "Purpose in Life among Very Old Men." *Advances in Aging Research* 2, no. 3 (2013): 100–105.

Heidegger, Martin. *Being and Time*. Albany: State University of New York Press, 2010/1953.

Hendryx, Michael, and Melissa M. Ahern. "Relations Between Health Indicators and Residential Proximity to Coal Mining in West Virginia." *American Journal of Public Health* 98, no. 4 (2008): 669–71.

Hendryx, Michael, Leah Wolfe, Juhua Luo, and Bo Webb. "Self-Reported Cancer Rates in Two Rural Areas of West Virginia with and without Mountaintop Coal Mining." *Journal of Community Health* 37, no. 2 (2012): 320–27.

Hengel, Karen M. Oude, Birgitte M. Blatter, Goedele A. Geuskens, Lando L. J. Koppes, and Paulien M. Bongers. "Factors Associated with the Ability and Willingness to Continue Working Until the Age of 65 in Construction Workers." *International Archives of Occupational and Environmental Health* 85, no. 7 (2012): 783–90.

Herbenick, Debby, Michael Reece, Vanessa Schick, Stephanie A. Sanders, Brian Dodge, and J. Dennis Fortenberry. "Sexual Behavior in the United States: Results from a National Probability Sample of Men And Women Ages 14–94." *Journal of Sexual Medicine* 7, no. S5 (2010): 255–65.

Heron, Melonie. *Deaths: Leading Causes for 2014*. National Vital Statistics Reports 65, no 5. Hyattsville, MD: National Center for Health Statistics, 2016.

Higgs, Paul, and Chris Gilleard. "Frailty, Abjection and the 'Othering' of the Fourth Age." *Health Sociology Review* 23, no. 1 (2014): 10–19.

Higgs, Paul, and Ian Rees Jones. *Medical Sociology and Old Age: Towards a Sociology of Health in Later Life*. New York: Routledge, 2009.

Higgs, Paul, and Fiona McGowan. "Aging, Embodiment and the Negotiation of the Third and Fourth Ages." In *Aging Men, Masculinities and Modern Medicine*, edited by Antje Kampf, Barbara L. Marshall, and Alan Petersen, 21–34. New York: Routledge, 2013.

Hillman, Jennifer. "Sexual Issues and Aging within the Context of Work with Older Adult Patients." *Professional Psychology: Research and Practice* 39, no. 3 (2008): 290–97.

Hinchliff, Sharron, and Merryn Gott. "Intimacy, Commitment, and Adaptation: Sexual Relationships within Long-Term Marriages." *Journal of Social and Personal Relationships* 21, no. 5 (2004): 595–609.

Hirschberger, Gilad, and Dan Shaham. "The Impermanence of All Things: An Existentialist Stance on Personal and Social Change." In *Meaning, Mortality, and Choice: The Social Psychology of Existential Concerns*, edited by Phillip R. Shaver and Mario Mikulincer, 111–25. Washington, DC: American Psychological Association, 2012.

Holley, Sarah R., Claudia M. Haase, and Robert W. Levenson. "Age-Related Changes in Demand-Withdraw Communication Behaviors." *Journal of Marriage and Family* 75, no. 4 (2013): 822–36.

Holmes, Thomas H., and Richard H. Rahe. "The Social Readjustment Rating Scale." *Journal of Psychosomatic Research* 11, no. 2 (1967): 213–18.

Holstein, Martha B., and Meredith Minkler. "Self, Society, and the 'New Gerontology.'" *The Gerontologist* 43, no. 6 (2003): 787–96.

Hooker, Steven P., Sara Wilcox, Ericka L. Burroughs, Carol E. Rheaume, and Will Courtenay. "The Potential Influence of Masculine Identity on Health-Improving Behavior in Midlife and Older African American Men." *Journal of Men's Health* 9, no. 2 (2012): 79–88.

Horiuchi, Shiro. "Major Causes of the Rapid Longevity Extension in Postwar Japan." *Japanese Journal of Population* 9, no. 1 (2011): 162–71.

Howe, Anna L., Andrew E. Jones, and Cheryl Tilse. "What's in a Name? Similarities and Differences in International Terms and Meanings for Older Peoples' Housing with Services." *Ageing and Society* 33, no. 4 (2013): 547–78.

Howell, Robert. "I'm Not the Man I Was: Reflections on Becoming a Widower." *Illness, Crisis & Loss* 21, no. 1 (2013): 3–13.

Hughes, Mary Elizabeth, Linda J. Waite, Tracey A. LaPierre, and Ye Luo. "All in the Family: The Impact of Caring for Grandchildren on Grandparents' Health." *Journals of Gerontology Series B: Psychological Sciences and Social Sciences* 62, no. 2 (2007): S108–19.

Hunter, Andrea G., and James Earl Davis. "Hidden Voices of Black Men: The Meaning, Structure, and Complexity of Manhood." *Journal of Black Studies* 25, no. 1 (1994): 20–40.

Hurd Clarke, Laura, and Erica Bennett. "'You Learn to Live with All the Things That Are Wrong with You': Gender and the Experience of Multiple Chronic Conditions in Later Life." *Ageing & Society* 33, no. 2 (2013): 342–60.

Hurd Clarke, Laura, Erica V. Bennett, and Chris Liu. "Aging and Masculinity: Portrayals in Men's Magazines." *Journal of Aging Studies* 31 (2014): 26–33.

Hurd Clarke, Laura, Meridith Griffin, and PACC Research Team. "Failing Bodies: Body Image and Multiple Chronic Conditions in Later Life." *Qualitative Health Research* 18, no. 8 (2008): 1084–95.

Hurd Clarke, Laura, and Alexandra Korotchenko. "'I Know It Exists . . . But I Haven't Experienced It Personally': Older Canadian Men's Perceptions of Ageism as a Distant Social Problem." *Ageing and Society* 36, no. 8 (2016): 1757–73.

Hyde, Zoë, Leon Flicker, Graeme J. Hankey, Osvaldo P. Almeida, Kieran A. McCaul, S. A. Chubb, and Bu B. Yeap. "Prevalence and Predictors of Sexual Problems in Men Aged 75–95 Years: A Population-Based Study." *Journal of Sexual Medicine* 9, no. 2 (2012): 442–53.

Idler, Ellen L. "Discussion: Gender Differences in Self-Rated Health, in Mortality, and in the Relationship Between the Two." *The Gerontologist* 43, no. 3 (2003): 372–75.

Idler, Ellen, Howard Leventhal, Julie McLaughlin, and Elaine Leventhal. "In Sickness but Not in Health: Self-ratings, Identity, and Mortality." *Journal of Health and Social Behavior* 45, no. 3 (2004): 336–56.

Inhorn, Marcia C., and Emily A. Wentzell. "Embodying Emergent Masculinities: Men Engaging with Reproductive and Sexual Health Technologies in the Middle East and Mexico." *American Ethnologist* 38, no. 4 (2011): 801–15.

Isherwood, Linda M., Debra S. King, and Mary A. Luszcz. "A Longitudinal Analysis of Social Engagement in Late-Life Widowhood." *International Journal of Aging and Human Development* 74, no. 3 (2012): 211–29.

———. "Widowhood in the Fourth Age: Support Exchange, Relationships and Social Participation." *Ageing and Society* 37, no. 1 (2017): 188–212.

Jackson, David. *Exploring Aging Masculinities: The Body, Sexuality, and Social Lives.* London: Palgrave Macmillan, 2016.

James, Sherman A. "John Henryism and the Health of African-Americans." *Culture, Medicine and Psychiatry* 18, no. 2 (1994): 163–82.

James, Sherman A., Nora L. Keenan, David Strogatz, Steven R. Browning, and Joanne M. Garrett. "Socioeconomic Status, John Henryism, and Blood Pressure in Black Adults. The Pitt County Study." *American Journal of Epidemiology* 135, no. 1 (1992): 59–67.

Johnson, Julia, Sheena Rolph, and Randall Smith. *Residential Care Transformed: Revisiting "The Last Refuge."* New York: Palgrave/Macmillan, 2010.

Jones, Julie, and Steve Pugh. "Ageing Gay Men: Lessons from the Sociology of Embodiment." *Men and Masculinities* 7, no. 3 (2005): 248–60.

Joyce, Kelly, and Meika Loe. "A Sociological Approach to Ageing, Technology and Health." *Sociology of Health & Illness* 32, no. 2 (2010): 171–80.

Kaminski, Patricia L., and Bert Hayslip Jr. "Gender Differences in Body Esteem among Older Adults." *Journal of Women & Aging* 18, no. 3 (2006): 19–35.

Karlsson, Sofie Ghazanfareeon, and Klas Borell. "Intimacy and Autonomy, Gender and Ageing: Living Apart Together." *Ageing International* 27, no. 4 (2002): 11–26.

Karlsson, Sofie Ghazanfareeon, Stina Johansson, Arne Gerdner, and Klas Borell. "Caring While Living Apart." *Journal of Gerontological Social Work* 49, no. 4 (2007): 3–27.

Karp, David A. "A Decade of Reminders: Changing Age Consciousness Between Fifty and Sixty Years Old." *The Gerontologist* 28, no. 6 (1988): 727–38.

Karraker, Amelia, John DeLamater, and Christine R. Schwartz. "Sexual Frequency Decline from Midlife to Later Life." *Journals of Gerontology Series B: Psychological Sciences and Social Sciences* 66, no. 4 (2011): 502–12.

Katz, Stephen. "Imaging the Life-Span: From Premodern Miracles to Postmodern Fantasies." In *Images of Aging: Cultural Representations of Later Life*, edited by Michael Featherstone and Andrew Wernick, 61–75. New York: Routledge, 1995.

Katz, Stephen, and Barbara Marshall. "New Sex for Old: Lifestyle, Consumerism, and the Ethics of Aging Well." *Journal of Aging Studies* 17, no. 1 (2003): 3–16.

Kaufman, Gayle, and Glen H. Elder. "Revisiting Age Identity: A Research Note." *Journal of Aging Studies* 16, no. 2 (2002): 169–76.

Kaufman, Sharon. *The Ageless Self: Sources of Meaning in Late Life.* Minneapolis: University of Minnesota Press, 1986.

Kayser, Karen, Lisa E. Watson, and Joel T. Andrade. "Cancer as a 'We-Disease': Examining the Process of Coping from a Relational Perspective." *Families, Systems, & Health* 25, no. 4 (2007): 404–18.

Keene, Jennifer R., Anastasia H. Prokos, and Barbara Held. "Grandfather Caregivers: Race and Ethnic Differences in Poverty." *Sociological Inquiry* 82, no. 1 (2012): 49–77.

Kidder, Tracy. *Old Friends*. New York: Houghton-Mifflin, 1993.

Kim, Hyun-Jun, and Karen I. Fredriksen-Goldsen. "Living Arrangement and Loneliness among Lesbian, Gay, and Bisexual Older Adults." *The Gerontologist* 56, no. 3 (2014): 548–58.

Kimmel, Michael S. *Guyland: The Perilous World Where Boys Become Men*. New York: Harper Perennial, 2008.

Kimmel, Michael S., Jeff Hearn, and R. W. Connell. *Handbook of Studies on Men & Masculinities*. Thousand Oaks, CA: Sage Publications, 2005.

Ko, Dennis T., Jack V. Tu, Peter C. Austin, Harindra C. Wijeysundera, Zaza Samadashvili, Helen Guo, Warren J. Cantor, and Edward L. Hannan. "Prevalence and Extent of Obstructive Coronary Artery Disease among Patients Undergoing Elective Coronary Catheterization in New York State and Ontario." *Journal of the American Medical Association* 310, no. 2 (2013): 163–69.

Kontos, Pia, Alisa Grigorovich, Alexis P. Kontos, and Karen-Lee Miller. "Citizenship, Human Rights, and Dementia: Towards a New Embodied Relational Ethic of Sexuality." *Dementia* 15, no. 3 (2016): 315–29.

Kontula, Osmo, and Elina Haavio-Mannila. "The Impact of Aging on Human Sexual Activity and Sexual Desire." *Journal of Sex Research* 46, no. 1 (2009): 46–56.

Koren, Chaya. "Men's Vulnerability–Women's Resilience: From Widowhood to Late-Life Repartnering." *International Psychogeriatrics* 28, no. 5 (2016): 719–31.

Kraaij, Vivian, Ella Arensman, and Philip Spinhoven. "Negative Life Events and Depression in Elderly Persons: A Meta-Analysis." *Journals of Gerontology Series B: Psychological Sciences and Social Sciences* 57, no. 1 (2002): P87–P94.

Kreider, Rose Marie, and Renee Ellis. *Number, Timing, and Duration of Marriages and Divorces: 2009*. US Department of Commerce, Economics and Statistics Administration, US Census Bureau, 2011.

Kulik, Liat. "Marital Equality and the Quality of Long-Term Marriage in Later Life." *Ageing and Society* 22, no. 4 (2002): 459–81.

Kulik, Liat, Shulamith Walfisch, and Gabriel Liberman. "Spousal Conflict Resolution Strategies and Marital Relations in Late Adulthood." *Personal Relationships* 23, no. 3 (2016): 456–74.

Kupelian, Varant, Carol L. Link, Raymond C. Rosen, and John B. McKinlay. "Socioeconomic Status, Not Race/Ethnicity, Contributes to Variation in the Prevalence of Erectile Dysfunction: Results from the Boston Area Community Health (BACH) Survey." *Journal of Sexual Medicine* 5, no. 6 (2008): 1325–33.

Labrecque, Lindsay T., and Mark A. Whisman. "Attitudes Toward and Prevalence of Extramarital Sex and Descriptions of Extramarital Partners in the 21st Century." *Journal of Family Psychology* 31, no. 7 (2017): 952.

Lang, Frieder R. "Regulation of Social Relationships in Later Adulthood." *Journals of Gerontology Series B: Psychological Sciences and Social Sciences* 56, no. 6 (2001): P321–26.

Laslett, Peter. *A Fresh Map of Life: The Emergence of the Third Age*. Cambridge: Harvard University Press, 1991.

Laumann, Edward O., Suzanne West, Dale Glasser, Culley Carson, Raymond Rosen, and Jeong-han Kang. "Prevalence and Correlates of Erectile Dysfunction by Race and Ethnicity among Men Aged 40 or Older in the United States: From the Male Attitudes Regarding Sexual Health Survey." *Journal of Sexual Medicine* 4, no. 1 (2007): 57–65.

Laursen, Birgitte Schantz, Kim Overvad, Anders Schou Olesen, Charlotte Delmar, and Lars Arendt-Nielsen. "Ongoing Pain, Sexual Desire, and Frequency of Sexual Intercourse in Females with Different Chronic Pain Syndromes." *Sexuality and Disability* 24, no. 1 (2006): 27–37.

Law, Cheryl, and Magdala Peixoto Labre. "Cultural Standards of Attractiveness: A Thirty-Year Look at Changes in Male Images in Magazines." *Journalism & Mass Communication Quarterly* 79, no. 3 (2002): 697–711.

Laz, Cheryl. "Age Embodied." *Journal of Aging Studies* 17, no. 4 (2003): 503–19.

Leder, Drew. *The Absent Body*. Chicago: University of Chicago Press, 1990.

Lee, Adrian. "Signposts of Aging: The Transitions to Later Life of a Sample of Older Gay Men." *Ageing International* 29, no. 4 (2004): 368–84.

Leeson, George W. "Out of the Shadows: Are Grandfathers Defining Their Own Roles in the Modern Family in Denmark?" In *Grandfathers: Global Perspectives*, edited by Ann Buchanan and Anna Rotkirch, 69–88. London: Palgrave Macmillan, 2016.

Leonard, William, Duane Duncan, and Catherine Barrett. "What a Difference a Gay Makes: The Construction of the 'Older Gay Man.'" In *Aging Men, Masculinities, and Modern Medicine*, edited by Antje Kampf, Barbara L. Marshall, and Alan Petersen, 105–20. New York: Routledge, 2013.

Lesperance, Duane. "Legacy, Influence and Keeping the Distance: Two Grandfathers, Three Stories." *Journal of Men's Studies* 18, no. 3 (2010): 199–217.

Levy, Anneliese, and Tina Cartwright. "Men's Strategies for Preserving Emotional Well-Being in Advanced Prostate Cancer: An Interpretative Phenomenological Analysis." *Psychology & Health* 30, no. 10 (2015): 1164–82.

Levy, Becca R. "Mind Matters: Cognitive and Physical Effects of Aging Self-Stereotypes." *Journals of Gerontology Series B: Psychological Sciences and Social Sciences* 58, no. 4 (2003): P203–11.

Levy, Becca R., Martin D. Slade, Suzanne R. Kunkel, and Stanislav V. Kasl. "Longevity Increased by Positive Self-Perceptions of Aging." *Journal of Personality and Social Psychology* 83, no. 2 (2002): 261–70.

Levy, Judith A. "Sex and Sexuality in Later Life Stages." In *Sexuality Across the Life Course*, edited by Alice S. Rossi, 287–309. Chicago: University of Chicago Press, 1994.

Lewin, Alisa C. "Health and Relationship Quality Later in Life: A Comparison of Living Apart Together (LAT), First Marriages, Remarriages, and Cohabitation." *Journal of Family Issues* 38, no. 12 (2017): 1754–74.

Liechty, Toni, and M. Rebecca Genoe. "Older Men's Perceptions of Leisure and Aging." *Leisure Sciences* 35, no. 5 (2013): 438–54.

Liechty, Toni, Nuno F. Ribeiro, Katherine Sveinson, and Laura Dahlstrom. "'It's about What I Can Do With My Body': Body Image and Embodied Experiences of Aging among Older Canadian Men." *International Journal of Men's Health* 13, no. 1 (2014): 3–21.

Lin, I-Fen, and Susan L. Brown. "Unmarried Boomers Confront Old Age: A National Portrait." *The Gerontologist* 52, no. 2 (2012): 153–65.

Lin, I-Fen, Susan L. Brown, Matthew R. Wright, and Anna M. Hammersmith. "Antecedents of Gray Divorce: A Life Course Perspective." *Journals of Gerontology Series B: Psychological Sciences and Social Sciences*, December 15, 2016 (ahead of print). https://doi.org/10.1093/geronb/gbw164.

Lincoln, C. Eric, and Lawrence H. Mamiya. *The Black Church in the African-American Experience*. Durham, NC: Duke University Press, 1990.

Lindau, Stacy Tessler, and Natalia Gavrilova. "Sex, Health, and Years of Sexually Active Life Gained Due to Good Health: Evidence from Two US Population Based Cross Sectional Surveys of Ageing." *BMJ* 340 (2010): c810.

Lindau, Stacy Tessler, L. Philip Schumm, Edward O. Laumann, Wendy Levinson, Colm A. O'Muircheartaigh, and Linda J. Waite. "A Study of Sexuality and Health among Older Adults in the United States." *New England Journal of Medicine* 357, no. 8 (2007): 762–74.

Lloyd, Liz. "The Fourth Age." In *Routledge Handbook of Cultural Gerontology*, edited by Julia Twigg and Wendy Martin, 261–68. New York: Routledge, 2015.

Lloyd, Liz, Michael Calnan, Ailsa Cameron, Jane Seymour, and Randall Smith. "Identity in the Fourth Age: Perseverance, Adaptation and Maintaining Dignity." *Ageing & Society* 34, no. 1 (2014): 1–19.

Lodge, Amy C. "Sexuality in Long-Term Relationships." In *Handbook of the Sociology of Sexualities*, edited by John DeLamater and Rebecca Plante, 243–59. New York: Springer, 2015.

Lodge, Amy C., and Debra Umberson. "Age and Embodied Masculinities: Midlife Gay and Heterosexual Men Talk about Their Bodies." *Journal of Aging Studies* 27, no. 3 (2013): 225–32.

———. "All Shook Up: Sexuality of Mid- to Later Life Married Couples." *Journal of Marriage and Family* 74, no. 3 (2012): 428–43.

Loe, Meika. "Fixing Broken Masculinity: Viagra as a Technology for the Production of Gender and Sexuality." *Sexuality and Culture* 5, no. 3 (2001): 97–125.

Lomranz, Jacob, and Yael Benyamini. "The Ability to Live with Incongruence: Aintegration— the Concept and Its Operationalization." *Journal of Adult Development* 23, no. 2 (2016): 79–92.

Lopata, Helen Z. *Widowhood in an American City*. Cambridge, MA: Schenkman, 1973.

———. *Women as Widows: Support Systems*. New York: Elsevier, 1979.

Lorber, Judith. "Believing Is Seeing: Biology as Ideology." *Gender & Society* 7, no. 4 (1993): 568–81.

Luescher, Kurt, and Karl Pillemer. "Intergenerational Ambivalence: A New Approach to the Study of Parent-Child Relations in Later Life." *Journal of Marriage and Family* 60, no. 2 (1998): 413–25.

Luoma, Jason B., Catherine E. Martin, and Jane L. Pearson. "Contact with Mental Health and Primary Care Providers Before Suicide: A Review of the Evidence." *American Journal of Psychiatry* 159, no. 6 (2002): 909–16.

Lupton, Deborah. *Medicine as Culture: Illness, Disease and the Body*. 3rd ed. Thousand Oaks, CA: Sage Publications, 1994.

Maccoby, Eleanor. *The Psychology of Sex Differences*. Stanford, CA: Stanford University Press, 1974.

Mahieu, Lieslot, and Chris Gastmans. "Older Residents' Perspectives on Aged Sexuality in Institutionalized Elderly Care: A Systematic Literature Review." *International Journal of Nursing Studies* 52, no. 12 (2015): 1891–1905.

Majors, Richard, and Janet Mancini Billson. *Cool Pose: The Dilemmas of Black Manhood in America*. New York: Touchstone, 1992.

Maliski, Sally L., Steve Rivera, Sarah Connor, Griselda Lopez, and Mark S. Litwin. "Renegotiating Masculine Identity After Prostate Cancer Treatment." *Qualitative Health Research* 18, no. 12 (2008): 1609–20.

Mamo, Laura, and Jennifer R. Fishman. "Potency in All the Right Places: Viagra as a Technology of the Gendered Body." *Body & Society* 7, no. 4 (2001): 13–35.

Maneerat, Sonthaya, Sang-arun Isaramalai, and Umaporn Boonyasopun. "A Conceptual Structure of Resilience among Thai Elderly." *International Journal of Behavioral Science* 6, no. 1 (2011): 24–40.

Mann, Robin. "Out of the Shadows?: Grandfatherhood, Age and Masculinities." *Journal of Aging Studies* 21, no. 4 (2007): 281–91.

Mann, Robin, Hafiz T. A. Khan, and George W. Leeson. "Variations in Grandchildren's Perceptions of their Grandfathers and Grandmothers: Dynamics of Age and Gender." *Journal of Intergenerational Relationships* 11, no. 4 (2013): 380–95.

Mann, Robin, and George Leeson. "Grandfathers in Contemporary Families in Britain: Evidence from Qualitative Research." *Journal of Intergenerational Relationships* 8, no. 3 (2010): 234–48.

Mann, Robin, Anna Tarrant, and George W. Leeson. "Grandfatherhood: Shifting Masculinities in Later Life." *Sociology* 50, no. 3 (2016): 594–610.

Mannheim, Karl. *Essays in the Sociology of Knowledge*. London: Routledge & Kegan Paul, 1952.

———. *An Introduction to the Sociology of Knowledge*. London: Routledge & Kegan Paul, 1936.

Manning, Wendy D., and Susan L. Brown. "The Demography of Unions among Older Americans, 1980–Present: A Family Change Approach." In *Handbook of Sociology of Ag-*

ing, edited by Richard A. Settersten and Jacqueline L. Angel, 193–210. New York: Springer, 2011.

Markides, Kyriakos S., and Karl Eschbach. "Hispanic Paradox in Adult Mortality in the United States." In *International Handbook of Adult Mortality*, edited by Richard G. Rogers and Eileen M. Crimmins, 227–40. New York: Springer, 2011.

Marmot, Michael. *The Status Syndrome: How Social Standing Affects Our Health and Longevity*. New York: Owl Books, 2005.

Marshall, Barbara L. "The Graying of 'Sexual Health': A Critical Research Agenda." *Canadian Review of Sociology/Revue Canadienne de Sociologie* 48, no. 4 (2011): 390–413.

———. "Rejuvenation's Return: Anti-aging and Re-masculinization in Biomedical Discourse on the 'Aging Male.'" *Medicine Studies* 1, no. 3 (2009): 249–65.

Marshall, Barbara L., and Stephen Katz. "Forever Functional: Sexual Fitness and the Ageing Male Body." *Body & Society* 8, no. 4 (2002): 43–70.

Marshall, Victor W., and Philippa J. Clarke. "Agency and Social Structure in Aging and Life Course Research." In *SAGE Handbook of Social Gerontology*, edited by Dale Dannefer and Chris Phillipson, 294–305. Thousand Oaks, CA: Sage Publications, 2010.

Martin, Emily. "The Egg and the Sperm: How Science Has Constructed a Romance Based on Stereotypical Male-Female Roles." *Signs* 16, no. 3 (1991): 485–501.

Martin-Matthews, Anne. *Widowhood in Later Life*. New York: Harcourt Brace, 1991.

Masten, Ann S. "Ordinary Magic: Resilience Process in Development." *American Psychologist*, 56, no. 3 (2001): 227–38.

Masten, Ann S., and Margaret O'Dougherty Wright. "Resilience Over the Lifespan: Developmental Perspectives on Resistance, Recovery, and Transformation." In *Handbook of Adult Resilience*, edited by John W. Reich, Alex J. Zautra, and John Stuart Hall, 213–37. New York: Guilford, 2010.

Matthews, Sarah H. *The Social World of Old Women: Management of Self-Identity*. Beverly Hills: Sage Publications, 1979.

McCrae, Robert R., and Paul T. Costa. "Psychological Resilience among Widowed Men and Women: A 10-Year Follow-up of a National Sample." *Journal of Social Issues* 44, no. 3 (1988): 129–42.

McFadden, Susan. "Foreword." In *Spiritual Resiliency and Aging*, edited by Janet L. Ramsey and Rosemary Blieszner, vii–x. Amityville, NY: Baywood, 2012.

McGinley, Ann C. "Identities Cubed: Perspectives on Multidimensional Masculinities Theory." Scholarly Works Paper 761, 2013. Accessed March 23, 2014. http://scholars.law.unlv. edu/facpub/761.

McGinley, Ann C., and Frank Rudy Cooper. "Introduction: Masculinities, Multidimensionality, and Law: Why They Need One Another." In *Masculinities and the Law: A Multidimensional Approach*, edited by Frank Rudy Cooper and Ann C, McGinley, 1–21. New York: New York University Press, 2012.

McLaren, Angus. *Impotence: A Cultural History*. Chicago: University of Chicago Press, 2007.

McVittie, Chris, and Joyce Willock. "'You Can't Fight Windmills': How Older Men Do Health, Ill Health, and Masculinities." *Qualitative Health Research* 16, no. 6 (2006): 788–801.

Meadows, Robert, and Kate Davidson. "Maintaining Manliness in Later Life: Hegemonic Masculinities and Emphasized Femininities." In *Age Matters: Realigning Feminist Thinking*, edited by Toni Calasanti and Kathleen F. Slevin, 295–312. New York: Routledge, 2006.

Ménard, A. Dana, Peggy J. Kleinplatz, Lianne Rosen, Shannon Lawless, Nicholas Paradis, Meghan Campbell, and Jonathan D. Huber. "Individual and Relational Contributors to Optimal Sexual Experiences in Older Men and Women." *Sexual and Relationship Therapy* 30, no. 1 (2015): 78–93.

Merleau-Ponty, Maurice. *Phenomenology of Perception*. Translated by Colin Smith. New York: Routledge, 1995.

Middleton, Harry. *The Earth Is Enough: Growing Up in a World of Flyfishing, Trout & Old Men*. Boulder: Pruett Publishing, 1989.

Minello, Karla, and Deborah Nixon. "'Hope I Never Stop': Older Men and Their Two-Wheeled Love Affairs." *Annals of Leisure Research* 20, no. 1 (2017): 75–95.

Minkler, Meredith, and Thomas A. Cole. "Political and Moral Economy: Not Such Strange Bedfellows." In *Critical Perspectives on Aging: The Political and Moral Economy of Growing Old*, edited by Meredith Minkler and Carol L. Estes, 37–50. Amityville, NY: Baywood, 1991.

Minkler, Meredith, and Carroll L. Estes. *Critical Gerontology: Perspectives from Political and Moral Economy*. New York: Baywood, 1991.

Mitchell, Kirstin R., Philip Prah, Catherine H. Mercer, Jessica Datta, Clare Tanton, Wendy Macdowall, Andrew J. Copas, et al. "Medicated Sex in Britain: Evidence from the Third National Survey of Sexual Attitudes and Lifestyles." *Sexually Transmitted Infections* 92, no. 1 (2016): 32–38.

Montenegro, Xenia P. *The Divorce Experience: A Study of Divorce at Midlife and Beyond*. Washington, DC: AARP, 2004.

Moore, Alinde J., and Dorothy C. Stratton. *Resilient Widowers: Older Men Speak for Themselves*. New York: Springer Publishing Company, 2002.

Moore, Andrew J., Jane C. Richardson, Julius Sim, Miriam Bernard, and Kelvin P. Jordan. "Older People's Perceptions of Remaining Physically Active and Living with Chronic Pain." *Qualitative Health Research* 24, no. 6 (2014): 761–72.

Moore, Stephen D., and Janice Capel Anderson. "Taking It Like a Man: Masculinity in 4 Maccabees." *Journal of Biblical Literature* 117, no. 2 (1998): 249–73.

Moss, Miriam S., and Sidney Z. Moss. "Remarriage of Widowed Persons: A Triadic Relationship." In *Continuing Bonds: New Understandings of Grief*, edited by Dennis Klass, Phyllis R. Silverman, and Steven L. Nickman, 163–78. New York: Taylor & Francis, 1996.

———. "Some Aspects of the Elderly Widow(er)'s Persistent Tie with the Deceased Spouse." *Omega: Journal of Death and Dying* 15, no 3 (1985): 195–206.

Moustgaard, Heta, and Pekka Martikainen. "Nonmarital Cohabitation among Older Finnish Men and Women: Socioeconomic Characteristics and Forms of Union Dissolution." *Journals of Gerontology Series B: Psychological Sciences and Social Sciences* 64, no. 4 (2009): 507–16.

Mueller, Margaret M., and Glen H. Elder. "Family Contingencies across the Generations: Grandparent-Grandchild Relationships in Holistic Perspective." *Journal of Marriage and Family* 65, no. 2 (2003): 404–17.

Murray, Joanna, Justine Schneider, Sube Banerjee, and Anthony Mann. "EUROCARE: A Cross-National Study of Co-resident Spouse Carers for People with Alzheimer's Disease: II—A Qualitative Analysis of the Experience of Caregiving." *International Journal of Geriatric Psychiatry* 14, no. 8 (1999): 662–67.

Murray, Sarah H., Robin R. Milhausen, Cynthia A. Graham, and Leon Kuczynski. "A Qualitative Exploration of Factors That Affect Sexual Desire among Men Aged 30 to 65 in Long-Term Relationships." *Journal of Sex Research* 54, no. 3 (2017): 319–30.

Nakagawa, Gordon. "Deformed Subjects, Docile Bodies: Disciplinary Practices and Subject-Constitution in Stories of Japanese-American Internment." In *Narrative and Social Control: Critical Perspectives*, edited by Denis Mumby, 143–63. Newbury Park, CA: Sage Publications, 1993.

National Alliance for Caregiving. *Caregiving in the US*. Washington, DC: National Alliance for Caregiving and the AARP Public Policy Institute, 2015. Accessed February 11, 2017. http://www.caregiving.org/wp-content/uploads/2015/05/2015_CaregivingintheUS_Final-Report-June-4_WEB.pdf.

Navon, Liora, and Amira Morag. "Liminality as Biographical Disruption: Unclassifiability Following Hormonal Therapy for Advanced Prostate Cancer." *Social Science & Medicine* 58, no. 11 (2004): 2337–47.

Neimeyer, Robert A. "Widowhood, Grief and the Quest for Meaning: A Narrative Perspective on Resilience." In *Spousal Bereavement in Late Life*, edited by Deborah S. Carr, Randolph M. Nesse, and Camille B. Wortman, 227–52. New York: Springer, 2009.

Neugarten, Bernice L. "Age Groups in American Society and the Rise of the Young-Old." *Annals of the American Academy of Political and Social Science* 415, no. 1 (1974): 187–98.

———. "Time, Age, and Life-Cycle." *American Journal of Psychiatry* 136, no. 7 (1979): 887–94.

Newman, Katherine. *A Different Shade of Gray: Mid-Life and Beyond in the Inner City.* New York: The New Press, 2003.

Nilsson, Margareta, Anneli Sarvimäki, and Sirkka-Liisa Ekman. "Feeling Old: Being in a Phase of Transition in Later Life." *Nursing Inquiry* 7, no. 1 (2000): 41–49.

Nixon, Darren. "'I Can't Put a Smiley Face On': Working-Class Masculinity, Emotional Labour and Service Work in the 'New Economy.'" *Gender, Work & Organization* 16, no. 3 (2009): 300–22.

Noël-Miller, Claire M. "Partner Caregiving in Older Cohabiting Couples." *Journals of Gerontology Series B: Psychological Sciences and Social Sciences* 66, no. 3 (2011): 341–53.

Noone, Jack H., and Christine Stephens. "Men, Masculine Identities, and Health Care Utilisation." *Sociology of Health & Illness* 30, no. 5 (2008): 711–25.

Öberg, Peter. "The Absent Body—A Social Gerontological Paradox." *Ageing and Society* 16, no. 6 (1996): 701–19.

———. "Images versus Experience of the Aging Body." In *Aging Bodies: Images and Everyday Experience*, edited by Christopher Faircloth, 103–39. Walnut Creek, CA: AltaMira Press, 2003.

Öberg, Peter, and Torbjörn Bildtgård. "Diversity of Union Forms and Importance for Well-Being in Later Life." Poster presented at the Gerontological Society of America annual meeting, Washington, DC, November 5–9, 2014. Abstracted in *The Gerontologist* 54, no. S2 (2014): 195.

Öberg, Peter, and Lars Tornstam. "Body Images among Men and Women of Different Ages." *Ageing & Society* 19, no. 5 (1999): 629–44.

O'Brien, Rosaleen, Graham Hart, and Kate Hunt. "'Standing Out from the Herd': Men Renegotiating Masculinity in Relation to Their Experience of Illness." *International Journal of Men's Health* 6, no. 3 (2007): 178–200.

O'Brien, Rosaleen, Kate Hunt, and Graham Hart. "'The Average Scottish Man Has a Cigarette Hanging Out of His Mouth, Lying There with a Portion of Chips': Prospects for Change in Scottish Men's Constructions of Masculinity and Their Health-Related Beliefs and Behaviours." *Critical Public Health* 19, no. 3-4 (2009): 363–81.

———. "'It's Caveman Stuff, but That Is to a Certain Extent How Guys Still Operate': Men's Accounts of Masculinity and Help Seeking." *Social Science & Medicine* 61, no. 3 (2005): 503–16.

Office of National Statistics. *Life Expectancy at Birth and at Age 65 by Local Areas in the United Kingdom: 2006–08 to 2010–12.* April 4, 2014. Accessed January 10, 2017.

———. *Life Expectancy at Birth and at Age 65 by Local Areas in England and Wales: 2012 to 2014.* November 4, 2015. Accessed January 10, 2017.

———. *Population Estimates by Marital Status and Living Arrangements: England and Wales, 2002 to 2015.* July 13, 2016. Accessed January 10, 2017.

Ojala, Hanna, Toni Calasanti, Neal King, and Ilkka Pietilä. "Natural(ly) Men: Masculinity and Gendered Anti-ageing Practices in Finland and the USA." *Ageing & Society* 36, no. 2 (2016): 356–75.

Ojala, Hanna, Ilkka Pietilä, and Pirjo Nikander. "Immune to Ageism? Men's Perceptions of Age-Based Discrimination in Everyday Contexts." *Journal of Aging Studies* 39 (2016): 44–53.

Oksuzyan, Anna, Eileen Crimmins, Yasuhiko Saito, Angela O'Rand, James W. Vaupel, and Kaare Christensen. "Cross-National Comparison of Sex Differences in Health and Mortality in Denmark, Japan and the US." *European Journal of Epidemiology* 25, no. 7 (2010): 471–80.

Oliffe, John. "Constructions of Masculinity following Prostatectomy-Induced Impotence." *Social Science and Medicine* 60, no. 10 (2005): 2249–59.

Oliffe, John L., Christina S. E. Han, John S. Ogrodniczuk, J. Craig Phillips, and Philippe Roy. "Suicide from the Perspectives of Older Men Who Experience Depression: A Gender Analysis." *American Journal of Men's Health* 5, no. 5 (2011): 444–54.

Oliffe, John L., Brian Rasmussen, Joan L. Bottorff, Mary T. Kelly, Paul M. Galdas, Alison Phinney, and John S. Ogrodniczuk. "Masculinities, Work, and Retirement among Older

Men Who Experience Depression." *Qualitative Health Research* 23, no. 12 (2013): 1626–37.

Oster, Candice, Clare McGuiness, Amy Duncan, and Deborah Turnbull. "Masculinity and Men's Participation in Colorectal Cancer Screening." *Psychology of Men & Masculinity* 16, no. 3 (2015): 254–63.

Palacios-Ceña, Domingo, Pilar Carrasco-Garrido, Valentín Hernández-Barrera, Cristina Alonso-Blanco, Rodrigo Jiménez-García, and César Fernández-de-las-Peñas. "Sexual Behaviors among Older Adults in Spain: Results from a Population-Based National Sexual Health Survey." *Journal of Sexual Medicine* 9, no. 1 (2012): 121–29.

Parkes, C. Murray, Bernard Benjamin, and Roy G. Fitzgerald. "Broken Heart: A Statistical Study of Increased Mortality among Widowers." *British Medical Journal* 1, no. 5646 (1969): 740–43.

Parkes, C. Murray, and Robert S. Weiss. *Recovery from Bereavement*. New York: Basic Books, 1983.

Pearlin, Leonard I. "The Sociological Study of Stress." *Journal of Health and Social Behavior* 30, no. 3 (1989): 241–56.

Perelman, Michael, Ridwan Shabsigh, Allen Seftel, Stanley Althof, and Dan Lockhart. "Attitudes of Men with Erectile Dysfunction: A Cross-National Survey." *Journal of Sexual Medicine* 2, no. 3 (2005): 397–406.

Perrig-Chiello, Pasqualina, Stefanie Spahni, François Höpflinger, and Deborah Carr. "Cohort and Gender Differences in Psychosocial Adjustment to Later-Life Widowhood." *Journals of Gerontology Series B: Psychological Sciences and Social Sciences* 71, no. 4 (2016): 765–74.

Phoenix, Cassandra, and Andrew C. Sparkes. "Being Fred: Big Stories, Small Stories and the Accomplishment of a Positive Ageing Identity." *Qualitative Research* 9, no. 2 (2009): 219–36.

Piatczanyn, Steven A., Kate M. Bennett, and Laura K. Soulsby. "'We Were in a Partnership That Wasn't Recognized by Anyone Else': Examining the Effects of Male Gay Partner Bereavement, Masculinity, and Identity." *Men and Masculinities* 19, no. 2 (2016): 167–91.

Pinquart, Martin. "Loneliness in Married, Widowed, Divorced, and Never-Married Older Adults." *Journal of Social and Personal Relationships* 20, no. 1 (2003): 31–53.

Pirhonen, Jari, Hanna Ojala, Kirsi Lumme-Sandt, and Ilkka Pietilä. "'Old but Not That Old': Finnish Community-Dwelling People Aged 90+ Negotiating Their Autonomy." *Ageing and Society* 36, no. 8 (2016): 1625–44.

Platt, Stephen. "Suicide in Men: What Is the Problem?" *Trends in Urology & Men's Health* 8, no. 4 (2017): 9–12.

Ploubidis, George B., Richard J. Silverwood, Bianca DeStavola, and Emily Grundy. "Life-Course Partnership Status and Biomarkers in Midlife: Evidence from the 1958 British Birth Cohort." *American Journal of Public Health* 105, no. 8 (2015): 1596–1603.

Polivka, Larry. "Postmodern Aging and the Loss of Meaning." *Journal of Aging and Identity* 5, no. 4 (2000): 225–35.

Pope, Mark, Edward A. Wierzalis, Bob Barret, and Michael Rankins. "Sexual and Intimacy Issues for Aging Gay Men." *Adultspan Journal* 6, no. 2 (2007): 68–82.

Potts, Annie, Nicola Gavey, Victoria M. Grace, and Tiina Vares. "The Downside of Viagra: Women's Experiences and Concerns." *Sociology of Health & Illness* 25, no. 7 (2003): 697–719.

Potts, Annie, Victoria Grace, Nicola Gavey, and Tiina Vares. "'Viagra Stories': Challenging 'Erectile Dysfunction.'" *Social Science & Medicine* 59, no. 3 (2004): 489–99.

Potts, Annie, Victoria M. Grace, Tiina Vares, and Nicola Gavey. "'Sex for Life'? Men's Counter-Stories on 'Erectile Dysfunction,' Male Sexuality and Ageing." *Sociology of Health & Illness* 28, no. 3 (2006): 306–29.

Powell, Jason L. *Social Theory and Aging*. New York: Rowman & Littlefield, 2006.

Powell, Jason L., and Charles F. Longino. "Towards the Postmodernization of Aging: The Body and Social Theory." *Journal of Aging and Identity* 6, no. 4 (2001): 199–207.

Powers, John. *A Bull of a Man: Images of Masculinity, Sex, and the Body in Indian Buddhism*. Cambridge, MA: Harvard University Press, 2009.

Pruchno, Rachel A., Francine P. Cartwright, and Maureen Wilson-Genderson. "Effects of Marital Closeness on the Transition from Caregiving to Widowhood." *Aging and Mental Health* 13, no. 6 (2009): 808–17.

Pudrovska, Tetyana, Scott Schieman, and Deborah Carr. "Strains of Singlehood in Later Life: Do Race and Gender Matter?" *Journals of Gerontology Series B: Psychological Sciences and Social Sciences* 61, no. 6 (2006): S315–22.

Pugh, Stephen. "The Forgotten: A Community without a Generation—Older Lesbians and Gay Men." In *Handbook of Lesbian and Gay Studies*, edited by Diane Richardson and Steven Seidman, 161–81. London: Sage Publications, 2002.

Quincey, Kerry, Iain Williamson, and Sue Winstanley. "'Marginalised Malignancies': A Qualitative Synthesis of Men's Accounts of Living with Breast Cancer." *Social Science & Medicine* 149 (2016): 17–25.

Ramello, Stefano. "Same Sex Acts Involving Older Men. An Ethnographic Study." *Journal of Aging Studies* 27, no. 2 (2013): 121–34.

Randall, William L. "Aging, Irony, and Wisdom: On the Narrative Psychology of Later Life." *Theory & Psychology* 23, no. 2 (2013a): 164–83.

———. "The Importance of Being Ironic: Narrative Openness and Personal Resilience in Later Life." *The Gerontologist* 53, no. 1 (2013b): 9-16.

Randall, William, Clive Baldwin, Sue McKenzie-Mohr, Elizabeth McKim, and Dolores Furlong. "Narrative and Resilience: A Comparative Analysis of How Older Adults Story Their Lives." *Journal of Aging Studies* 34 (2015): 155–61.

Reboussin, Beth A., W. Jack Rejeski, Kathleen A. Martin, Kelley Callahan, Andrea L. Dunn, Abby C. King, and James F. Sallis. "Correlates of Satisfaction with Body Function and Body Appearance in Middle- and Older Aged Adults: The Activity Counseling Trial (ACT)." *Psychology and Health* 15, no. 2 (2000): 239–54.

Reitzes, Donald C., and Elizabeth J. Mutran. "Grandparenthood: Factors Influencing Frequency of Grandparent–Grandchildren Contact and Grandparent Role Satisfaction." *Journals of Gerontology Series B: Psychological Sciences and Social Sciences* 59, no. 1 (2004a): S9–16.

———. "Grandparent Identity, Intergenerational Family Identity, and Well-Being." *Journals of Gerontology Series B: Psychological Sciences and Social Sciences* 59, no. 4 (2004b): S213–19.

Ribeiro, Oscar. "Elderly Men on Ageing Families." In *Families in Later Life: Emerging Themes and Challenges*, edited by Liliana Sousa, 97–134. New York: Nova Science Publishers, 2009.

Ribeiro, Oscar, and Constanca Paúl. "Older Male Carers and the Positive Aspects of Care." *Ageing & Society* 28, no. 2 (2008): 165–83.

Ribeiro, Oscar, Constança Paúl, and Conceição Nogueira. "Real Men, Real Husbands: Caregiving and Masculinities in Later Life." *Journal of Aging Studies* 21, no. 4 (2007): 302–13.

Richardson, Noel. "'The "Buck" Stops with Me'—Reconciling Men's Lay Conceptualisations of Responsibility for Health with Men's Health Policy." *Health Sociology Review* 19, no. 4 (2010): 419–36.

Richardson, Virginia E. "Length of Caregiving and Well-Being among Older Widowers: Implications for the Dual Process Model of Bereavement." *Omega: Journal of Death and Dying* 61, no. 4 (2010): 333–56.

Richardson, Virginia E., and Shantha Balaswamy. "Coping with Bereavement among Elderly Widowers." *Omega: Journal of Death and Dying* 43, no. 2 (2001): 129–44.

Riggs, Anne. "Men, Friends and Widowhood: Toward Successful Ageing." *Australasian Journal on Ageing* 16, no. 4 (1997): 182–85.

Roberto, Karen A., Katherine R. Allen, and Rosemary Blieszner. "Grandfathers' Perceptions and Expectations of Relationships with Their Adult Grandchildren." *Journal of Family Issues* 22, no. 4 (2001): 407–26.

Robertson, Steve. "'Not Living Life in Too Much of an Excess': Lay Men Understanding Health and Well-Being." *Health:* 10, no. 2 (2006): 175–89.

———. *Understanding Men and Health: Masculinities, Identity and Well-Being*. New York: Open University Press, 2007.

Robinson, Tom, and Mark Callister. "Body Image of Older Adults in Magazine Advertisements: A Content Analysis of Their Body Shape and Portrayal." *Journal of Magazine and New Media Research* 10, no. 1 (2008): 1–16.

Rosenfeld, Dana, and Christopher Faircloth. *Medicalized Masculinities*. Philadelphia: Temple University Press, 2006.

Rosenfeld, Michael J., and Reuben J. Thomas. "Searching for a Mate: The Rise of the Internet as a Social Intermediary." *American Sociological Review* 77, no. 4 (2012): 523–47.

Rostow, Eugene V. "The Japanese American Cases—A Disaster." *Yale Law Journal* 54, no. 3 (1945): 489–533.

Rowe, John W., and Robert L. Kahn. *Successful Aging*. New York: Pantheon Books, 1998.

———. "Successful Aging 2.0: Conceptual Expansions for the 21st Century." *Journals of Gerontology Series B: Psychological Sciences and Social Sciences* 70, no. 4 (2015): 593–96.

Rowles, Graham D. "Place and Personal Identity in Old Age: Observations from Appalachia." *Journal of Environmental Psychology* 3, no. 4 (1983): 299–313.

Rowntree, Margaret R. "'Comfortable in My Own Skin': A New Form of Sexual Freedom for Ageing Baby Boomers." *Journal of Aging Studies* 31 (2014): 150–58.

Rozanova, Julia. "Discourse of Successful Aging in the *Globe & Mail*: Insights from Critical Gerontology." *Journal of Aging Studies* 24, no. 4 (2010): 213–22.

Rubin, David C., and Dorthe Berntsen. "People over Forty Feel 20% Younger Than Their Age: Subjective Age across the Lifespan." *Psychonomic Bulletin & Review* 13, no. 5 (2006): 776–80.

Rubinstein, Robert L. "Childlessness, Legacy, and Generativity." *Generations* 20 (1996): 58–60.

———. "Never Married Elderly as a Social Type: Re-evaluating Some Images." *The Gerontologist* 27, no. 1 (1987): 108–13.

———. *Singular Paths: Old Men Living Alone*. New York: Columbia University Press, 1986.

Russell, Cherry, and Maree Porter. "Single Older Men in Disadvantaged Households: Narratives of Meaning around Everyday Life." *Ageing International* 28, no. 4 (2003): 359–71.

Russell, Richard. "Men Doing 'Women's Work': Elderly Men Caregivers and the Gendered Construction of Care Work." *Journal of Men's Studies* 15, no. 1 (2007): 1–18.

———. "Their Story, My Story: Health of Older Men as Caregivers." *Generations* 32, no. 1 (2008): 62–67.

Rutter, Michael. "Resilience as a Dynamic Concept." *Development and Psychopathology* 24, no. 2 (2012): 335–44.

Sahil, Sara. *Judith Butler: Routledge Critical Thinkers*. New York: Routledge, 2007.

Sand, Michael S., William Fisher, Raymond Rosen, Julia Heiman, and Ian Eardley. "Erectile Dysfunction and Constructs of Masculinity and Quality of Life in the Multinational Men's Attitudes to Life Events and Sexuality (MALES) Study." *Journal of Sexual Medicine* 5, no. 3 (2008): 583–94.

Sandberg, Linn. "Affirmative Old Age—The Ageing Body and Feminist Theories on Difference." *International Journal of Ageing and Later Life* 8, no. 1 (2013a): 11–40.

———. *Getting Intimate: A Feminist Analysis of Old Age, Masculinity and Sexuality*. PhD diss., Linköping University, 2011. Linköping Studies in Arts and Sciences, Vol. 527. Accessed May 2013.

———. "In Lust We Trust? Masculinity and Sexual Desire in Later Life." *Men and Masculinities* 19, no. 2 (2016): 192–208.

———. "Just Feeling a Naked Body Close to You: Men, Sexuality and Intimacy in Later Life." *Sexualities* 16, no. 3-4 (2013b): 261–82.

Sattari, Maryam. "Breast Cancer in Male-to-Female Transgender Patients: A Case for Caution." *Clinical Breast Cancer* 15, no. 1 (2015): e67–69.

Saxton, Benjamin, and Thomas R. Cole. "No Country for Old Men: A Search for Masculinity in Later Life." *International Journal of Ageing and Later Life* 7, no. 2 (2012): 97–116.

Schaan, Barbara. "Widowhood and Depression among Older Europeans—The Role of Gender, Caregiving, Marital Quality, and Regional Context." *Journals of Gerontology Series B: Psychological Sciences and Social Sciences* 68, no. 3 (2013): 431–42.

Scherrer, Kristin S. "Images of Sexuality and Aging in Gerontological Literature." *Sexuality Research and Social Policy* 6, no. 4 (2009): 5–12.

Schilling, Oliver. "Development of Life Satisfaction in Old Age: Another View on the 'Paradox.'" *Social Indicators Research* 75, no. 2 (2006): 241–71.

Schimmele, Christoph M., and Zheng Wu. "Repartnering After Union Dissolution in Later Life." *Journal of Marriage and Family* 78, no. 4 (2016): 1013–31.

Schrock, Douglas, and Michael Schwalbe. "Men, Masculinity, and Manhood Acts." *Annual Review of Sociology 35* (2009): 277–95.

Schwartz, Christine R., and Nikki L. Graf. "Assortative Matching among Same-Sex and Different-Sex Couples in the United States, 1990–2000." *Demographic Research* 21 (2009): 843–78.

Schwartz, Pepper, Sarah Diefendorf, and Anne McGlynn-Wright. "Sexuality in Aging." In *Handbook of Sexuality and Psychology*, edited by Deborah Tolman and Lisa Diamond, 523–51. Washington, DC: American Psychological Association, 2014.

Segal, Lynne. *Slow Motion: Changing Masculinities, Changing Men*. New Brunswick, NJ: Rutgers University Press, 1990.

Seidler, Victor J. *Transforming Masculinities: Men, Cultures, Bodies, Power, Sex and Love*. New York: Taylor and Francis, 2006.

Seidman, Steven. "Constructing Sex as a Domain of Pleasure and Self-Expression: Sexual Ideology in the Sixties." *Theory, Culture & Society* 6, no. 2 (1989): 293–315.

Sentell, Edgar. "Suicide and the Life Insurance Death Claim." *FDCC Quarterly* 58, no. 3 (2008): 363–80.

Seymour-Smith, Sarah, and Margaret Wetherell. "'What He Hasn't Told You . . .': Investigating the Micro-Politics of Gendered Support in Heterosexual Couples' Co-constructed Accounts of Illness." *Feminism & Psychology* 16, no. 1 (2006): 105–27.

Shah, Sunil M., Iain M. Carey, Tess Harris, Stephen DeWilde, Christina R. Victor, and Derek G. Cook. "Do Good Health and Material Circumstances Protect Older People from the Increased Risk of Death After Bereavement?" *American Journal of Epidemiology* 176, no. 8 (2012): 689–98.

Shapiro, Adam, and Corey Lee M. Keyes. "Marital Status and Social Well-Being: Are the Married Always Better Off?" *Social Indicators Research* 88, no. 2 (2008): 329–46.

Shernoff, Michael. *Gay Widowers: Life After the Death of a Partner*. New York: Routledge, 2013.

Shilling, Chris. *The Body and Social Theory*. 2nd ed. Thousand Oaks, CA: Sage Publications, 2003.

———. "Educating the Body: Physical Capital and the Production of Social Inequalities." *Sociology* 25, no. 4 (1991): 653–72.

———. "Embodiment, Experience and Theory: In Defense of the Sociological Tradition." *Sociological Review* 49, no. 3 (2001): 327–44.

Shippy, R. Andrew, Marjorie H. Cantor, and Mark Brennan. "Social Networks of Aging Gay Men." *Journal of Men's Studies* 13, no. 1 (2004): 107–20.

Siegel, Rebecca L., Kimberly D. Miller, and Ahmedin Jemal. "Cancer Statistics, 2016." *CA: A Cancer Journal for Clinicians* 66, no. 1 (2016): 7–30.

Simpson-Young, Virginia, and Cherry Russell. "The Licensed Social Club: A Resource for Independence in Later Life." *Ageing International* 34, no. 4 (2009): 216–36.

Slevin, Kate F. "Disciplining Bodies: The Aging Experiences of Older Heterosexual and Gay Men." *Generations* 32, no. 1 (2008): 36–42.

Slevin, Kate F., and Thomas J. Linneman. "Old Gay Men's Bodies and Masculinities." *Men and Masculinities* 12, no. 4 (2010): 483–507.

Smith, James A., Annette Braunack-Mayer, Gary Wittert, and Megan Warin. "'It's Sort of Like Being a Detective': Understanding How Australian Men Self-Monitor Their Health Prior to Seeking Help." *BMC Health Services Research* 8, no. 1 (2008): 56.

———. "'I've Been Independent for So Damn Long!': Independence, Masculinity and Aging in a Help Seeking Context." *Journal of Aging Studies* 21, no. 4 (2007): 325–35.

Solimeo, Samantha. "Sex and Gender in Older Adults' Experience of Parkinson's Disease." *Journals of Gerontology Series B: Psychological Sciences and Social Sciences* 63, no. 1 (2008): S42–48.

———. *With Shaking Hands: Aging with Parkinson's Disease in America's Heartland.* Philadelphia: Rutgers University Press, 2009.

Sorenson, Penny, and Neil J. Cooper. "Reshaping the Family Man: A Grounded Theory Study of the Meaning of Grandfatherhood." *Journal of Men's Studies* 18, no. 2 (2010): 117–36.

Sparkes, Andrew C. "The Fatal Flaw: A Narrative of the Fragile Body-Self." *Qualitative Inquiry* 2, no. 4 (1996): 463–94.

Spector-Mersel, Gabriela. "Never-Aging Stories: Western Hegemonic Masculinity Scripts." *Journal of Gender Studies* 15, no. 1 (2006): 67–82.

Springer, Kristen W., and Dawne M. Mouzon. "'Macho Men' and Preventive Health Care: Implications for Older Men in Different Social Classes." *Journal of Health and Social Behavior* 52, no. 2 (2011): 212–27.

Stepler, Renee. *Smaller Share of Women Ages 65 and Older Are Living Alone: More Are Living with Spouse or Children.* Washington, DC: Pew Research Center, February 2016.

Stern, Lori. "Sex and Seniors: The 70-Year Itch." *Health Day*, January 20, 2017. Accessed March 6, 2017. https://consumer.healthday.com/encyclopedia/aging-1/misc-aging-news-10/sex-and-seniors-the-70-year-itch-647575.html.

Stevens, Nan. "Gender and Adaptation to Widowhood in Later Life." *Ageing and Society* 15, no. 1 (1995): 37–58.

Stevens, Nan, and Gerben J. Westerhof. "Partners and Others: Social Provisions and Loneliness among Married Dutch Men and Women in the Second Half of Life." *Journal of Social and Personal Relationships* 23, no. 6 (2006): 921–41.

StGeorge, Jennifer M., and Richard J. Fletcher. "Men's Experiences of Grandfatherhood: A Welcome Surprise." *International Journal of Aging and Human Development* 78, no. 4 (2014): 351–78.

Stroebe, Margaret S. "The Broken Heart Phenomenon: An Examination of the Mortality of Bereavement." *Journal of Community & Applied Social Psychology* 4, no. 1 (1994): 47–61.

Stroebe, Margaret, and Henk Schut. "The Dual Process Model of Coping with Bereavement: A Decade On." *Omega: Journal of Death and Dying* 61, no. 4 (2010): 273–89.

Stroebe, Margaret, Wolfgang Stroebe, and Henk Schut. "Gender Differences in Adjustment to Bereavement: An Empirical and Theoretical Review." *Review of General Psychology* 5, no. 1 (2001): 62–83.

Strohm, Charles Q., Judith Seltzer, Susan Cochran, and Vickie M. Mays. "'Living Apart Together' Relationships in the United States." *Demographic Research* 21, no. 7 (2009): 177–214. https://doi.org/10.4054/DemRes.2009.21.7.

Strom, Robert D., and Paris S. Strom. "Assessment of Intergenerational Communication and Relationships." *Educational Gerontology* 41, no. 1 (2015): 41–52.

Subramanyam, Malavika A., Sherman A. James, Ana V. Diez-Roux, DeMarc A. Hickson, Daniel Sarpong, Mario Sims, Herman A. Taylor, and Sharon B. Wyatt. "Socioeconomic Status, John Henryism and Blood Pressure among African-Americans in the Jackson Heart Study." *Social Science & Medicine* 93 (2013): 139–46.

Suen, Yiu Tung. "Older Single Gay Men's Body Talk: Resisting and Rigidifying the Ageing Discourse in the Gay Community." *Journal of Homosexuality* 64, no. 3 (2017): 397–414.

———. "To Date or Not to Date, That Is the Question: Older Single Gay Men's Concerns about Dating." *Sexual and Relationship Therapy* 30, no. 1 (2015): 143–55.

Szinovacz, Maximiliane E., and Anne M. Schaffer. "Effects of Retirement on Marital Conflict Tactics." *Journal of Family Issues* 21, no. 3 (2000): 367–89.

Szymczak, Julia E., and Peter Conrad. "Medicalizing the Aging Male Body: Andropause and Baldness." In *Medicalized Masculinities*, edited by Dana Rosenfled and Christopher Faircloth, 89–111. Philadelphia: Temple University Press, 2006.

Tan, Hui-Meng, Wah Yun Low, Chirk Jenn Ng, Kuang-Kuo Chen, Minoru Sugita, Nobuhisa Ishii, Ken Marumo, et al. "Prevalence and Correlates of Erectile Dysfunction (ED) and Treatment Seeking for ED in Asian Men: The Asian Men's Attitudes to Life Events and Sexuality (MALES) Study." *Journal of Sexual Medicine* 4, no. 6 (2007): 1582–92.

Tannenbaum, Cara, and Blye Frank. "Masculinity and Health in Late Life Men." *American Journal of Men's Health* 5, no. 3 (2011): 243–54.

Tarrant, Anna. "Constructing a Social Geography of Grandparenthood: A New Focus for Intergenerationality." *Area* 42, no. 2 (2010): 190–97.

———. "Grandfathering: The Construction of New Identities and Masculinities." In *Contemporary Grandparenting: Changing Family Relations in Global Contexts*, edited by Sara Arber and Virpi Timonen, 181–202. Chicago: University of Chicago Press, 2012.

Taylor, Larry W. "The Transition to Mid-Life Divorce." *Review of Economics of the Household* 9, no. 2 (2011): 251–71.

Tergesen, Anne. "The Long (Long) Wait to Be a Grandparent." *Wall Street Journal*, March 30, 2014. Accessed May 1, 2018. https://www.wsj.com/articles/the-wait-to-become-a-grandparent-gets-longer-1396020375.

Tetley, Josie, David M. Lee, James Nazroo, and Sharron Hinchliff. "Let's Talk about Sex—What Do Older Men and Women Say about Their Sexual Relations and Sexual Activities? A Qualitative Analysis of ELSA Wave 6 Data." *Ageing and Society* 38, no. 3 (2018): 497–521.

Thoits, Peggy A. "Identity Structures and Psychological Well-Being: Gender and Marital Status Comparisons." *Social Psychology Quarterly* 55, no. 3 (1992): 236–56.

Thompson, Edward H. "Guest Editorial." *Journal of Men's Studies* 13, no. 1 (2004): 1–4.

———. *Older Men's Lives*. Thousand Oaks, CA: Sage Publications, 1994.

Thompson, Edward H., and Kaitlyn Barnes. "The Meaning of Sexual Performance among Men with and without Erectile Dysfunction." *Psychology of Men and Masculinity* 14, no. 3 (2013): 271–80.

Thompson, Edward H., and Lenard W. Kaye. *A Man's Guide to Healthy Aging: Stay Smart, Strong, and Active*. Baltimore, MD: Johns Hopkins University Press, 2013.

Thompson, Edward H., and Kaitlyn Barnes Langendoerfer. "Older Men's Blueprint for 'Being a Man.'" *Men and Masculinities* 19, no. 2 (2016): 119–47.

Thompson, Edward H., and Alexandra Leichthammer. "'You've Gotta Be Kidding Me': Male Breast Cancer." Paper presented at the annual meeting of the Gerontological Society of America, New Orleans, LA, November 19–23, 2000. Abstracted in *The Gerontologist* 50, no. S3 (2010): 77.

Thompson, Edward H., Joseph H. Pleck, and David L. Ferrera. "Men and Masculinities: Scales for Masculinity Ideology and Masculinity-Related Constructs." *Sex Roles* 27, no. 11 (1992): 573–607.

Thompson, Edward H., and Patrick M. Whearty. "Older Men's Social Participation: The Importance of Masculinity Ideology." *Journal of Men's Studies*, 13, no. 1 (2004): 5–24.

Thompson, Neil. "The Ontology of Masculinity: The Roots of Manhood." In *Men Coping with Grief*, edited by Dale A. Lund, 27–35. Amityville, NY: Baywood, 2001.

Thompson, Paul Richard, Catherine Itzin, and Michele Abendstern. *I Don't Feel Old: The Experience of Later Life*. New York: Oxford University Press, 1990.

Tiefer, Leonore. "In Pursuit of the Perfect Penis: The Medicalization of Male Sexuality." *American Behavioral Scientist* 29, no. 5 (1986): 579–99.

Tolhurst, Edward, and Bernhard Weicht. "Preserving Personhood: The Strategies of Men Negotiating the Experience of Dementia." *Journal of Aging Studies* 40 (2017): 29–35.

Torgé, Cristina Joy. "Freedom and Imperative: Mutual Care between Older Spouses with Physical Disabilities." *Journal of Family Nursing* 20, no. 2 (2014): 204–25.

Townsend, Nicholas. *The Package Deal: Marriage, Work, and Fatherhood in Men's Lives*. Philadelphia: Temple University Press, 2002.

Trompeter, Susan E., Ricki Bettencourt, and Elizabeth Barrett-Connor. "Sexual Activity and Satisfaction in Healthy Community-Dwelling Older Women." *American Journal of Medicine* 125, no. 1 (2012): 37–43.

Tulle, Emmanuelle. "Running to Run: Embodiment, Structure and Agency amongst Veteran Elite Runners." *Sociology* 41, no. 2 (2007): 329–46.

———. "Sense and Structure: Toward a Sociology of Old Bodies." In *The Need for Theory: Critical Approaches to Social Gerontology,* edited by Simon Biggs, Ariela Lowenstein, and Jon Hendricks, 91–104. Amityville, New York: Baywood, 2003.

―――. "Theorising Embodiment and Ageing." In *Routledge Handbook of Cultural Gerontology*, edited by Julia Twigg and Wendy Martin, 125–32. New York: Routledge, 2015.

Tulle-Winton, Emmanuelle. "Old Bodies." In *The Body, Culture and Society: An Introduction*, edited by Philip Hancock, Bill Hughes, Elizabeth Jagger, Kevin Paterson, Rachel Russell, Emmanuelle Tulle-Winton, and Melissa Tyler, 64–83. Buckingham, UK: Open University, 2000.

Turcotte, Martin. *Living Apart Together*. Statistics Canada, March 2013. Accessed March 12, 2017. http://www.statcan.gc.ca/pub/75-006-x/2013001/article/11771-eng.pdf.

Turner, Bryan S. "Aging and Identity: Some Reflections on the Somatization of the Self." In *Images of Aging: Cultural Representations of Later Life*, edited by Mike Feathersone and Andrew Wernick, 245–60. New York: Routledge, 1995.

―――. *The Body and Society*. 2nd ed. Thousand Oaks, CA: Sage Publications, 1996.

―――. *Regulating Bodies: Essays in Medical Sociology*. New York: Routledge, 1992.

―――. "Strategic Generations: Historical Change, Literary Expression, and Generational Politics." In *Generations, Culture and Society*, edited by June Edmunds and Bryan S. Turner, 13–29. Philadelphia: Open University Press, 2002.

Turra, Cassio M., and Noreen Goldman. "Socioeconomic Differences in Mortality among US Adults: Insights into the Hispanic Paradox." *Journals of Gerontology Series B: Psychological Sciences and Social Sciences* 62, no. 3 (2007): S184–92.

Uhlenberg, Peter, and Bradley G. Hammill. "Frequency of Grandparent Contact with Grandchild Sets: Six Factors That Make a Difference." *The Gerontologist* 38, no. 3 (1998): 276–85.

Umberson, Debra, and Jennifer Karas Montez. "Social Relationships and Health: A Flashpoint for Health Policy." *Journal of Health and Social Behavior* 51, no. 1_suppl (2010): S54–S66.

Umberson, Debra, Mieke Beth Thomeer, and Amy C. Lodge. "Intimacy and Emotion Work in Lesbian, Gay, and Heterosexual Relationships." *Journal of Marriage and Family* 77, no. 2 (2015): 542–56.

Ungerson, Clare. "Why Do Women Care?" In *Labour of Love: Women, Work and Caring*, edited by Janet Finch and Dulcie Groves, 69–86. London: Routledge and Kegan Paul, 1983.

United Nations, Department of Economic and Social Affairs, Population Division. *World Population Ageing 2015* (ST/ESA/SER.A/390). New York: United Nations, 2015.

Unützer, Jürgen. "Late-Life Depression." *New England Journal of Medicine* 357, no. 22 (2007): 2269–76.

US Census Bureau. *Marital Status of People 15 Years and Over, by Age, Sex, and Personal Earnings*. Washington, DC: US Department of Commerce, 2015.

―――. *Statistical Abstract of the United States: 2012*. Washington, DC: US Department of Commerce, 2012.

van den Hoonaard, Deborah K. *By Himself: The Older Man's Experience of Widowhood*. Toronto: University of Toronto Press, 2010.

―――. "Experiences of Living Alone: Widows' and Widowers' Perspectives." *Housing Studies* 24, no. 6 (2009): 737–53.

Vares, Tiina, and Virginia Braun. "Spreading the Word, but What Word Is That? Viagra and Male Sexuality in Popular Culture." *Sexualities* 9, no. 3 (2006): 315–32.

Vesnaver, Elisabeth, Heather H. Keller, Olga Sutherland, Scott B. Maitland, and Julie L. Locher. "Alone at the Table: Food Behavior and the Loss of Commensality in Widowhood." *Journals of Gerontology Series B: Psychological Sciences and Social Sciences* 71, no. 6 (2016): 1059–69.

Vespa, Jonathan. "Relationship Transitions among Older Cohabitors: The Role of Health, Wealth, and Family Ties." *Journal of Marriage and Family* 75, no. 4 (2013): 933–49.

―――. "Union Formation in Later Life: Economic Determinants of Cohabitation and Remarriage among Older Adults." *Demography* 49, no. 3 (2012): 1103–25.

Vincent, Norah. *Self-Made Man: One Woman's Year Disguised as a Man*. New York: Penguin, 2006.

Vinick, Barbara H., and David J. Ekerdt. "The Transition to Retirement: Responses of Husbands and Wives." In *Growing Old in America*, 4th ed., edited by Beth Hess and Elizabeth Markson, 305–17. New Brunswick, NJ: Transaction Books, 1991.

Waite, Linda J., James Iveniuk, Edward O. Laumann, and Martha K. McClintock. "Sexuality in Older Couples: Individual and Dyadic Characteristics." *Archives of Sexual Behavior* 46, no. 2 (2017): 605–18.

Waite, Linda J., Edward O. Laumann, Aniruddha Das, and L. Philip Schumm. "Sexuality: Measures of Partnerships, Practices, Attitudes, and Problems in the National Social Life, Health, and Aging Study." *Journals of Gerontology Series B: Psychological Sciences and Social Sciences* 64, no. S1 (2009): i56–66.

Waldrop, Deborah P., Joseph A. Weber, Shondel L. Herald, Julie Pruett, Kathy Cooper, and Kevin Juoavicius. "Wisdom and Life Experience: How Grandfathers Mentor Their Grandchildren." *Journal of Aging and Identity* 4, no. 1 (1999): 33–46.

Wang, Haidong, Austin E. Schumacher, Carly E. Levitz, Ali H. Mokdad, and Christopher J. L. Murray. "Left Behind: Widening Disparities for Males and Females in US County Life Expectancy, 1985–2010." *Population Health Metrics* 11, no. 1 (2013): 8. https://doi.org/10.1186/1478-7954-11-8.

Wang, Wendy, and Kim Parker. *Record Share of Americans Have Never Married*. Washington, DC: Pew Research Center's Social and Demographic Trends, 2014.

Ward, Richard, and Caroline Holland. "'If I Look Old, I Will Be Treated Old': Hair and Later-Life Image Dilemmas." *Ageing & Society* 31, no. 2 (2011): 288–307.

Warnock, Eleanor. "Elderly Japanese Fill Jobs: Nation's Low Birthrate, Lack of Immigration Create Openings at Desperate Companies." *Wall Street Journal*, November 30, 2016: A4.

Wassersug, Richard J. "Mastering Emasculation." *Journal of Clinical Oncology* 27, no. 4 (2009): 634–36.

Weeks, Jeffrey. *Sexuality and Its Discontents: Meanings, Myths and Modern Sexualities*. New York: Routledge, 1985.

Weiss, Robert Stuart, and Scott A. Bass. *Challenges of the Third Age: Meaning and Purpose in Later Life*. New York: Oxford University Press, 2002.

Wenger, Lisa M., and John L. Oliffe. "Men Managing Cancer: A Gender Analysis." *Sociology of Health & Illness* 36, no. 1 (2014): 108–22.

Wentzell, Emily. "Aging Respectably by Rejecting Medicalization: Mexican Men's Reasons for Not Using Erectile Dysfunction Drugs." *Medical Anthropology Quarterly* 27, no. 1 (2013a): 3–22.

———. "How Did Erectile Dysfunction Become 'Natural'? A Review of the Critical Social Scientific Literature on Medical Treatment for Male Sexual Dysfunction." *Journal of Sex Research* 54, no. 4-5 (2017): 486–506.

Wentzell, Emily A. *Maturing Masculinities: Aging, Chronic Illness, and Viagra in Mexico*. Durham, NC: Duke University Press, 2013b.

West, Candace, and Don H. Zimmerman. "Doing Gender." *Gender & Society* 1, no. 2 (1987): 125–51.

West, Loraine A., Samantha Cole, Daniel Goodkind, and Wan He. *65+ in the United States: 2010*. Washington, DC: Government Printing Office, 2014.

Whitehead, Stephen M. *Men and Masculinities*. Malden, MA: Polity Press, 2002.

Whitley, Deborah M., and Esme Fuller-Thomson. "The Health of the Nation's Custodial Grandfathers and Older Single Fathers: Findings from the Behavior Risk Factor Surveillance System." *American Journal of Men's Health* 11, no. 6 (2017): 1614–26.

Wienke, Chris, and Gretchen J. Hill. "Does the 'Marriage Benefit' Extend to Partners in Gay and Lesbian Relationships? Evidence from a Random Sample of Sexually Active Adults." *Journal of Family Issues* 30, no. 2 (2009): 259–89.

Wiersma, Elaine, and Stephanie Chesser. "Masculinity, Ageing Bodies, and Leisure." *Annals of Leisure Research* 14, no. 2-3 (2011): 242–59.

Wierzalis, Edward A., Bob Barret, Mark Pope, and Michael Rankins. "Gay Men and Aging: Sex and Intimacy." In *Lesbian, Gay, Bisexual, and Transgender Aging: Research and Clinical Perspectives*, edited by Douglas Kimmel, Tara Rose, and Steven David, 91–109. New York: Columbia University Press, 2006.

Wild, Kirsty, Janine L. Wiles, and Ruth E. S. Allen. "Resilience: Thoughts on the Value of the Concept for Critical Gerontology." *Ageing and Society* 33, no. 1 (2013): 137–58.

Wiles, Janine L., Kirsty Wild, Ngaire Kerse, and Ruth E. S. Allen. "Resilience from the Point of View of Older People: 'There's Still Life Beyond a Funny Knee.'" *Social Science & Medicine* 74, no. 3 (2012): 416–24.

Wiley, Diana, and Walter M. Bortz. "Sexuality and Aging—Usual and Successful." *Journals of Gerontology Series A: Biological Sciences and Medical Sciences* 51, no. 3 (1996): M142–46.

Williams, Kristi. "Has the Future of Marriage Arrived? A Contemporary Examination of Gender, Marriage, and Psychological Well-Being." *Journal of Health and Social Behavior* 44, no. 4 (2003): 470–87.

Williams, Mark Edward, and Karen I. Fredriksen-Goldsen. "Same-Sex Partnerships and the Health of Older Adults." *Journal of Community Psychology* 42, no. 5 (2014): 558–70.

Willson, Andrea E., Kim M. Shuey, and Glen H. Elder, Jr. "Cumulative Advantage Processes as Mechanisms of Inequality in Life Course Health." *American Journal of Sociology* 112, no. 6 (2007): 1886–1924.

Wilson, Ben, and Steve Smallwood. "The Proportion of Marriages Ending in Divorce." *Population Trends* 131 (Spring 2008): 28–36.

World Health Organization. *Preventing Suicide: A Global Imperative*. Geneva: World Health Organization, 2014.

Wright, Matthew R., and Susan L. Brown. "Psychological Well-Being among Older Adults: The Role of Partnership Status." *Journal of Marriage and Family* 79, no. 3 (2017): 833–49.

Wright, Rosemary. *What a Drag It Is Getting Old: Awareness and Appraisal of Age Related Change in White Men Born Between 1946 And 1955*. Unpublished PhD diss., Wichita State University, 2015. Accessed December 15, 2016. http://soar.wichita.edu/bitstream/handle/10057/11613/d15027_Wright.pdf.

Wu, Zheng, and Christoph Schimmele. "Uncoupling in Late Life." *Generations* 31, no. 3 (2007): 41–46.

Wu, Zheng, Christoph M. Schimmele, and Nadia Ouellet. "Repartnering After Widowhood." *Journals of Gerontology Series B: Psychological Sciences and Social Sciences* 70, no. 3 (2015): 496–507.

Zola, Irving Kenneth. "Bringing Our Bodies and Ourselves Back In: Reflections on a Past, Present, and Future 'Medical Sociology.'" *Journal of Health and Social Behavior* 32, no. 1 (1991): 1–16.

———. "Medicine as an Institution of Social Control." *Sociological Review* 20, no. 4 (1972): 487–504.

———. *Missing Pieces: A Chronicle of Living with a Disability*. Philadelphia: Temple University Press, 1982.

Index

affirmative old age, 72
age consciousness, 40, 50, 51, 56, 63, 70
age performances, 54
age relations, 33–34
age reminders, 61, 63, 71, 87
aged, by culture, 6, 59, 211
ageism, 18, 24, 25, 33, 34, 35, 36–37, 40,
    59, 65, 117, 169; embodied, 5, 8, 35,
    51, 196
agency, in late life, 9, 26, 28, 38, 39, 42,
    52, 73, 103, 210, 211–213, 213
aging masculinities, 1, 6, 7, 8, 11, 12, 24,
    26, 41–45, 74, 80, 84, 93–94, 105, 120,
    150, 154, 178, 188, 203, 221, 223–225;
    fields of, 6, 31, 38, 42, 43, 71, 85, 88,
    205, 224, 226; and impermanence, 84;
    practices of, 24, 74, 79, 80, 91–92, 92,
    130, 213, 224, 226, 227; and
    responsibility, 91, 92, 93, 94. *See also*
    impermanence, embodied
aging: becoming genderless, 1, 3, 5, 10;
    and comorbidities, 51, 71, 80, 81, 85,
    96, 98, 102; corporeal, 4, 6, 25, 28, 35,
    38–39, 40, 45, 47, 51, 53, 55;
    embodiment of, 6, 35, 53, 65, 74, 80,
    84, 93, 224, 227; masks of and
    masquerading, 51–53, 54, 67, 68; a
    personal responsibility, 40, 54, 56, 59,
    62, 66, 71, 72, 79, 80, 84, 91, 92, 94,
    125

antiaging enterprise, 47, 65, 69, 115, 117,
    209
antiaging narratives, 69, 82, 117

bereavement, 193–196, 197–199; and
    resilience, 218
biomedical lens, 5, 40, 48
biomedicalization, 61, 68, 116, 117
blended families, 175
bodies, oppression of, 48, 49
body aesthetics, 47, 55, 55–57, 59, 64, 66,
    169
body appearance, 50, 51, 52, 54, 56–57,
    58, 59, 63, 64, 66, 108
body consciousness, 47, 48, 50, 51, 52, 64
body functioning, 47, 56, 57–59, 65, 73,
    117, 156
body limitations, coming to terms with,
    104–106, 106, 119–120
body work, 52, 61, 64–67, 184
body, as a project, 61, 62, 64, 64–66, 75
body, corporeal, 34, 47, 51, 55
Bourdieu, Pierre, 2, 8, 26–27, 28–29,
    30–31, 32, 38, 43, 49, 61–63, 75, 83,
    120, 151, 209, 224
Butler, Judith, 23, 24, 54

cancers, gendered, 108–112
capital: community, 95, 97, 102, 218, 220,
    223; cultural, 8, 26, 28, 29, 44, 210,
    223; masculine, 7, 10, 12, 35, 41, 43,

About the Author

Men, Masculinities, and Aging will testify that I am from the social constructionist tradition within sociology, which is rooted in voices such as Peter Berger and Thomas Luckman's *The Social Construction of Knowledge*, Erving Goffman's *Presentation of Self in Everyday Life*, and Georg Simmel's attention to forms of sociation. As a sociologist, I am keenly interested in social relations and social patterns. Men's interaction, whether it is with other men or the stories they tell about the reimagined persons embedded in fogged memories, are the social relations that principally interest me.

I joined the faculty at the College of the Holy Cross (Worcester, Massachusetts) in the late 1970s as a trial run to see if teaching in an elite small liberal arts college was for me. I had only known large universities. By the end of year four, I was hooked. Creating courses was a privilege. The students were amazing; they read the heavy load assigned, thoughtfully discussed their changing understanding of people's lives. In fall 1987 I taught an undergraduate course on Sociology of Men for the first time as a college honors seminar. The syllabus noted, "Many social science and humanities courses offer some information about men as historical figures, evil patriarchs, anonymous fathers, coercive husbands, and other caricatures. However, very few courses raise questions about ordinary men's lives. This course is designed to be gender conscious and systematically examine men's lives— their experiences as men within the matrix of masculinities encountered in our culture, their anxieties and emotions, their relations with women, children, and other men." All the students in the seminar were nonmajors by college rule, all very bright, and this group of men and women helped me begin my journey of wrestling with understanding men's lives.

By the beginning of the 1990s, I began presenting my thinking about aging men at academic conferences and then published the first edited collection of original work examining the everyday lives of older men (*Older Men's Lives*) in the SAGE series on Men and Masculinity. I argued at that time that aging men are invisible within people's thinking about men. Inside sociology and more so within social gerontology, this is no longer the case.

I am now an emeritus professor no longer grading papers or teaching and mentoring undergraduates. I thoroughly enjoy hiking. Not long overnight treks, but I could be easily convinced to hike the Grand Canyon rim to rim. The Zen of fishing is solace. I have grown children—Stephen and Natalie— and an incredibly loving and supportive wife, Ruth. This book is dedicated to Ruth.

Diversity and Aging

Series Editor: Toni Calasanti, Virginia Tech

The elder population is not only growing in size, but also becoming more diverse—including differences in gender, race, ethnicity, class, and sexuality—and the experiences of aging people can vary dramatically. Books in this series explore this diversity, focusing on the ways that these social inequalities, along with ageism, shape experiences of growing old. The series will illustrate the challenges and opportunities that diversity and aging present for society, both now and in the future.

Titles in Series